PRIORITIES AND PATHWAYS IN SERVICES REFORM

Part II – Political Economy Studies

World Scientific Studies in International Economics

(ISSN: 1793-3641)

Vol. 22 International Trade Policy Formation: Theory and Politics
by Wolfgang Mayer (University of Cincinnati, USA)

Vol. 23 Priorities and Pathways in Services Reform:
Part I — Quantitative Studies
edited by Philippa Dee (Australian National University, Australia)

Vol. 24 Globalizing Information: The Economics of International Technology Trade
by Keith E Maskus (University of Colorado at Boulder, USA)

Vol. 25 Priorities and Pathways in Services Reform: Part II — Political Economy Studies
edited by Christopher Findlay (University of Adelaide, Australia)

Vol. 26 World Trade Organization and International Trade Law: Antidumping, Subsidies and Trade Agreements
by Gary N Horlick (Law Offices of Gary N Horlick, USA & University of Bern, Switzerland)

Vol. 27 European Economic Integration and Fragmentation of Production
edited by Lucia Tajoli (Politecnico di Milano, Italy)

Vol. 28 Services Trade Reform: Making Sense of It
by Philippa Dee (Australian National University, Australia)

Vol. 29 The Social Value of the Financial Sector: Too Big to Fail or Just Too Big?
edited by Viral V Acharya (New York University, USA & Centre for Economic Policy (CEPR), UK), Thorsten Beck (Tilburg University, The Netherlands & Centre for Economic Policy (CEPR), UK), Douglas D Evanoff (Federal Reserve Bank of Chicago, USA), George G Kaufman (Loyola University Chicago, USA), & Richard Portes (London Business School, UK & Centre for Economic Policy (CEPR), UK)

Vol. 30 Economics and Politics of Trade Policy
by Douglas R Nelson (Tulane University, USA)

The complete list of the published volumes in the series can be found at
http://www.worldscientific.com/series/wssie.

25 World Scientific Studies in International Economics

PRIORITIES AND PATHWAYS IN SERVICES REFORM

Part II — Political Economy Studies

Editor

Christopher Findlay

University of Adelaide, Australia

World Scientific

NEW JERSEY • LONDON • SINGAPORE • BEIJING • SHANGHAI • HONG KONG • TAIPEI • CHENNAI

Published by

World Scientific Publishing Co. Pte. Ltd.
5 Toh Tuck Link, Singapore 596224
USA office: 27 Warren Street, Suite 401-402, Hackensack, NJ 07601
UK office: 57 Shelton Street, Covent Garden, London WC2H 9HE

British Library Cataloguing-in-Publication Data
A catalogue record for this book is available from the British Library.

World Scientific Studies in International Economics — Vol. 25
PRIORITIES AND PATHWAYS IN SERVICES REFORM
Part II — Political Economy Studies

ISBN 978-981-4504-68-3

In-house Editor: Ms. Sandhya Venkatesh

Printed in Singapore by World Scientific Printers.

Preface

Chapters in this volume examine what it takes to overcome political resistance to services policy reform, by reporting on actual reform experiences in some of these sectors and economies. There are many examples of reform, some outstanding successes, some only partially done and some reversed. The volume seeks to understand the contributors to these outcomes.

A companion volume presents empirical studies designed to quantify impediments to services trade and investment.

In 2006 the Australian Research Council funded a joint project involving the Australian National University, the University of Adelaide and the Australian Productivity Commission to assess priorities for services reform. I would like to thank Professor Jenny Corbett from the Australian National University for leading the project, Professor Philippa Dee for her principal role in the research and for her contribution as editor of the companion volume, and Paul Gretton from the Productivity Commission for coordinating the support and input from that institution.

There were strong synergies between the ARC project and emerging concerns within APEC member countries. In 2004, APEC Leaders had signed on to a Leaders' Agenda to Implement Structural Reform (LAISR), wherein they recognised the value of well executed structural reform, underpinned by institutional capacity building, for achieving sustainable economic growth and supporting APEC's goal of trade and investment liberalisation. The newly-created APEC Policy Support Unit saw the benefits of studies that could demonstrate the potential benefits from structural reforms in key infrastructure industries. The studies here are also derived from this project.

I would also like to thank Philip Gaetjens, then Director of the Policy Support Unit, and Nathan Zhivov, Policy Advisor, for their enthusiasm in organising such a project, which contributed some of the chapters in this book.

Christopher Findlay

December 2012

Contents

Contributors

Fabien Bertho is Trade Economist, The University of Adelaide and Research Fellow, Groupe d'Economie Mondiale (Sciences Po, Paris).

Rupa Chanda is Professor in Economics and Social Sciences, Indian Institute of Management in Bangalore (IIMB).

Ronald Duncan is Emeritus Professor at the Crawford School of Public Policy, the Australian National University.

Christopher Findlay is Executive Dean and Professor in Economics at the Faculty of the Professions, University of Adelaide.

Paul Furlong is Professor of European Studies, Cardiff School of European Languages, Translation and Politics, Cardiff University.

Pralok Gupta is Consultant (Assistant Professor)-Services and Investment, Centre for WTO Studies, Indian Institute of Foreign Trade, New Delhi.

Dave Heatley is Principal Advisor, New Zealand Productivity Commission. This research was undertaken while a Research Fellow at the New Zealand Institute for the Study of Competition and Regulation.

Seung-Hoon Lee is Professor, Seoul National University; former Chairman of the Korean Electricity Commission (2001-2004); President of Korean Society of Electricity Industry Studies.

Anne McNaughton is Senior Lecturer ANU College of Law, Australian National University.

Deunden Nikomborirak is Research Director at Thailand Development Research Institute and Secretary to the Minister of Finance, Finance Ministry (2007–2008).

Margot Schwass is Freelance writer and editor; case-writer for Australia New Zealand School of Government (ANZSOG).

Alexandra Sidorenko is Senior Adjunct Lecturer, University of Adelaide.

Narong Pomlaktong, Rattana Jongwilaiwan, Prakai Theerawattanakul, and Rapee Pholpanich Thailand Development Research Institute.

Raimundo Soto is Professor of Economics, Institute of Economics, School of Economics and Business Administration, Pontificia Universidad Católica de Chile.

Fan Ying is Associate Professor, School of International Trade and Economics, University of International Business and Economics.

List of Tables

List of Figures

Abbreviations

2G	Second-generation wireless telephone technology
ANZESC	Australian & New Zealand/Eastern Shipping Conference
APEC	Asia Pacific Economic Cooperation
ARC	Auckland Regional Council
ARTA	Auckland Regional Transport Authority
ASEAN	Association of South East Asian Nations
AUD	Australian Dollar
BLMP	Baseload marginal price
BMTA	Bangkok Mass Transit Authority
BPO	business process outsourcing
BTU	British Thermal Unit
CAP	Compania de Aceros del Pacífico
CARB	California Air Resource Board
CBP	Cost-based pool
CCF	Capital Construction Fund
CCS/KOM	Competitive Capacity Selection
CLTCB	Central Land Transport Control Board
CPI – X	Price cap regulation
CSA/DPM	Capacity Supply Agreements
CSV	Compania Sudamericana de Valores
DIPP	Department of Industrial Policy and Promotion
DLT	Department of Land Transport
DOT	Department of Telecommunications
DPEIDC	Department of Public Enterprises, Information and Development Corporation
DPTS	Division of Postal and Telecommunication Services
dwt	deadweight tonnage
EBIT	Earnings before interest and tax
EC	European Community
ECJ	European Court of Justice

EEC	European Economic Community
EFE	Empresa de Ferrocarriles del Estado
EGAT	Electricity Generating Authority of Thailand
EPPO	Electricity Policy and Planning Office
ERC	Electricity Regulatory Commission
ERRA	European Energy Regulators Regional Association
EU	European Union
FAS	Federal Antimonopoly Service
FDI	Foreign direct investment
FEPASA	Ferrocarriles del Pacífico
FGC	Federal Grid Company
FIE	Foreign-invested enterprises
FMC	Federal Maritime Commission
FTE	Full time equivalent
FTS	Federal Tariff Service
FWA	Fair Work Act
GAO	Government Accountability Office
GATS	General Agreement on Trade in Services
GDP	Gross domestic product
Gencos	Generating companies
GRDI	Global Retail Development Index
GSP	Gas separation plants
GW	Gigawatt
ICAI	Institute of Chartered Accountants of India
ICCC	Independent Consumer and Competition Commission
ICRIER	Indian Council for Research on International Economic Relations
ICT	Information and communication technology
IDGC	Inter-regional distribution grid companies
IEA	International Energy Agency
ILO	International Labour Organization
IMI	Internal Market Information
INR	Indian Rupee
IPBC	Independent Public Business Corporation
IPP	Independent power producers
ISCR	Institute for the Study of Competition and Regulation
ISP	Internet Service Provider
ITE	Income Tax Exemption
KDI	Korea Development Institute
KEPCO	Korea Electric Power Corporation
KOREC	Korean Electricity Commission
KPX	Korea Power Exchange
KRW	South Korean won

kWh	Kilowatt hours
LLP	Limited Liability Partnership
LNG	Liquified natural gas
LPG	Liquified Petroleum Gas
LTPC	Land Transport Policy Committee
MOCIE	Ministry of Commerce, Industry and Energy
MRSK	Russian acronym for inter-regional distribution grid companies
MSP	Maritime Security Program
MW	Megawatt
MWh	Megawatt hour
NBC	National Broadcasting Commission
NEC	National Executive Committee
NEPO	National Energy Policy Office
NESDB	National Economic and Social Development Board
NGO	Non-government Organisation
NGV	Natural Gas for Vehicles
NICTA	National Information and Communications Technology Authority
NTC	National Telecommunication Commission
NTP	National Telecommunications Policy
NZ	New Zealand
NZD	New Zealand Dollar
NZRC	New Zealand Rail Corporation
OECD	Organization for Economic Co-operation and Development
OSP	Other Service Providers
OSRA	Ocean Shipping Reform Act
PANGTEL	Papua New Guinea Telecommunications Authority
PDR	People's Democratic Republic
PGK	Papua New Guinea Kina
PJM	Pennsylvania–New Jersey–Maryland
PLTCB	Provincial Land Transport Control Board
PMC	Pacific Mobile Communications Ltd
PNG	Papua New Guinea
PPA	Power purchase agreement
PSC	Points of Single Contact
PTC	Post and Telecommunication Corporation
PTT	Petroleum Authority of Thailand
PTTEP	PTT Exploration and Production
PTTNGD	PTT Natural Gas Distribution Company
RAB	Regulatory Asset Base
RAO-UES	United Energy Systems of Russia
RDG	Rail Development Group
RMB	Chinese renminbi

Ro/Ro	Roll-on/Roll-off
RUB	Russian ruble
SAFE	State Administration of Foreign Exchange
SME	Small and medium enterprises
SMP	System marginal price
SPP	Small independent power producers
TC	Commodity charge
TD	Demand charge
TDRI	Thailand Development Research Institute
TFA	Trade Facilitation Agreement
TFEU	The Treaty on the Functioning of the European Union
TGC	Territory generation company
THB	Thai baht
TRAI	Telecommunications Regulatory Authority of India
TRANSAP	Transporte Ferroviario Andrés Pirazolli S.A.
UK	United Kingdom
UNCTAD	United Nations Conference on Trade and Development
US	United States
USA	United States of America
USD	United States dollar
USITC	United States International Trade Commission
USO	Universal service obligation
VAT	Value added tax
VISA	Voluntary Intermodal Sealift Agreement
WACC	Weighted average cost of capital
WGC	Wholesale generation company
WTO	World Trade Organization

Chapter 1

Overview[1]

Christopher Findlay

1.1 Introduction

Services markets are often highly regulated and international trade and investment in services is restricted as a result. According to other research, there are significant gains from reform of both domestic regulation and regimes applying to international providers of services, yet those results are often debated and progress on reform has been slow around the world (see for example, François and Hoekman, 2010). This is the second of two volumes that are designed to help fill the gap in the research which is evident in this debate.

The first volume (*Priorities and Pathways in Services Reform: Modelling and Quantitative Studies*) contains up-to-date assessment and evaluations of the impact of policy in a range of services markets in different countries. This work is brought together in the form of cross-country modelling of the impact of a cooperative reform programme among APEC members. Missing from the work that has been produced to date on policy reform and its effects is an understanding of what makes reform successful. Quantifying the benefits of reform is necessary

[1] This chapter is based on a paper produced with funding from the Asia Pacific Economic Cooperation's Policy Support Unit and material from that paper is reproduced with its permission. Information is taken from The Impacts and Benefits of Structural Reforms in the Transport, Energy and Telecommunications Sectors in APEC Economies APEC#211-SE-01.1. The views expressed in this chapter are those of the authors and do not necessarily represent those of the APEC Secretariat or APEC Member Economies.

but not sufficient to bring reform about. In this second volume, there is an effort to begin to fill that gap in understanding by reporting the experiences of reform in different sectors and various countries.

The studies in this volume refer to the telecommunications, energy and transport sectors. The provision of these services is regulated for many reasons. Because of the nature of the production process of services, one reason for regulation is the risk of monopoly and the consequence of higher prices for consumers. Managing reform to deal with this issue is a key focus in this volume. This includes attention to which elements of the provision of a service have the features of a natural monopoly and which do not, how to separate these elements and how to manage the former.

There are also other reasons for regulation, including those related to the lack of information held by consumers, and for whom relevant information is revealed only as the service is consumed. Policy packages which will respond to these issues efficiently are identified and compared to those policies actually in place. The differences between actual and efficient policy that are observed make the case for reform.

Case studies of reform in each sector are presented. In some cases, particularly in telecommunications, reform has been an outstanding success. In other cases, the results are mixed – reforms have stalled or even reversed, that is, the reform has been undone and aspects of the earlier regime have been reinstated. We aim to identify the contributing factors to the variation in the process of reform and we summarise the results in final remarks about ten key lessons for successful reform. These include work on empirical studies like those reported in the companion volume on modelling and quantitative studies.

In this chapter, the main results from the following chapters are identified. Considered first are the chapters related to telecommunications, then those related to the energy sector (gas and electricity) followed by transport (which includes mention of rail, sea and road transport). The volume includes country studies of China, India and the EU which are then reviewed. The volume concludes with a statement of the ten lessons of reforms that are reviewed in the other chapters.

1.2 Telecommunications

One rationale for regulating telecommunications is to avoid the abuse of market power, when at least some elements of the telecommunications network have the characteristics of a natural monopoly and where the exercise of that monopoly power would be likely to create greater economic damage than might occur as a result of any regulatory issues. Another key objective is often to regulate to ensure that the industry meets universal service obligations, that is, to meet community expectations of the level of access to services of particular quality.

Technology changes rapidly in this sector and so judgments about which elements of the process of delivering service may constitute a natural monopoly also change. The current consensus is that there are few elements of mobile technology that provide the basis for a natural monopoly, while in fixed-line networks the 'last mile' (the copper wire connection, and the ducts or infrastructure associated with it, between an individual subscriber and the first switch in the network) may still have natural monopoly characteristics. The regulatory challenge is to prevent the economic waste associated with duplication of the bottleneck facility (the 'last mile') while encouraging competition elsewhere in the network.

One of the common regulatory approaches to this problem is to establish an access regime, whereby other providers pay a wholesale charge for access to the incumbent's bottleneck facility, so they can offer retail services (e.g. retail telephony or ISP services) that use this facility. If the access charge is set appropriately, this can encourage competition in retail services while discouraging inefficient duplication of the 'last mile'. If the access charge is set too high, retail competition will be thwarted and there will be an incentive for inefficient duplication of the last mile, but if the access charge is set too low, the incumbent will have little incentive to invest to maintain or extend the bottleneck facility. A common regulatory solution is to price access at long-run incremental cost – a charge that includes a capital component towards maintenance and eventual replacement of the asset, but does not include any 'super normal' profits for the incumbent.

Nevertheless, other aspects of the regulatory regime may still limit competition indirectly. Typically, subscriber access charges were kept low enough to encourage participation by the poor, and usage charges were then increased to cover costs, particularly on long-distance calls. Universal service obligations, that is, to provide services to all households, including poor or isolated households, were traditionally met in many economies by cross-subsidies in this form which were built into the incumbent's retail pricing structure. However, when competition is introduced, entrants are attracted to the most profitable parts of the market and the cross-subsidies cannot be sustained. The failure of some developing economies to find ways other than cross-subsidisation to fund universal service obligations is constraining the development of competition in telecommunications (telecom), even where the economies have made commitments to do so.

The growth of the telecom sector itself adds to GDP, but the initial impact of liberalisation or competitive market entry is often a contraction of the workforce. This is partly a response to competitive pressures by the incumbent to become more efficient. More importantly, over time it is due to the response by the incumbent to accelerate the adoption of new digital technologies, which are far less labour intensive. New technologies are associated with innovation in services in two ways: firstly, through more effective delivery channels, such as internet-based mobile cellular services; and secondly, through new services, for example converged services such as internet and mobile TV. As new entrants make their mark, users become more aware of the benefits and availability of telecoms and new services create new markets, so employment in the sector grows again. Further details of the experiences of reform are reported in Chapter 2 for Papua New Guinea.

While the fixed-line service remained in the hands of a government enterprise in Papua New Guinea (PNG), competition was introduced into the mobile sector when entrant Digicel joined the incumbent B-Mobile. The number of mobile phone subscribers (through B-Mobile) was estimated to be between 130,000 and 140,000 prior to the entrance of Digicel in July 2007. By 2010, these two firms claimed to have over 500,000 customers each, which suggests a remarkable 700% growth in the total number of mobile phone subscribers. This result could be regarded as achieving universal coverage. Average peak and off-peak domestic call billing rates fell by 11% for peak times and by 51% for off-peak times after the introduction of Digicel. Average peak and off-peak international call rates fell by 40% and 38%, respectively. Furthermore, calling rates for both carriers and for both domestic and international calls have moved from 30-second billing increments to per second billing increments.

Digicel claims to have provided employment opportunities to some 300 people of whom 90% were Papua New Guineans, and indirect employment for about 500 people through dealer stores, top-up vendors, distributors, etc. Furthermore, it has committed itself to a busy community relations programme. In a land with a terrain as difficult as PNG's, the benefits to the many remote communities of being able to interact with other people cannot be underestimated. Already the availability of mobile phone services has done much for social interaction as well as being helpful in medical emergencies. Moreover, the mobile banking initiatives now underway will be enormously helpful because, hitherto, banking services in rural areas have been very limited. The provision of market pricing information through mobile phone services will also be very helpful because the livelihood of the bulk of the population is from agricultural and fishing activities.

The chapter on assessing the effects of policy reform in a multisectoral setting (Chapter 10) in the companion volume includes some discussion of the implications of technological change for 'convergence', where broadband services can provide both data and voice traffic. It is argued there that regulatory structures should acknowledge this development and not hinder the evolution of the technologies for delivering those services and providing competition for incumbents. One challenge however is that the role of regulation is to deal with 'natural monopoly' components of the network, and the nature and extent of the natural monopoly problem depends on the particular technology in question. Thus, given the rapid development and proliferation of technologies, there may be no 'one-size-fits-all' best approach to regulation. Since there is also uncertainty about the evolution of technology, the suggestion is made that regulatory regimes be internally consistent. For example, economies making a commitment to fibre-optic technologies could put more regulatory effort into the design of access regimes, because of the nature of those technologies, than economies relying more on mobile and fixed wireless technologies.

1.3 Energy

The network infrastructure in the energy sector has natural monopoly characteristics. Examples include high-pressure gas transmission pipelines and (perhaps) lower pressure distribution pipelines. However, efficiency in production and distribution can be improved by promoting competition in all areas including the production and import of gas and in gas retailing, that is, competition for supply into the pipeline system and in the extraction from that system. An additional benefit of retail competition is that it allows retailers to offer bundles of services, such as combined electricity and gas services.

Traditionally, natural gas markets were either local – the gas was used where it was produced – or bilateral – gas consumption and production occurred at either end of a gas pipeline. Now liquefied natural gas (LNG) technology has made it possible to ship gas from a single source to multiple markets. The international market for gas can thus be expected to become much more competitive over time, in the same way that oil markets have become 'thick', making it easier for importing economies to 'shop around'. This can be expected to promote competitive importing. Arrangements for access to pipeline systems also allow liquefied petroleum gas (LPG) to be replaced by reticulated LNG. However, LNG terminals are themselves expensive and highly capital intensive, and may display natural monopoly characteristics, depending on their capacity relative to market size. Thus, in the future, competitive importing may require arrangements that allow users other than the owners to have access to LNG facilities as well as for pipelines. These are called third party regimes.

In general, reforms in natural gas markets have been less extensive than in electricity (which is reviewed below). In part, this is because the scope for competition in natural gas production depends on access to different sources of supply. A gas market reform plan in Thailand (reviewed in Chapter 3) was developed in the late 1990s which would have separated the gas transmission pipeline from the retail trading operations and from production. However, when implemented, following a change of government, the main change was the privatisation of the gas company. There was no separation, nor was an independent regulator established as had been planned. The goal had become the mobilisation of funds to invest in the network. From this perspective, the change was remarkably successful, and offshore gas fields were connected. A side effect was that domestic capacity increased so quickly that imports fell, but there were no evident efficiency gains, prices remained controlled and questions remain about the quality of gas supplied relative to global benchmarks. While prices remained relatively low, despite the lack of competition in the market, this was due to access to low cost gas from domestic sources and government subsidies. As growth continues and local sources are used up, this situation is not likely to continue.

Like gas pipelines, lines for the transmission of electricity may possess natural monopoly characteristics, but industry performance can be enhanced by encouraging competition in electricity generation (and perhaps retail distribution). Recent technological advances, such as cogeneration (of electricity and usable heat) have changed the economics of generating electricity and created options for competitive supply. Transmission costs are mostly fixed. A regulatory regime that encourages competition in electricity generation would:

- unbundle those activities that are considered to be competitive (generation and retailing) from those that are thought to be natural monopoly activities (transmission), so as to avoid conflicts of interest in promoting competition; and
- allow third party access by guaranteeing open and non-discriminatory access for all generators to the transmission grid (subject to available transmission capacity).

Some consideration of the price-setting mechanism is also required. The choice has been controversial. One option is to introduce a wholesale pool, or spot market, for electricity (either mandatory or optional). However, in a wholesale price pool there is the possibility of dominant generators using their market power to play a 'game' by manipulating the bidding system to deliver electricity at prices that are above cost. Thus, while the United Kingdom established a wholesale electricity market in March 1990, the 'gaming' problem led to the pool being replaced by a system of bilateral contracts in March 2001. It was not clear that an alternative price-setting mechanism, such as long-term contracts between generators and retailers, would deliver lower prices than a wholesale pool, as the underlying problem was the same in both regimes – the market power of the generators. In any event, there are vertical economies between generation and retail. To the extent that vertical integration of these activities increases the proportion of wholesale transactions that are intra-firm transactions, it may mean that explicit wholesale markets will tend to be thin. For this reason, the use of a wholesale price pool rather than long-term contracts may be contentious.

Other, less controversial, aspects of a pro-competitive regulatory regime include:

- allowing new generators to enter the market and new sources of supply generally, such as wind and solar, and allowing different demand management mechanisms;
- allowing customers (sometimes large customers such as retailers or large industrial users, sometimes all retail customers) to purchase electricity directly from the generator or retailer of their choice; and
- introducing a regulator independent of industry players and day-to-day political influence.

Previous research has confirmed the benefits of true retail competition, which includes both choice of generator and choice in billing and contract terms. However, retail competition is only likely to be as extensive as competition in generation, because vertical economies mean that non-integrated retail companies have little chance of success at any reasonable scale.

The extent of reform of the Russian electricity sector (examined in Chapter 4) is remarkable. The Californian experience of reform has not been a deterrent in Russia. In California, reform, which was argued to be incomplete, was followed by blackouts and by attempts by suppliers to extract higher prices from newly created markets. In Russia, the reforms have been designed with these lessons in mind. There has been a complete transformation of the system to separation and a wholesale market. The motivation was the urgency to mobilise investment in capacity. Demand for electric energy had been rising with an upturn in economic activity since 1999 but capacity was not expected to be sufficient. Reform was conceived around the idea of maintaining government regulation over the natural monopoly components of the sector, while introducing competition and private investment in the generating segment. The outcome in Russia has included restructuring and private ownership (2003–08); price deregulation according to a schedule and full competition in generation (by 2011); and competition by ensuring third party access to network infrastructure. Price regulation remains to 2015 for retail consumers. The consequence was significant increases in capacity but further reform will be valuable. Higher payments for the provision of capacity would add to the incentive for private investment in generation. Regulatory risks remain high, with government interventions to curb the rise in retail tariffs by changing the rules of the wholesale markets. There is also a risk of reversal towards the greater role of government-owned companies in generation, and in operating the network and retail sectors.

Korean reforms in the electricity market (reviewed in Chapter 5) were begun in 2000 and led to the separation of the generators from the distribution company. Little progress has been made since then. The original company continued to own the generators, even though the next step in the reform would have been to sell them. The reforms stalled because of resistance, especially from labour unions, coinciding with a new government which was not committed to the original reform plan.

The partial reforms may have created some efficiency gains, though researchers continue to debate their significance and there are conflicting conclusions. Some indicators such as reliability show positive results. The heat efficiency of the generation facilities and the maintenance of frequency and voltage seem to have also improved after restructuring. There was a substantial rise in the capacity utilisation rate of coal-fired plants and a subsequent reduction in generation cost after the divestiture. The utilisation rate surged. The gains arise from improved management after the divestiture. A pattern of cross-subsidies (including from profits from constructing generation capacity) keeps industry-user prices low but this reduces incentives for those who benefit in this way to support reforms. The subsidies may also not be sustainable with expectations of falling greenhouse gas emissions.

In electricity generation, the lack of a set of significant changes all at once, that is, the lack of a set of 'big bang' initiatives, is partly because introducing competition into generation and retail usually involves a highly complex regulatory process. In electricity, the 'product' is completely non-storable. New capacity needs to be brought on stream in a way that does not overload the system or risk system stability in the network, which would result in a reduction in quality of supply. The regulatory requirements for competitive new producers and/or wholesalers to gain access to existing transmission and distribution networks must be compatible with the technical requirements for the safety and physical integrity of the system.

1.4 Transport

Rail services consist of the construction, ownership and maintenance of railway track, the purchase, ownership and maintenance of railway rolling stock (carriages, etc.), and the operation of railway rolling stock along railway lines to provide passenger and freight transportation services. The track, having incurred the up-front costs of investment, can carry extra traffic at zero cost. It therefore has the characteristic of a natural monopoly. However, at the point of congestion, extra traffic generates additional costs. So, prior to the point of congestion, the aim of economic regulation should be to ensure that its capacity is utilised effectively without the application of monopoly power – this may be referred to as static efficiency. Beyond the point of congestion, the aim of economic regulation should be to ensure that there is an efficient level of investment in new track infrastructure – the objective here is dynamic efficiency.

One way to ensure the efficient use of rail track infrastructure is to encourage competition in the provision of 'above-the-rail' rail passenger and freight services. However, historically, rail services in many economies have been provided by a single, integrated, often government-owned monopoly. Thus structural reform of rail services has tended to proceed by encouraging private sector participation in the provision of rail services, while making use of the existing track infrastructure, through contractual arrangements. Sometimes reform has also involved the privatisation of the incumbent service provider and/or the structural separation of the ownership and maintenance of track infrastructure from the provision of rail transport services. The rationale for structural separation is to reduce conflicts of interest – otherwise the owner of the track infrastructure would have an incentive to use its control of that infrastructure to thwart competitors.

Research on the European rail system has found that a combination of vertical separation and horizontal competition provides significant benefit. It was also found that efficiency and productivity levels in economies that only introduced vertical separation are similar to those in economies that did nothing. Free entry of new operators is critical for better performance. In this respect, the experience of reform in southern Chile reported in Chapter 6 is of great interest.

The government-owned rail corporation in Chile sold its southern operations to the private sector. Later a second private operator entered the market, prompted by a change in sanitary and environmental regulations that prohibited truck transport of sulphuric acid through urban areas, thus leading a major mining operation to transfer the service to the private railway. These carriers had non-exclusive 20-year contracts or 'concessions' that allow free entry of carriers to facilities and require the payment of fixed and variable tariffs for the use of the infrastructure. The track remained in the hands of the state organisation, which was required to provide maintenance and facilities. Tariffs were around 40% lower than those prevailing before privatisation, indicating a substantial benefit to consumers.

Both private carriers operated by exploiting market niches rather than providing a full range of services to the general public. They concentrated their business on the transport of bulk commodities in large volumes (paper pulp, iron ore, etc.) and not on general freight, where competition from trucks was intense. Although rail traffic volumes did not increase in the initial years after privatisation, revenue and traffic per worker increased markedly.

The slow beginning was the result of numerous issues relating to labour and line rehabilitation. After a decade of operations, traffic and revenue per worker expanded markedly. Determining the fixed and variable fees for track use has been controversial. The track operator, on the presumption that the marginal social cost of using rail transport is low, has noted that trucks are not charged the marginal social cost of their use of roads, and has labelled this unfair competition.

Rail in New Zealand (Chapter 7) provides another interesting example of the processes of reform. Railways were run by a government department until 1982 when it was converted to a corporate management system, although retained in government ownership, and required to make a profit. In 1990 work began to prepare the 'core rail operations' for privatisation which then occurred in 1993. The business changed to another private owner in 2004, with the understanding it would sell the track to the government for NZD1, which would then reinvest in the infrastructure but with the private firm maintaining operations. However, both track and operations returned to government ownership in 2008.

The NZ case shows that partial reform, such as maintaining control of fares without subsidies and restrictions on exit, is not consistent with a sustainable role for private operators, especially in a situation where the features of the transport services to be provided may not suit the use of rail. However, privatisation was associated with some improvements in performance and the introduction of tendering for rail services in Auckland (reviewed below) was associated with higher patronage and improved service quality.

The process of privatisation in the NZ rail system did have a significant effect on performance. Marketing research led to an improved understanding of customer needs. Rail volumes for the bulk goods segment increased by 5.5% p.a. over 1994–97 in response to rail transport price falls of 7% p.a. In the export goods segment volumes grew at 12% p.a. in response to price falls of 4.4% p.a. Significant improvements were found in customer satisfaction surveys conducted in 2000 and 2003, with positive responses to the question 'Would you recommend (the operator) to another potential customer?' improving from just over 30% to nearly 80%. The operator improved productivity and returned the first operating profits for rail in many years. Costs were reduced, including by cutting uneconomic services. Freight volumes grew, peaking in 2000 and rail's share of the land freight market peaked at 29% in 1998. However, over this period profits were not covering the cost of capital and debt was increasing, while track maintenance was neglected. There were constraints due to the combination of the underlying economics of rail transport and the constraints on operations imposed by the government. This led eventually to the return of the track to the government.

In 2002 tenders were called for the operation of the Auckland (NZ's capital city) urban rail system. The government retained ownership of the track and provided subsidies for fares (which were NZD7-8 per trip). However, the winning tenderer also improved service quality with more services, higher frequencies, greater punctuality and better trains. Services increased from 635 per week in 2005 to 1,475 in 2009. In March 2005 only 77% of trains arrived on time and this figure was over 85% for most of 2009. Over five years, 21 of the 41 stations on the network were upgraded. Patronage doubled between 2005 and 2010. The fare subsidies (in part offsetting, it was argued, the lack of congestion pricing for roads) were able to be combined with better performance. Now being planned is how to electrify the track. This is expected to increase patronage and lower the subsidy per passenger.

The experience of rail reform shows that the decision to vertically separate network businesses is not straightforward, since it can lead to the loss of the advantages of economies of joint management. Integrated rail operators make better choices about investments in tracks compared to those focusing only on operations. They are more aware of the trade-offs involved. The advantage of separation, on the other hand, is that it changes the incentives of the track operator to favour larger volumes of traffic. There is no incentive to hold back competitors. If separation is not undertaken, then some mechanism to support competition has to be identified, such as providing contracts for access to the track by competitors.

Key rationales for regulating maritime services are to minimise the damage from natural monopoly and to meet safety requirements. A clear assessment of the location of facilities, within the series of services provided, that provide the basis of the natural monopoly is important in the consideration of regulation. The common assessment is that international shipping is subject to competition in many markets, that is, the provision of shipping services is usually not a natural monopoly. However, the management of ports in some locations may have natural monopoly characteristics, depending on the scale of the port facilities relative to traffic. In many economies, the provision of port services has been reserved as a state-owned monopoly. In these cases, not only was there no competition in providing port services but many port services (e.g. pilotage, towing, tug assistance, use of navigational aids, use of berthing services, waste disposal, anchorage and casting off) were deemed to be mandatory, meaning that ships visiting a port had to pay for them whether they used them or not. A final point to note here is that some economies have restrictive regulations governing access to ports (e.g. determining which ships and which cargoes can visit which ports). These arrangements have proved to be costly. However, it may be possible to encourage competition between ports as well as to encourage competition for the right to operate existing port facilities.

Another arrangement common in maritime services is the application of restrictions on cabotage rights. Cabotage is the transport of goods or passengers between two points in the same economy. Many economies reserve such domestic shipping either for domestically owned ships or for ships that fly that economy's flag. Such cabotage restrictions clearly reduce competition, although they have proved resistant to reform through WTO trade negotiating channels. Such restrictions have been shown to be costly, especially for developing economies, as in research reviewed in Chapter 8.

The Australian approach to cabotage has not been to remove the regulation but to change the manner of its implementation. The use of a permit system, introduced in the 1990s, has had two effects. At first, it sustained a downward trend in real interstate non-bulk freight rate which was already underway since the early 1980s due to technological factors and to rationalisation of manning scales introduced by the Australian government. The impact of the change in coastal shipping policy is clear from the mid-1990s, when the decrease of the freight rate for journeys between eastern and western Australia accelerated despite rising fuel prices. Rates were 40% lower in 2005 compared to the start of the 1990s. A second effect was that the size of the Australian fleet decreased in deadweight tonnage (carrying capacity) by almost half between 1999 and

2007, with a much larger decrease in the coastal fleet. At the same time capacity utilisation increased and productivity more than doubled. However, as the capacity of Australian ships declined, there was pressure for new policies to 'revive' the industry and the balance has swung back towards the operation of the regulatory system in a more protectionist manner.

In the US, only vessels owned by a US corporation can carry freight on domestic routes – a company's maximum foreign equity is 25%, 75% of its employees must be US citizens and cabotage is reserved for ships built in the US. Any domestic leg of an international journey is covered by these rules. Subsidies are also provided to US shipyards to make this policy feasible. However, the higher cost of domestic freight by this mode has led to a substitution to other modes and the volume of domestic freight by sea has fallen, as has the size of the US fleet. The size of the shipbuilding sector has also declined. Businesses which consign freight have been lobbying against the regulation but have not been effective due to the concentrated influence of the remaining shipping companies (now a duopoly). The complexity of the policy package and the lack of transparency mean that any assessment is not straightforward.

Studies of the economic characteristics of road transport suggest that there is little need for intervention by government to ensure efficient allocation of resources, except to ensure that there is competition and that safety, environmental and other externality considerations are taken fully into account. In particular, there is little evidence of economies of scale in either trucking or bus operations. Nevertheless, the damage that vehicles do to roads rises dramatically with increasing axle weight.[2] A key rationale for regulating road freight and passenger services is therefore to limit road damage, to provide a mechanism for recovering the maintenance costs of the damage that is done and sometimes (as in the case of toll roads) to recover construction costs. Another rationale is to deal with road congestion.

[2] Damage being related to axle loads and not total loads means that vehicle design and load limits are critical components in designing and maintaining roads.

In some economies, licensing requirements, price controls and other regulatory restrictions can extend beyond those required for legitimate purposes, and can be used to restrict entry into and limit competition within the industry, to the benefit of existing road service providers. Sometimes such entry barriers and price restrictions are imposed and/or enforced by professional bodies or representatives of trade and commercial interests, rather than by governments. In these cases, structural reform can follow naturally from systematic reviews of anti-competitive regulation.

In other economies, overly restrictive road transport regulations may arise from the desire to give protection to railways and/or bus operators. It may be possible to phase out such road transport regulations following structural reforms in rail that improve the productivity of the rail transport sector.

Another source of inefficiency in some cases is the over-exploitation of road transport as a source of revenue (through licence fees, charges for trip permits, etc.) for regional and local levels of government, in the absence of more efficient revenue sources, as well as road transport being a source of informal payments to police and other agents. Thus reform of road regulation may be contingent on better systems of public sector management as well as broader anti-corruption strategies.

A further issue is price control, with caps on fares designed to achieve higher levels of access for poorer households or those living further from city centres. However, these controls can lead to unintended (and possibly unwanted) market responses. The case of passenger vans in Bangkok is reviewed in Chapter 9.

The bus services in Thailand had a feature that is familiar in regimes with fare control – the quantity demanded exceeded that supplied. This created the opportunity for new entrants at unregulated prices. These new services, or 'vans', were strictly illegal at first in the mid-1980s, but later were licensed. The vans charged higher prices but offered shorter, faster routes with guaranteed seats, although they were also smaller vehicles than buses, and required passengers to go to terminals. The vans competed with buses and were eventually brought within a licensing system with a cap on the number of licences available (although many continue to operate outside that system). However, the initial stage of their development could be regarded as an experiment with deregulation. When the vans were re-regulated and licensed, the fees charged for access to the van terminals and for their use were also increased by the investors in those facilities, attempting to capture some of the profits that re-regulation made possible.

Another issue is the lack of pricing for road congestion in Thailand and also in the freight sector in particular for the costs of road usage by heavy trucks. The vans have added to road congestion in Bangkok, and while the vans are not supposed to stop at bus stops or elsewhere to pick up, they do so if the police fail to enforce that requirement. This further slows down the traffic flow. While congestion pricing has an advantage of allocating available space in the road system more efficiently, there is a problem if the authority collecting the congestion pricing revenue is also the constructor of the road system, which is the case in Thailand. The incentives then are to under-invest in the road capacity and collect revenue from the congestion charges.

1.5 Country Studies

This volume includes a review of services sector policy and its evolution in China, India and the EU.

The review of the experience in China (Chapter 10) finds that the development of China has reached a turning point. The previous export-led model of growth is being replaced and there is an effort to rebalance the economy, which includes a greater role for the services sector. The role that the services sector plays in contributing to productivity growth elsewhere in the economy is noted. Previous regulation of the sector has however impeded the development of the international competitiveness of the services sector. China did make ambitious commitments on services at the time of accession to the WTO but implementation of those commitments remains in issue in some sectors. There are also concerns about the degrees of concentration in some services sectors. The experience of China therefore illustrates some of the challenges of reform. Examples are provided of the complementary relationship between commitments to openness and the development of new institutions and other domestic reforms.

Liberalisation of services in India (examined in Chapter 11) was part of a wider reform programme. The review identifies the domestic political constraints to reform in some sectors. It also finds that commitments in trade agreements have lagged behind unilateral action, which has led the reform process. A number of lessons are evident in India's services sector reform – reform is not a smooth process and political will is important since reform inevitably triggers conflicts between interest groups which has to be resolved; reform has been marked by examples of learning by doing; and the pace of reform in different sectors is linked to the structure of domestic markets (including the role of government owned firms). The experience in India also shows how difficult it is to balance efficiency and equity objectives. The study concludes that "instituting appropriate regulatory bodies, clearly defining their roles, and improving governance, are just as important as pursuing liberalisation."

Original proposals for services market integration in the European Union (EU), reviewed in Chapter 12, were to apply the principle of mutual recognition. The approach proved contentious, with Member States concerned about their own right to regulate. The outcome in the Services Directive was instead a regime in which states applied their own regulation but according to principles including non-discrimination, proportionality and necessity. Even more important, the directive requires that members continue to defend any measures they have in place. It is argued in Chapter 12 that this process will be the key to integration of these markets. However, the description of the processes involved makes it clear that the institutional strengths of members and the EU are critical to success. Where those structures do not exist, the directive would be less likely to deliver the results expected in the EU. While hard mutual evaluation between nation states is unlikely outside the EU (although APEC could develop a 'soft' version), other economies can and should have their own hard internal evaluation mechanisms.

1.6 Ten Lessons of Reforms to Date

In this section, ten general lessons of the reform in the case study economies to date are put forward. The themes of these lessons include the values of transparency, of having a clear view about goals and of having the expectation of continuing change.

1.6.1 *Competition is more important than ownership*

The review of reform to date finds that the value of competition and contestability and the value of preceding changes in ownership by the introduction of competition are particularly important. Privatisation without competition can lead to the continuation of the same problems under a new owner. At the very least, competition for the market or regulation of the critical infrastructure, whose owners might otherwise capture the gains from trade, is required. This is illustrated for instance in the case studies on markets for gas and electricity. Whether or not different stages of the production of the services are separated (independent of ownership), the focus should be on the introduction of competition.

At the same time, there may be some concerns about introducing competition. For example, the result may be market structures in which a small number of firms compete, that is, oligopolies. Foreign firms might enter and try to drive out competitors by lowering prices, that is, by predatory behaviour. In that case, the application of competition policy is appropriate but in doing so capacity building and training skilled staff in the competition policy institution may be valuable.

1.6.2 *Take a forward-looking view and provide a leadership commitment*

A forward-looking view, that is, maintaining concentration on reform, and explaining a desirable end point of reform, helps avoid landing in an 'undesirable equilibrium' and then becoming stuck at that point because of the emergence of new vested interests. It is also important that there is a commitment by leaders to structural reform (e.g. to a set of national development goals) and that they have the ability to explain structural reforms.

To illustrate the consequences of not meeting this condition, consider for example an urban transport system where not taking some action results in the system descending into congestion. From that situation, however, a number of vested interests extract significant benefit and there is little pressure for further policy change. The situation with urban transport in Bangkok is an example. Another example is undertaking a partial reform, such as privatisation in gas or electricity but then not proceeding past that point. The experiences of gas in Thailand and electricity in Korea highlight the challenges.

1.6.3 *Be aware of 'the gap' in regulatory practice*

It is important to have some sense of 'the gap', that is, how far away the current regime is from 'good practice'. This level of performance is not the same as 'best practice' in global terms but it is the regulatory process that would be regarded as efficient at the state of development. Regional cooperation organisations like APEC have a key role to play in sharing this experience and expertise, as discussed with reference to the gas markets in the previous section. Reform in electricity is also complex, and concerns remain about the Californian experience. The designers of electricity reform in Russia drew on advice and experience from the rest of the world to design a new system.

1.6.4 *Know the costs of the current regime*

For reform to occur, it is important that the community has some sense of the costs of the gap in performance. This gap might be evident in various dimensions, for example, low quality services or prices too high. High prices are not the only cost of incorrect policy choices or a lack of action by policy-makers. It could also be, as in many energy markets, that prices are too low when the environmental impacts of consumption or production are taken into account. Gas markets provide examples of this situation.

Other points that help make the case for change are:

- the scope for efficiency gains, like those available from electricity reform, or even a partial reform, as in Korea;
- the greater capacity to respond to other shocks or developments, such as responding to climate change;
- the easing of fiscal constraints and interests from within the industry itself, such as its capacity to raise finance, which was a driver of reform in Russia;
- responding to technological change which leaves some interests 'stranded' or without value, as is becoming more apparent in telecommunications; and
- responding to environmental impacts, including congestion, which may be worsened by inappropriate regulation, as in the case of Bangkok.

Modelling results can be used to demonstrate the gains from reform. In the companion volume, model results are presented in which it is found that APEC-wide, the projected gains from structural reforms are more than three times as big as the gains from further liberalisation of merchandise trade (see Dee, 2012).

An argument for reform based on efficiency gains to the general public may be very difficult to implement and manage, since, as noted in the companion volume, reforms of the type examined there cannot generate significant gains without also generating significant structural adjustments (Dee, 2012). There may also be concern that reform will crowd out domestically-owned businesses in favour of foreign-invested firms. It is also noted in the companion volume that to some extent, reforms can provide their own reward, in terms of stimulating activity and increasing the resilience of the economy, but prudent macroeconomic management is also crucial. In addition, according to the modelling results reported there, crowding out of domestic providers is not of particularly great practical concern. It is also noted that services trade reform, when comprehensive, can benefit domestic new entrants, who can become a counterweight to the fear of such crowding out.

How else could efficiency gains be presented as a benefit to the public or small business in order to mobilise further support for reform? Some more appealing communication of the challenges as well as the likely gains will be important. The cases in this study include instances where service quality improved because of reform, for example, the van market in Bangkok.

1.6.5 *The commitment to structural reform is continuous*

In the past, there may not have been a performance gap of note in relation to the application of regulatory policy, but as times change, gaps in performance may emerge. For example, investment in capacity may lag behind the growth in demand – this was a driver of reform in the electricity sector in Russia where a key figure in the industry played a lead role in identifying that particular 'gap' in performance. New technologies may also provide new sources of competition and undermine the rationale for existing regulation, as in telecommunications. Equally, new bottlenecks may emerge because of technological change and demand attention, so the regulatory focus has to shift. In maritime transport, for example, a key issue is no longer the anti-competitive behaviour of shipping companies but the management of ports.

The choice, therefore, is not simply one between good and bad practice that is considered at one point of time. There is value in adjusting the regime as new gaps between current and good practice emerge. This is not easy. Also, it is important to avoid the problems of 'reform indigestion', that is, a build-up of valuable reforms which are not implemented. Monitoring of performance and reporting on it is part of the process to avoid this type of indigestion.

1.6.6 *Promote engagement from within*

Is there pressure from the regulated businesses within a sector and can this pressure become a force for reform?

Relevant sources of this pressure might be:

- an internal weakness and poor performance;
- failure to meet expectations from shareholders;
- actions by competitors (who might operate in a different regulatory environment, for example, the same market in technical terms providing substitute services but a different institutional setting);
- difficulty in meeting financing constraints; and
- a reaction from downstream sectors to poor performance, such as a low quality of services from an infrastructure operator.

Reform happens faster when it is motivated from within. However, referring to an earlier principle, the experience indicates that a clearly defined end point is required for a particular reform initiative since otherwise, incumbents can recapture the process of designing policy and direct it to their own ends. It is valuable to monitor the competitive and regulatory benchmarks set by other countries. It is easier to prevent special pleading from particular regulated industries for regulation in their favour if structural reform is taken as a package across all state-owned enterprises, or at least a group of them. It also helps to achieve a good result to establish structural reform as part of a 'better governance' campaign or a budget 'clean-up'.

1.6.7 *Use experiments*

Experiments can be useful to demonstrate the value of reform. The experience of the passenger van market in Bangkok, although not originally officially sanctioned and later re-captured by regulation, is an example of a market-led, natural experiment that grew out of an earlier period of regulation. Experiments can be useful to break bottlenecks to change – they demonstrate benefits in smaller areas, even regions, or parts of markets. Criteria for selection (or acceptance) of experiments might be the extent of change required or the capability to execute change and the capacity to quantify effects. Complementary research efforts are important to capture the experience and distribute the messages to interested parties.

1.6.8 *Use independent evaluation for designing options*

Independent evaluation of policy is very important, either in the formal government sector or utilising the 'second track' of institutions with links to government. Those organisations, by maintaining a focus on the public interest, help to offset the lobbying efforts of the vested interests who pursue policy in their own interest. They also can challenge the 'good performer' myth, that is, the proposition that a structure looks to be working well because it is profitable (perhaps too much so) or financing its own investment and maintaining capacity (perhaps to too great an extent). This myth is a contributor to the lack of progress of reform in the gas market in Thailand. These review agencies are also important in that they identify options, engage the stakeholders in a process to choose between options, maintain attention on the case for efficiency, then propose a reform plan, publicise targets, monitor reform and report back on progress.

1.6.9 *Coordinate when it matters*

Some problems demand coordination of the application of policy across infrastructure services in order to achieve an efficient solution, for example, in public transport where coordination across modes is important to avoid congestion. This is also relevant to logistics, where policy across a number of modes of transport has to be coordinated. It is illustrated in the case of Thailand with respect to investment in road networks. Critical activities include:

- establishing a formal process in which all relevant parties are involved;
- providing funding for it;
- providing the process with relevant powers to make changes to policies and practices;
- including all the stakeholders, not just suppliers but also users of the services – public and private - from the beginning;
- having a functional organisation; and
- monitoring progress.

Other examples of the value of coordination include setting up integrated ticketing systems, which requires as much coordination as network-wide traffic signal coordination. Other structures, for example railways and highways, are easier to operate on their own account. However, when co-ordination is critical, the question is how to get it done? This requires leadership and external advice.

1.6.10 *Meet universal service obligations*

Viet Nam in the telecommunications sector demonstrates yet again the value of dealing with universal service obligations directly. To embed them in the commitments of incumbents creates a disincentive for reform. Separating them out from other policy objectives makes the cost transparent.

1.7 Conclusion

The importance of structural reform economies is illustrated in the chapters in this volume. This conclusion makes two points about the value of clarity about the purpose of reform and the benefits from regional cooperation.

Effective structural reform is adopted for a purpose and to achieve a stated outcome. A key to progress is first to be clear about that purpose and the outcomes sought. The focus in this volume was the introduction of competition in markets where there was a risk of the abuse of a position of natural monopoly. It was found that reforms can stall or be diverted if the ultimate goal is lost from sight and not referred to regularly. The impacts of reform and their economy-wide effects with respect to these goals are also worthy of regular attention. Evidence of gaps between good practice, given the stage of development and the costs of those gaps, are drivers of reform. The pace of reform is important. But in the end what matters is the outcome.

Structural reforms, as is evident from the case studies here, are challenging and require a significant political commitment amid the economic and political complexities in all economies. These results suggest the value of regional cooperation to build an even stronger structural reform agenda and work programmes across groups of economies. Structural reform will be a continuing process, as growth, changes in economic structures, new technologies and market responses to existing regulation continue to change the situations in which economies and their regulatory systems operate. Steady adaptation is required, not least because expectations will rise as development proceeds. Pressure from the rest of the world, both in terms of competition from other economies and new commitments for cooperation, create further forces for change. The sharing of experience of the design and implementation of policy remains a priority. Given the specification of the goals of reform, another area of cooperation is the design and implementation of reporting systems and monitoring arrangements for the progress of reform.

Chapter 2

Telecommunications in Papua New Guinea[1]

Ronald Duncan[2]

2.1 Introduction

Telecommunications reform, specifically reform of the market for mobile phone services, has been adopted in five Pacific island economies in recent years. Reform of this market in Papua New Guinea (PNG) was perhaps the most difficult of the five cases, particularly with respect to the political struggle over the nature and pace of the reform. This study illustrates the benefits of being able to lock in domestic reforms through international commitments – in this case through the World Trade Organization's (WTO) telecommunications commitments.

This study also illustrates the problems that regulatory capture can give rise to in trying to bring about reform. PNG's Independent Consumer and Competition Commission (ICCC), which was initially given the power to issue licences to mobile phone providers, fought a gallant battle to ensure competition. However, this eventually resulted in the loss of its role as an independent regulator of telecommunications.

---

[1] This chapter is based on a paper produced with funding from the Asia Pacific Economic Cooperation's Policy Support Unit and material from that paper is reproduced with its permission. Information is taken from The Impacts and Benefits of Structural Reforms in the Transport, Energy and Telecommunications Sectors in APEC Economies APEC#211-SE-01.1. The views expressed in this paper are those of the authors and do not necessarily represent those of the APEC Secretariat or APEC Member Economies.

[2] Crawford School of Public Policy, The Australian National University, Canberra, Australian Capital Territory (ronald.duncan@anu.edu.au).

This study also demonstrates the potent power of consumers realising the benefits of market reform and the irresistible force that consumer power can exert with respect to reforms.

2.2 Historical Background[3]

A plan for a national telephone system in PNG was drawn up in 1964 when the Telecommunication Division of the Department of Posts and Telegraph was established and 'overseas' expert advice was sought from Australia. A telephone service was subsequently introduced.

In 1973 the Department of Information and Communication Services was established when the National Broadcasting Commission (NBC) was set up to take over the PNG branch of the Australian Broadcasting Commission. The NBC became the broadcasting arm of the department. This was a vital event in PNG's history. Given the very rugged topography and the isolation of many clans, radio played a crucial role in the dissemination of information throughout the land, using an extensive network of provincial radio stations. Radio has subsequently played a huge role in building a more cohesive society from what was then more than 1,000 diverse tribes.

After gaining independence from Australia in September 1975, the Department of Information and Communication Services was responsible for information services, communication policy, and research and development. The newly-formed Department of Public Utilities took over the functions and the responsibilities of the Department of Posts and Telegraphs and became the Division of Postal and Telecommunication Services (DPTS). DPTS continued to function as a separate organisation until it was incorporated as the Post and Telecommunication Corporation (PTC) in October 1982.

On 9 September 1981 an executive steering committee was set up to examine ways and means of making a change in the status of the Postal and Telecommunications Services Division to a 'legal commercial

[3] This section draws on Sinclair (1984), Sinclair (1993), Stanley (2008a) and Stanley (2008b).

entity'. This committee presented its report to the National Executive Committee (NEC; effectively the Cabinet) on 16 December 1981 and the NEC gave approval to draft enabling legislation. The bill was passed by the National Parliament on 15 February 1982—the Post and Telecommunication Corporation Act 1982.

Due to a change in government policy in 1996, the PTC was split up and corporatised. The split saw the creation of Telikom PNG Ltd, Post PNG Ltd, and the PNG Telecommunications Authority (PANGTEL).

In 1997 the Department of Information and Communication Services was reduced to the Office of Information and Communication and there were tighter constraints on its resources. This resulted in a situation where it was not able to implement its mandated responsibilities. After the 2002 general elections, however, a new government established the Department of Public Enterprises, Information and Development Corporation (DPEIDC). Its core functions included national information and communication policy, rural connectivity and development, and the integrated government information system. It was also required under the government's Medium Term Development Strategy (2005–10) to expand telecommunication infrastructure and services.

With the re-establishment of the Ministry for Information and Communication Services in 2007, all matters relating to the PANGTEL, NBC and the Office of Information and Communication were placed under its administration.

2.2.1 *Telikom PNG Ltd*

Under the Telikom PNG Limited Act 1996, Telikom PNG Ltd was responsible for providing telecommunication services for profit and with a consideration of community service obligations. Under the Telecommunications Act 1996, Telikom was given exclusive rights up to 2001 to provide all forms of telecommunications services within PNG and between PNG and other economies. Through a regulatory contract with the ICCC, Telikom was granted another five-year monopoly, from 2002 until 17 October 2007, over fixed-line and mobile services, and the international gateway.

2.2.2 *PANGTEL*

PANGTEL was established on 1 January 1997 under the Telecommunications Act 1996. Its creation was part of the government's policy to corporatise PTC and to divide it into three different organisations: two service delivery companies incorporated as public companies under the Companies Act and one regulatory and licensing authority. PANGTEL became the sole technical regulator and licensing authority of telecommunications and broadcasting in PNG. The telecommunications industry comprises all private and government-owned companies that are involved in the provision of fixed and mobile telecommunications services such as voice, facsimile, data, cellular phones, video and audio programmes to the general public. The radio communications sector includes radio frequency spectrum and satellite orbital positions. The radio frequency spectrum is managed according to the Radio Spectrum Act 1996.

PANGTEL's main operational functions with respect to mobile telephony include:

- the granting of licences to carriers and suppliers of telecommunication services and equipment;
- establishing performance standards for any carrier and monitoring compliance with the standards;
- regulation of the telecommunications industry to ensure competitiveness;
- protection of consumers of telecommunications services;
- promotion of fairness and efficiency in the industry;
- provision of arbitration to conflicting parties in the industry; and
- monitoring the development of telecommunication services.

2.2.3 *Independent Competition and Consumer Commission*

The powers and functions of the Independent Competition and Consumer Commission are set out in the Independent Competition and Consumer Commission Act 2002. The ICCC was established as part of the government's economic reforms in implementing its privatisation policy.

Generally, the ICCC has very wide powers relating to price regulation, licensing, industry regulation through regulatory contracts, and ensuring compliance with the competition and consumer protection provisions of its legislation.

With respect to licensing, its powers relate to giving approval either for acquisitions or new entrants to a market and to the administration of Part IV of the ICCC Act, which deals with competitive market conduct. The ICCC is required under this part of its Act to consider all aspects of market conduct rules. When the ICCC is satisfied that the proposed activity will not have any negative effect, but rather enhance competition, it may grant the necessary approval or licence. It is in this context that the ICCC assumed authority to award carrier licences to two new entrants to the deregulated mobile phone industry.

As the principal regulator of the telecommunications sector, the ICCC was required to ensure that the provision of telecommunications services under the Telecommunications Act were fulfilled. The exception was any provision relating to the technical regulation of the sector, which was the responsibility of PANGTEL. Where the ICCC and PANGTEL were given concurrent powers, the agencies were required to consult before making any decision. In the event that they were unable to agree, the views of the ICCC would prevail.

However, the ICCC's powers with respect to mobile phone licences were removed and now rest with the Minister for Information and Communication. The ICCC participates through representation on the ICT Licensing Committee and makes recommendations to the Minister for Information and Communication for approval and awarding of SERVCO licences.

2.2.4 *Pacific Mobile Communications Ltd*

Pacific Mobile Communications Ltd (PMC), a wholly-owned subsidiary of Telikom PNG Ltd, was established in 2002. PMC is responsible for the provision of internet gateway services. It is also involved in the mobile phone sector, trading as Bmobile Ltd (Bemobile). Since Telikom is the sole distributor and wholesaler of bandwidth, PMC, the operator of the internet gateway, leases bandwidth from Telikom and resells it to internet service providers under the brand name 'Tiare'. As a wholly-owned subsidiary of Telikom PNG, Bemobile is regulated by the licences, codes, and rules established under the Telecommunications Act 1996.

2.2.5 *Independent Public Business Corporation*

The Independent Public Business Corporation (IPBC) came into being on 30 June 2002 under the Independent Public Business Corporation Act 2002. The IPBC holds the majority of state-owned commercial assets in trust and is expected to manage those assets prudently for the benefit of the State. The IPBC reports to the Minister for Public Enterprises.

2.2.6 *Universal service obligations*

One of the key objectives of PNG's information and communication technology (ICT) policy has been the provision of access to telecommunications for all users, with particular emphasis on the rural population. Strategy guidelines have been set. These include the provision of funding for rural telecommunications and encouraging local and provincial governments to improve access to telecommunications for all citizens. The rural development obligations and the Rural Development Fund in the Telecommunications Act 1996 focused on basic telephony becoming 'reasonably' accessible to all. Consultation between the minister and PANGTEL declares specific areas for rural development obligations. Operators declared by PANGTEL to be universal service carriers may access the Rural Development Fund to pursue infrastructure developments. Funding for the Rural Development Fund is sourced from levies paid by operators and interest from the fund's investments.

2.3 Development of ICT Policy[4]

In December 2005 the NEC handed down a decision to open the market in mobile phone services. Since this decision, several policies and pieces of legislation have been drafted, amended and repealed. Prior to the introduction of mobile services, only two pieces of ICT legislation had been implemented. These were, first, a Communication Policy drafted as a result of a Communication Policy seminar in 1978. Second, in 1992 the Department of Information and Communication was instructed to begin the process of formulating a coherent national ICT policy (Department of Communication and Information, 2008, pp. 2–3). The result was the National Policy on Information and Communication of Papua New Guinea adopted in 1994. This latter policy was more comprehensive in setting out general guidelines on defining ownership, access and content. It emphasised the role of the publicly-owned telecommunications operator in providing access to rural communities and extending the network to complement economic development. Privatisation plans for the incumbent operator were mentioned. The introduction of competition was not.

The main objective of the ICT policy approved in 2005 was to use telecommunications for economic development. The government's stated preference was to establish electronic connectivity for disseminating information to the general public and as a means of reaching out to the public and outside world (e-government, e-commerce and e-education); however, Telikom's infrastructure through which these services were to be provided was limited and in need of major modernisation. Therefore, rehabilitation of Telikom was said to be a government priority. According to the same NEC decision, competition was to be introduced in the mobile sector. However, Telikom was inadequately prepared for competition. The lack of ability of Telikom to operate effectively in a competitive market seems to have been the key issue that drove much of the political intervention in the reform programme that led to regulatory uncertainty in 2007 and 2008.

[4] This section draws extensively on Ofa (2011).

The capacity of Telikom to serve rural and isolated communities was severely constrained due to the difficult geographic terrain, the largely rural population and the diversity of languages and culture within PNG. However, geography and the largely rural population were not the main reasons for Telikom's underperformance. A new administration in 2002 set out to rehabilitate Telikom. Poor management was seen as one of the major contributors to inefficiencies. The Prime Minister reported to Parliament in 2005 that Telikom at one time had six managing directors over an 11-month period. The government stabilised the management structure and hired experts to assist in providing strategic direction to the chairman and the board. The results were a series of positive business initiatives, including the appointment of international firms to formulate strategic policies and further the network expansion of fixed-line services.

There were three key statements in the NEC's decision in December 2005. Firstly, through its regulatory contract with ICCC, Telikom PNG Ltd was to terminate its mobile phone monopoly by 31 March 2006. Secondly, ICCC was mandated to select, via public tender, two new licensees to compete with Telikom's B-Mobile service. Thirdly, March 2007 was the date set for open competition in mobile services.

Following the government's decision to introduce competition, in January 2006 the ICCC released a press statement outlining the processes it would follow in fulfilling its obligations (ICCC, 2006, pp. 1–2). There were to be four main steps. Firstly, the public tender process would begin on 7 March 2006 and submissions would close in May 2006. Secondly, the assessment of the applications would be undertaken by the ICCC, with the two new mobile providers being announced by mid-October 2006. (In fact, the licensees were announced in September 2006.) Thirdly, construction of network infrastructure for the mobile entrants was tentatively scheduled for December 2006. Fourthly, licences would be issued: these were issued on 27 March 2007 to Digicel PNG and GreenCom. The former commenced operations on 17 July 2007. GreenCom has since gone into receivership.

2.3.1 *Policy uncertainty*

The ICCC was required to consult with Telikom on the processes to be followed by Telikom in terminating its monopoly over mobile services. In surrendering its exclusivity rights, Telikom required the ICCC to fulfil several conditions. The ICCC claimed that these were addressed and amended the contract agreement with Telikom to reflect the termination of exclusive rights over mobile services.

However, in September 2006, Telikom claimed that the conditions were not fulfilled and that it did not consent to the release of its monopoly rights (ICCC, 2007, p. 1). Moreover, the government released a National ICT Policy in the same month that effectively reversed the NEC's decision in December 2005 to liberalise mobile services. Notwithstanding the uncertainty, the ICCC kept to its timeline and announced the two new licensees in March 2007.

Three public entities pressured the ICCC to stall the mobile liberalisation programme. Firstly, Telikom commenced three separate judicial proceedings to challenge the ICCC's actions: one through an Appeal Panel and the other two through the court system. However, the Appeal Panel ruled in favour of the ICCC. The first court decision also dismissed Telikom's claim for abuse of process (Supreme Court of Papua New Guinea, 2008, p. 1). Telikom voluntarily discontinued the second court proceeding.

Secondly, the IPBC—the sole shareholder of Telikom—advocated a position that would have prevented the introduction of mobile competition (Abe, 2007a, p. 4). Thirdly, the minister responsible for the DPEIDC pushed for the policy reversal in order to allow for the rehabilitation of Telikom's capacity to compete effectively.

This reversal attempt referred to the September 2006 National ICT Policy, which stated that Digicel should not be granted a licence for immediate competition but that there should be staged competition. However, the licence that the ICCC granted in March 2007 was based on the NEC's decision in 2005, which had not been amended before Digicel began to establish its infrastructure network in September 2006. Although the ICT Policy was passed in September 2006, coinciding with the announcement of the result of the tender process, it was rather late as the ICCC had followed its public tender process mapped out from January 2006, soon after the NEC's decision in 2005.

Two reasons for the policy reversal were put forward in the National ICT Policy. Firstly, that Telikom's network was technically not capable of interconnecting to another carrier's network and, therefore, customers of one carrier would not be able to call customers of another carrier. Digicel requested interconnection with Telikom three months before its official launch in May 2007 (Joku, 2008). Digicel only began testing interconnection with Telikom on 31 January 2008 and nation-wide connection was not possible until July 2008. Much of the delay was focused on the technical capacity of Telikom to allow interconnection. Also, the numbering plan in Telikom's network limited subscribers to 400,000 mobile telephone numbers.

Secondly, it was claimed that the "ICCC has both a regulatory function under the ICCC Act (2002) and the regulatory authority to issue and revoke licences under the Telecommunications Act (1996)... which is a conflict of interest and ought not be allowed to subsist" (DPEIDC, 2006, p. 32). The National ICT Policy recommended that the ICCC's power to issue and revoke licences return to a committee comprised of representatives from PANGTEL and the ICCC, with a former Chief Justice in the chair. This recommendation would have effectively returned licensing power to government control not to an independent entity.

The National ICT Policy was never implemented. No publicly accessible document is available to shed light on why this was so, although its timing does provide hints about the purpose of the policy. The policy was finalised at the same time that the ICCC announced the results of the public tender process for the two new mobile service providers. The ICCC timeline set for March 2007 was based on the December 2005 NEC decision.

In March 2007 Digicel launched several mobile stations. In accordance with its legislative mandate, PANGTEL issued Digicel with a spectrum licence. However, several days later it withdrew the licences stating 'amended ICT policy' as the reason for withdrawal. PANGTEL's Acting Director-General was reported as saying that under the amended ICT policy, access to spectrum would be restricted to NETCO, the proposed new operator of all telecommunications infrastructure. Digicel obtained a court order shortly afterwards that overrode PANGTEL's action and allowed it to continue operations.

The ICT policy was reviewed again in early 2007. A Telecommunications Blueprint was developed in May 2007, which was the basis for the May 2007 National ICT Policy. The May 2007 policy reflected the recommendations of the draft September 2006 National ICT Policy in three crucial regulatory areas. Firstly, there was a recommendation for the adoption of the 'NETCO/SERVCO model' in which Telikom retained an indefinite monopoly over NETCO infrastructure, whereas SERVCO would be opened for new licences. Secondly, competition (SERVCO services) would only commence after 1 June 2008. Thirdly, the government, through DPEIDC, would establish new committees to oversee licensing issues and the overall ICT policy. The authority of the ICCC to issue and revoke licences would be 'removed and will rest with the Minister for the DPEIDC' (DPEIDC 2007, p.12).

The May 2007 policy was never implemented, however, due to pressure from key stakeholders, including Digicel. Subsequently, the latest ICT Policy (March 2009) gave the power to issue and revoke licences to a new body, the National Information and Communication Authority (NICTA). NICTA is primarily composed of PANGTEL staff and assets.

2.3.2 *Multilateral policy restraints*

Digicel was methodical but diplomatic in how it dealt with the policy uncertainties. Digicel pressured the government through two main channels. Firstly, it negotiated directly with the government on ensuring security for its investment. Digicel met with the Prime Minister early in March and was given an assurance that Digicel's investment and licence to operate in PNG were protected. Digicel continued to engage in regulatory dialogue with Telikom, the ICCC, PANGTEL and the government to ensure that its initial licence, based on the December 2005 NEC decision, was protected. Digicel was also assisted in protecting its investment through government-to-government dialogue channels between the Irish and PNG governments (Digicel is an Irish company) (*Islands Business*, 3 September 2007).

Digicel's main investment concerns up to the May 2007 ICT Policy were basically two-fold: the withdrawal of Digicel's spectrum licence by PANGTEL in March 2007 and concern over the NETCO 'model' through which Telikom controlled the international gateway. The chief executive officer of Digicel PNG was reported as saying that:

> with only one gateway operating, people will experience higher calling rates, lower quality of calls due to network congestion as well as limited international roaming services [and] to remove Digicel's international gateway would be a step backward from the current open market approach. The people have tasted the benefits of competition and have the right to continue to enjoy those benefits – lower prices, better quality, increased coverage and introduction of new services (Digicel, 2008).

There is evidence that Digicel PNG also relied on PNG's WTO commitments on telecommunications reform to protect its investment and to ensure that it was able to operate mobile services. Two events in the telecommunications reform process strengthen the case for this point. Firstly, the latest ICT Policy stated that the model proposed was consistent with PNG's WTO obligations (Department of Communications and Information, 2009, p. 22). This indicates that the government was trying to ensure that the policy is compatible with its WTO commitments. Secondly, the September 2006 National ICT Policy had argued for a phased liberalisation under which, in phase 1, Telikom retained its monopoly over the international gateways. The two ICT policies issued in 2008 adopted similar frameworks. There was no timeframe indicated in the 2008 ICT policies as to when phase 2 would begin. However, the March 2009 ICT Policy came up with a clear timeframe and set milestones to be achieved.

2.3.3 *Domestic restraints*

Local business communities in PNG also put pressure on the government. The Port Moresby Chamber of Commerce made known its concerns that the government had not consulted with them on the policy.

As noted above, the ICCC also resisted changes in the government's policy (Abe, 2007). Since the ICCC's involvement with the reform programme in December 2005, its position was to act as the independent regulator for telecommunications services and to provide competition in the mobile service sector through the granting of licences. The ICCC's role in accordance with its legislation was effective during the reform programme on one key regulatory aspect – independence. Maintaining independence amid commercial and political interference was achieved by the ICCC, although it may have contributed to the loss of its power to grant and revoke telecommunications licences. On 24 November 2009 the National Information and Communications Technology Authority (NICTA) bill was passed. This legislation transferred the telecommunications regulatory functions previously administered by the ICCC to NICTA. Now the ICCC is responsible only for issuing mobile licences and for ensuring that mobile carriers are rolling out infrastructure as planned.

2.4 The Benefits from Opening the Mobile Phone Market

As mentioned earlier the government tender process was completed in September 2006. Two carriers were selected: Digicel, which had been successful in privatising the telephony market in the Caribbean; and GreenCom, an Indonesian engineering and telecommunications company (now in liquidation). In March 2007 mobile carrier licences were issued to Digicel and GreenCom by the ICCC, while PANGTEL issued the spectrum licences. Digicel PNG Ltd commenced operations on 17 July 2007 and has since extended its services to most of PNG.

In setting up its services, Digicel made two strategic moves. It established widespread coverage very quickly and put mobile phones into the hands of as many Papua New Guineans as quickly and as cheaply as possible. The novelty of having a mobile phone and of being able to call relatives and friends over large distances in an economy where physical movement is so difficult gave a huge impetus to Digicel's efforts to retain its licence. Essentially, the public pressure from consumers to retain Digicel's licence became impossible to resist.

Digicel claims to have invested in excess of PGK450 million in the PNG mobile telecommunications market in 2008 and 2009 (Batten *et al.*, 2009). This investment has had a large impact on the coverage and quality of domestic services, with mobile phone coverage now very extensive. The quality of international connections has also improved, with a substantial amount of the investment going towards enhancing an international gateway. Moreover, there are plans for an additional PGK1 billion investment in rolling out further services over the next three years (Stanley, 2008b). Extending coverage to most of PNG is anticipated.

ICCC and World Bank estimates placed the number of mobile phone subscribers (through Bemobile) at 130,000–140,000 prior to the entrance of Digicel in July 2007. While exact industry figures are not available, Telikom and Digicel now claim to have over 500,000 customers each. This suggests a remarkable 700% growth in the number of mobile phone subscribers (Batten *et al.*, 2009).

Average peak time and off-peak time domestic call billing rates have fallen by 11% and 51% respectively since the introduction of Digicel (Table 2.1). Average peak and off-peak international call rates have fallen by 40% and 38% respectively. As well, calling rates for both carriers and for both domestic and international calls have moved from 30 second billing increments to per second billing increments. Charges by Bemobile and Digicel are generally similar, except when special pricing events are being run.

Table 2.1 Average call rates for domestic and international phone calls, 2008 (PGK/minute).

Charges	Peak	Off-peak
Domestic		
Pre-Digicel	K1.80	K1.60
Post-Digicel (Sept. 2008)	K0.99	K0.49
International		
Pre-Digicel	K2.45	K1.60
Post-Digicel (Sept. 2008)	K1.48	K0.99

Source: Batten *et al.* (2009), Table 4.

Digicel has a wide range of market products and services, such as a pre-paid handset pack, 24/7 customer care, post-paid price plans, international text messaging, missed call alerts and other promotional products such as 'talk-for-free' and 'Happy Fridays'. It claims to have provided employment opportunities to some 300 people of whom 90% are Papua New Guineans and indirect employment for about 500 people through dealer stores, top-up vendors, distributors, etc. Furthermore, it has committed itself to community relations programmes such as Operation Open Heart, Street Vendors and to providing technical support to St John's Ambulance and Food for Schools, and sponsorship of the Pukpuk national rugby 7s team at the South Pacific Games in Samoa (*The National*, 12 September 2007).

On 26 June 2008 the long-awaited interconnection of Bemobile and Digicel services was achieved. Previously, they had been operating on separate and unconnected networks. The interconnection ended the rather bizarre situation where many consumers carried two mobile phones, one for calling through Digicel and the other for calling through Bemobile.

Mobile phone sector reform and growth has made a strong contribution to PNG's GDP. Following the entry of Digicel in 2007, the contribution of the transport, storage and communication sector to total and non-mining GDP almost doubled – from 2.7% and 3%, respectively, in 2006 to 5.1% and 5.7%, respectively, in 2008 (Batten *et al.*, 2009). The sector contributed just over 20% of total GDP growth for 2008. With total GDP growth estimated at 7.16%, this means that the sector contributed approximately 1.4 percentage points to GDP growth in 2008.

Since the introduction of competition, Telikom has adapted by selling 50% of the equity in its mobile service (Bemobile) for PGK130 million. The 50% equity investment was contributed by a "consortium of companies, including the US-based Trilogy International Partners LLC (20%), GEMS Ltd (20%), PNG's National Superannuation Fund (5%) and Nambawan Super Ltd (5%)" (*Post Courier*, September 2008). With separate ownership and management of the mobile service, it is anticipated that Bemobile will be able to compete with Digicel.

2.5 Locking-in Policy through WTO Commitments

The multilateral policy restraint provided by the WTO's telecommunications commitments has been very important in progressing mobile telephony reform in PNG. The main difference between this form of policy restraint and domestic policy restraint provided by an independent regulator is in the domestic and international costs of policy reversal by governments.[5] Commitments on telecommunication's liberalisation reform in the WTO are legally binding and failure to adhere to the commitments can be challenged by member economies through the WTO's Dispute Settlement Body. Bosworth and Duncan (2002, p. 10) capture this argument in suggesting that:

> the main economic benefit to be gained… from WTO membership is help in facilitating policy reforms that liberalize trade and, as a by-product, support a market economy... By 'locking in' such reforms internationally, WTO accession [commitments] provide governments with a defence mechanism against future policy backsliding or 'de-liberalization' in response to domestic protectionist pressures.

The telecommunications regulatory reforms in PNG encountered challenges that the domestic independent regulator dealt with to the best of its ability. However, the frequent policy changes over the past five years point to the limited ability of the independent regulator to provide credibility to the reform process. Actions instigated through various channels by the Irish-owned Digicel operator, including the European Commission reminding the PNG government of its WTO obligations, provide evidence that multilateral policy restraints can provide credibility to the telecommunications reform process. The government recognised

[5] International reputation, borrowing capacity, aid programmes, and political and socio-economic partnerships of economies are at stake when departing from international rules.

its WTO obligations as evidenced by revisions to PNG's ICT policy in 2008 and 2009.

2.6 Conclusion

Notwithstanding an eventful process to liberalise the mobile telephony market in PNG, the benefits are already large and appear likely to become much larger in the future. Call rates have been reduced significantly and coverage has increased hugely and looks to become almost universal. In a land with a terrain as difficult as PNG's, the benefits to the many remote communities of being able to interact with other people cannot be underestimated. Already the availability of mobile phone services has done much for social interaction as well as being helpful in medical emergencies. Moreover, the mobile banking initiatives now underway will be enormously helpful. Until now, banking services in rural areas have been very limited. Further, the provision of market pricing information through mobile phone services will be very helpful because the livelihood of the bulk of the population is from agricultural and fishing activities.

However, the liberalisation of the mobile phone sector has been a difficult experience at a political level. In this there are several lessons for PNG and other economies. One of the main lessons is that regulatory capture provides incentives for government to reverse commitments on telecommunications reform. The eventual 'internal reform' of the ICCC since its involvement in the telecommunications reform process in 2005, culminating in the removal of its autonomous power to grant licences and essentially giving this power back to the minister responsible for telecommunications, shows the vulnerability of domestic policy restraints to vested political interests.

The publicly-owned telecommunications operator, Telikom, needed significant rehabilitation time and funding to prepare for open competition. The government may not have been clear about the necessary rehabilitation following the NEC's decision in December 2005. Since then, seven national ICT policies were passed over about three years. These frequent policy changes created significant uncertainty about investment regulations. Nevertheless, when PNG authorities were reminded of the WTO telecommunications commitments, it realigned its policies to those commitments. This multilateral policy restraint, therefore, provided credibility to the reform programme and gave confidence to international and domestic investors.

Another lesson is that technical assistance in making the case for reforms is vital. Once it was seen that the introduced competition would have significant benefits, including for those in rural and isolated areas, the general public's support for the liberalisation of the mobile service sector increased dramatically. As a result, it became much more difficult to resist or reverse the reform. Therefore, convincing the public that services will improve and prices will be reduced is critical to gaining their support for the introduction of competition.

Chapter 3

Gas in Thailand[1]

Deunden Nikomborirak[2]

3.1 Introduction

In 2009, Thailand ranked 27th in terms of natural gas production (28.7 million m^3) and 40th in terms of proven natural gas reserves (317,100 million m^3) according to the US Central Intelligence Agency (2009). Thailand has a vast natural gas supply in the Gulf of Siam and the Andaman Sea. However, domestic supply was not able to keep up with the surge in demand prompted by escalating global petroleum prices and government subsidies of the use of natural gas for vehicles (NGV) and home cooking (liquefied natural gas; LNG). During 2004–09 demand for natural gas increased on average 5.26% per year compared with 0.4% for petroleum. Thailand has been an importer of natural gas since 1998 (Figure 3.1).

The bulk of the demand for natural gas in Thailand comes from the power generation sector which relies heavily on natural gas. In 2009

[1] This case chapter is based on a paper produced with funding from the Asia Pacific Economic Cooperation's Policy Support Unit and material from that paper is reproduced with its permission. Information is taken from The Impacts and Benefits of Structural Reforms in the Transport, Energy and Telecommunications Sectors in APEC Economies APEC#211-SE-01.1. The views expressed in this paper are those of the authors and do not necessarily represent those of the APEC Secretariat or APEC Member Economies.

[2] Research Director at Thailand Development Research Institute (deunden@tdri.or.th) and Secretary to the Minister of Finance, Finance Ministry (2007–2008).

more than 70% of consumption went to electricity generating plants, with the remaining 17% going to gas separation plants and 11% to industrial use (Figure 3.2).

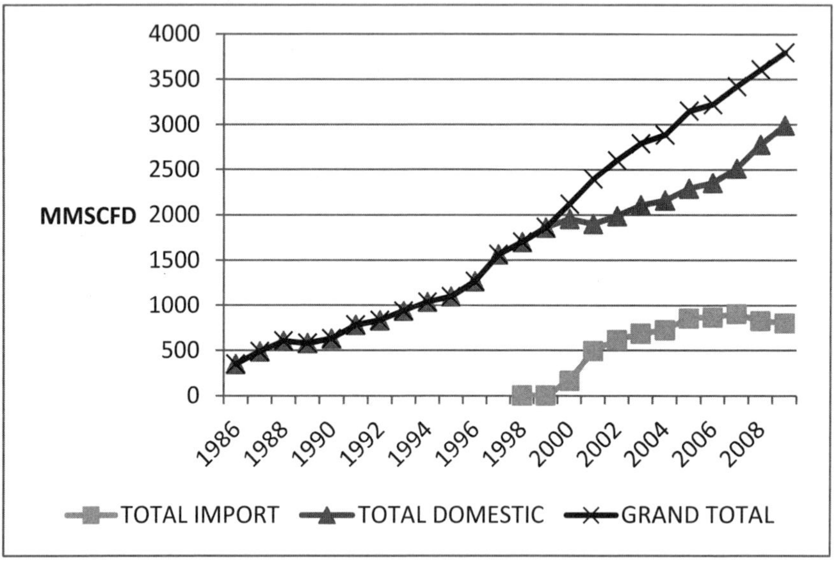

Figure 3.1 Thailand's Natural Gas Supply, 1986–2009 (millions of standard cubic feet per day).
Source: Energy Policy and Planning Office.
Note: MMSCFD = millions of standard cubic feet per day.

A reform plan for the gas sector was developed in the late 1990s. This plan included extensive change. However, in 2001 a new government adopted a policy of support of national champions which focussed on privatisation and corporate development rather than market reform and the introduction of competition. This case study explains how the reform plan was adjusted in the light of the adoption of that policy and identifies some of the economic consequences of doing so. The first step is to provide some background information on the gas industry.

3.2 The Structure of the Gas Industry in Thailand

3.2.1 *Domestic competition*

The gas industry in Thailand is dominated by two players – the Petroleum Authority of Thailand (PTT) on the supply side and the Electricity Generating Authority of Thailand (EGAT) on the demand side. Both entities are majority government owned, although PTT is now a listed company with 49% of its equity share floated on the stock market and the remainder held by the Ministry of Finance.

PTT, with few minor exceptions, acts as the sole purchaser, transporter and distributor of natural gas in Thailand. PTT purchases all indigenous gas from the producers, including PTT Exploration and Production (PTTEP), its subsidiary, and transmits this through its pipeline system to consumers. Its network of pipelines in Thailand currently stretches 3,100km, linking all commercial offshore gas fields to EGAT's power plants, its own five gas separation plants (GSPs), as well as some 200 industrial users. Many of the industrial users are petrochemical companies and gas distribution companies in which PTT owns a controlling share.

In the petroleum sector, the company holds a majority equity share in several refineries whose production capacity contribute to more than 80% of the economy's total refinery capacity. It is also the largest player in retail distribution (petrol stations), international trading activities and the downstream petrochemical industry.

Limited private participation in pipeline construction (at the distribution level) has been introduced with the establishment of PTT Natural Gas Distribution Company (PTTNGD), a joint venture pipeline owned 49% by PTT and the balance by private investors. However, there is no mandatory third party access to PTT's gas transmission pipelines network, and so there is no competition in the distribution market. Certain power plants construct their own pipelines to connect to PTT's.

On the demand side, EGAT is by far the largest consumer of natural gas in Thailand. Although Figure 3.2 shows its gas consumption share is only 32%, the government-owned electricity generating enterprise holds a major equity share in many of the independent power producers (IPPs). As a result, sales to EGAT's group of electricity generating plants account for roughly half of Thailand's total natural gas supply.

The second largest group of customers comprises the gas separation plants, all of which belong to PTT. The third largest group comprises the small independent power producers (SPPs). These power producers supply electricity to EGAT's grid at a predetermined price. As for industrial customers, whose number totalled roughly 240 in 2009, many are downstream petrochemical companies affiliated with the PTT. All PTT contracts, whether with suppliers or consumers, are on a long-term (25–30 years) take or pay basis.

To conclude, there is little market competition in the vertical structure of the natural gas industry. Exploration and production where foreign players maintain a majority share in the market may be an exception. Although PTTEP's market share in exploration is roughly 25% in terms of sales, the company also holds equity shares that range from 5% to 40% in many of the exploration projects undertaken by its main competitor, Chevron.

3.2.2 *Foreign commercial presence*

The presence of foreign operators in the Thai gas industry has been confined to the exploration and production of natural gas. The Petroleum Act 1971 and the Energy Industry Act 2007 are the two main laws governing the gas industry. However, foreign investment issues are dealt with by the Foreign Business Act 1999. The foreign equity share is not restricted for businesses related to the production of tangible products, but for service businesses, foreign equity is limited to a minority portion. Hence, foreign companies that seek to operate gas transmission, trading and distribution services are required to seek a joint venture with a local partner.

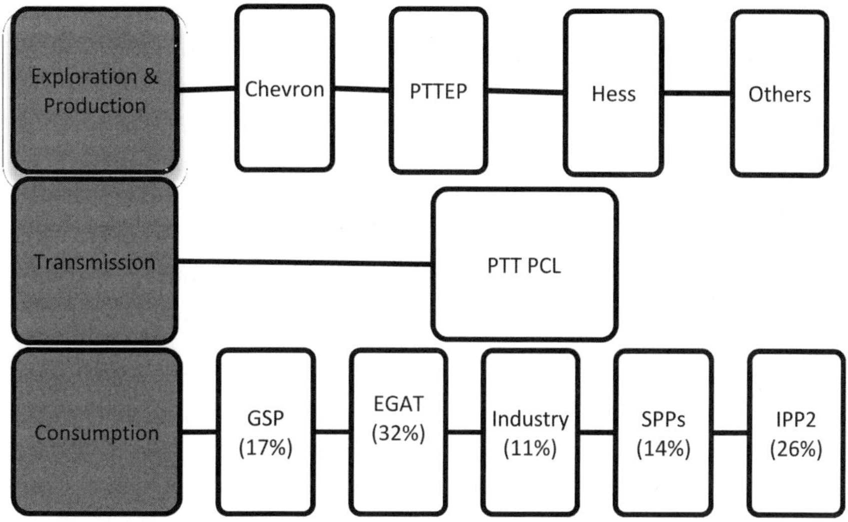

Figure 3.2 The Current Structure of the Thai Gas Industry.

The employment of foreigners in Thailand is governed by an act entitled the Working of Aliens Act BE2521 (1978). Generally, when considering whether to allow a foreign worker to enter the economy to work, the Department of Employment will consider whether the opening can be filled by a Thai, whether the foreign worker is qualified and whether the job fits the need of Thailand. Moreover, all foreign and Thai companies are required to observe the 4:1 ratio of the number of Thai to foreign employees at all times according to the Order of Immigration Office No. 110/2546 (2003). This may pose a problem for companies that require highly specialised staff to undertake work before production that will require local workers. The Board of Investment is able to waive this restriction. Promoted companies are allowed to bring in skilled workers and professionals. Gas exploration and production businesses are not among the list of promoted companies, unlike their downstream gas transmission and petrochemical counterparts.

3.2.3 *Cross-border competition*

While there is cross-border supply of natural gas both through pipelines and in the form of LNG, cross-border competition in natural gas is not established. Presently, there are several joint development gas exploration and production projects between PTT and its counterparts in neighbouring economies such as Myanmar, Malaysia and Cambodia (Figure 3.3).

Pipelines connect offshore gas fields to electricity generation plants or gas liquefaction, condensation or separation plants mainly to serve Thailand's domestic demand.

The cross-border pipeline network between Burma and Thailand includes the Yadana–Ratchaburi pipeline (completed 1999) and the Yetagun–Ratchaburi pipeline (completed September 2000). On the horizon are projects to deliver gas to Malaysia and Thailand from the Malaysia–Thailand Joint Development Area.

Work to develop a regional natural gas market has been in progress for over a decade. ASEAN's proposal for a 'Trans-ASEAN Gas Pipeline' and APEC's concept of an 'Asian Gas Grid' both recognise natural gas' superior fuel qualities and the logic of linking ASEAN's natural gas production centres with markets in neighbouring economies. Both concepts are designed to catalyse cross-border linkages connecting national gas grids. According to Sovacool (2009), the establishment of national gas grids faces three challenges.

Firstly, Lao PDR, Myanmar and Cambodia are poorer economies with vast reserves of natural resources, relative to Thailand, which is perceived to be a much more advanced economy with a large demand for energy. Thus, the flow of energy within the region is likely to be one way. Secondly, the energy business in the region remains dominated by government enterprises – PTT (Thailand), Petronas (Malaysia) and Pertamina (Indonesia). Competition that would undermine the status of each of these enterprises may be resisted by their government owners in order to protect national assets. Thirdly, the planned integrated natural gas pipeline is estimated to require an investment totalling USD16 billion to construct the additional 5,600km of pipeline needed to connect centres of demand in the region. It is unlikely that private investors would be willing to inject capital into a project of such a scale given that there is a lack of certainty concerning the pricing, that regulatory regimes are yet to be harmonised across borders and that gas market structures may continue to accommodate single-buyer regimes.

Competition from compressed LNG is conceivable, especially since Indonesia and Malaysia are among the five largest worldwide exporters of LNG. Indeed, to secure its gas supply, besides developing new gas fields in joint cooperation with neighbouring economies, Thailand has come to rely increasingly on imported LNG. PTT has undertaken to construct Thailand's first LNG terminal (in Rayong in the northern industrial zone on the eastern coast). The facility includes a tank terminal, a jetty and a 5 million ton storage facility that will be enlarged to accommodate 10 million tons in a second phase. The terminal is scheduled to start operating in 2011. However, in the absence of third party access to PTT's pipeline, there is unlikely to be any competition in the import of LNG.

3.3 Government Policy

Greacen (2005) categorises the Thai government's policy towards the development of the domestic energy market into three distinct periods – the 'Nationalist Era' (1950–90), the 'Neo-Liberal Era' (1990–2000) and the 'National Champion Era' (2001–05), the time of his presentation.

The Nationalist Era saw the establishment of government-owned utilities that were self-regulating monopolies based on the cost-plus price regulatory scheme. PTT was established in 1978.

The Neo-Liberal Era was a period during which the government was dominated by technocrats whose concerns were focused mainly on introducing greater competition into utility markets monopolised by government enterprises. During the period, some EGAT power plants were spun off to become listed companies on the stock market. IPPs and SPPs were introduced to foster private competition in the power generation market.

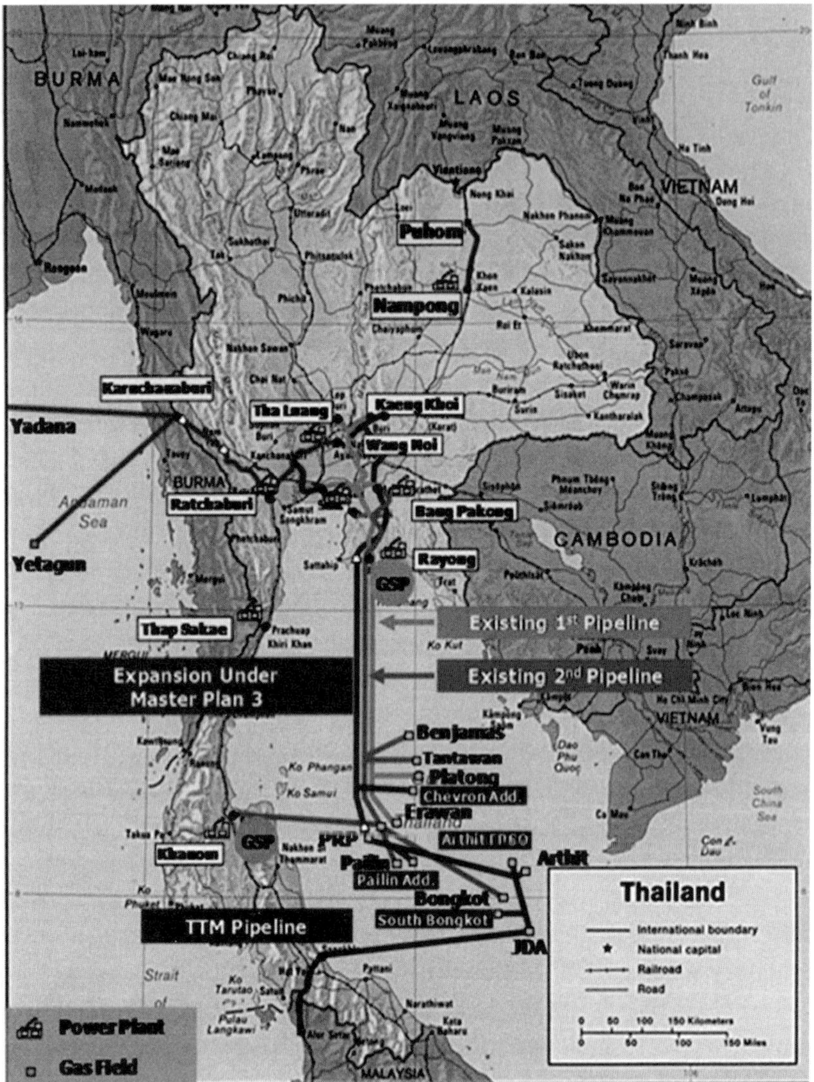

Figure 3.3 Thailand's Regional Natural Gas Pipeline Network and its Neighbours.
Source: PTT

The National Energy Policy Office (NEPO)[3] floated the idea of creating a 'power pool' in 2000. A draft law on the rules governing the power pool was also proposed in the following year.

Although no reform took place in the gas industry during this era, the Ministry of Finance introduced a comprehensive plan for government enterprise reform. It proposed restructuring, liberalisation and regulation of the markets in which government enterprises dominated – telecommunications, transport and energy (gas, oil and power). This 'Master Plan for State Enterprise Reform 1998' offered a clear direction for developing the gas industry (Figure 3.4).

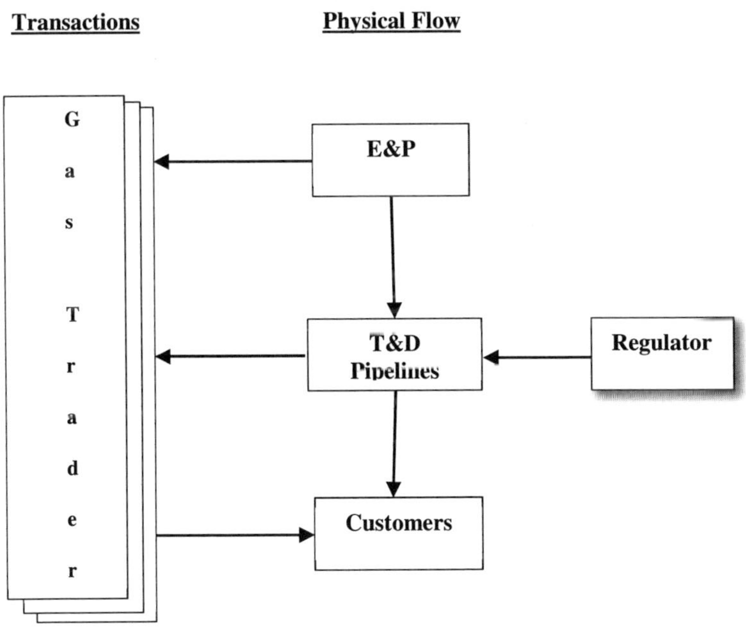

Figure 3.4 Future Gas Industry Structure as Perceived in 1998.
***Source*:** Master Plan for State Enterprise Reform 1998, http://www.mof.go.th/sepc/sepcfn2.htm
Note: E&P: Exploration and Production (Including PTTEP). T&D Pipelines: Transmission and Distribution Pipelines

[3] The office is currently known as the Energy Policy and Planning Office (EPPO), Ministry of Energy.

The competitive market model described in the plan contained two key reforms: the separation of the transmission network from production and trade functions, and third party access. The separation of PTT's gas transmission pipeline function, either by accounting or legal methods, from its gas trading business was a pre-condition to promoting competition. Full legal separation by a corporatised entity would not only facilitate competition in the production, trade and distribution of gas, but also would allow more transparent and efficient regulation of the industry.

The establishment of third party access to gas transmission pipelines is a means of facilitating the development of competition in gas supply. The provision of access to these facilities by third parties on fair terms and conditions would allow consumers to purchase gas from upstream producers or continue to purchase the bundled service of gas transmission and supply from the pipeline owner.

'Special Purpose Pipelines' were proposed in the plan of 1998. Developers of new pipelines were to be granted a franchise under terms that would have allowed them to negotiate use of the pipeline with a limited number of customers. Under this approach, the broad framework for access would be well defined, but the actual terms and conditions (such as tariffs) would be set by negotiation. This would have allowed a level of commercial control on the part of the owner, which may have led to an abuse of this position in terms of monopolistic pricing of the transmission service. To balance these matters, a dispute resolution process would have been necessary to address disputes arising from the negotiation process, with recourse to a predefined means of arbitration.

The Neo-Liberal Era ended in 2000 and was replaced, under a new government, by the 'national champion model'. PTT was listed on the stock market in 2001 so that public funding could be mobilised to facilitate the planned expansion of the enterprise. However, the government retained a majority equity share: only 49% of the equity was floated.

Under the national champion strategy, privatisation took place without any of the market reform envisioned in the 1998 master plan. There was no separation of the monopolistic gas transmission business from the potentially competitive trading and distribution businesses and an independent energy regulatory body was not immediately established. Privatised operations conferred some benefits on the company, but without the introduction of competition these were not likely to be passed to consumers. As a listed company, for example, it was able to mobilise private capital to finance its expansion while its commitments to shareholders provided it with a framework to respond to community or government expectations about the services it might provide.

PTT shares sold out in 77 seconds. The price of the share went from THB35 at its IPO in November 2001 to THB183 at the end of 2003. The share price went up 70% in a single month when the government approved the proposed THB100 billion gas transmission pipeline plan with a guaranteed rate of return at 16% (Greacen and Greacen, 2004). PTT now contributes 48.7% of the Thai Stock Exchange's total value (Nikomborirak and Sirikarn, 2009).

A landmark court case decision in which the Supreme Court ruled against the privatisation of EGAT prompted the same group of NGOs to try to revisit the case of PTT. In August 2006 the Federation of Consumers and its affiliated organisations filed lawsuits, petitioning for the two Royal Decrees pertinent to the privatisation to be revoked and the company re-nationalised. In December 2007 the Administrative Court delivered a verdict that fell short of delisting the company, but required it to transfer all land acquired through expropriation and all assets (i.e. gas pipelines) attached therewith to the Ministry of Finance (PTT website, 2007). In practice, PTT continues to operate these pipelines as if they were its own but it does not have legal ownership of these particular pipelines and it has to pay the Ministry of Finance an annual access fee calculated as a fixed percentage of its total transmission revenue (this is 10–30% depending on the size of the revenue).

Corporate governance in the government-owned enterprises remains an issue. The National Anti-Corruption Commission is proposing a ban on government officials becoming directors in government-owned enterprises due to the conflict of roles. Members of Parliament and Senators raised concerns in Parliament about this conflict of roles among directors of government-owned enterprises. These issues may also limit the scope for further reform.

The national champion era came to an end in 2006 when the government originally elected in 2001 was replaced. During the period from September 2006 to February 2008 the neo-liberal era was revived. The Energy Industry Act, which established a fully fledged energy regulatory body, was passed in 2007. However, the time span of that government was too short to implement the reform. A new government was elected in 2008 but there has been no further policy change since that time.

3.4 The Regulatory Regime

3.4.1 *The institution*

The gas industry in Thailand is governed by two major laws; the Petroleum Act 1971 stipulates rules concerning the extraction and production of natural gas, and the Energy Industry Act 2007 prescribes rules on the transmission of natural gas, compression of gas into liquid form, distribution of gas and wholesale and retail sale of gas. The Petroleum Act assigns the regulatory power to the Electricity Policy and Planning Office (EPPO) in the Ministry of Energy, which also oversees energy policy work. The Energy Industry Act established a regulatory body, the Electricity Regulatory Commission (ERC), for the gas and electricity generation industry. Regulations governing the petroleum industry and the exploration for and production of fossil fuel (including gas) were not included in this law. This was to preserve the Ministry of Energy's regulatory role, set out in the Petroleum Act.

Section 9(6) of the Energy Industry Act stipulates that the Minister of Energy is responsible for setting the quality and standard of energy services. Section 64 similarly grants the Minister (with approval from the National Energy Policy Commission) the authority to set policy and guidelines with regard to the pricing of energy services. As a result the ERC applies the form of regulation (rate of return regulation or price cap) chosen by EPPO, but decides on the actual tariff within that method. The ERC was granted the power of whether to allow the service provider to pass on certain costs to consumers. For example, it refused to allow

PTT to pass on costs incurred from the destruction of its offshore gas exploration platform near the Oceania Islands.

It is interesting to compare the ERC's regulatory power with that of its telecommunications counterpart, the National Telecommunication Commission (NTC), which was established by the Telecommunications Act in 2001. The NTC's broad regulatory power and financial independence guarantee its autonomy. This is partly due to the fact that unlike the NTC, the independence of the energy regulator was not mandated in the constitution. However issues of accountability and transparency of the NTC remain and need to be balanced with independence (Nikomborirak and Cheevasittiyanon, 2009).

3.4.2 *Regulatory rules*

The key features of the existing regulatory regime governing the structure of the natural gas market, the access to the market and the tariff regulation are discussed below.

There are no legal restrictions on the structure of gas undertakings (no vertical separation requirement). PTT and its subsidiaries are engaged in the entire gas supply chain from exploration, production and transmission through to trade, import and distribution to retail.

There are no legal restrictions on new entries into any of the natural gas business subsectors, including the importation of LNG. However, PTT's monopoly in transmission and, hence, the buying and selling of gas, amount to barriers to entry. As there is not yet third party access to PTT's proprietary transmission network and no third party access to its gas terminal facilities, entry is practically impossible.

While the market-oriented reforms have not been adopted, there is an extensive system of price regulation, at least for natural gas. While some of its parameters could be debated (for example, the rates of return on investment built into the formulas), the regulatory system covers the key areas where there is a risk of the application of monopoly power over prices.

The wholesale gas price comprises the wellhead gas price, a marketing margin, the transmission tariff and the distribution tariff. These components are determined as follows:

- The wellhead gas price is specified in the gas purchase contract signed between the producer and PTT. It is normally indexed with the price of fuel oil, the exchange rate, and the consumer and producer price index. The price for natural gas produced from the Gulf of Thailand is roughly USD2 per million BTU, one-half the price of that in the USA and one-third of that in Japan where it is in the ranges of USD5–6 (Energy website, n.d.). Gas procured from joint development with neighbouring Malaysia and Myanmar is slightly more expensive at USD2.3–2.75. Significantly lower wellhead gas prices are common for less mature gas fields.
- The marketing margin is regulated by the EPPO. The current rate of the pooled gas price (the weighted average price of gas purchased from various production sources) is 1.75% for sales to IPPs and EGAT and 9.33% for SPPs. The higher margin reflects the higher risks that PTT has to bear as SPP contracts are shorter (five years vs. 20–25 years) and allow an SPP to switch from one source of energy to another, depending on the price level. For example, an SPP may choose to use LPG instead of natural gas. However, at the time of writing, the rate was being revised downward as statistics show that SPPs rarely exercise the option. Hence, the risk involved with the contract may have been overestimated, but since 1999 a cap of THB2.15 (which translates into less than 1% considering the current price of natural gas) has been imposed.
- The transmission tariff is set by EPPO with approval from the Minister of Energy. The tariff is uniform for all gas customers. The current tariff is made up of the demand charge (TD) component to cover fixed costs and CPI - X for the commodity charge (TC) to cover variable costs. The rate of return on capital used for the demand charge is 18% for older pipelines and 12% for new pipelines (pipelines installed after 2007). The x value used in the price cap has always been 2%; the cap is revised every five years or when a new investment qualifies for a revision of the capital allowance.

- The distribution tariff is unregulated. PTT negotiates a price with its customers.

In contrast to the cost-based approach to pricing natural gas, the wholesale price of LPG has been capped since 2006 at USD330 per ton compared with USD550–700 per ton for imported LPG. The government pays the difference between the import price and the capped price: this gap has increased since 2004 when those prices were about the same and the gap is now around THB9/kg. This system also discourages PTT from manufacturing LPG as the government only subsidises imported LPG. The production of domestic LPG is 350,000 tons per month, which is not enough for the likely increase in demand, resulting at present in 74,000 tons of LPG being imported monthly. The additional one-year extension of the LPG price cap will be a burden for the Oil Fund since it will require a subsidy of THB740 million per month (USD22.42 million) for imported LPG (EPPO, n.d.).

Similarly, the price of NGV has been capped since January 2007 at USD258 per ton, while the global price is roughly USD424 per ton. Originally, the regulated price was to be adjusted upward gradually under a laddering model so that it would reflect actual costs by 2014. Governments have chosen to postpone these increases.[4]

Unlike the case of domestic production of LPG, however, PTT is promptly compensated for the NGV it produces. Thus, there is no shortage of domestic supply as in the case of LPG. EPPO estimated that maintaining a price cap on NGV will cost taxpayers roughly USD9 million per month. LPG demand has been increasing so the cost of the subsidy may increase.[5] Another issue in meeting this demand is that the controlled price leaves no room for a distribution margin which reduces the incentive to open new stations.

---

[4] See, for example, http://www.siamdailynews.com/2009/09/29/govt-to-pin-prices-of-lpg-ngv-ft-until-aug-2010/.

[5] http://www.bangkokpost.com/breakingnews/156365/ptt-ngv-usage-soars

3.5 The Performance of the Thai Gas Industry and PTT

How has this regulatory model performed in terms of the development of the gas market and the players involved? Broadly, the results of this assessment show a strong growth in the capacity of the distribution system but questions remain about the level of gas prices compared to those in the rest of the world.

3.5.1 *The Thai gas industry*

The demand for and supply of natural gas in Thailand expanded at a very high rate from 1986 to 1999 when large reserves of natural gas were discovered in the Gulf of Siam (Table 3.1).

Table 3.1 Gas Supply and Demand Growth, 1986–2009.

Average per period	Supply	Demand
1986–94	15.23	15.23
1995–99	12.54	12.55
2000–04	3.06	14.2
2005–09	6.55	5.77

***Source*:** Calculated from Data Provided by EPPO.

Domestic supply was able to keep up with demand until the end of the 20th century. During 2000–04 demand outpaced supply as there was no new investment in new transmission pipeline capacity. However, when the ownership issues were clarified, PTT was able to mobilise capital from the equity market to expand its transmission pipeline network connecting new offshore gas fields to its onshore gas separation plants and its onshore gas fields to various power plants in 2006–07 (Figure 3.5). As a result, the growth in domestic gas supply during 2005–09 exceeded that of demand such that the volume of imported gas fell (Figure 3.1).

The natural gas industry, therefore, has undergone relatively healthy growth in terms of supply. PTT has been effective in seeking and developing new sources of natural gas supply overseas and investing in transmission capacity. The relatively high allowable rate of return on investment (internal rate of return on equity of 18%) is above the risk-adjusted rate for capital borrowing in the market place. These conditions have provided the incentives for PTT to expand its transmission pipeline network to facilitate growth in domestic gas supply. Earnings before interest and tax (EBIT) as a proportion of net sales for the gas operation has been higher than that in the petroleum and petrochemical businesses which operate in more competitive markets (Figure 3.6).

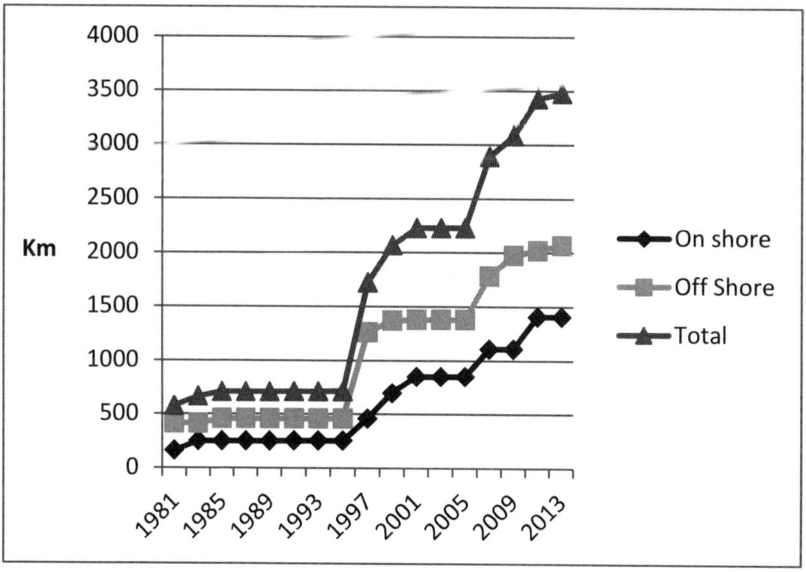

Figure 3.5 The Length of Natural Gas Pipeline, 1981–2012 (km).
Source: PTT Annual Report 2009. History of Gas Transmission *www.pttplc.com/Files/Document/Pdf/Gas/Gas_en2.pdf*, pipelines investment plan

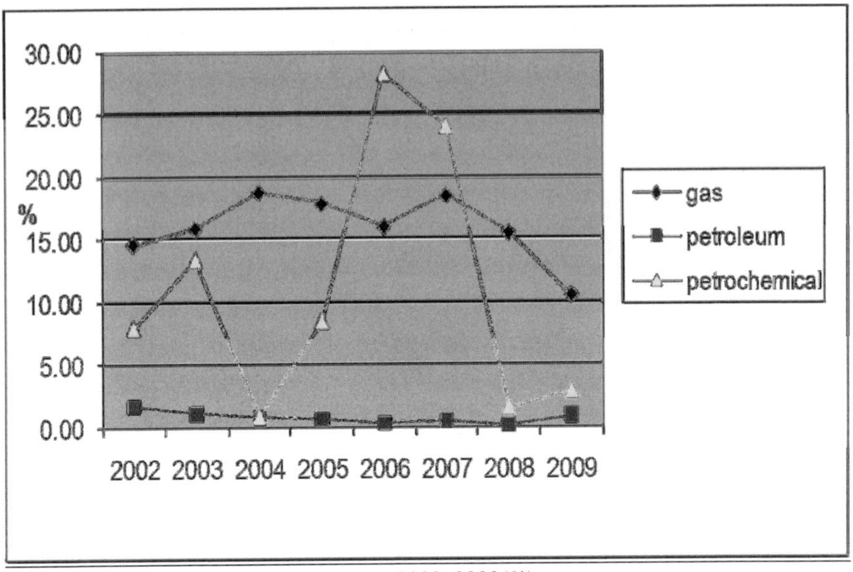

Figure 3.6 PTT's EBIT/Net Sales Ratio, 2002–2009(%).
Source**:** PTT Annual Reports.

PTT has performed well to meet the rapid growth of domestic demand for gas. The enterprise has also been one of the most efficient among its government-owned peers. A study by Hunt and Mantajit (2005) found that the pre-privatisation PTT was relatively efficient when compared with its counterparts in Japan, UK and Malaysia. The company was therefore able to take good advantage of access to direct financing once it became a listed company.

3.5.2 *Gas prices*

The price of natural gas depends on the wellhead prices plus the various margins. As noted above, the wellhead price is relatively low in Thailand. Lower wellhead gas prices due to lower cost of production and proximity of gas supply to demand also allowed the retail price of natural gas to be lower than that prevailing in other economies that do not have their own gas supplies while also allowing PTT to retain its margins. According to the study by Asia Pacific Energy Research Centre (2003), retail natural gas prices in Thailand have always been well below those of Chinese Taipei, Korea or Japan. Meanwhile NGV users enjoy subsidised retail tariffs.

3.5.3 *Gas quality*

According to Laoonual *et al.* (2007), Thailand did not have a quality standard of natural gas like that established by the California Air Resource Board (CARB), the 'clean air agency' of California. The quality of NGV produced varied widely depending on the particular gas field. Natural gas from onshore fields in north-eastern Thailand on average contains 76% methane and 13% carbon dioxide, while that from offshore fields in Myanmar contains 72.4% methane, 6.2% carbon dioxide and 16% nitrogen. According to the CARB, natural gas traded must have a combined carbon dioxide and nitrogen component not exceeding 1.4% and a methane number not less than 80 (except in some locations which have a minimum of 73). In standards found in other economies, the carbon dioxide component is usually required to remain below 3%. Hence, the quality of natural gas in Thailand, in particular that from the onshore fields in the eastern region, is below the international standard. NGV in Thailand may not be cleaner than LPG or gasoline in the absence of proper separation of carbon dioxide from the raw gas supply. In July 2009 the Department of Energy Business established a standard for natural gas to be used for NGV, but these standards are still inferior to the international ones.

3.6 Conclusion

The case of gas in Thailand illustrates a number of aspects of structural reform. These include the forces which cause an extensive reform strategy to shift and evolve in the process of implementation. At the same time, this case illustrates that a reform plan which is less extensive than originally conceived can have significant effects. Thailand's gas sector also illustrates a situation common in the region of energy prices below world market levels – substantial energy subsidies. As energy prices rise, this policy, however, may not be sustainable for fiscal reasons, and the forces which might emerge in Thailand may also be important in other economies.

The sequence of events was that a 1998 master plan laid out the reform of the gas sector in Thailand. This included the separation of production and transmission and the introduction of competition at all stages. The government entity, PTT, would be corporatised and privatised. An independent regulator would be established. This plan was overtaken, however, by a change of government in 2001 and its adoption of a strategy of focussing on the promotion of national champions, which involved more emphasis on development of some key enterprises to contribute to a wider set of policy goals, than on competition in the marketplace. A minority share of PTT was sold to private owners but other elements of market reform were not adopted. More recently, and following another change of government in 2006, a regulatory agency has been established with extensive systems of cost-based regulation at least for natural gas. Other elements of the market reform agenda have still not been implemented.

One of the significant consequences of this reform package has been rapid growth in the capacity of the gas system. Since its listing in 2001, PTT has grown rapidly and performed well to meet the rapid growth in domestic demand for natural gas by its constant search for and development of new sources of gas in neighbouring economies and expansion of transmission capacity accordingly. Its rapid infrastructure roll out was a response to the relatively generous allowable rate of return for its transmission tariff.

Meanwhile, gas prices have remained relatively low, because of a large domestic and regional gas supply and a government subsidy at the wellhead level. This approach to pricing involves distortions to consumption decisions. The low prices are not a reflection of competition in distribution and transmission, which remains absent.

The two current issues are therefore pricing and the lack of competition in distribution and transmission. Competition could be introduced. The steps to doing so include:

- requiring PTT to divest its equity share in many of upstream and downstream gas businesses and to allow third party access to the transmission pipelines; and
- enforcing the competition law, which is important in a market that is so highly concentrated – PTT's current immunity from the Trade Competition Act 1999 would be abolished in that case.

On the other main issue of pricing, there are no significant forces for further reform either from within the sector or from its customers. PTT's main customers are power plants and its own gas separation plants. Although fewer than 300 customers are industrial users, many of them are petrochemical plants and natural gas distribution companies also affiliated with PTT. PTT's integrated operations and its control of the critical infrastructure reduce the incentives for it to maximise throughput in order to earn its target rate of return. Meanwhile, the retail price of NGV and the wholesale price of LPG are controlled at a rate well below cost. Thus, consumers enjoy low gas prices and have less interest in reforms of gas policy.

However, this situation may not be sustainable, because of the fiscal consequences of the current policy package. A source of pressure for reform may be that the local gas supply is running out and PTT will have to import an increasing volume of more expensive LNG from distant places. For now, government import subsidies have sheltered consumers from rising costs. The pressure for reform could mount if fiscal pressures cause these subsidies to be abolished. However, because LPG is used in many households for cooking, a change of policy involves political risks, despite the fiscal implications of the lack of reform.

Chapter 4

Electricity in Russia[1]

Alexandra Sidorenko[2]

4.1 Introduction

The Russian Federation has embarked on, and achieved, significant progress on what seems to be the 'textbook version' of the comprehensive electricity sector privatisation, restructuring, competition and regulatory reform programme (Joskow, 2008b), following the lead of the United Kingdom and applying the market design of the Pennsylvania–New Jersey–Maryland (PJM) model from the United States of America (USA).

As Pollitt (2007) remarks, "what seems to be the case is that the pursuit of electricity reform through to its logical conclusion is only likely to happen in jurisdictions where there is strong ideological commitment to competition in energy markets. This will partly be driven by resource conditions ... but significantly by whether there is a fundamental belief that electricity prices should be left to the market".

In the case of the Russian Federation, the progress to date demonstrated that strong commitment to market reform and leadership was the key condition for keeping the reform on track despite its

[1] This chapter is based on a paper produced with funding from the Asia Pacific Economic Cooperation's Policy Support Unit and material from that paper is reproduced with its permission. Information is taken from The Impacts and Benefits of Structural Reforms in the Transport, Energy and Telecommunications Sectors in APEC Economies APEC#211-SE-01.1. The views expressed in this paper are those of the authors and do not necessarily represent those of the APEC Secretariat or APEC Member Economies.

[2] Senior Adjunct Lecturer, University of Adelaide (alexandra.sidorenko@adelaide.edu.au). More details of the legal documents associated with the reform are available on request.

unpopularity. It looked like the Russian reform had successfully passed the point of no return and the only way was forward, fine-tuning the wholesale market mechanism, aligning price signals and incentives, enforcing competition policy, increasing energy efficiency and fostering investment in modern technology, both public and private. However, the post-2011 policy developments highlight the fact that the regulatory risks are still high, and the danger of reform reversal, at least in spirit if not by the letter, is still there. The government has to maintain the focus on the goals of the reform to remain successful.

This case study outlines the scope and progress of the reform and some of its effects to date.

4.2 Electricity System in Russia

The Russian Federation is one of the top electricity generating economies in the world:

- It is the fourth largest generator after the USA, China and Japan, producing 5% of the world's electricity (International Energy Agency (IEA), 2009, and IEA, 2011, *World Energy Outlook*).
- In 2009 there were more than 700 generating plants in Russia with a total installed capacity of 211,846MW.
- Domestic electricity generation was 957.1 million MWh, domestic consumption 942.8 million MWh (SO, 2010b).
- Russia was a net exporter of electricity (exports account for 2% of domestic supply, imports 0.3%) (FSS, 2010).
- The composition of the installed generating capacity in Russia by type of fuel was 68% thermal, 11% nuclear, and 21% hydro.
- The regional composition varied, with Siberia relying on hydropower stations (47% of capacity), the North-East on nuclear generation (27%), and the Urals almost exclusively on thermal generation (94% of installed capacity) (SO, 2010b).

The Russian unified electrical energy system was created during the Soviet times as the backbone for the economic growth in an industry-oriented planned economy. Following the collapse of the Soviet Union, in 1992 the Russian Federation government transferred most of the electricity assets to the open joint stock company 'United Energy Systems of Russia' (RAO-UES).

At the onset of the reform, RAO-UES owned 72% of the economy's installed generating capacity and 95% of its transmission grid.[3] It had 72 regional vertically integrated subsidiaries called 'AO-Energos'. The dispatching and system operation services also belonged to RAO-UES.

In 1998 Anatoliy Chubais became the president of RAO-UES. His team was behind the concept of electricity reform and its implementation in Russia. Chubais' background as one of the architects of voucher privatisation and major market-oriented reforms of the early 1990s shaped his approach to the task of reforming the electricity sector. Chubais was responding to a number of challenges faced by RAO-UES.

Chubais had to deal with a number of issues. Payment arrears were plaguing RAO-UES's bottom line during the transition years and there were no funds to maintain, even less to expand, the infrastructure.[4] A related motivation for the reform of the electricity sector came from the so-called 'Chubais cross', a diagram based on the existing and projected installed capacity, with the intersection in 2008 (Chubais, 2007). Chubais observed that in 1990 electricity consumption was 1,074 billion kWh. This fell to 809 billion kWh in 1998 and then steadily increased. By 2006 it had reached the 1992 level and Chubais estimated that at the rate of growth at that time the historic high of 1990 would be reached again in 2008. He went on to forecast consumption of 1,198 billion KWh in 2010. He then estimated it would be necessary for Russia to build a substantial

---

[3] http://www.rao-ees.ru/ru/info/history/show.cgi?prof.htm.

[4] In 1998 salaries and wages of RAO-UES staff were on average three months in arrears, cash payments for electricity supply were less than 17% of the total owing, and more than 20 RAO-UES companies were on the verge of bankruptcy. Corporate debts of RAO-UES reached about USD10 billion at the beginning of 1998.
http://www.rao-ees.ru/en/invest/reporting/reports/report2007/4.htm

amount of capacity over the 2006–10 period to meet this growth in demand.[5]

The observations by Chubais were the basis of a case for reform in order to finance the construction of the new capacity. In retrospect, the timing of the capacity exhaustion could have been delayed by the Global Financial Crisis of 2008–2009: as noted above, consumption in 2009 was actually only 943 billion kWh and capacity in 2009 was about the same level as it was in 1991. At the time, the perception was that the value of the reform was acute.

Reform was conceived around the idea of maintaining government regulation over the natural monopoly components of the sector, while introducing competition and private investment in the generating segment. The large-scale reform of the electric power sector was launched in 2001.[6] Its stated goals included:

- Private ownership (2003–08);
- Price liberalisation and full competition in generation (by 2011); and
- Third party access to network infrastructure.

Pricing mechanisms for electricity tariffs were to be changed to stimulate investment, which had been inadequate for many years:

- The average input of new generating capacity over 1991–2000 was just 600–1,500MW per year, compared to 6,000–7,000MW per year on average over 1976–85 (Palamarchuk and Voropai, 2006).

---

[5] Chubais' estimate was that Russia would require 40.9GW of capacity over the period 2006-2010 and the context was that Russia had built only 23GW over the previous 15 years.

[6] Reform began with the signing of Resolution #526 'On the Restructuring of the Electric Power Industry of the Russian Federation'.

- In 2007 about two-thirds of all installed capacity had been commissioned at least 25 years earlier (Abdurafikov, 2009, and Figure 4.1).
- With the accepted power infrastructure lifetime values, the depreciation of transmission lines had reached 50% in 2009, thermal generation 60–70% and hydroelectric power generation 80%.[7]
- The August 2009 accident at Sayano-Shushenskaya hydropower station highlighted the need for urgent investment to replace aging and failing infrastructure.

  USD572–888 billion over 2009–30.[8] The IEA 2011 *World Energy Outlook* estimates Russia's required investment in electrical energy assets at USD615 billion (in 2010 constant dollars) over 2011–35, with more that USD260 billion directed to transmission and distribution.[9]

Manufacturing and mining were among the largest users of electric power (Figure 4.2), and a competitive modern electricity sector was essential for their performance. Energy saving measures were also becoming more important and are recognised in recent legislation. The main elements of the policy to increase efficiency in the electricity energy sector using renewable sources were adopted by the Russian Federation government on 8 January 2009. The share of renewable energy (excluding hydropower generators with installed capacity greater than 25 MW) in total generation was scheduled to increase from 1.5% in 2010 to 4.5% in 2020.[10]

[7] http://www.gazeta.ru/business/2010/01/25/3316190.shtml.

[8] http://minenergo.gov.ru/activity/energostrategy/pr_4.php.

[9] IEA 2011 *World Energy Outlook*

[10] http://minenergo.gov.ru/activity/plan/2010-2012_3/1.php.

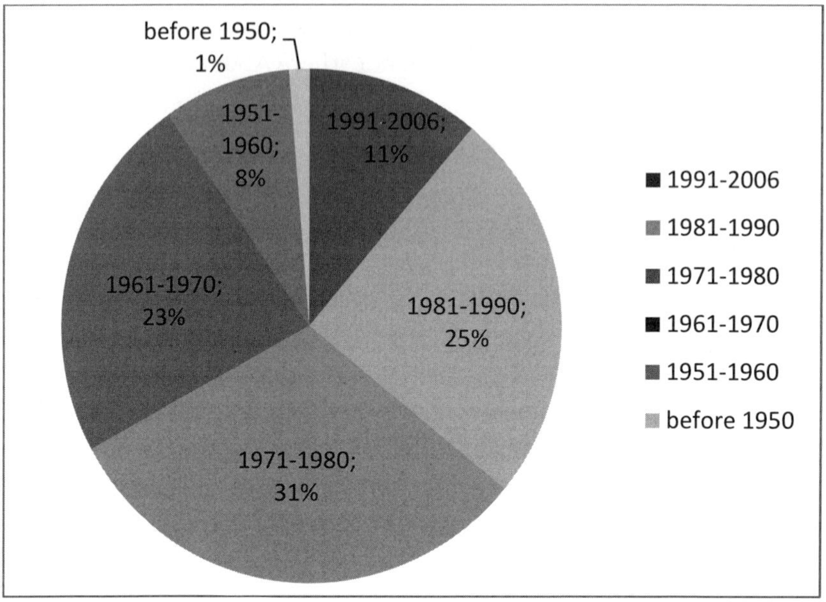

Figure 4.1 Distribution of Installed Capacity by Commissioning Year, 2007.
***Source*:** Abdurafikov (2009).

4.3 Policy Reform

Reform of the electrical energy sector was initiated in 1997, with the draft resolution 'The main directions of the State Policy on Restructuring the Electric Power Industry in the Russian Federation' adopted by the government in 2000. The Arthur Andersen consulting company was chosen to assist in the development of the restructuring model. The large-scale reform of the electric power sector was launched in 2001 with the signing of Resolution No. 526 'On the Restructuring of the Electric Power Industry of the Russian Federation'.

Before the reform 72 vertically integrated regional energy subsidiaries of RAO-UES (AO-Energos) controlled most of the electric power assets in Russia. RAO-UES coordinated the unbundling of its regional subsidiaries with regional authorities. In August 2002 procedures for establishing the wholesale and territory generation companies (WGCs and TGCs), distribution grid companies and inter-regional grid companies were approved by the RAO-UES Board. In the course of reform, transmission and distributing network assets were separated, hydroelectric and nuclear generating assets moved to designated government-owned companies (RusHydro and RosAtom), and generating assets were split among six newly-created WGCs and 14 TGCs[11] and offered for privatisation.

On 1 July 2008 RAO-UES ceased to exist as a company, having completed both horizontal and vertical separation. The resulting industry structure by the time of RAO-UES demise is presented in Table 4.1.

4.3.1 Ownership

The target industry structure and market design was based on international best practice in electricity sector restructuring. There was political will to implement liberalisation of the generation sector and to introduce third party access to the transmission and distribution infrastructure, which was to remain under majority government control. Incumbent hydroelectric power stations (previously part of RAO-UES), were transferred to the RusHydro company, with mandatory majority government ownership. Nuclear generation remained under full government ownership and supervision through the RosEnergoAtom company.

[11] TGCs included combined electricity and heat generation plants with the obligation to provide heating services to households and other connected customers. Heat tariffs have also been subject to government regulation. Reform of central heating infrastructure assets is much less advanced than the reform of the electricity sector. Heating remains subsidised to the households through regulated tariffs and must-run orders to combined heat and energy generators in the winter season.

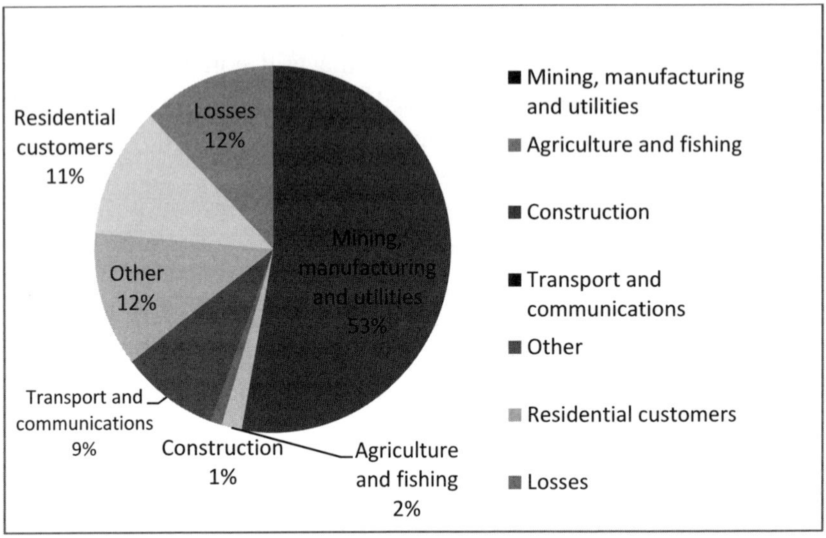

Figure 4.2 Electricity Consumption by Final Use, 2007.

Table 4.1 Electric Power Industry Structure and Market Concentration, 2008.

Name of firm	Service provided: Generation Transmission Retail	Year the firm first offered services	Market share	Owners of capital and their respective shares (domestic/foreign/ government)
FGC	Transmission	2002/1992	100%	25%-1 private/ 75%+1 gov
MRSK	Transmission (regional)	2003	90-100%	
System Operator	Network technical supervision	2002	100%	100% govt
RusHydro	Generation (hydro)	2004	13%	40 %/60% govt
RosEnergo Atom (RosAtom)	Generation (nuclear)	1992	12%	100% govt
Distribution/ retail companies	More than 540	Various (reorganised during reform)	Some regions are highly concentrated	Various (public/private with different level of local governments share)
Generating companies	More than 700	Various (reorganised during reform)	HHI=601 on the national level, but concentrated on regional level analysis	Mostly private, with foreign equity participate on in three large WGCs (control about 11% of generating capacity).

By 2008, the role of the private sector in the electricity industry was already significant: 48.5% of companies in the electricity, gas and water sector were private, contributing 54% to the total sector revenue and 34.5% employment. There were 1,469 companies with (joint) foreign ownership – 3.8% of the total number of companies in the sector – producing 13.5% of the total sector revenue and employing 5.2% of the sector's workforce (Industry of Russia, 2008). A federal law had imposed a 25% limit on foreign participation in the assets of the corporatised incumbent UES.[12] This restriction was later removed in the course of the reform.

The first foreign entry into electricity assets was by portfolio investors and private funds who bought shares in RAO-UES and then its spin-offs. In 2007–08 strategic investors entered. From their entry and to date, E.ON (Germany), Enel (Italy) and Fortum (Finland) remain the three largest foreign investors in Russian generation assets.

Restructuring of the AO-Energos was launched at the end of 2001, starting with Belgorod-energo. In parallel with this, a wholesale market for electricity (and capacity) was set up to enable trading in electricity at unregulated prices. The active divestment of RAO-UES's generating assets in 2007 attracted the attention of foreign investors who gained control over 17.3GW of capacity, or almost one-third of generation capacity privatised in 2007 (UniCredit, 2008).[13] By 2008, about 11% of Russian generation assets were controlled by foreign companies which also took up investment obligations associated with the privatisation (see Table 4.2).

[12] No. 74-FZ of 7 May 1998 'On managing common stock of the Russian joint-stock energy and electricity company 'United Energy System of Russia' and stock of other joint-stock electric energy companies in federal ownership'.

[13] In 2007 eight large generating companies (WGC-2,3,4,5 and TGC-1,3,5,8) were sold by RAO-UES for USD20 billion (installed capacity 57,400MW, about 27% of the national installed capacity). WGC-5 was bought by foreign investor Enel (Italy) and WGC-4 by E.ON (Germany).

The Federal Grid Company (FGC, or FSK in the Russian acronym) was established in June 2002 as an open joint stock company fully owned by RAO-UES. The transmission assets of its regional subsidiary AO-Energos were brought under FGC control in March 2003. There is mandatory majority government ownership of the national transmission grid incumbents FGC (75% + 1 share) and System Operator (100%).

In 2009, the network assets of FCG were spread over 73 regions of the Russian Federation, covering an area of 13.6 million km^2. They included 118,000km of trunk transmission lines and 757 transformer stations with a total capacity of over 286,000MVA (voltage 35–1150kV).[14]

Table 4.2 Generation Sector Market Structure, 2008–2011, and Investment Obligations.

Generation company's name	Initial largest owners (2008)	Largest owner 2011	Installed electricity generation capacity, 2007, GW	Investment obligations 2008-2012, GW
OGC-1	FGC, Roshydro	Inter RAO	9.5	3.5
OGC-2	Gazprom	Gazprom	8.7	2.8
OGC-3	Norilsk Nikel	Inter RAO	8.5	2.1
OGC-4	E.ON (Germany)	E.ON (Germany)	8.6	2.4
OGC-5	Enel (Italy)	Enel (Italy), Inter RAO (26.5%)	8.7	1.8
OGC-6	Gazprom	Gazprom	9.1	1.9
TGC-1	Gazprom, Fortum (Finland)	Gazprom, Fortum (Finland)	6.2	4.4
TGC-2	Sintez	Sintez	2.5	1.5
TGC-3 Mosenergo	Gazprom, Moscow City	Gazprom, Moscow City	10.7	4.2
TGC-4 Kvadra	Onexim (Prohorov)	Onexim (Prohorov)	3.3	1.4
TGC-5	IES (Vekselberg)	IES (Vekselberg)	2.5	0.4
TGC-6	IES, FGC	IES, Inter RAO	3.1	0.5
TGC-7 Volzhskaya TGC	IES, FGC	IES, FGC	6.9	0.5
TGC-8 Southern TGC	Lukoil	Lukoil	3.3	1.5

[14] http://www.fsk-ees.ru/investors_about.html.

Table 4.2 (Continued)

TGC-9	IES	IES	3.3	1.7
TGC-10	Fortum (Finland)	Fortum (Finland)	2.8	2.3
TGC-11	SUEK, E4, Lukoil	Inter RAO	2	0.5
TGC-12 Kuzbassenergo	SUEK	SUEK	4.4	1.1
TGC-13 Yenisei TGC	SUEK	SUEK	2.5	0.5
TGC-14*	Energopromsbyt	Energopromsbyt	0.6	0.05
OGCs and TGCs together			107	35
Independent regional thermal generators (e.g. Eurosibenergo)	regional governments plus private domestic	34	34	n.a.
Far East	Federal and regional governments	9	9	0.8
Other isolated areas plus stand-alone generation	mostly private domestic companies plus Inter RAO**	17	17	n.a.
RosHydro	Federal government	25	25	4.9
RosAtom	Federal government	23	23	n.a.
Total domestic			215	

Source: Solanko (2011) and Gore *et al.* (2012).

FGC required significant investment in modernisation and in the extension of the national high-voltage grid. According to FGC data, in 2010 the average depreciation of the network's physical assets was 41%, including 65% depreciation of transformer and other auxiliary equipment, 35% depreciation of transmission lines and 23% depreciation of buildings and facilities.[15]

Special rules apply to the new transmission assets built by other operators. Article 10.2 of the Federal Law 'On Electric Power Industry' stipulates that any entity can construct a transmission grid subject to building approvals (Article 42). Once connected to the national grid, transmission assets with a rated capacity greater than or equal to 330kV, and other transmission assets with a rated capacity 220–330kV providing a critical connection between significant generation and load centres, become part of the national grid. The owners cannot exit without the

[15] http://www.fsk-ees.ru/evolution_strategy.html.

approval of FGC, which collects transmission charges on their behalf based on the established tariffs and reimburses the owners.[16]

At the onset of structural reform, 72 vertically integrated regional energy companies (AO-Energos) controlled most of the distribution lines in Russia. Subsidiary companies of RAO-UES held 85% of distribution lines, with the rest belonging to four independent AO-Energos and municipal utility companies (Standard & Poor's, 2008).

As part of the restructuring process, 66 AO-Energos belonging to RAO-UES were unbundled and their distribution assets transferred to separate companies. Seven inter-regional grid companies were established in December 2003. In April 2004 the configuration of inter-regional distribution grid companies (IDGC, or MRSK in the Russian acronym) was approved[17] and 12 inter-regional distribution companies (MRSKs) spin-offs had been formed.[18] MRSKs are publicly listed and majority government-owned (53%), with more than 300,000 shareholders.

4.3.2 Regulation

The basic model of WGCs was approved in September 2003. Discussion of mergers between AO-Energos to form a single TGC started in December 2003. A lease-based model was used. The first WGC (#5) and the first two TGCs (#9 and #14) were established in September 2004. Hydroelectric power assets were consolidated in a separate WGC, RusHydro, in October 2004.

Mandatory unbundling provisions in force from 1 April 2006 mean that a company is forbidden to own or lease assets in the transmission or

---

[16] Article 7.2 of Federal Law 'On Electric Power Industry' and Russian Federation Government Decree No. 41 of 26 January 2006 'On Criteria for the Assignment of Electric Grid Facilities to the Unified National (All-Russian) Power Grid'.

[17] The first four IDGCs were established in October 2004: MRSK-1 UES of Centre and Northern Caucasus, MRSK -2 UES of North-West, MRSK -3 UES of Urals and MRSK - 4 UES of Siberia.

[18] http://www.holding-mrsk.ru/about/facts/spravka/. The grid network of ten voltage categories (0.4–220kV) under MRSK-Holding is 2 million km; 637 million MWh were transferred through the grid in 2008.

dispatch of electricity and in its generation and/or distribution. Since 1 January 2008 the same measures apply to a company's affiliates operating in the same price zone of the wholesale market (currently there are two price zones – Europe/Urals and Siberia).

Exemptions include Guaranteeing Suppliers (the Suppliers of Last Resort) – designated distribution companies with USO to residential and other consumers; isolated systems where there is no competition, and where electricity is generated for the provider's own use. Most of the regions in the Russian Federation have companies which are exempt from the unbundling requirement.

The types of economic entities allowed bundled operations are:

- Supplying network companies – activities in transmission and distribution;
- Supplying companies with subscribers – transmission and distribution to connected customers as part of the operations; not the main economic activity;
- Energy-industrial conglomerates – combined transmission and distribution; secondary function (not the main activity). Examples are large production facilities in metallurgy, the paper industry, oil refineries, petrochemical industry, etc.;
- Nuclear power facilities; and
- Suppliers to military and other strategic entities.

Unbundling was performed in several ways, including the transfer of network assets to a different owner or the transfer of customer supply contracts to another distribution company or guaranteeing supplier.

The entry of independent power producers was facilitated by the development of the wholesale electricity market and the setting of rules for third party access to transmission lines (see below). Independent generators with a total generating capacity of at least 25MW, and 5MW minimum at each connection node, can become participants in the wholesale market.

It was envisaged that the development of new generation capacity would be largely funded by private investors but, until recently, regulated electricity tariffs in Russia had failed to reward investment in new capacity (Table 4.3).

Table 4.3 Selected Comparisons of International Electricity Prices, 2007 (US cent/kWh).

Economy	Industrial	Households
Austria	15.41	25.72
Czech Republic	15.12	19.15
Denmark	–	39.60
Finland	9.69	17.24
France	5.95	16.90
Hungary	16.97	22.34
Ireland	18.59	26.72
Italy	28.98	30.53
Korea	6.02	8.86
Mexico	12.60	9.61
Netherlands	–	24.26
New Zealand	7.14	16.44
Norway	6.36	16.39
Poland	11.93	19.30
Portugal	13.13	21.97
Slovak Republic	17.39	21.96
Spain	12.52	21.80
Switzerland	9.38	15.43
Chinese Taipei	6.72	8.56
Turkey	13.88	16.48
UK	14.59	23.13
USA	7.02	11.35
Russia*	4.50	4.50

Source: IEA (2009), *data for Russia MED (2007).

Some features of the electricity markets include a long lag between committing to new capacity and the ability to supply it; the high cost of new energy compared to old or installed; the lack of certainty of future electricity price, and the presence of generating plants with different cost structures (competition with hydro and nuclear generating facilities) (Belyaev, 2005).

In 2004 electricity tariffs were US1.5 cent/kWh in the European part of Russia. Belyaev (2005) explains such low tariffs as a failure to account for capital costs as a result of 'gratis' privatisation of electric power industry assets in the early 1990s which led to the creation of the RAO-UES monopoly and its regional electricity monopolies AO-Energos. Prices for natural gas, a major fuel for thermal power generators, were regulated and the level was low. There was virtually no investment activity in replacement and new assets, hence there was no investment component included in the electricity tariffs.

Based on the analysis of cost structure for new and installed generation capacity (Table 4.4), Belyaev concluded that the deregulated electricity market will be characterised by a permanent capacity shortage. A similar argument recognises that the investment in new generation capacity should be rewarded either through higher tariffs or through capacity payments. Capacity payment mechanism embedded in the wholesale electricity or capacity market design is discussed below.

Table 4.4 Cost Components of Old and New Generation Plants, 2005 (US cent/kWh).

OLD						NEW				
Type	Depreciation	O&M	Fuel	Cost of capital	Total	Depreciation	O&M	Fuel	ROI	Total
CFP	0.54	0.69	1.19	-	2.42	0.54	0.53	1.19	3.68	5.94
GFP	0.40	0.44	1.84	-	2.68	0.40	0.34	1.34	2.05	4.13
NPP	0.44	0.53	0.40	-	1.37	0.44	0.41	0.40	3.76	5.01

Source: Belyaev (2005).
Note: CFP = coal-fired plant, GFP = gas-fired plant, NPP = nuclear power plant; ROI = return on investment, O&M = operation and maintenance.

The 2003 legislation stipulated the rules for gaining non-discriminatory access to transmission and distribution networks. Transmission tariffs and technological connection fees are regulated by the Federal Tariff Service (FTS). In 2008 there were 120 companies with direct connection to FGC, including distribution network companies (56% of connections), independent network companies (9%), retail distributors (17%) and large consumers of energy (18%).

The formula for transmission tariffs changed in 2006 from the actual amount transmitted (in MWh) to a declared capacity (in MW per month).

Base transmission tariffs increased from USD1,478/MW per month in 2006 to USD2,236/MW per month in 2008, with additional payments for transmission losses differentiated by region.[19]

Distribution tariffs are also set by the FTS (FTS Order No. 20-e/2 6 August 2004, as amended on 31 December 2009, 'On approval of instructional guidelines for the calculation of regulated tariffs and prices for electric (thermal) power in the retail (consumer) market'. The move to the Regulatory Asset Base (RAB) regulation of network charges created necessary price signals to increase investment in transmission and distribution assets (see Box 4.1 below).

The Administrator of Trading System (ATS) was founded by 28 bodies representing market participants (generators and consumers) and regulators.[20] It is a not-for-profit organisation whose responsibilities include managing trading and settlement in the wholesale electricity market (maintaining a registry of participants, registering contracts, data collection, development of rules and methodologies, dispute resolution, etc.). A Market Council oversees operations of the wholesale electricity (capacity) market.[21]

---

[19] The transmission tariff is differentiated by voltage of the lines required to supply the energy. Four categories are specified: high voltage (110kV and above); medium first (35kV), medium second (20kV down to 1kV) and low (0.4kV and below). The higher the voltage, the less transformation losses are associated with electricity delivery to the customer, hence the lower the tariff. Distribution surcharge is included in the final tariff and is also regulated by the FTS.

[20] The wholesale market for electrical energy and capacity was first tested in Russia in the late 1990s. The earlier model, FOREM, was based on Federal Law No. 41-FZ of 14 April 1995 'On State Regulation of Tariffs for Electric and Thermal Power in the Russian Federation', and the Decree # 793 'On Federal (national) wholesale electricity power (capacity) market' (12 July 1996). The rules and structure of the new wholesale market, NOREM, are based on Federal Law No. 35-FZ, 'On the Electric Power Industry (26 March 2003); #36-FZ, 'On Specific Features of Functioning of Electric Power Industry During the Transitional Period and on Introduction of Amendments into Certain Legislative Acts of the Russian Federation and on Recognizing Certain Legislative Acts of the Russian Federation to Have Lost Their Force in Connection with Adoption' (26 March 2003) and Russian Federation Government Resolution No. 576 'On Federal Bodies of Executive Power Authorized to Provide State Control over Activities Performed by the Administrator of Trading System of the Wholesale Power (Capacity) Market' (16 September 2003).

[21] http://www.np-ats.ru/.

The 'System Operator - Central Dispatch Administration of the Unified Energy System' (SO-CDA) was established in July 2002 to provide paid dispatch services. On 1 April 2003 the dispatch functions of AO-Energos were transferred to regional dispatch administrators — subsidiaries of SO-CDA — increasing the number of SO dispatch branches from 20 in 2003 to 60 by 2004. SO is a technical body responsible for the technical security and uninterrupted supply of the national electrical grid.[22]

- Simulation trading at the new wholesale market started in September 2002.
- Originally there were 87 wholesale market participants. During 2002 wholesale market rules were developed, including payments for the ATS and SO services.
- The wholesale market model during the transitional phase was approved in March 2003.
- In October 2003 wholesale market regulations were adopted. Template contracts for joining the wholesale market were approved and the dispute settling mechanism established.
- The first trading in the competitive power sector ('5–15% total') was on 1 November 2003, with six registered buyers and seven sellers and 13,000MWh traded at average weighted price RUB260/MWh.
- By the end of the first year of operation, the Russian wholesale electricity market became the fifth in Europe and the ninth in the world in terms of the volume traded.
- Out of 128 participants of the wholesale market in the first year, 54 were independent from the incumbent.[23]

The current design of the wholesale market has been influenced by the Pennsylvania–New Jersey–Maryland (PJM) interconnection model,

---

[22] http://www.so-ups.ru/.

[23] The balancing market was launched in October 2005 (Government Decree No. 620 of 17 October 2005 'On Amending the Russian Government Decree on the Deviations Sector of the Transitional Wholesale Power [Capacity] Market').

including its nodal pricing approach and Financial Transmission Rights (FTR) mechanism to hedge price differences between the nodes. The role of the latter is fulfilled by Free Bilateral Contracts (Oksanen *et al.*, 2009).

The Russian national electricity system is composed of seven united energy systems: Centre, Middle Volga, Urals, North-West, South and Siberia. The energy system of the East operates as a separate synchronous zone, with manual control over the 220kV connection with the Siberian system.

The national wholesale market is divided into 29 zones of 'free energy flow' which become technically isolated at peak hours due to congestion on interconnecting transmission lines. Of these 29 zones, only three zones (Centre, Urals and Siberia) display workable competition in generation.[24] There are two price zones – Europe (Centre/Urals) and Siberia – in which wholesale spot electricity prices are determined. The transmission links between the zones are weak, not allowing for trade between price zones. The third largest region, Russia's Far East, is not part of the wholesale market due to its remoteness and lack of connections (Palamarchuk and Voropai, 2009). There are also non-price zones or islands with limited connections to the wholesale market. Transmission capacity even within the same price zones is often congested, including the links between the Urals and the Middle Volga/Centre, and the North-West to and from the centre (SO, 2010a).

At the end of 2009, 82% of the technological reserve capacity was used in the Central subdivision of the market, signalling the need for additional capacity and facilitation of flows between the zones. Newly installed or modernised generating capacity comprised 1,377MW, or 0.7% of the existing stock at the beginning of 2009. Introduction of a competitive wholesale electricity market in Central/Urals zone was meant to send a price signal to stimulate investment in capacity and alleviate congestion.

The major suppliers to the wholesale market are six WGCs with cross-territorial operations, 14 TGCs and the government-owned nuclear

---

[24] Characterised by a Herfindahl-Hirschman index below 0.25, see Gore *et al.* (2012), Table 3.

energy consortium RosEnergoAtom, importers and independent generators (with total generating capacity of at least 25MW and 5MW minimum at each connection node). Buyers are distribution companies, including guaranteeing suppliers, exporters and large industrial consumers (with connected demand capacities of at least 20MVA, and a minimum 2MVA at each connection node, although for direct consumers and local distribution companies the latter limit was reduced to 1MVA from 1 August 2007, and then to 750kVA from 1 February 2008). In 2009 there were 7,913 nodes and 12,151 branches in the wholesale electricity (capacity) market trading model (SO, 2010a).

Until the introduction of the wholesale market, most of the electricity was supplied at regulated prices through long-term (usually five-year) vested contracts. These regulated 'take-or-pay' contracts defined both the volume and prices of the electricity (capacity), and customers were required to make the full agreed payments regardless of actual consumption. The tariffs under these contracts were regulated by the FTS. The phasing out of regulated (vested) take-or-pay contracts has allowed for a gradual transition to market liberalisation.

As part of the liberalisation process, the share of electricity which can be traded on the wholesale market at unregulated prices increased gradually.

As of 2011, regulated contracts in wholesale market price zones can only be concluded for the supply of electricity and capacity to residential customers (who still pay regulated retail prices, as explained below) and to last-resort suppliers operating in the North Caucasus republics, the Tyva Republic and the Republic of Buryatia.[25]

The difference between the FTS tariffs for the regulated contracts and the equilibrium wholesale market price was significant. In the European Russia/Urals price zone in 2008 the average market price was RUB708/MWh compared with the FTS price of RUB425/MWh (or US2.8 cent/kWh vs. US1.7 cent/kWh). In the Siberian zone, it was RUB500/MWh compared to RUB219/MWh (or US2.0 cent/kWh vs. US0.9 cent/kWh), respectively (ATS, 2010). The highest prices were observed in the South (due to high transmission losses), and the lowest in

[25] http://www.en.np-sr.ru/abouttheelectricityindustry/electricityandcapacitymarkets/wholesalemarket/

the Urals (low generation costs and large proportion of price-taking suppliers).

There are two major forms of electricity trading in the 'unregulated' wholesale market – bilateral contracts and a day-ahead market.[26] Bilateral contracts allow the parties to supply electricity directly to buyers (wholesale market participants) at contractual prices. The day-ahead market is composed of bids from suppliers and buyers for next day consumption. A buyer with excess capacity purchased through bilateral contract can sell their spare electricity on a day-ahead market. Similarly, a generator who needs additional capacity to fulfil contractual obligation can purchase additional amounts on a day-ahead market. The bids are processed by the ATS and the equilibrium price is determined using the nodal pricing model. As a result, an hourly supply schedule is designed with dispatch instructions sent to the suppliers and buyers for the day ahead. The balancing market ensures that deviations from the scheduled supply and demand are met in real time (here, the participants are unsuccessful bidders from the day-ahead market who offer to supply electricity, and buyers with controlled loads). In 2008, prices were calculated for more than 6,000 nodes in European Russia/Urals and more than 600 nodes in Siberia, taking into account generation costs, transmission losses and congestion charges (Oksanen *et al.*, 2009)

Wholesale electricity spot prices were designed to cover the variable costs of generation. Fixed costs including capital expenditure were to be covered by capacity payments, with a separate capacity trading market introduced in 2008. Capacity is a special commodity that, when purchased, gives the wholesale market participant the right to demand that the capacity seller maintains their generating equipment in a state of availability to generate electricity of a defined quality and in the volume required to meet that participant's needs. From 1 June 2008 capacity has been traded based on competitive capacity selection conducted by the System Operator. Prior to 2008, suppliers received payment only for 85% of installed capacity of their generation equipment and for buyers payment for this capacity was included in the flat-rate tariff for electricity. Now there are separate payments for electricity and capacity.

---

[26] http://www.rao-ees.ru/en/reforming/market/show.cgi?market.htm.

As with electricity, starting from 2011, capacity may only be supplied under regulated contracts in volumes required to supply residential consumers. There are regulated tariffs set by the FTS for some other types of capacity (e.g. the capacity and electricity produced by 'must-run' generators, the capacity in zones determined to have limited competition).

The capacity market is designed to ensure reliable and sustainable electricity supply. When selling capacity, suppliers are obliged to maintain their generation equipment in proper condition and to use it in accordance with the requirements imposed by the System Operator. To encourage new investments, the new long-term capacity market[27] allows capacity to be selected for four years ahead, thus guaranteeing the supplier capacity payments during the construction of new facilities. In addition, new capacity can be commissioned under Capacity Supply Agreements (DPM in Russian acronym), with the prices of capacity calculated from operating and capital costs.[28] The Capacity Supply Agreements were the major tool for investors in generating capacity to ensure guaranteed return on their investments for 15 years. All new capacity approved under the 'GenSkhema' – the Government General Scheme 2008 of power sector industry development to 2020 attracts the CSA/DPA capacity payments.[29]

Other types of capacity payments include long-term agreements between hydro and nuclear generators and System Operator, guaranteeing return on investment for a 20-year period. The rest of the capacity including old (installed) capacity participates in the capacity market (Competitive Capacity Selection, or KOM in Russian acronym). The preference for selection of capacity for the year ahead is given, in decreasing order, to nuclear plants and plants ensuring system reliability;

[27] The long-term market followed amendments to the wholesale market rules in Russian Federation Government Decree No. 89 of 24 February 2010 'On issues of competitive tendering of long-term capacity in the wholesale electricity/capacity market'.

[28] Russian Federation Government Decree No. 238 of 13 April 2010 'On pricing parameters of capacity traded in wholesale electricity/capacity market during transition period'.

[29] Russian Federation Government Resolution No. 215-p of 22 February 2008 'General Scheme of Development of Electric Power Industry to 2020'.

'must-run' cogeneration heat-energy plants in the winter period, technical minimum of power plants and hydro-power plants; generators accepting regulated tariffs to supply households; those on free bilateral supply contracts, and finally those selected at Competitive Capacity Selection/KOM auction (Gore *et al.*, 2012). Installed capacity not selected in the Competitive Capacity Selection/KOM process is not entitled to capacity payments and can only supply energy on the day-ahead spot market or be decommissioned. If decommissioning is impossible for technical reasons, these generators receive the status of forced generator and are compensated by a regulated forced generation tariff formula (Milyutin, 2011).

Electricity grids of several neighbouring economies work in parallel with the Russian grid: Belarus, Estonia, Latvia, Lithuania, Georgia, Azerbaijan, Kazakhstan, Ukraine, Moldova and Mongolia. Electricity grids of Uzbekistan, Kyrgyz Republic and (until the end of 2009) Tajikistan are also connected via the Kazakhstan grid (SO, 2010b). Direct transformation links exist with the grids of Finland (through Vyborg), Norway (several generators in the Kolsk system are supplying directly), and connection from the Far East to China (SO, 2010b). The operating system frequency of the Russian national grid is 50Hz. Peak loads occur in the winter months, with historic demand maximums reached or exceeded during 17–21 December 2009 in all regional energy sub-systems of the national grid (SO, 2010b).

Power failures can occur when the grid frequency falls outside the normal range, which is 50Hz +- 0.05Hz. This can happen during peak demand when there are insufficient spinning reserves to ensure normal frequency. The Moscow black-out of 25 May 2005 was caused by the failure of local distribution lines (110kV) raising the concern about the classification of network lines as 'transmission' or 'distribution' in terms of government supervision (Renaissance Capital, 2005). Figure 4.3 illustrates deviations from optimal frequency over 2004–09. Note that there is no clear trend in terms of changes in system reliability following the structural reform.

Russia imports electricity from Kazakhstan (Northern regions) and Kyrgyzstan (transit)/Central Asia, Ukraine and Lithuania; and exports to

Finland/Nord Pool, Belarus, Kazakhstan (Western regions), and Georgia, Armenia, Mongolia and China (Inter RAO, 2008).

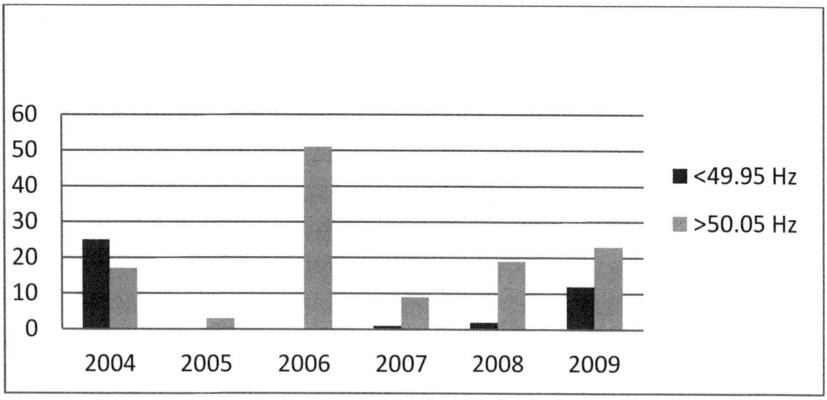

Figure 4.3 Technical Reliability of RAO-UES Operations, 2004–2009 (Quality: operation time outside the normal frequency range of the UAES, minutes). ***Source:*** SO (2010a).

The electricity system of Russia's Far East is independent from the European and Siberian markets and accounts for less than 10% of national total generation and consumption (Palamarchuk and Voropai, 2006). Growing demand from neighbouring China creates an opportunity for developing this regional system. China has approved plans to construct 5,000km of 500kV transmission lines along the Russia–China border. Since 2005 about 492,000MWh of electricity has been exported annually to China, with the planned increase to 3.8 million MWh/year by 2015 (Drugov, 2008). Various interconnection projects have been proposed and discussed (e.g. Belyaev *et al.*, 2005; Yoon *et al.*, 2006; Lee *et al.*, 2007).

Large industrial users (with connected demand capacity of at least 20MVA, and a minimum of 2MVA in each connection node) can purchase electricity (capacity) directly from the wholesale market. For direct consumers and local distribution companies the required capacity limit was reduced to 1MVA from 1 August 2007, and then to 750kVA from 1 February 2008. This move facilitated further entry into the wholesale market by potential buyers.

There is limited competition in retail distribution to date. There are examples of Federal Antimonopoly Service (FAS) investigations into the state of competition in the distribution sector. It is worth noting that the introduction of retail competition has been slow in many economies undertaking reform (Joskow, 2008), and Russia does not appear to be an exception. Kuleshov *et al.* (2012) study the level of competition in the Russian retail electricity market and find that the current level of market competition is either inactive or sub-active.

The guaranteeing supplier receiving electricity through vested (regulated) contracts is obliged to sell the full amount at regulated retail tariffs. Residential customers are supplied exclusively at regulated tariffs. Any amount of electricity purchased at free wholesale market prices can be supplied at prices above the regulated tariffs. Independent distribution companies – participants in the wholesale market – can supply to any customer at unregulated prices. While the free bilateral contracts allow wholesale market participants to hedge their risks for future increases in the wholesale price, similar contracts do not exist for retail market participants.

Previously the rules for setting wholesale electricity tariffs in regulated contracts were based on cost-plus reimbursement (Russian Federation Government Resolution No.109 of 26 February 2004 'On Formation of Prices for Electric and Thermal Power in the Russian Federation'). The allowable rate of return on invested capital was set to be between the government bond rate and the refinancing rate of the Central Bank of Russian Federation (13–14% in 2004 and 8.5–9% in 2009[30]). A similar approach was followed in the methodology for setting transmission charges.[31]

The allowable rate of return in the cost-plus formula often underestimated risk premiums associated with the economic activity of the regulated utilities, did not stimulate necessary investments and did

[30]http://www.cbr.ru/eng/print.asp?file=/eng/statistics/credit_statistics/refinancing_rates_e.htm.

[31] Federal Tariff Service Resolution No. 56-e/1 of 21 March 2006 'On approval of methodology for calculation of tariffs for transmission services in the unified national (all-Russian) electricity grid'.

not promote efficiency.[32] An Investment Guarantee Mechanism was briefly introduced to compensate for investment in new capacity by levying a surcharge on the SO's tariff.

In the distribution or retail sector, residential tariffs were price-cap adjusted for CPI. One of the criticisms was that the expected inflation was lower than realised over 2002–05, and the prospective adjustor failed to compensate for an actual increase in costs. The real revenues of the sector were stagnant in 2002–05: the average profitability dropped from 15.7% in 2002 to below 10% by 2005, with half of all enterprises making losses (Milov, 2005).

The deficiency of cost-plus approaches to regulated pricing was recognised, and a new Regulated Asset Base (RAB) formula for distribution tariffs was introduced in July 2008. The new formula was implemented in five regional pilot projects, with the consequent roll-out to other regions in 2009–10. Challenges include the determination of the asset base for RAB regulatory purposes: all new investments are included in the RAB calculations for the next accounting period. Hence there is a delay between the outlay of funds and the opportunity to recoup them through higher tariffs. RAB regulation has been applied for FGC transmission assets since 2010 and extended to high-voltage inter-regional distribution networks of MRSK in 2011.

The Federal Energy Commission (FEC) was established in 1995.[33] In 2001 the FEC assumed other anti-monopoly control functions in infrastructure sectors (such as transport) and government regulation of tariffs. Regional Energy Commissions (RECs) were formed to support the FEC activities with the role of regulating local tariffs for electricity and heat. In 2004 the Federal Tariff Service (FTS) was formed to take

[32] Tariff levels for 2004–06 were set in the Russian Federation Government Decree No. 1754-r of December 1, 2003 'On Approval of the Program for Changing State Regulated Prices (Tariffs) in Electric Power Industry'.

[33] Presidential Decree No. 1194 'On Federal Energy Commission of Russian Federation' to regulate natural monopoly in the energy sector (based on the Federal Law No. 41-FZ of 14 April 1995 'On State Regulation of Tariffs for Electric and Thermal Power in the Russian Federation', and Federal Law No. 147-FZ of 17 August 1995 'On Natural Monopolies'). The FTS was formed based on the Russian Federation Government Decree No. 204 'On Federal Tariff Service' (9 April 2004).

over the FEC's functions. Responsibilities of the FTS include developing pricing and tariff methodologies, setting maximum and minimum price caps and tariffs (Box 4.1). Regional tariffs are set jointly with the RECs.

Box 4.1 RAB Formula for Distribution Tariffs.

The cost-plus formula was superseded with the Regulated Asset Base (RAB) methodology (Russian Federation Government Resolution No. 459 of 18 June 2008 'On changes to the RF Government Resolution No. 109 of 26 February 2004 On Formation of Prices for Electric and Thermal Power in the Russian Federation', with technical details provided in Annex to the Federal Tariff Service Resolution No. 231-e of 26 June 2008 'Methodology for regulation of tariffs using the return on invested capital approach'). The new methodology formulated the rules for calculating regulatory capital value, reporting requirements for new investments and formula for an allowable rate of return. Tariffs set for longer term (3–5 year) contracts are adjusted on an annual basis. Operating costs are adjusted for CPI, anticipated changes in business assets and an efficiency parameter (currently 1%, but possibly up to 2.5% reduction in operating costs p.a.). Any efficiency gains due to the reduction of transmission or distribution losses and to the reduction of operating costs remain with the company and are not taken into account in the annual review of tariffs (do not affect the allowable total revenue figure). The allowable return on capital (both equity and debt) is set once for the whole regulation period using the WACC formula. Return on debt is set to the average of return on corporate bonds issued by the regulated industries. Return on equity is set equal to the return on government bonds (4–6 year duration) plus risk premium for the regulated companies. Investment plans of the regulated company are coordinated with the FTS, and with the regulator's approval, earn the rate of return including the regional adjustor (higher allowable return in the areas of shortage). The investment activities are a separate item for accounting purposes and separated by geographic region (a federal subject of the Russian Federation). Calculation of the initial regulatory capital value is performed by an independent expert. Transmission assets which are being fully funded by connecting charges are not included in the calculation of invested capital. The regulator receives an annual update on implementation of the agreed investment programme and adjusts the values of the RAB and the return on RAB, and tariffs accordingly. In the distribution sector, RAB regulation has been in place for eight MRSK regional branches and Tomsk distribution company since 1 January 2010, with an additional 22 branches switching to RAB by 1 July 2010. All the remaining regions were on the RAB tariff formula by 1 January 2011. The regulators (FTS and RECs) approve RAB parameters for each of the MRSKs. There is a perceived problem of regulatory valuations of the capital base being lower than accepted market valuation (ATON, 2010).

Other regulators include:

- Federal Antimonopoly Service: competition supervision, including approval of mergers and acquisitions, regulation of market conduct, and consumer protection. Oversees non-discriminatory third-party access to the transmission grid. Regulates the activities of the Administrator of Trading System.
- Administrator of Trading System (ATS) – NOREM (wholesale electricity or capacity market operator) is a not-for-profit organisation with government involvement. Responsibilities of ATS include managing trading and settlement in the wholesale electricity market (maintaining a registry of participants, registering contracts, data collection, development of rules and methodologies, dispute resolution, etc.).
- Market Council oversees operations of the wholesale electricity (capacity) market, develops rules and procedures, and oversees pricing of capacity delivered through Capacity Supply Agreements/DPM.
- Rostekhnadzor (Russian Technical Supervision Agency) regulates technical protocols and norms in the construction and operation of the components of thc electricity sector.
- System Operator – the technical body responsible for the technical security or uninterrupted supply of the national electrical grid. System Operator is responsible for running the Competitive Capacity Selection market.

Market competition and abuse of monopoly power in the electrical energy sector is under the direct supervision of the FAS, a government agency in the Russian Federation. For the purposes of market definition, there is a single market for electrical energy and capacity in Russia. Distribution companies supply electricity to the retail markets through retailers and guaranteeing suppliers. In 2008 both regulated and free (wholesale market determined) tariffs were in place. Supply to residential customers and other customers classified as such, including municipal utility companies, was conducted using regulated tariffs. The regions or territories outside the boundaries of the wholesale market were supplied using regulated tariffs (FAS, 2009a).

The FAS registry in 2008 included 540 distribution companies including 260 guaranteeing suppliers in 82 regions of the Russian Federation. Most of the regions have several distribution companies, usually coinciding with municipal divisions. At this level of geographic disaggregation, many sub-regional distribution markets appeared highly concentrated.

Distribution companies belonged to one of the following categories:

(1) Distributors — spin-offs from RAO-UES AO-Energos ('AO-energosbyt'). There were 70 such distributors on the FAS registry, all of them participants in the wholesale market. Some of these distributors were active in more than one region: e.g. 'Far East energy company' operates in several regions of the Russian Far East; Mosenergosbyt in both Moscow city and Moscow oblast (region); Petersburg energosbyt company in St Petersburg city and Leningradskaya oblast;

(2) Independent distribution companies – participants of the wholesale electricity (capacity) market and serving primarily large industrial customers. Some of these were also present in more than one geographic subdivision of the retail market: e.g. Rusenergosbyt (Moscow) was active in trading and supply of electrical energy in 45 regions, serving the needs of the Russian Railways; Mezhregionenergosbyt (Moscow) in 39 regions; Siburenergomanagement (Voronezh) in 13 regions; RN-Energo (Moscow) in six regions; Energoservice Trading House (Moscow) in seven regions; Transneftservice (Moscow) in 34 regions; and Mechel-Energo in four regions;

(3) Other retailers including municipal companies, non-members of the wholesale market. These distributors purchased energy from

guaranteeing suppliers, other distributors or directly from generators, some of whom are second-tier guaranteeing suppliers.

According to FAS (2009b), the share of type (1) distributors on most of their geographic markets exceeded 75%; in some regions they were the monopolistic suppliers. All of these distributors were granted the guaranteeing supplier status. In the regions with multiple distributors, often only AO-Energos could purchase electricity on the wholesale market and re-sell it to other guaranteeing suppliers. At the same time, there was growing competition between retail distributors.

Since 1 April 2006 a company has been forbidden to own or lease assets in the transmission or dispatch of electricity and in its generation and/or distribution. Since 1 January 2008 these measures have applied also to a company's affiliates operating in the same price zone of the wholesale market (currently European Russia/Urals and Siberia).

Challenges facing FAS in enforcing this law include enforcement mechanisms which are not clearly specified and the difficulty of keeping track of the owners of affiliated entities. Breaches of the law on the separation of natural monopoly and competitive activities in the electrical energy sector are brought by FAS to courts on a case-by-case basis. Uniform practices in solving such cases are not yet established.

Some third-tier distribution companies attempting to purchase electricity for further distribution from large distributors or guaranteeing suppliers complain about anti-competitive requests, such as pre-payment for the electricity or other arbitrary conditions.

Overall, FAS estimates that the level of competition in distribution and retail remains low, and most markets appear highly concentrated. In 2008 there were almost 3,000 complaints to FAS regarding anti-competitive behaviour in the electricity sector. About one-third of these cases were investigated, with 60% of them resulting in orders by FAS to stop the offending action. Most of the complaints pertained to the refusal of guaranteeing suppliers to grant connections to the independent distributors, unreasonable conditions of supply, disconnection of services, etc. Box 4.2 outlines some of the barriers to entry in distribution.

Box 4.2 Barriers to Market Entry by New Distributing Companies.

1) Administrative barriers, such as:
   - postponement of tendering for the status of guaranteeing supplier within the established geographic market to 2010;
   - failure by the Ministry of Energy to approve rules and develop sample documents for the earlier tender to provide guaranteeing supplier services, in breach of the May 2008 deadline;
   - control over retail tariffs for guaranteeing suppliers;
   - lack of consistency in application of tariff policy (e.g. approval of one-part tariffs for transmission charges by local tariff regulators while the two-part tariffs were still contractually in place)
2) Economic barriers, such as:
   - Requirements to reimburse the guaranteeing supplier when switching to an alternative supplier if breaking the contract within its duration (normally one year);
   - High cost of installing metering equipment to connect to the wholesale market;
   - Customer receipts arrears;
   - Unauthorised or unaccounted for electricity consumption;
   - Cross-subsidies;
   - Arrears of payments for supply to communal utilities;
   - Investment needs to maintain infrastructure;
   - Inefficiencies in transmission and distribution networks, including technical dilapidation, disputed ownership of distribution lines, large distances from the point of connection to wholesale purchasers to final consumers;
   - Abuse of market power by guaranteeing suppliers, barriers to entry by independent distributors by refusing them on the grounds that they are not final consumers.
3) Technological barriers:
   - Lack of automatic metering and accounting systems to participate in the wholesale electricity market.

Source: FAS (2009a).

Guaranteeing Suppliers (Suppliers of Last Resort) are designated distribution companies with USO to residential and other consumers. The guaranteeing supplier receiving electricity through vested (regulated) contracts is obliged to sell the full amount at regulated retail tariffs.

Residential customers are supplied exclusively at regulated tariffs. The situation is to be preserved until 2015. In 2008, residential customers accounted for 11% of total electricity consumption.

The need to bring electricity tariffs in line with economic costs has long been publicly recognised in Russia.[34] Residential electricity tariffs were often used as a policy instrument in election campaigns at sub-federal level, with tariffs kept artificially low in pre-election years (Yudashkina and Pobochy, 2007).

Cross-subsidisation took many forms in Russia – between industrial and residential users, heat and electricity tariffs, geographic regions, implicit subsidies from regulated natural gas prices and electricity tariff discounts for special categories of customers (e.g. veterans, pensioners, low income). The government provided USD90 million in direct subsidies for electricity tariffs in the Far East in 2004, in addition to USD280 million fuel subsidies in Far North regions.[35] The full extent of cross-subsidies is difficult to estimate. The pre-reform range was USD4.5–12 billion per year (Milov, 2005; Renaissance Capital, 2006). RAO-UES estimated electricity cross-subsidies in 2007 to amount to RUB115 billion (USD4.5 billion), a 34% annual increase over USD3.3 billion in 2006.[36]

Major steps in the elimination of cross-subsidy between residential and industrial customers occurred over 2003–04, with the gap between residential and industrial tariffs closing by the end of 2004. By 2004 the residential tariffs temporarily reached the level of industrial tariffs and in 2005 exceeded them at 1 RUB/kWh (or US3.4 cent/kWh) (Kurronen, 2006). In the transitional wholesale market arrangements of 2003–11 residential tariffs were kept regulated, most of the time below the competitively determined wholesale price. Retail tariffs still remained below the full economic costs but were expected to rise to reflect the full

[34] The Government Decree No. 1231 'On gradual elimination of cross-subsidies in electric power industry and on bringing residential electricity tariffs in line with actual costs of generation, transmission and distribution' of 26 September 1997 has set the elimination in action.

[35] http://budgetrf.info/?tag=dotacia.

[36] http://www.rao-ees.ru/en/invest/reporting/reports/report2007/8_3.htm.

costs of distribution and retailing. The efficiency of electricity use remained low, and the need for energy-saving measures became apparent.

The 2010 Budget of the Russian Federation assumptions of average electricity tariffs included:[37]

- an increase in average electricity tariffs for all users from US4.5 cent/kWh in 2007 to US7 cent/kWh in 2011 and US10.5 cent/kWh in 2020.
- Residential tariffs were forecast to increase more steeply, from US4.5 cent/kWh in 2007 to US7.1 cent/kWh in 2011 and US15.3 cent/kWh in 2020.
- Residential tariffs would be subject to government regulation at least until 2015.
- Tariffs in the regulated segment of the electricity market were set annually. From 1 January 2010, 60% of all electricity was scheduled to be purchased at the unregulated wholesale market but residential customers would continue to be supplied at regulated tariffs.
- Full elimination of cross-subsidies in residential electricity tariffs was envisaged by 2015.
- Domestic prices for natural gas would also be brought in line with the world price by 2020.
- In each of three growth scenarios used for 2010 budget projections residential electricity tariffs were set to increase by 1.35–2 times over 2011–15.

Following the budget announcement there were a number of public protests across Russia against the forthcoming increase in electricity, transport and residential utility tariffs.

4.3.3 Review of the implementation of reform

The changes in policy since 2003 are summarised in Table 4.5. Implementation of the reform of such depth and magnitude in a relatively

---

[37] http://budgetrf.info/?tag=dotacia

short time (one decade) has presented multiple challenges. The population in general resisted the reform, unimpressed by the idea of higher retail electricity tariffs. Keeping the residential segment shielded from free market prices was a trade-off to liberalise other segments of the electricity sector.

During 2002–05 there were delays in passing the necessary legislation and starting the reform. The Duma (2007) and Presidential (2008) elections added to the uncertainty as to the future progress of the reform. The Renaissance Capital (2005) report highlighted the industry's disappointment with the discrepancy between the announced reform milestones and their implementation.

Table 4.5 Changes in Policy, 2003–2008.

Area of policy change (market access, ownership or regulation)	Year of change	Description of change
Structure	2003–08	Restructuring of incumbent operator RAO-UES based on: • vertical unbundling of contestable activities from network services and system operation; first accounting and then structural separation; and • horizontal unbundling of contestable components of the value chain, to facilitate competition in generation, retail and repair and maintenance services.
Ownership, structure	2003–08	All assets owned or controlled by RAO-UES, all existing assets of regional energos and any other public utility enterprises owning or operating electricity infrastructure were subject to restructuring. Restructuring of RAO-UES resulted in creation of 6 wholesale generating companies, 14 territory generation companies, and international trading and generation company Inter RAO. All hydroelectric power assets were transferred to RusHydro. Nuclear generation assets are under RosEnergoAtom. All high-voltage transmission grid assets were transferred to the Federal Grid Company, and regional distribution networks to an Inter-regional Transmission Company. Technical supervision of the electricity network is performed by the System Operator. Privatisation of generating assets.

Table 4.5 (Continued)

Market access, competition	2003	Third-party access to the grid for independent generators and re-organised wholesale and regional generating companies. Horizontal unbundling of retailing functions, including the creation of guaranteeing suppliers to serve regulated consumers and to operate as a retailer of last resort.
Regulation, market access	2003	Wholesale electricity and capacity market has allowed competitive supply in the market not covered by vesting (regulated) contracts. Creation of an Administrator of Trading System. Next day market, balancing market, financial transfer rights market and market for derivatives.
Regulation	2003	Elimination of licensing requirement for economic activity 'generation, transmission and distribution of electrical energy'. Technical standards and norms (Rosteckhnadzor).
Market access	2003–08	Entry of foreign utilities and strategic investors in electricity infrastructure. Currently, E.ON (Germany), Enel (Italy) and Fortum (Finland).
Regulation	2008–	Move from cost-plus to RAB tariff formula for network assets, Return on investment regulation for generation or capacity payments. Price caps for capacity payments in non-price zones.

Tightly regulated by regional energy commissions, consumer tariffs often did not leave any room for regulated distributors' required capital expenditure. The shortfall between the usage fees and costs was often covered through connection fees introduced in 2006. For 2008–12 the connection fees for new customers and for existing users requiring additional capacity were expected to cover the capital costs and connection fees for new customers and for existing users requiring additional capacity were expected to cover the capital costs and investment. Reliance on connection fees has the drawback of increased volatility of MRSK's revenues. In an economic downturn, the demand for new connections and additional capacity falls, so funding for investment projects dries up (Standard & Poor's, 2008).

The incentive for distribution companies to recoup shortfalls of tariff revenues over the cost of investment and maintenance through connection charges created a significant barrier to small and medium enterprises (SMEs) seeking a new connection. In response, the Russian

Federation Government mandated a simplified procedure for technical connections.[38]

It is important to recognise that the original investment programme, formulated in the economic boom years, has been halted by the financial and economic crisis of 2008–09. As noted above, electricity consumption failed to grow at the rate that Chubais has expected and in hindsight the growth in capacity was not required as urgently as he had predicted.

The data from the Ministry of Economic Development and Trade demonstrates that, despite the recession, the electricity, water and gas sector fell by only 5.2% in physical output, and actually increased by 2.4 times in revenue over 2008–09 to RUB200 billion (USD8 billion) (MED, 2010b). Improved financial performance of the sector was definitely attributed to the increase in tariffs as part of the reform implementation. Processing and manufacturing industries in energy-using sectors were hit particularly hard by both falling demand for their goods and rising electricity costs. This is a (rather painful) example of when price signals generate incentives to increase efficiency – both technical efficiency, through energy-saving measures, and allocative efficiency, by considering the longer term viability of the energy-using sector – given the true economic cost of electricity and other energy sources. These efficiency gains, and the reductions they make possible in the energy intensity of the economy, have been an important benefit of the reforms to date and of the further stages of its implementation which are planned.

Investment targets in generation for 2008 and were not fully met.[39] Russian Prime Minister Vladimir Putin criticised private owners of

---

[38] By Resolution No. 334 of 21 April 2009, since 5 May 2009 the connection fee for the maximum capacity of 15kW should not exceed RUB550 (USD18). Customers requiring connection of 15–100kW are given the option to pay the connection charge in instalments within three years from the connection date. Information disclosure requirements were imposed on distribution companies to facilitate transparency of their connection fee decisions (FAS, 2009b). The decision has led to a 30% increase in connection applications from SMEs over 2008–09 (for <15kW connections), and a 50–60% increase in the requested total capacity (MED, 2010a).

[39] In 2008 the national energy system received an addition of 11,000km of transmission or distribution lines (76% of the planned facilities), transformation stations with total capacity 22,570MVA (90% of planned capacity) and 2,004MW of generating capacity (68% of the planned) http://minenergo.gov.ru/activity/plan/2010-2012_3/1.php.

generating assets for lagging behind with their investment programmes. The industry response was that recent changes in economic conditions forced the postponement. Following economic recovery and improved investment outlook, the investment in generation returned back on track. In 2011, 5 845MW of new generation was installed, most of which (4,815MW or 82%) was supplied by private investors, including 4,067MW installed through Capacity Supply Agreements (CSA/DPM). Foreign-owned generating companies (E.ON, Enel and Fortum) installed 2,051MW of this new capacity. With 11% share of generation assets, foreign-owned generating companies contributed to 35% of new installed capacity in 2011 (Ministry of Energy, 2012: 13). Expected commissioning of new generation assets in 2012 is 6GW.[40] The recent data suggest that private generation investors honour their investment commitments, and that CSA/DPM provides an effective mechanism to reward investment in capacity.

Capacity markets are justified on the premises that the energy-only wholesale markets often fail to create price signals for an optimal level of investment in generating capacity, especially when the demand is near capacity. Well-designed forward capacity markets are supported in Joskow (2006) and Joskow (2008a) as the tool to overcome the 'missing money' problem which arises when the price-cap regulated wholesale prices fail to reflect the true economic cost of scarcity (measured, for example, as a value of lost load). As a result, going prices fail to generate sufficient revenue to cover both the operating and capital investment costs, and under-investment occurs. The Russian model includes two traded commodities – electricity and capacity.

Wholesale electricity prices at the day-ahead market are based on marginal (variable) costs, covering mostly the fuel component. Fixed costs of generation are covered through capacity payments in the capacity market, with an annual competitive selection of future capacity suppliers (to supply starting year of selection +4). The amount of capacity payment is differentiated by new or old energy, between type of fuel (nuclear, hydro, gas, coal), and for new capacity under CSA/DPM it

---

40 Ministry of Energy 2012 data, http://minenergo.gov.ru/activity/powerindustry/powerdirection/investpolit/

is calculated for each generator based on a rate of return formula. Clarifications of the capacity payment rules and mechanisms and liberalisation of tariffs would help resolve uncertainty that stifled investment in the generation sector. [41]

Presentations by foreign investors in the Russian generation sector to the European Energy Regulators Regional Association (ERRA) conference in 2011 painted a picture of malfunctioning capacity markets.[42] Acknowledging that the wholesale electricity spot market is functioning reasonably well, representatives of Fortum, Enel and E.ON stressed that there were a number of problems with the capacity market. Firstly, almost 75% of capacity in 2011, supplied in 27 out of 29 capacity or energy free flow zones, were subject to price caps for capacity payments and forced generation (capacity payment for which did not cover fixed costs). Price caps were found to be too low to support investment in capacity upgrade and modernisation. Old and dilapidated assets were not allowed to be decommissioned and had to be run at a loss. Government was seen as expressing preference for development of nuclear and hydro assets, through preferential long-term capacity agreements (Fortum submission).

CSA/DPM granted for new capacity in power plants privatised during the first phase of restructuring (2007–08) were also getting more favourable terms compared to the new rules of capacity trade through Competitive Capacity Selection (CCS/KOM). Price caps applicable to generating capacity selected at CCS/KOM were below the estimated economic cost of capacity provision (Enel submission). The KOM was postponed until 2012, and the launch of longer-term four-year competitive capacity selection was deferred until 2013. Rules for capacity market were enacted in March 2011 retroactively, applicable from October 2010. In the existing CSA/DPM calculations, the WACC

[41] Russian Federation Government Decree No. 238 of 13 April 2010 'On pricing parameters of capacity traded in wholesale electricity/capacity market during transition period' and Russian Federation Government Decree No. 89 of 24 February 2010 'On issues of competitive tendering of long-term capacity in the wholesale electricity/capacity market'.

[42] http://www.energy-regulators.eu/portal/page/portal/EER_HOME/ EER_ INTERNATIONAL/CEER-

value was revised downwards, from 14% to 13%, without providing much explanation.

Milyutin (2011) provides an official FTS estimate of the long-term capacity payment model, in which only 14% of capacity is supplied at KOM without price caps. Almost 60% of capacity is not traded and supplied at competitive markets, but through the mechanism of CSA/DPM (5% total), forced or most expensive generation (12%), nuclear and hydro-power long-term supply agreements (17%) and household sector supply (25% total). It appears that in the short- to medium-term capacity payments under the effective price-cap mechanism will remain inadequate to compensate for future costs of investment into generation.

Cross-subsidies to households and other municipal users through regulated tariffs remain high, estimated at USD6.6 billion or 10% of total electricity sector revenue (Cooke *et al.*, 2012). Removal of such subsidies has been postponed until at least 2014. Unwinding household energy subsidies requires political will and determination. Recent attempts by the government to curtail rises in tariffs flag the difficulties with keeping the earlier commitment of bringing household retail tariffs to the cost-reflective level.

The Russian government has been torn in the dilemma of avoiding sharp increases in electricity prices without reneging on the reform. With the target of electricity tariff growth of 15% exceeded early in 2011, the government intervened by 'manual steering' of capacity payments and price smoothing in the wholesale day-ahead market.[43] The rise in retail electricity prices early in 2011 was due to the 15-47% increase in transmission and distribution tariffs through RAB regulation to allow for capital expenditure, an 15% increase in regulated price of natural gas, and an 12-13% increase in capacity payments for new generation capacity commissioned as a result of CSA/DPM and long-term agreements for nuclear and hydro-power (E.ON submission to ERRA 2011). The government intervened to curtail tariff explosion and managed to keep the increase in electricity tariffs at below the 15% target (Ministry of Energy, 2012: 36).

---

[43] Russian Federation Government Decree No. 929 of 14 November 2009 'Special regime of electricity price calculation in the event of sharp increase in price'.

Large energy consumers such as Deripaska's aluminium conglomerate RUSAL supported the government's attempt to keep tariffs down, demanding reversal of network tariff increases and review of DPM projects among other intervention measures.[44]

Recent M&A activities in the electrical energy market has seen the transition of Inter RAO from a relatively small actor in generation (1.8GW in 2008) to an influential player holding 10% of the generation market share in 2011 (Gore *et al.*, 2012). With Russian state gas monopolist Gazprom holding the largest market portfolio of generation assets (TGC-1, TGC-3 Mosenego and WGC-2) through its subsidiary Gazprom Energoholding, the share of indirectly state-controlled generation can reach 60 percent of the market.

Examples of recent integration are:

- Horizontal integration by combining WGC and TGC within the same price zone or geographic area (Inter RAO and Gazprom M&A activities);
- Vertical integration through fuel supplier's acquisition of generation assets (e.g. Gazprom for natural gas and SUEK for coal);
- Vertical integration by merger of generation and retail distribution or guaranteed supplier (e.g. RusHydro, IES, Gazprom, Lukoil, Enel, Inter RAO) (Gore *et al.*, 2012).

Russian market competition watchdog FAS stopped the Inter RAO move to acquire 75% of TGC-4 Kvadra in its July 2011 decision, to prevent the potential market power impact on the Centre free-flow area.[45] The role of state-affiliated companies is increasing as part of their investment plans. For example, Gazprom Energoholding has investment commitments through CSA/DPM to supply 9GW until 2016, which corresponds to almost one-third of total new generation assets.[46]

[44] See, for example, disagreement in valuation of the new investment project with CSA/DPM component, in the negotiations on purchase by Deripaska's RUSAL of Vekselberg/IES assets in TGK-9. http://m.gazeta.ru/business/2012/03/26/4105417.shtml

[45] http://investcafe.ru/blogs/voronkov/posts/11376

[46] Based on Ministry of Energy 2012 data, http://minenergo.gov.ru/activity/powerindustry/powersector/structure/organization/

In May 2012, the Government of the Russian Federation voiced an intention, supported by the Ministry of Energy, to consolidate the inter-regional distribution grid company MRSK with the transmission Federal Grid Company FSK. The final decision was expected in September 2012.

There are proposals voiced by some officials to give the function of the Supplier of Last Resort to Inter RAO. With the recent aggressive expansion in generation, Inter RAO may become a vertically integrated generator-retailer, a mini-version of the demised RAO-UES. Some analysts foresee a reversal of reform towards creating a state-controlled generation sector dominated by Gazprom, Inter RAO, RusHydro and RosAtom, a state network monopoly combining FSK and MRSK transmission and distribution grid assets, and Inter RAO-dominated Guaranteeing Supplier retail sector.[47] Cancellation of regular bidding for the Guaranteeing Supplier status introduced in the recent government decree indirectly supports this possibility.[48] Recent changes in retail supply market regulation eliminated opportunity for retailers to earn profits from wholesale electricity or capacity trades.[49] The largest chunk of retail suppliers' profit originated from mismatch of peak consumption by their customers and the peak price of requested capacity traded at the wholesale market. From 1 April 2012, these profits were eliminated due to regulatory tightening, with major negative effect on the retail suppliers' bottom line (ATON, 2012). Some analysts argue that it is only a question of time until the Inter RAO will be called to step in to pick the portfolio of bankrupt retail suppliers, to become a federal Supplier of Last Resort.

---

[47] Online Conference 'Electric Power Industry: Consequences of Recent Reforms', 15 May 2012, http://www.finam.ru/analysis/conf0000100441/default.asp

[48] Russian Federation Government Decree No. 1242 of 31 December 2010 'On changes to certain legislative acts of the Government of Russian Federation on the rules of wholesale electricity market operations'.

[49] Russian Federation Government Decree No. 877 of 4 November 2011 'On changes in certain Government legislative acts in order to improve relations between suppliers and customers of the retail electricity market'.

> Consolidation into government ownership after unbundling and privatisation is an unusual development based on IEA experience and may have implications for competitive neutrality and efficient market operations and development in longer term. (Cooke *et al.*, 2012)

The imminent rise in energy tariffs calls upon bringing the matters of energy efficiency to the forefront of the discussion. Current energy intensity use in the Russian economy is a multiple of that in the developed world. There are large untapped resources of demand- and supply-side management, including replacement of dilapidated generating and manufacturing plant and equipment (Nigmatullin, 2011).

4.4 Conclusion

The electricity sector in Russia has experienced significant reform since 2003, in terms of ownership, pricing and access to new competitors. The commitment to price reform has led to the scope for efficiency gains in energy use. The transition of pricing to world market levels has been an important contributor to support for the implementation of reform, but the commitment remains to reach the global benchmarks.

One of the prime motivations for the reform was to create incentives for new investment. Foreign investors have been attracted to the sector. However, the slower than expected growth in electricity consumption, including the impact of the Global Financial Crisis, has allowed a delay in those investments. The maintenance of an investment programme remains an issue, and some uncertainties related to the design of the reforms are yet to be resolved.

The progress of reform and its significance in Russia can be put into context by consideration of the lessons from the experience in California in 2001. Several issues underpinned the electricity crisis there at that time: the lack of investment in new generating capacity during the reform period when market rules were being developed; the strategic behaviour of the generators to withhold capacity and bid up wholesale prices, and the inability of retailers to pass the increased wholesale costs to consumers due to retail price caps.

The following observations not only highlight the new stages of the reform but also illustrate the ways in which the reform programme in Russia has learnt from the experience in California:

(1) *Investment in new capacity*. It appears that investment in new capacity has been postponed until the rules of the wholesale market become clear and tested. Owners of the privatised RAO-UES generating assets have had their investment programmes approved but much of the investment concentrates in replacing dilapidated assets and upgrading existing assets. There have been virtually no greenfield investments until recently. Changes to the capacity payment mechanisms resulting from government intervention to combat rising electricity tariffs have resulted in increased uncertainty and investors' anxiety.

(2) *Strategic behaviour of generators and market power*. The new rules for capacity payments impose heavy penalties on generators withholding declared capacity or using a different mix of capacity from that approved by the System Operator. Generators operating in the markets with limited interconnection are subject to price-cap regulation by FTS and FAS. Base-load nuclear and hydro-generating assets remain fully or majority publicly owned, with the majority of private suppliers operating thermal plants with comparable cost structure. All of the above make the occurrence of California-type changes to the market design less likely.

(3) *Retail price caps and inability to pass costs to final users*. With the scheduled liberalisation of the wholesale market to 2011, most customers will be supplied at unregulated wholesale market tariffs. Residential customers will be supplied at regulated tariffs until 2014, with the level of residential tariffs gradually brought in line with the full economic cost. Industrial and other users will be supplied at market prices. Voluntary bilateral contracts between suppliers and buyers of electricity or capacity allow retail distribution companies to hedge their price risks and

purchase contractual amounts at mutually agreed prices. Any price increase at wholesale markets can be passed on to industrial and other non-residential customers, who are not subject to price caps.

(4) *Regulatory risks and dangers of reform reversal.* Recent government interventions, such as price-control of capacity payments and wholesale price smoothing, give negative signals to the market participants. Progress of the reform to date and its success should not be taken for granted. Continuing effort is required to ensure competitive and efficient market structure of the Russian electric power industry in future.

Chapter 5

Electricity in Korea[1]

Seung-Hoon Lee[2]

5.1 Introduction

A sufficient and stable power supply was, and still is, the most important condition for a developing economy in undertaking ambitious industrialisation projects. The Korea Electric Power Corporation (KEPCO), which has charge of supplying electricity to the entire nation as a state monopolist, was created in 1961 by consolidating three state-owned and operated electricity supply companies in Korea; one generation–transmission company and two distribution–sales companies. KEPCO supported the rapid industrialisation of Korea by supplying sufficient power at low tariffs without outside subsidies, by successful expansion of the capacity for generation and the transmission–distribution grid in a timely manner.

The growth of KEPCO was paralleled by the rapid industrialisation of the Korean economy. In the 1980s it became the nation's largest company by asset value, and the second largest by the number of

---

[1] This case chapter is based on a paper produced with funding from the Asia Pacific Economic Cooperation's Policy Support Unit and material from that paper is reproduced with its permission. Information is taken from The Impacts and Benefits of Structural Reforms in the Transport, Energy and Telecommunications Sectors in APEC Economies APEC#211-SE-01.1. The views expressed in this paper are those of the authors and do not necessarily represent those of the APEC Secretariat or APEC Member Economies.

[2] Professor, Seoul National University; former Chairman of the Korean Electricity Commission (2001-2004); President of Korean Society of Electricity Industry Studies (shoonlee@snu.ac.kr).

employees, behind Korea Telecommunications. The Korean government decided to sell 49% of its stock in KEPCO to the general public in an attempt to invite private capital to the power sector. The government still holds over 50% of the total stocks in KEPCO. Also, a small portion of new investment was allowed in private generators in the form of independent power plants under long-term power purchase agreements with KEPCO.

The operation of the Korean economy depended upon public sector investment to a substantial extent, since the Korean government made extensive use of public enterprises during the process of economic development, not only in basic infrastructure but also in energy and material industries such as oil refining, gas, electricity, steel and petrochemicals. In other economies the petrochemical and steel industries are usually under private, not public, control. The Korean petrochemical and steel industries, however, began through state initiative in the early stages of economic development when private capital was not sufficient and therefore not able to invest in these capital-intensive industries. The Korean government established many public enterprises in those sectors, aiming at the import substitution of basic materials. The major market for their outputs was Korea's manufacturing sector, which was rapidly growing as a successful export industry under the vigorous export drive policy of the Korean government. The public enterprises had once produced as much as 15% of the total value added of the entire national economy.

With the accelerated growth of the private sector, the Korean government initiated privatisation of many public enterprises. Though there were no objections to privatising material industries, public opinion was divided over privatising network industries such as telecommunications and electricity. A substantial portion of the population maintained the idea that there must be proper mechanisms for the provision of these universal services, and the regulated operation under public ownership was essential for this purpose.

At the same time, other countries (economies) shifted towards competition, restructuring network industries. Research institutes and academics advised the Korean government to initiate restructuring in line with this trend. On the other hand, the industries and their labour unions opposed what they referred to as an 'untested' experiment.

There are, however, differences and similarities between sectors. Consider the trends of change in electricity and telecommunications. A new entrant is able to compete in the telecommunications industry only after a slight institutional re-arrangement due to technological change. More extensive change is, however, required for electricity, in particular, to unbundle generation from grid operation in order to guarantee fair open access of energy traders to the grid. Third party access under functional unbundling prevailed in systems where traditional grid operators were private utilities under regulation, who objected to attempts to intrude upon their property rights. On the other hand, open access under structural unbundling seems more likely in systems where traditional monopolies were state enterprises. Examples of the former are the USA, Germany and Japan, and examples of the latter are the UK and Nord Pool economies. However, resistance to change from the incumbent could still be expected in those cases.

In the case of Korea, the size of KEPCO was a matter for consideration in the design of reform. KEPCO had not only monopolised the supply of electricity, but also now comprised many associated businesses. In particular, it had undertaken all the construction works of its own generation plants: other construction and engineering companies could join in projects only as subcontractors. This approach added to its size but also invited criticism of its corporate governance structure, which contributed to the pressure for reform.

The proposal for restructuring the electricity industry to accommodate competition attained political support, and the Korean government finally decided to initiate restructuring. The National Assembly passed the relevant legislation in 2000, and restructuring began in April 2001.

5.2 Restructuring and Reaction

The original restructuring plan comprised three stages:

(1) Divesting the generation sector from KEPCO to initiate the creation of a competitive wholesale market;
(2) Divesting the distribution sector from KEPCO to complete the wholesale market; and
(3) Creating a competitive retail market.

Stage 3 was planned to be completed by 2009. The plan was, however, suspended before Stage 2.[1]

To begin Stage 1 the Korean government created six generation companies (one nuclear-hydro and five thermal). It also established the Korea Power Exchange (KPX) which was to take charge of the system's operation and to mediate wholesale trading of power between generators and retail suppliers, including other buyers such as large-scale customers. Thus the function of KEPCO was to be limited to being a grid company and a retailer, without engaging in generation. Though KEPCO would become the only buyer, the wholesale price was to be determined by the KPX.

The Korean Electricity Commission (KOREC) was established under the Ministry of Commerce, Industry and Energy (MOCIE). KOREC was headed by a chairman and eight commissioners, who are all part-time members, except for one full-time commissioner who was the chief energy policy-maker of the MOCIE, whose role was also to take care of the remaining tasks of restructuring the industry.

KOREC was not an independent body, since it was designed to report to the Minister of Commerce, Industry and Energy. This structure was due to the fact that KOREC was also in charge of the policy implementation of further restructuring, for which the Minister had to be responsible. It was understood that KOREC would be made independent as soon as the task of restructuring was completed.

KOREC was to approve electricity tariffs and oversee the quality of electricity and security of the system. It also was to review the fundamental qualifications of the applicants for the businesses in the electricity industry such as generation, transmission, distribution and rctail. All applications were to be approved unless they violated conditions stipulated in the law, and without discriminating against foreign entrants. Approval was permanent as long as applicants abided by the regulations and there were no licence fees. Since the transmission business was to be monopolised by KEPCO for the time being, and the distribution–supply business would be made open in later stages, all the applications were expected to be, and were, concentrated in generation.

Long-term power purchase agreements (PPAs) were honoured for all pre-existing contracts with private generators, which had obtained approval before restructuring. New private power plants, however, were no longer eligible for PPAs. They had to sell their power only through the KPX at market prices, and could only sell it directly to consumers when trading was made feasible.

There was no explicit legal restriction on foreign ownership: there had been, and are still, several generators under full or partial foreign ownership. Most of them sold off their shares and withdrew their investment from Korea during the past decade. The withdrawals, however, were not due to the government's restriction on foreign ownership but were a voluntary choice. As for portfolio investment, about 25% of the total outstanding KEPCO shares were in the hands of foreign investors in September 2008, and a similar level has been maintained.

5.2.1 *Basic nature of the Korean model*

The KPX operated a cost-based pool (CBP) to determine real time wholesale equilibrium prices, which equate electricity supply and demand on an hourly basis. Demand was determined by the amount of power consumption, and supply by marginal cost, reflecting the merit order of the generators adjusted for the real time availability. So the equilibrium price was determined by the marginal cost of the marginal generator, called the system marginal price (SMP).

Since the pricing by SMP may not recover fixed costs, for the marginal generator in particular, a fixed amount of compensation was allowed under the title of a 'capacity payment'. So the final payment to the generators was composed of the SMP, which represents the level of the marginal cost for generation, a capacity payment and compensation for ancillary services. This system was essentially similar to the old UK system – the England-Wales pool.

The Korean wholesale market, however, was different from that in the UK in its dual structure. The KPX priced wholesale power in two ways. Generators were divided into two groups: nuclear and coal-fired generators (baseload group) and oil-fired and gas-fired generators (general group). Each group had its own marginal price and capacity payment. The marginal cost of the 'marginal' baseload generator, usually a coal-fired one, was called the baseload marginal price (BLMP), while that of the real marginal generator maintained its original name of SMP. The BLMP is much lower than the SMP. Each baseload generator is paid by BLMP and the general group by SMP for their energy. Since the baseload generator is more costly to build, its capacity payment is set higher than that of a general generator. A baseload generator incurred losses through the BLMP, and recovered them through the higher capacity payment.

This feature of the Korean CBP was introduced to comply with ongoing retail tariff regulation. If the same SMP were paid to all the baseload generators, KEPCO would encounter a substantial rise in cost for its acquisition of wholesale power. This would drive KEPCO to a deficit under the fixed retail tariff. The government had to either repeal the tariff regulation or adopt dual wholesale pricing. As a transitory measure, the government adopted the dual pricing system.

The new law allowed large-scale customers' direct purchase of power from generators. However, this measure was delayed until the transmission tariffs could be established and retail tariffs liberalised. Direct purchase was not likely to take place then. All the large-scale customers, most of whom were industrial consumers, were enjoying subsidised low tariffs. Also, the big residential complexes which paid high tariffs to subsidise industrial consumers were not ready to form collective units to bargain.

This model was only supposed to last until deregulation of the retail tariff and the start-up of retail market operations in subsequent stages. The CBP market was to be replaced by an elaborate price-bidding pool, which would have involved the following measures:

- the generating companies (Gencos) were to be privatised individually,
- genuine open access to the grid was to be implemented,
- trading by bilateral contracts between customers and generators was to be introduced,
- retail tariffs were to be liberalised in order to accommodate the market determination of energy prices and
- retail supply market was to be made fully open.

The initial mechanism was designed only to cover the transitory initial phase.

The divestiture of the generation sector was incomplete in the sense that it was designed to let KEPCO own the entire share of stocks of each generation company. This was also just a transitory feature, since the Korean government planned to privatise all the thermal Gencos according to the original plan. Privatisation, however, would not be possible unless all the future conditions surrounding the electricity market became clear and reliable. Apparently, the uncertainty about future restructuring had the effect of discouraging potential buyers in the early stage of restructuring and none of the Gencos were sold.

5.2.2 *Reform put on hold*

In 2002 the Gencos' unions undertook a month-long strike against the restructuring, when the government attempted to privatise a Genco. However, the restructuring proceeded on schedule under the support of the President who had initiated the restructuring. This support continued while he was in office but things began to change in 2003. Although the new president of that year belonged to the same political party as the outgoing president, there was evidence[3] that he was sceptical about privatising the power industry. The labour unions continued to demand a repeal of the entire restructuring plan. The issue at hand was the

---

[3] During the campaign, the President maintained it was desirable that network utility industries be under public control, except telecommunications which had already been privatised.

divestiture of the distribution sector, scheduled as part of Stage 2. The unions threatened another strike if the government proceeded according to the original restructuring plan.

The new President then decided not to push restructuring any further but to maintain it in its present status. There was no further restructuring but there was no return to the previous system either. The consequence was a higher level of uncertainty among private investors. Private investment in the generation sector was limited only to capacity expansion of pre-existing generators, and no new private generator entered the market. Though the total installed capacity expanded from 55GW to 75GW during the past decade, the expansion was mainly driven by the six Gencos owned by KEPCO. Exceptions to this are the renewable generators of 803.64MW capacity, which are subsidised by a scheme independent of the market, and the district suppliers with approved capacity of 1.5GW (see below).

5.2.3 *Retail tariffs and cross-subsidisation*

The retail rates of electricity in Korea are set by the standard principle of rate of return regulation. Although the figures vary over time, it is generally accepted that the rates for agricultural and industrial users are set below cost, while those for other users are above cost. There is a special discounted rate for late night consumption. This rate is set just to cover the marginal cost of nuclear generation and intended to encourage the consumption of residual midnight power from nuclear plants.

Table 5.1 summarises the trends of electricity prices for each usage and total. Retail tariffs are set by the rate of return regulation modified by some progressive schemes. So the figures in the table are not the market prices but the average of regulated tariffs, and they do not directly reveal any effect of restructuring. The prices have been rising consistently, reflecting the rising costs until 2001, and then fixed at almost the same level in order to control inflation. In 2008 KEPCO incurred a loss of KRW1 trillion due to the substantial increase in fuel prices.

This rate structure generated cross-subsidisation within Korean electricity consumption. Firstly, residential and commercial consumers paid higher tariffs for power in order to subsidise agricultural and industrial consumers. Industrial consumers represent up to half of Korea's total power consumption. Such cross-subsidisation provided incentives for Korean industry to rely heavily upon high electricity consumption, while other economies are endeavouring to conserve energy. This is a legacy of an export-driven policy, which provided the manufacturing industry with a wide range of subsidies. Cheap power helped the export-led growth of the Korean economy significantly. At the same time, however, it nurtured an industry structure which consumes too much power and which cannot survive with a price that would recover costs.

Secondly, urban consumers paid much higher tariffs than the incurred costs. This was done in order to subsidise consumers residing in remote mountain regions and isolated islands who pay the same rates as the urban consumers. It is interesting to note that the tariffs for tap water, which is as essential as electricity, differ across regions. Perhaps this is because water is supplied by separate municipal governments while electricity is supplied by a nationwide monopoly.

Thirdly, the midnight discount rate is only for power consumed by approved heating and air conditioning equipment. This programme is intended to encourage consumption of midnight power that is left over from nuclear generation. It has proven very effective. Load factors have improved so much that costly liquefied natural gas (LNG) must be burned now in order to meet increased midnight demand for power. At the same time, the programme generated a strong interest group, led by the equipment producers, who strongly opposed its repeal, even though the need for the programme is no longer present.

Table 5.1 Trends in Average Prices, 1994–2008 (KRW per kWh).

Year	Residential	Industrial	Agricultural	Total
1994	85.95	46.14	34.59	59.39
1995	86.47	47.14	36.17	61.28
1996	88.95	48.37	37.11	62.99
1997	92.05	49.86	38.96	65.26
1998	96.60	55.01	44.31	72.08
1999	96.41	54.78	44.04	71.59
2000	94.72	58.30	43.04	74.65
2001	91.57	61.56	43.51	77.06
2002	87.01	59.02	42.37	73.88
2003	88.00	60.30	43.45	74.68
2004	90.94	60.23	41.95	74.58
2005	91.07	60.25	41.67	74.46
2006	93.70	61.92	42.96	76.43
2007	94.78	64.56	42.45	77.85
2008	97.58	66.24	42.38	78.76

***Source*:** KEPCO statistics 2010.

5.2.4 *Emergence of district suppliers*

As the electricity rates for residential consumers were set high, there was strong demand from the private sector to enter the power market for large residential complexes. They built gas turbine generators in urban residential complexes, mostly doing cogeneration, and sold power to the complexes at rates slightly lower than KEPCO's. Furthermore, they were allowed to sell excess power to KEPCO at reasonable rates. This emergence of district suppliers prompted KEPCO and KOREX to set the transmission tariff, opening the door for direct trading by bilateral contract between generators and large-scale customers.

District suppliers sell their power to their customers at prices which are similar to the retail tariffs of KEPCO. They may obtain back-up power from KEPCO at industrial or general rates, which are lower than the residential rate, or directly from the wholesale market. Their left-over power may be sold back to KEPCO at the real time SMP. Rising oil prices have discouraged their activities.

In total, 22 district suppliers were approved across 28 districts from October 2004 to July 2008, and the total capacity approval reached 1512.25MW. Operations started in four districts and suppliers withdrew from two districts. The initial enthusiasm cooled down, because the soaring oil price substantially eroded its profitability. The cross-subsidising rate structure removes the incentive for large-scale customers to trade directly with generators, even though the transmission tariffs are set clearly.

5.3 Present Status

The lack of continued restructuring has had a number of consequences. No new private generator has entered the market except for the renewable generators and the district suppliers. Also the tightly controlled retail tariff has caused a serious financial imbalance between KEPCO and the Gencos. Every spot price then became subject to a ceiling to try to solve this problem and the wholesale market shifted to serving the role of allocating earnings artificially between KEPCO and the Gencos.

A new President belonging to a different party was elected in 2008 and to date the new President has not announced further reforms in the electricity industry. Meanwhile the labour unions continue to push the government not to pursue further restructuring actions. The Minister of Commerce, Industry and Energy, in his nomination hearing at the National Assembly, then said he would subject the restructuring of the power industry to a thorough review by the Korea Development Institute (KDI), a national think tank. KDI has recently released its final report, which proposes to resume restructuring by divesting the retail sector from KEPCO to begin retail competition. The Minister, however, announced that it is not yet the right time to begin retail competition. Instead he decided that all the Gencos will be controlled not by KEPCO but by government, in contrast to the demand to repeal all the restructuring and go back to the old system. He also promised to introduce an electricity rate system chained to oil prices.

5.4 Statistical Features of Korea's Electricity Industry

5.4.1 *Price trends*

KEPCO attained a good reputation for its supply of electricity at a low price to support the industrialisation of Korea. Figure 5.1 shows the trend of average prices.

The trend does not indicate any direct effect of restructuring. The price of KRW78.76 per kWh (US6.6 cents) in 2008 was much cheaper than the price of US9.74 cents in the USA in the same year. Except for the years from 2008 of soaring oil prices, KEPCO managed its operations without requiring fiscal support from the government.

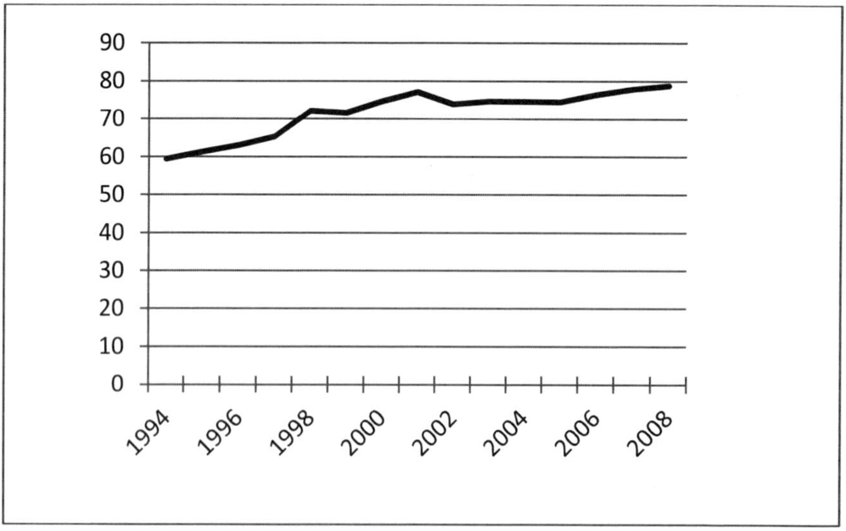

Figure 5.1 Trend of average power prices, 1994–2008 (KRW/kWh).

5.4.2 *Trend of total power losses*

Transmission–distribution loss has reduced over time to 4.01% in 2008 (Figure 5.2). Improvement was evident well before the restructuring, and the trend was not interrupted by restructuring (though the trends in Figure 5.2 do not reflect the effect of restructuring).

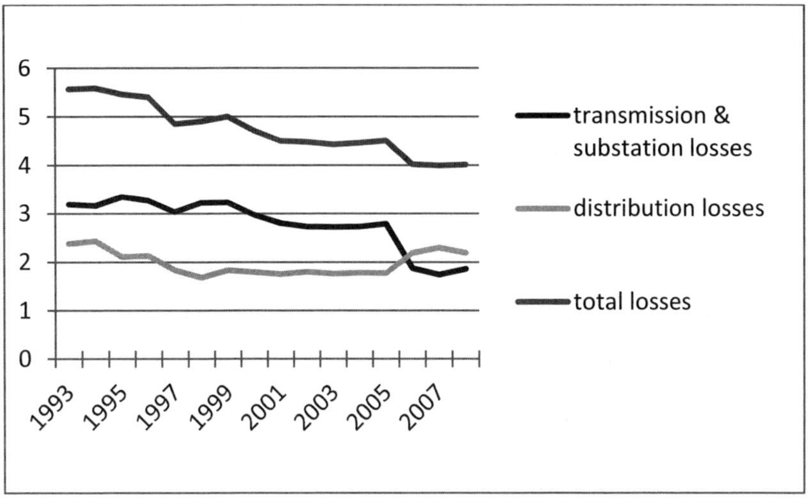

Figure 5.2 Trends of losses, 1993–2008(%).

The loss rate of 4.01% is remarkable in comparison with the USA's 6.5% in 2007. While Korea cannot be compared with the USA in terms of area, it appears that KEPCO managed the grid operation extremely well.

5.4.3 *Efficiency gains from restructuring?*

Although the future of restructuring is quite uncertain, several studies have examined whether any efficiency gains were made through restructuring. The restructuring is incomplete and the relevant data are insufficient so, as yet, there are no convincing conclusions.

Since there has not been market competition in earnest, any gains would appear to arise from improved management after the divestiture. The planned outage, which in 2000 required 25.0 days across 109 units of generators, dropped following restructuring to be 19.4 days across 117 units in 2003 (Samil Consultant, 2003). The heat efficiency of the generation facilities and the maintenance of frequency and voltage also seem to have improved after restructuring (Tables 5.2 and 5.3, respectively; The Korean Society for Electricity Industry Study, 2007).

Table 5.2 Trend of Heat Efficiency of Generators, 1998–2004 (%).

Year	1998	1999	2000	2001	2002	2003	2004
Heat efficiency	39.45	39.51	39.45	39.57	39.96	39.94	40.66

Source: The Korean Society for Electricity Industry Study, 2007.

Table 5.3 Maintenance of Frequency and Voltage 1998–2005 (%).

Year	1998	1999	2000	2001	2002	2003	2004	2005
Frequency	99.17	99.28	99.33	99.41	99.45	99.70	99.74	99.70
Voltage	99.35	99.57	99.79	99.84	99.88	99.94	99.96	99.96

Source: The Korean Society for Electricity Industry Study, 2007.

There was a substantial rise in the capacity utilisation rate of coal-fired plants and a subsequent reduction in generation cost of the Gencos after the divestiture (The Korean Society for Electricity Industry Study, 2005). The rate rose from 74.8% in 1999 to 89.0% in 2003, and the cumulative cost savings were estimated as KRW602 billion for 2001–03. Kim, Knittel and Cho (2006) and Kim and Kim (2008) reported similar results. It is important to note, however, that Lee and Kim (2008) criticise the models used, claiming that they give rise to conflicting conclusions about the efficiency gains of restructuring.

In terms of financial performance, the (recent) hike in oil and coal prices since 2008 drove up the wholesale price of power. As a result, KEPCO was pushed into deficit under the fixed retail tariff. This resulted in price ceilings on the wholesale price and substantially reduced the Gencos' profits. KEPCO at the same time has observed that the Gencos have paid higher prices for the coal they import, since each Genco was not able to command the same strong market power that KEPCO did before the restructure. However, this point can be debated, since even KEPCO is not likely to have substantial buying power in the world coal market.

5.5 Politics of Reform

All reform encounters political resistance as well as support. When the Korean electricity industry reform was initiated, this author's observation was that the bureaucracy, following the President's instruction, pushed the reform very aggressively. The management of KEPCO also complied with the government's direction. The labour unions objected to the reform explicitly although their month-long strike was in vain. The general public was not sure of the reform, since the idea of a competitive power market was novel. However, the move to reform was firm and steady while the political leader was clearly fully convinced of its merits.

The situation changed substantially when a new president signalled that he was not convinced about the value of reform. This author's assessment and observation was that bureaucrats lost their enthusiasm; KEPCO managers began to express their opposition publicly. For example, the present chief executive officer of KEPCO said before the National Assembly that he believes that the electricity industry must go back to its original form, that is, a KEPCO monopoly. The labour unions started systematic campaigns involving opponents from academia and industry. People generally appeared to become more sceptical, and the negative impact of the Californian electricity situation contributed to this.

Some recent experience provides an example of how competition might work and therefore could help reinvigorate the progress of reform. This involves the use of smart grids in line with a green power policy. To improve the efficiency of energy consumption the Korean government promoted the introduction of the smart grid into the electricity system. Jeju Island was selected for testing a smart grid: an extensive experiment was underway until 2011. A smart grid will inform each consumer of the real time cost and price of power if the competitive market is at work. A display panel will provide the information so the consumer can decide then whether to use power or not. Consumers are unlikely to respond to the real time cost if it does not reduce their power bill, but many certainly will respond to the real time price in order to save money.

This experience could deliver the message that a competitive market is more appropriate for the system based on the smart grid than the traditional regulated monopoly. The large telecommunications companies KT and SK (which are the full names of those companies) are aggressive with respect to the smart grid. There is the prospect of competition between the traditional giant of the electricity sector and two giants of telecommunications.

The patterns of electricity consumption in Korea remain an issue, and may also contribute to the momentum for further reform. Consumption data indicate that the Korean electricity industry is characterised by 'too much consumption', which is encouraged by the low tariffs. Per capita power consumption of Korea was very close to Japan's in 2009. However, Korea's per capita income was only half that of Japan's. Korea consumed 497kWh of electricity in order to produce USD1,000 of GDP, while Japan, the USA and the UK each consumed only 30-60% as much.

5.6 Conclusion

As explained in this case study, an extensive programme of reform was proposed in Korea, but a change in circumstances and apparently in the evaluation of the reform by political leaders has altered the process of its implementation. The main reform to date has been the separation of the generation companies, although without a change of ownership. There is some evidence of an effect on various dimensions of efficiency, though its significance is debated. Competition has not been introduced. Drivers of further reform may not be fiscal constraints, since KEPCO has performed well in financial terms. However there is evidence of the benefits of competition emerging in new models of systems of supply and an apparent interest from the telecommunications companies in the electricity market. Prices have risen closer to world market benchmarks but remain below them. This approach to pricing, and the cross subsidies to industry, lead to higher levels of consumption which remains an issue.

What might be the next steps in reform? In 2007 a research group proposed that KEPCO divest its retail sector so that each Genco could take over the retail business and start competing in the retail market, without divesting its distribution sector (The Korean Society for Electricity Industry Study, 2007). The idea was motivated in part by the experience in Texas. There, fierce retail competition was used to drive retail prices down. However, it also resulted in certain retailers becoming insolvent. The customers, who had signed contracts with the insolvent retailer, were stranded without a supply of electricity. However, if a retailer is backed by its own generation business, this acts as a 'physical' hedge against fluctuations in the wholesale electricity price. As a result, the retailer is less likely to go bankrupt easily and the customers are less likely to be left stranded. Such an approach is common amongst electricity generators or retailers in Australia. This proposal, while opposed by those against further restructuring, deserves attention.

Further restructuring could also involve a) divesting the construction and retail businesses from KEPCO, b) bringing the Gencos into the retail business, and c) creating an energy market by abandoning regulation of the retail rate. There would be resistance from the interest groups who gain from the current structure of cross-subsidisation. Their position (now) seems to be supported by political leaders as well as the general public, based on the perception that KEPCO is an excellent utility which can supply electricity at low prices without any state subsidy. In many efficiency measures KEPCO is indeed an excellent utility, but it is not desirable for the present system to continue to encourage high electricity consumption in Korea. More extensive and convincing analysis and presentation of information would be valuable for successful further restructuring of the Korean electricity industry.

Chapter 6

Rail Transport in Chile[1]

Raimundo Soto[2]

6.1 Introduction

Railways played a significant role in Chilean social life for almost a century. Between 1860 and 1950 railroads were an exemplar of modernisation, integration and economic development. By 1950, nevertheless, the industry started to decline, unable to compete with more efficient means of transportation (buses and trucks). By the mid-1970s railroads were bankrupt, surviving through government subsidies. Two decades later, passenger services had almost disappeared (accounting for less than 1% of total traffic). Freight operations, on the contrary, had been privatised and revitalised, and concentrated on small profitable market niches usually in remote areas of the economy (Thompson and Angerstein, 1997).

This paper reviews the Chilean case and analyses the current standing and operations of the industry, focusing on the reforms, public sector involvement, regulation, market entry, vertical integration, externalities and political factors. The Chilean economy underwent a massive

---

[1] This case chapter is based on a paper produced with funding from the Asia Pacific Economic Cooperation's Policy Support Unit and material from that paper is reproduced with its permission. Information is taken from The Impacts and Benefits of Structural Reforms in the Transport, Energy and Telecommunications Sectors in APEC Economies APEC#211-SE-01.1. The views expressed in this paper are those of the authors and do not necessarily represent those of the APEC Secretariat or APEC Member Economies.

[2] Institute of Economics, School of Economics and Business Administration, Pontificia Universidad Católica de Chile (rsotom@uc.cl).

restructuring in the mid-1970s, which included opening to foreign trade, complete market deregulation, inflation control, macroeconomic stabilisation and, most importantly for our study, a complete reallocation of government subsidies. In this economic turnaround, despite the waste and inefficiency associated with the publicly-owned railroad monopoly, no specific reforms were devised for railroads. Fiscal reforms led to a substantial reduction in subsidies to the sector which, in turn, prompted managers to change operations, eliminate redundancies and inefficiencies, and divest assets to cut financial losses. The government did not consider a transition phase or compensation mechanisms for those affected negatively.

Perhaps uniquely, the Chilean reforms resulted in the coexistence of two different forms of private sector participation in freight operations: (1) privatisation of the entire Northern Railroad, including rolling stock and essential facilities (track, yards and terminals) without open-access clauses; and (2) contracting out or 'concessioning' freight in the Southern Railroad to private carriers who pay a fee for the use of the track and terminals while sharing these essential facilities with the remains of the publicly-owned passenger-services company. Both systems have led to substantial increases in transportation volumes, rising labour productivity and declining tariffs. Consumers benefitted from the reforms which are discussed below in more detail. The first step however is a review of the circumstances in which the rail system operates.

6.2 Chilean Geography and the Development of Railroads

To a large extent, the development of railways depends on geography. Since their inception, entrepreneurs and government authorities looked at railroads as a means to overcome isolation, improve connectivity, consolidate territorial integration and advance economic development. Historical and political events such as international conflicts have also shaped the development of railroads not only in Chile but also in most economies (see Atack *et al.* (2009) and references therein for the United States of America, and Thompson and Angerstein (1997) for Chile). This section provides a brief summary of the geographical and historical events leading to the development of the Chilean railroad industry. Readers with more interest in the detail of the reform are referred to section 6.3.

Chile is a long and relatively narrow economy (4,300km from north to south; and an average width of 180km), sandwiched between the Pacific Ocean and the Andes Mountains. The northern half is dominated by the Atacama Desert, rich in minerals but sparsely populated. The southern half, in contrast, concentrates most of the population and economic activities (except mining).

In such a peculiar geographical environment, it would have been natural to expect railroads to play a crucial role in economic development and social life. Indeed, one longitudinal railroad track and a number of branches would service most of the population and economic enterprises, providing efficient and cheap transport services to the public and a reasonable profit for investors (Figure 6.1). That was the tenet of railroad managers and the Chilean governments for decades, but history proved otherwise.

Chile's first railroad track was laid in 1851 to transport silver from the mines in the north to the seaport of Caldera. Other tracks mushroomed in following years, but a railway system did not take shape until the 1870s (Alliende, 2001). Private initiatives were initially supported with public funds due to the insufficient development of Chilean financial markets and the lack of private capital. Dissatisfied with the slow pace of expansion, the government started to acquire private railroads in the 1880s and embarked on an ambitious investment programme to connect all railways. From then on, the industry development was almost exclusively a public sector business.

Between 1870 and 1915 the government completed the Chilean railway system (Table 6.1). Massive investments in the northern railway were justified by the significant territorial expansion after the Nitrate War (1879–84) and were easily financed by taxes on nitrate exports.[3] By

---

[3] The Nitrate War (Spanish: Guerra del Pacífico) took place from 1879 through 1883. Chile fought against Bolivia and Peru over the mineral-rich Peruvian provinces of Tarapacá, Tacna, and Arica, and the Bolivian province of Antofagasta. Chilean enterprises, which largely exploited the area, saw their interests at stake when Peru

1915 some 3,500km of tracks were laid and interconnected. These tracks were of metric gauge (1m). The southern railway expanded similarly, laying around 3,800km of track, but of broad gauge (1.676m). By 1910 a publicly owned railroad linked Chile and Argentina (250km) using a cogged metric track and reaching altitudes of 3,200m. Finally, by 1913, a publicly owned railroad linked Chile and North Bolivia (500km) and one private company linked Chile and South Bolivia (c. 1,000km). These were the last investments in rail tracks until the 21st century.

By 1915 the main companies (Ferrocarril del Norte and Ferrocarril del Sur) were consolidated in one firm called EFE, an acronym for Empresa de Ferrocarriles del Estado. It has been argued that there was never a railway system because the two railroads remained disconnected by their differences not only in track gauge but also in market and development strategies. Later, this tacit separation would play a decisive role in the shape of the reforms.

A report by the EFE directors notes the history of challenges of managing a publicly-owned firm, including political interference, financial mismanagement, lack of maintenance of tracks, buildings and rolling stock, the low quality human capital of its labour force and disregard for customer satisfaction (EFE, 2009). In contrast, the only private railroad with significant operations (Antofagasta–Bolivia) remained profitable and expanded its operations, despite continuous political turmoil between the two economies.

---

nationalised all nitrate mines in Tarapaca, and Bolivia imposed a 10-cent tax on the Antofagasta Nitrate and Railway Company. As a result of the war, Chile acquired the Peruvian territory of Tarapacá, the disputed Bolivian department of Litoral (cutting Bolivia off from the sea), as well as temporary control over the Peruvian provinces of Tacna and Arica.

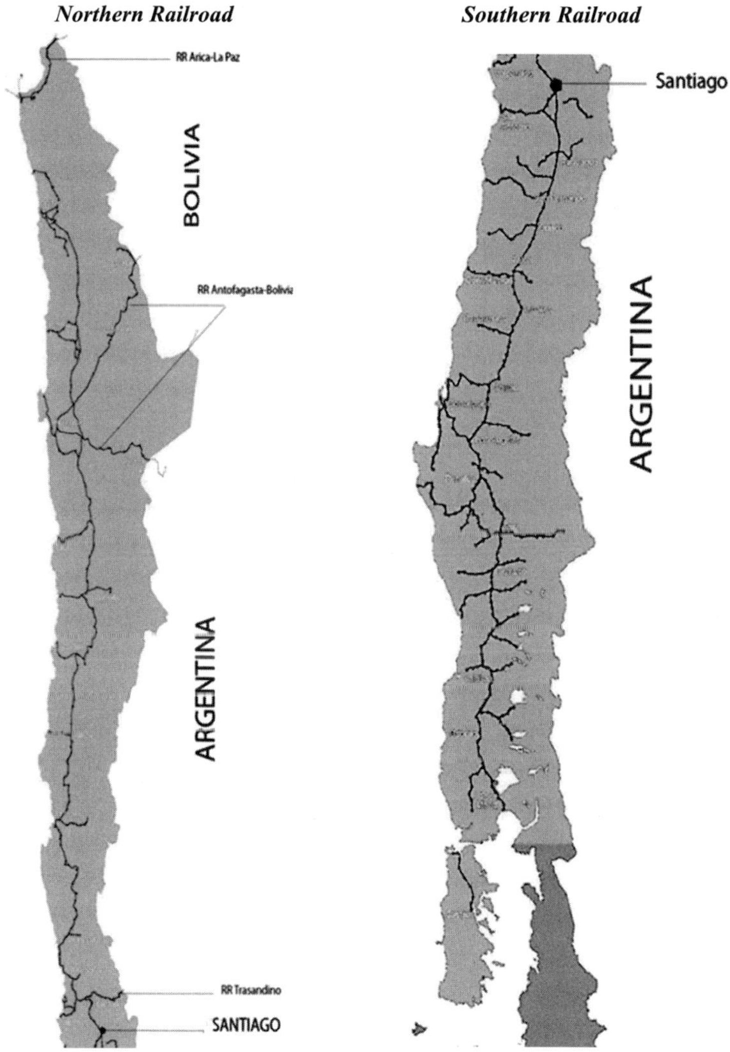

Figure 6.1 Main Railroads in Chile.

Table 6.1 Main Railroads in Chile.

Name of company	Length (km)	Track gauge (m)	Completed	Current operational status
Ferrocarril del Sur	1,254	1.676	1913	Passengers: operated by public firm
				Freight: private sector concessions
Ferrocarril del Norte	1,867	1.000	1915	Passengers: discontinued in 1975
				Freight: privatised in 1997
Ferrocarril Antofagasta-Bolivia	700	1.000	1888	Privately owned
				Transports freight and passengers
Ferrocarril Transandino	250	1.000	1910	Closed since 1984
Ferrocarril Arica-La Paz	204	1.435	1913	Privatised in 1996
				Bankrupt and closed since 2005
Ferrocarril Potrerillos	155	1.000	1928	Privately owned by mining operation (freight only)
Ferrocarril Tocopilla	124	1.067	1890	Privately owned by mining operation (freight only)
Ferrocarril de Huasco	100	1.000	1892	Privately owned by mining operation (freight only)
Ferrocarril de Romeral	38	1.000	1913	Privately owned by mining operation (freight only)

Source: Elaborated from work of Thompson and Angerstein (1997).

By the 1950s EFE began to feel the very strong competition from trucks and buses as a result of the extension of roads and paving. Continuous financial losses throughout the 1960s and into the mid-1970s led to a significant decline in service quality and massive injections of public funds to maintain operations. At the peak of its popularity in the 1950s EFE transported around 35% on average of the various markets in which it operated, i.e. freight and passenger. However, by the mid-1970s, the market shares in both freight and passenger transport were in single digits. Declining market share contributed to rising financial losses of the railway.

Table 6.2 Traffic Operations by EFE, 1960–2008.

	1960	1970	1980	1990	2000	2008
Passengers (millions)	26.4	21.1	9.4	8.8	9.5	10.0
Passenger*km (millions)	1,906	2,338	1,425	1,077	737	759
Freight (million tons)	13.0	19.0	16.7	19.1	22.0	27.2
Freight*km (millions)	1,952	2,532	1,942	2,804	3,134	4,292

Source: Based on Anuarios de Transporte y Comunicaciones, Instituto Nacional de Estadísticas de Chile.

6.3 Reforms in Chile's Railroad Industry

As in most economies, the reforms to the Chilean railroad industry were not devised as a sectoral programme but stemmed from macroeconomic and fiscal reforms initiated in the mid-1970s. As discussed in Thompson *et al.* (2001), a series of economic crises removed the government's ability to pay for losses in the railway. Railway reforms in Chile, however, predate those in Latin America, Africa and Europe by two decades. The economy-wide reform process included a vast array of measures aimed at deregulating the economy, achieving effective vertical and horizontal disintegration, opening all sectors to foreign competition and foreign investment, allowing and encouraging private sector initiatives and restricting public sector activities to subsidiary initiatives (poverty alleviation, control of externalities, human capital formation and the like) (Larraín and Vergara, 2000).

A significant goal of the Chilean reforms was the elimination of subsidies which could not be justified on social grounds. In this context the publicly-owned railroad monopoly was targeted for major restructuring. This did not include a transition phase or an adjustment plan. A second general goal of the reforms was to improve efficiency but in the case of the railroad, given the scale of the financial losses, efficiency was a secondary target (Thompson, 2001).

As a result of the fiscal reforms, all direct subsidies were eliminated, leading to the closure of a substantial number of branchlines and layoffs of personnel (the rail labour force fell from 15,000 workers in 1978 to 7,000 in 1981). Concurrently, the government deregulated the inter-urban passenger transport market and opened up imports of trucks and cars, thus increasing competition for EFE in both markets.

In order to cut subsidies, the government also required EFE to downsize operations. The Northern Railroad ceased all operations in 1975, its tracks as well as its rolling stock abandoned or sold to local private operators (see below). The Argentina–Chile Transandino Railroad ceased operations in 1984, the track was abandoned and covered by snow and mountain landslides. The publicly owned Chile–Bolivia Railroad remained in operation largely as a result of the provisions of the Peace Agreement after the Nitrate War, but it reduced activities to a minimum until it was privatised in 1997. By 2005 the Bolivian private company that acquired the railroad was bankrupt and its operations closed. The Southern Railroad continued to operate, but the government had to impose branch closures, layoffs and reduce frequencies to regain financial balance.

Despite the sizable government intervention, EFE did not become operationally profitable. The main longitudinal track of the Southern Railroad remained operative, yet financial and operative losses put continuous pressures on EFE and required further restructuring. More pressure came in the 1990s from the successful highway concession programme that improved substantially the quality and availability of paved roads, thereby reducing costs for trucks and buses. Between 1988 and 1990 EFE sold the remains of the Northern Railroad that had been closed for around 15 years to a public holding that subsequently restructured the company and privatised it in 1996. Other EFE assets such as yards, buildings, crossings and even the 'fiscal track' (the land on which the railroad tracks are laid) were divested in order to raise funds for continuing operations. In spite of the adjustment, EFE still required major support: for example, in 1994 it transported around 9 million passengers (less than 10% of total inter-urban traffic) and 17 million tons of freight, earning around USD39 million. Total costs, however, reached around USD80 million of which the payroll amounted to USD42 million. The USD51 million deficit was subsidised by the government.

Studies undertaken by the government and EFE in the early 1990s concluded that (1) a major legal restructuring of EFE was needed; (2) the freight business was profitable if properly managed by private-sector carriers; and (3) passenger services were not profitable but could be provided at a social benefit by a restructured EFE.

The legal restructuring of EFE was required in order to increase its capabilities to undertake new business, reinforce internal control and professionalise its management. In 1993 the government passed a new legal charter for EFE allowing for vertical and horizontal disintegration. The separation of freight and passenger activities was completed when EFE created a separate company – Ferrocarriles del Pacífico (FEPASA) – to handle its freight operations. In 1995 FEPASA was privatised to a joint venture of Chilean and foreign investors; EFE retained a participation of 18%. According to the concession contract, FEPASA has the right to carry for 20 years, accessing and using EFE tracks for which it has to pay fixed and variable tolls. FEPASA, nevertheless, does not hold exclusivity in access to the tracks. A second private carrier – Transporte Ferroviario Andrés Pirazolli S.A. (TRANSAP) – also signed contracts with EFE and started freight operations in 2001. In 2009 these two private carriers transported around 11 million tons (equivalent to 3.6% of the total freight transport in southern Chile), in what has become a small yet profitable market. EFE had previously complained of unfair competition from trucks on the grounds that road tolls were too low to cover their marginal cost. The success of FEPASA and TRANSAP indicates the effect may be small.

The second major restructuring of EFE was the creation in 1995 of several subsidiaries to serve the passenger market according to those segments of the railroad system where it was deemed to be socially justified. Only one of these new companies has succeeded financially, while the others required sizable subsidies to operate. The company maintained passenger services at a loss. Competition from buses dwarfed its market share; in 2008 only 9 million passengers were served by EFE, less than 1% of the total of passengers transported in southern Chile.

The third change to EFE's structure was to allow its current operations to be managed as a private company while the government retained the control of major investment plans. In principle, EFE was to inform the government on current operations but was required to obtain approval for capital investments. In practice the company operated as an unregulated unit due to loopholes in the 1993 law, while negotiating directly with the presidency for capital appropriations. The management of the company improved steadily over time, but constraints on providing services for political purposes continued to be an issue.

Over 2005–08 EFE embarked in a USD1 billion investment project to restart passenger services in southern Chile with new and refurbished rolling stock, improved building and terminals, and upgraded tracks. Contrary to Chile's tradition, the government did not undertake the mandatory social evaluation of the project. The project did not succeed; no new services were implemented, the refurbished rolling stock did not operate, and new buildings and terminals await their opening. There are several ongoing legal inquiries to determine responsibilities.

EFE's financial position has deteriorated markedly. Operational losses amounted to around USD65 million a year (2009), or roughly USD3 per passenger. The losses were expected to increase to around USD100 million for years to come as a result of debt service. A World Bank study has found that EFE was losing money in every single business undertaking (World Bank, 2007). Operational losses reduced somewhat between 2009 and 2011 (15% on average), largely as a result of contained costs and improved earnings from commuter passenger services, but the non-operational losses increased more markedly leading to a total loss of around USD200 million (EFE, 2011).

6.4 Regulation and Performance of Chile's Railroad Industry

This section reviews the rationale for government regulation in railroads and discusses the extent to which reforms and current regulations in Chile follow such rationale and how this, in turn, affects the performance of the Chilean industry.

6.4.1 *The rationale for regulation in railroads*

The fundamental rationale for government regulation in railroads is that infrastructure is almost inevitably a natural monopoly and is characterised by indivisibilities and economies of scale and scope (European Conference of Ministers of Transport, 2005). Regulation becomes crucial when network industries are vertically separated and competition is introduced. There are, however, particular characteristics of railways in Chile that would affect regulation. Whilst there is a desire to promote competition – as a means of promoting cost-minimisation or productive efficiency and of fostering innovation and traffic growth – there is still a dominant publicly-owned operator and owner of the track, EFE. Therefore, the regulator's role in promoting competition is particularly important, not only in preventing exploitation of monopoly power but also in facilitating access to the infrastructure. In practice this means not only regulating charges and access conditions but also the process of timetabling and the allocation of paths for trains, and possibly access to other essential facilities such as depots and terminals.

A further crucial point about rail, which tends to make it different to most other regulated utilities, is that there is a *prima facie* case for subsidy in terms of economies of scale within the sector and in terms of the failure to charge appropriately on competing modes. For these and for other political reasons, European governments have typically intervened heavily in rail industry decisions, particularly in the passenger sector. However, there remain debates as to how much to subsidise the industry and whether to channel the subsidy into the infrastructure or the operations. In this situation, an essential role of the regulator may be to protect private entrants from arbitrary decisions by the government, for instance, in regard to the level of finance it will provide to the infrastructure manager and, therefore, the capacity and quality of the infrastructure over which the private operators run. This can create potential conflicts between the regulator and the government.

In considering the arguments for regulating the access charges of the rail industry, there are three roles that a regulator might perform: (1) preventing the monopoly infrastructure manager from exploiting market power to the detriment of the public interest; (2) facilitating access to the infrastructure, in particular where the infrastructure manager is linked with one or more of the train operators; and (3) protecting the train operators from arbitrary decisions by the government regarding the level of finance it will provide to the infrastructure manager.

6.4.2 *Railroad regulation in Chile*

There is no railroad regulation in Chile beyond general security and environmental restrictions in the legal codes that apply to the transport sector (CITRA, 2008). Until 1993 EFE – and implicitly the entire sector – operated under the 1931 Railway Transportation Law, even when most of its provisions only pertained to publicly-owned railways and were obsolete or in direct opposition to other more modern regulatory provisions. For example, the 1931 law granted EFE the monopoly of railroad operations in Chile and restricted asset divestiture. In spite of this, EFE has privatised a substantial share of its activities, including all of the Northern Railroad. As mentioned, in 1993 EFE was given a new charter which changed it rights and obligations, but *de facto* the private and public sector continues to operate according to the 1931 law. This law is a slightly amended version of the 1925 law. Among other unusual provisions it requires transporting mail for free, free transporting of rolling stock from universities and granting free passes for authorities.

Likewise, there is no regulatory body in charge of railroad operations, nor an agency responsible for the strategic, long-term planning for the industry. Formally, the Ministry of Transport and Telecommunications is the industry authority (LIBRA, 2007). In practice it has never issued any significant regulation and its strategic planning activity comprises only a few, largely descriptive studies that do not relate directly to rail.

An historical explanation for the absence of regulation and regulatory agencies is the prevailing opinion that the publicly-owned monopoly would not require a regulatory body and that any regulation could be better channelled and implemented directly by EFE. In fact, over the years EFE has passed a series of internal regulations for its operations that became the norm for the few private-use railroads servicing mines and seaports in the north. However, this does not justify the lack of regulation after reforms and particularly after recent privatisations.

The 1993 Charter Act for EFE gave the company the capacity to undertake new businesses, divest assets, form joint ventures and disintegrate its operations vertically and horizontally. This, in practical terms, corresponds to a major change in regulation for the sector and certainly affected the operation of the entire industry.

The fact that this structural change was based in and affected mainly the public-sector indicates the nature of its limitations and the difficulties it poses for enacting much needed sector regulations (see below). In particular, the changes in the regulations channelled via the incumbent company used *ad hoc* procedures which increased regulatory risks and opened space for lobbying and capture.

6.4.3 *Unregulated privatisation*

Consider first the case of the Northern Railroad, FERRONOR. In a competitive bid in 1995 FERRONOR acquired the complete railroad, i.e. tracks, rolling stock, fiscal land, buildings, terminals and other facilities. According to Chilean law, the bidding process did not discriminate between domestic and foreign firms, nor did it require licensing, quotas or any restriction on the participation of the private sector in the railroad industry. Nine companies participated in the auction of the Northern Railroad, including foreign companies (such as Spanish RENFE, American Railroad Development Corporation and British RAILTEX), large size Chilean companies (Compania de Aceros del Pacífico, CAP and Compania Sudamericana de Valores, CSV) and consortia formed for the sole purposes of participating in the auction. FERRONOR was owned initially by Chile's APCO (45%) and USA's Rail America (55%): APCO purchased Rail America's share in 2001.

As a result of the privatisation, the Northern Railroad now operates as an unregulated, vertically integrated enterprise. The privatisation process considered no provisions for preventing the infrastructure monopoly from exploiting their market power or for facilitating non-discriminatory access to essential facilities (i.e. the track), although the government required the winning company to undertake the maintenance of the entire track.

Since privatisation FERRONOR concentrated its operations in a few segments of the market, eliminating small volume loads and general cargo, and focusing only on large operations (e.g. minerals and sulphuric acid) and long-term contracts. As noted by Thompson (1999), private-sector railway managers were not interested in carrying freight at rates equal to or below their marginal costs, and they expected all the traffic transported to at least help to finance fixed costs. Therefore, although the volumes transported have more than tripled with privatisation, some types of freight ceased to be transported by rail.

Table 6.3 provides information on the performance of FERRONOR after privatisation. There is evidence that the social benefits after privatisation may have been increased substantially. It can be seen that freight transport increased markedly for two years after privatisation, indicating that the privatised firm was able to restructure production towards more efficient use of resources. This is also indicated by the increase in physical labour productivity: transport in tons*km per worker increased by around 200%. However, four years after privatisation physical labour productivity and transport volumes had not grown, while revenues continued to rise. This would indicate a restructuring of operations towards more profitable segments of the market because tariff charges reduced after privatisation by around 36% (Thompson *et al.*, 2001).

A key, but largely unexplored, issue is whether forcing FERRONOR to grant access to its essential facilities would change market conditions for entry and efficiency. A mostly descriptive study by LIBRA (2007) indicates that entry in the short run is unlikely for several reasons, even if full access were granted. Firstly, the market for large volumes and long-term contracts is restricted to current mining operations and is unlikely to expand significantly in the future. Secondly, competition from trucks in general freight is intense and benefits from the absence of tolls on roads and lax environmental regulations. Thirdly, the rail track beyond what has been in use in the period 1990–2010 (17% total) is in poor condition and would require substantial investment to yield the high-quality and low-cost services required for trains to compete effectively with trucks.

Table 6.3 FERRONOR's Operations after Privatisation, 1997–2000 (%).

	1997	1998	1999	2000
Freight transported ('000 tons)	1,300	3,900	5,900	6,300
Total revenue (USD m)	7.9	15.3	21.0	23.7
Expenditures (USD m)	6.3	10.6	15.3	17.7
Productivity I (revenue per worker USD)	35,300	63,000	77,800	82,000
Productivity II (m ton*km/worker)	0.84	2.11	2.57	2.57

Source: Elaborated from The World Bank Railways Database.

In addition, FERRONOR allows other carriers to use the track, charging an unregulated toll that is directly negotiated between the parties. In principle, the ownership of an essential facility such as the track would indicate that FERRONOR could exercise monopoly power. However, the consumers are large mining operations with substantial resources and the ability of making credible threats to the company. This may have counterbalanced the potential market power of FERRONOR, but certainly a regulated price could benefit small consumers unable to negotiate on equal footing with the company. However, there have been no complaints to the Antitrust Commission against FERRONOR.

6.4.4 *Regulated concessions*

Consider, in contrast, the divestment of freight in the Southern Railroad. As indicated, EFE divested its freight operations by first creating a subsidiary FEPASA and then auctioning its concession to the private sector in 1995. Three companies bid for the 51% of FEPASA: Consorcio del Pacífico S.A., Compañía de Transportes Ferroviarios S.A. and Cruz Blanca S.A. The last named won with an offer of around USD30 million. The remaining 49% of the property was to remain in the hands of EFE (which expected annual dividends of around USD15 million), but it later sold an additional 30% of its participation to the International Financial Corporation of the World Bank and Latin American railway investors. A second private carrier – TRANSAP – entered the market in 2001. Concessions consist of non-exclusive 20-year contracts that allow free entry of carriers to facilities and require the payment of fixed and variable tariffs for the use of the infrastructure. The track remained in the hands of the government and, consequently, EFE is required to provide maintenance for the tracks and facilities as well as the path and to schedule services.

Following the trend in railroad reforms elsewhere, EFE concessions provided some elements of vertical disintegration and attempted to generate competition among carriers. As noted by Pietrantonio and Pelkmans (2004), vertical separation helps identify the true cost of running the railway and the eventual subsidy needed to allow safe and reliable infrastructure. Removing and preventing cross-subsidisation, in turn, creates fair conditions for potential entrants. Ideally, too, vertical separation helps reduce the asymmetries of information in the railway business, which is traditionally prone to hide cost structures and discourage performance.

Thompson *et al.* (2001) calculated that FEPASA tariffs were around 40% lower than those prevailing before privatisation, thus indicating a substantial benefit to consumers. Nevertheless, it should be acknowledged that both private carriers in the Southern Railroad have operated in the same manner as FERRONOR in the Northern Railroad (i.e. by exploiting market niches rather than providing a full range of services to the general public). They have concentrated their business on the transport of bulk commodities in large volumes (paper pulp, iron ore, etc.) and not in general freight, where competition from trucks is intense. This would indicate that the freight operations have benefitted mostly from better management, but not necessarily by improving efficiency to the point of being competitive with trucks beyond their current level.

Table 6.4 presents data on the performance of FEPASA. The effects of the change in management can be seen: although traffic volumes did not increase in the initial years after privatisation, revenue and traffic per worker increased markedly. This slow beginning was the result of problems relating to labour and line rehabilitation. It was only after a decade of operations that traffic and revenue per worker expanded markedly, indicating the long-run development of the market. Note FEPASA's relatively low profit levels.

The contract signed by FEPASA included the payment of a fixed fee to EFE for track maintenance and path and scheduling services. The subsequent entry of TRANSAP to the market indicates that this fixed payment was relatively low and did not deter entry. TRANSAP's entry was motivated by a change in sanitary and environmental regulations that prohibited truck transport of sulphuric acid through urban areas, thus leading a major mining operation to transfer the service to the private railway. In time, TRANSAP operations began to diversify which suggests that long-term contracts may be an important requirement to start operations as they guarantee the amortisation and recovery of fixed costs (typically in rolling stock and reputation) and lower risk.

Determining the fixed and variable fees is controversial. As noted by Pietrantonio and Pelkmans (2004) for the OECD, the adoption of marginal cost pricing is problematic on economic grounds. The drawbacks include arbitrary cost allocation rules in the presence of large economies of scope and relatively large common costs, a non- optimal

Table 6.4 FEPASA's Operations after Concessioning, 1995–2009(%).

	1995	1997	1999	2001	2009
Freight transported ('000 tons)	4,333	3,981	4,810	5,395	7,100
Total Revenue (USD m)	29.9	28.9	29.7	32.4	56.5
Expenditures (USD m)	26.0	24.8	32.2	32.4	53.0
Productivity I (revenue per worker USD)	57,700	68,800	68,000	64,800	114,342
Productivity II (m ton*km/worker)	1.52	1.73	2.31	2.61	2.69

Source: Elaborated from The World Bank Railways Database and FEPASA.

incentive system and, possibly, anti-competitive effects of two-part tariffs. EFE has complained of unfair competition from trucks as road tolls are too low to cover their marginal social cost and that this, in turn, artificially lowers the demand for rail transport of freight. It has asked for a permanent subsidy of around USD0.1 per ton*km transported.

Concession contracts are usually subject to renegotiation. In the Chilean case legal disputes arose with regard to EFE's inability to upgrade (and even maintain) the quality of tracks as required by the original contracts. There have been, however, no complaints about the fixed and variable tolls that private carriers must pay for the use of the essential facility (tracks and other facilities).

6.4.5 *Remnants of the past*

EFE continues operating passenger services despite incurring heavy losses (USD65 million in 2009 as noted above). The market share in inter-urban transport continues to shrink and the quality of services is low in terms of comfort and frequency. Accidents are relatively frequent (at a rate 10 times higher than that in the USA) and costly: the social cost of accidents was estimated at around USD16 million in 2007 alone (LIBRA, 2008).

The continuing losses of EFE indicate that the original purpose of the reforms, namely to avoid fiscal costs, has not been met, that subsidies continue to drain public resources and that a lack of safety leads to an increased social cost. Moreover, such losses negatively affect EFE's ability to raise funds for other important tasks such as the maintenance of the track and facilities and the upgrading of several railway components that have become bottlenecks for the operations of the system. These include expanding single to double tracks to eliminate traffic bottlenecks, improving communication systems, etc.

EFE's board of directors have acknowledged that, from a social point of view, only two of its commuter passenger services (Metrotren and Merval, operating between small towns adjacent to the main cities of Santiago and Valparaiso, respectively) are justifiable since financial losses are less than the estimated social value of the positive externalities derived from its operations (EFE, 2009). Passenger services should cease operations if they are not socially justifiable. The government, however, has been reluctant to undertake these measures and to bear the likely later political costs of closing down services. Decisions have been made in the opposite direction. In 2003 EFE embarked on a USD1 billion investment project to restart passenger services as noted above. Likewise, despite a negative social evaluation of the project, a suburban train system was launched in 2005 in Concepción with an implicit subsidy of USD0.41 per km/passenger.

This indicates the value of isolating the management of EFE from political pressures. Currently, the Chilean president directly appoints EFE's chairman and board thus adding the appearance of political considerations to the nomination and encouraging interest groups (e.g. regional authorities) to press for subsidised services. Measures aimed at higher levels of transparency, accountability and independence from political contingencies are an indispensable component of any successful reform proposal.

In addition, it would be advisable to separate passenger services from the track operations. EFE's board has proposed creating a separate company to manage the railroad infrastructure, probably as a first step for further privatisation (EFE, 2009). Independent observers have also suggested that subsidiaries should be created for the existing passenger services in order to make costs and resource allocation transparent. Alternatively, separating costs would provide sufficient information to undertake appropriate policy reforms, avoiding the coordination problems of having separate companies. Asmild *et al.* (2005) found that in 23 OECD economies there was a clear positive effect on operating efficiencies of the cost transparency following from accounting separation. However, whether there is an additional benefit through complete separation or whether the potential coordination problems outweigh the benefits remains unanswered.

6.5 Conclusion

For almost a century, railroads in Chile were an exemplar of modernisation, integration and economic development. By the 1970s railroads were bankrupt, surviving on government subsidies. Reforms initiated in the 1990s managed to revitalise freight transport by transferring operations to the private sector, but passenger services virtually disappeared.

The process of this reform of the freight industry provides examples of different types of reform: (1) unregulated vertically integrated privatisation; and (2) a regulated, vertically disintegrated concession with public control of the essential facilities. Neither of these reforms was designed to optimise the working of the industry, nor do they fit in an integrated transport regulated system. They stem from the government's desire to cut financial losses and to avoid political damage in running a bankrupt system. Reforms were made to a large extent on an *ad hoc* basis. Nevertheless, they complied with the standard Chilean norm of divesting publicly-held assets using competitive, non-discriminatory and largely transparent bidding processes.

Both reformed sectors achieved significant efficiency and welfare gains and, in this sense, reforms have improved the industry operations. Nevertheless, the starting point was quite low, making it easier to achieve such gains. The question remains of whether alternative divestiture procedures would have achieved better results.

In particular, the privatisation of the vertically integrated Northern Railroad without provisions for the open access to essential facilities such as the track, yards and terminals raises the question of potential market power on the part of the incumbent. Declining tariffs and absence of complaints indicates that potential monopoly power may have been counterbalanced by the large economic size of the mining operations that are the main customers of the railroad.

In contrast, freight concessions in the Southern Railroad using long-term contracts seem to have bridged the open-access issue successfully, but have not been able to provide an effective solution to managing the essential facility by the incumbent. While usage fees may provide for maintenance and system improvements, resources have been used to cover losses in passenger transport, a segment of the industry with no competitive advantages and apparently destined to disappear in the long run.

Reforms were dictated by fiscal balance reasons rather than aiming at improving the working of the railroad industry for consumers or with a strategic vision of the future needs of the transport sector. Consequently, reforms fell short of providing a more complete and efficient regulatory framework for the industry, in particular with regards to regulation in several areas. Four issues remain:

- Firstly, reforms reduced but did not stop losses of the incumbent public firm in passenger transport. Subsidies continue to consume public resources.
- Secondly, such losses negatively affect EFE's ability to undertake important tasks such as the maintenance of the track and facilities and the upgrading of those components that have become bottlenecks for the operations of the system.
- Thirdly, the reforms did not provide for an adequate institutional setting capable of isolating the management of EFE from political pressures. Likewise it did not increase transparency.
- Fourthly, the absence of a transport authority capable of integrating externalities, security considerations and environmental issues unnecessarily complicates the operation of railroads.

Chapter 7

Rail Transport in New Zealand[1]

Dave Heatley[2] and Margot Schwass[3]

7.1 Introduction

"The railways in New Zealand have never been regarded, or run, as a profit-making concern," wrote New Zealand's Minister of Railways, Gordon Coates, in 1923. Even the most unprofitable branch lines and services had an intangible value, he said: "They have opened up the economy, increased production and consequently the wealth of the Dominion" (Atkinson, 2007, p. 60). For much of the 20th century, rail was regarded not only as core government business but also as an iconic part of New Zealand's journey to prosperity. Notions that the railways should cover costs or provide a return on the capital invested were anathema to policy-makers and the public alike. To Minister Coates, running a railway solely on commercial grounds "would not be utilising the service in the true interests of [New Zealand]."

---

[1] This case chapter is based on a paper produced with funding from the Asia Pacific Economic Cooperation's Policy Support Unit and material from that paper is reproduced with its permission. Information is taken from The Impacts and Benefits of Structural Reforms in the Transport, Energy and Telecommunications Sectors in APEC Economies APEC#211-SE-01.1. The views expressed in this paper are those of the authors and do not necessarily represent those of the APEC Secretariat or APEC Member Economies.

[2] Dave Heatley, Principal Advisor, New Zealand Productivity Commission. This research was undertaken while a Research Fellow at the New Zealand Institute for the Study of Competition and Regulation (dave.heatley@productivity.govt.nz).

[3] Margot Schwass, writer and editor, Australia New Zealand School of Government (margot@schwass.co.nz).

Those traditional assumptions were swept aside in the 1980s. Corporatisation was followed by deregulation, privatisation and then the separation of infrastructure from rail operations. In 2008, however, rail became a government activity once more, with both the tracks and rail services owned and managed by the New Zealand Rail Corporation under the KiwiRail brand. After more than 25 years of policy shifts and U-turns, rail in New Zealand today is still far from 'a profit-making concern' and the need for significant government subsidies remains. There are conflicting views on rail's potential to contribute to New Zealand's economic development and environmental goals. Debate continues over how best to fund and run a railway 'in the true interests' of New Zealand.

This case study describes the arrangements under which rail has operated in New Zealand, and explores the policies and political imperatives that drove them. Figure 7.1 summarises the changes in policy. How has rail performed under the various models? Finally, given its ongoing economic performance problems, where might the future of rail in New Zealand lie?

The next section includes some detail of the history of the development of the rail network up to the creation of a corporate structure for the government-owned system in 1982. Those more interested in regulatory changes since then should turn to section 7.3.

7.2 A Short History of New Zealand Rail to the 1990s

7.2.1 *Building the railway, building the nation: 1860 to the 1920s*

Rail has been described as New Zealand's 'engine of colonisation' (Atkinson, 2007, p. 22). From the 1860s, railways helped open up the economy's interior, linking new European settlements to ports. The first railways were short lines built by provincial governments usually at very high cost. By 1880, with the economy's population still only 500,000,

- **1982** • The government Railways Department becomes the New Zealand Rail Corporation (NZRC), which operates the rail network (freight and passenger services) and the rail ferry service connecting the North and South Islands.
- **1986** • NZRC becomes a publicly-owned enterprise as the government pursues a far-reaching programme of economic liberalisation, including the privatisation of many state activities.
- **1990** • In preparation for privatisation, NZRC's core rail and ferry operations are transferred to a new entity, NZ Rail. NZRC retains ownership of the land under the tracks, and various non-core businesses (e.g. buses, property, etc.).
- **1993** • NZ Rail sold to a private consortium for NZD400 million by the National Government, which continues many of the previous government's economic policies.
- **1995** • NZ Rail renamed Tranz Rail.
- **1996** • Tranz Rail shares publicly floated.
- **2002** • Tranz Rail sells the Auckland commuter rail network to the government, and the operation of commuter trains becomes the responsibility of a subsidiary of the Auckland Regional Council. Ownership of the track network is transferred to the publicly-owned enterprise, NZRC (which in 2004 adopts the trading name ONTRACK).
- **2003** • Logistics and transport company Toll Group buys an 84% shareholding in Tranz Rail, which is renamed Toll NZ.
- **2004** • Operation of the Auckland commuter train services is sub-contracted to the private company Connex Group Australia (later Veolia Transport Auckland). The government buys the remaining track network beyond Auckland from Toll NZ and establishes ONTRACK to manage the tracks (structural separation).
- **2008** • The government buys the rail and ferry businesses from Toll NZ for NZD690 million and rebrands them as KiwiRail. Toll retains other non-core businesses. On the recommendation of the Rail Development Group, the government adopts a vertically integrated structure for rail operations. NZRC is the single entity responsible for both rail and ferry services, and for rail infrastructure. KiwiRail and ONTRACK (subsequently renamed 'KiwiRail Network') are separate operating units reporting to the NZRC Board.
- **2010** • The government announces the 'KiwiRail Turnaround Plan' - a 10-year, NZD4.6 billion plan 'designed to see the rail freight business become sustainable within a decade by getting it to a point where it funds its costs solely from customer revenue'.

Figure 7.1 Milestones in the Development of Railways in New Zealand, 1982–2010.

New Zealand had more than 1900km of track. Trains carried nearly 3 million passengers and 830,000 tons of freight a year (KiwiRail, 2012a).

The government's enthusiasm for railways continued well into the 20th century. While there were dreams of a national trunk line, it was also considered vital to establish branch lines connecting rural areas – with their farms, dairy factories, meat works, mills and mines – to export ports. Passenger services between major urban centres expanded too, and some extraordinary feats of engineering saw the North Island main trunk line finished in 1908 (its South Island counterpart was completed in 1945). Between 1870 and 1929 tens of millions of pounds were spent on rail construction, representing 48% of the economy's Public Works Fund (Atkinson, 2007, p. 57). By 1920 New Zealand Rail was carrying 28 million passengers and more than 6 million tons of freight.

7.2.2 *The end of the golden age: 1930 to the 1990s*

The rail network continued to expand, reaching its peak in 1952 at 5695km. However, it was not until 1962 – when rail ferries began sailing between the North and South Islands – that New Zealand had a fully integrated national rail network.

For much of the 20th century, rail remained a protected icon of national progress. Money was poured into enhancements – the transition from steam to diesel, the electrification of suburban lines, the introduction of railcars, the promotion of rail tourism – without any expectation that the costs would be recouped. Rail was effectively a public service, with the Railways Department New Zealand's largest employer.

Even while the network was expanding, rail was losing its pre-eminence. Increasing competition from road transport from the 1920s saw the start of the steady deterioration in rail's financial performance that has continued ever since (see Figure 7.2).

New Zealanders embraced the automobile early and enthusiastically, with ownership of cars more than doubling in the second half of the 1920s, from 71,403 to 150,571, by which time there was one car for every nine New Zealanders – then one of the highest rates of automobile ownership in the world (Atkinson, 2007, p. 100). Passenger rail travel began to fall almost immediately.

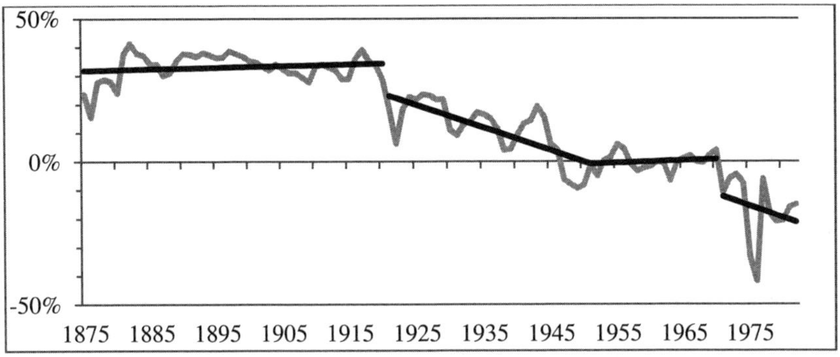

Figure 7.2 Rail Operating Profit/Loss as a Percentage of Revenue, 1875–1982
Source: Heatley (2009) p. 11.

For freight, the competition from trucks – whose greater flexibility and connectivity made them ideally suited to New Zealand's low freight volumes and sparse settlement patterns – represented a major threat. The government stepped in, offering generous freight concessions to ensure local producers used rail. Then, in 1936, legislation was introduced preventing trucks from carrying loads more than 30 miles (48km) and restricting new trucking operators to those that could prove a need for their services. The Railways Department expanded its Road Services Branch, which soon become one of the economy's largest bus operators (Atkinson, 2007, p. 102).

Despite these interventions, rail's already poor financial performance continued to decline. After an upsurge due to fuel rationing during and after World War II (Dravitzki and Lester, 2006, Figure 3), passenger travel dropped dramatically, apart from some resurgence in urban commuter services for the new suburbs established post-war (Atkinson, 2007, p. 215). The option of travelling from Auckland to Wellington within an hour by air, rather than 10 hours by train, increasingly enticed long-distance travellers. Rail freight services continued to lose market share to road.

The Railways Department continued to struggle financially and, eventually, its declining fortunes prompted drastic measures. Closures of the least profitable branch lines and services, which had begun in the 1950s, accelerated. In 1982 the Railways Department was corporatised, becoming the New Zealand Railways Corporation. With a new focus on profit-making, there were massive job losses – between 1982 and 1989 the workforce was cut by 54%. For a while rail's financial decline steadied. Like new technologies and regulatory protection previously, however, line closures and staff cuts were not enough to arrest the downward trend.

In the 1980s the transport sector felt the full force of the fourth Labour Government's deregulation programme. The restriction on road freight movements (which had steadily increased from 48 to 150km) was phased out, and by 1986 road transport operators were no longer subject to the Ministry of Transport's qualitative licensing system. At the same time, the permitted size and weight of trucks were growing steadily. The combined impact was immediate and dramatic: rail lost one-third of its freight market share between 1980 and 1988 (ISCR, 1999a, p. 13), and greater competition saw freight haulage prices fall by 25% (McKinnon, 1998, p. 213). If rail was to remain competitive, services and infrastructure (for both freight and passengers) needed modernising urgently.

All these factors, in conjunction with the reforming ideology of the times, drove the government's decision to sell rail to the private sector.

7.3 Privatisation

Deregulation, privatisation, asset sales and subsidy removal were central planks of the radical economic programme of the government elected in 1984. In its electoral term, a heavily-indebted, tightly-regulated economy that the new Prime Minister described as operating 'like a Polish shipyard' was transformed into a deregulated free market economy at a speed that astonished onlookers.

The privatisation mantra was continued by the new government that came to power in 1990. It saw selling government assets as a way to raise money while avoiding ongoing investment in them. In the case of rail, significant investment was urgently needed in both the track and rolling stock after years of cost cutting: who better to take on the task than the private sector? The same approach was applied to other areas previously seen as core government business. Telecommunications, electricity, the postal service and the national airline were all either privatised or became publicly-owned enterprises during this period. (In New Zealand, a publicly-owned enterprise is a corporation whose shares are wholly owned by the government, and whose principal objective is to operate as a successful business. Each enterprise has an independent board and management, and their responsibilities, together with those of the shareholding Minister, are clearly delineated under the State Owned Enterprises Act 1986.)

Preparations for selling New Zealand Rail began in 1990. In 1993 it was bought by a private consortium comprising Fay Richwhite and Company (local investment bankers), the Wisconsin Central Transportation Corporation and Berkshire Partners LLC. They paid NZD400 million, and renamed the business Tranz Rail.

A 'Core Lease' between the Crown and Tranz Rail gave the company an exclusive 40-year right (with a right of renewal for a further 40 years) to use the land under the then current network for the purposes of running a railway. There was no access regime for potential competitors (excepting provisions for heritage operators). Presumably, by granting exclusive rights the government received a higher sale price at privatisation.

Following the decision to prepare rail for privatisation in 1989, a focussed marketing effort led by non-rail staff (brought in for that purpose) segmented the freight market. This effort led to better understanding of customer needs and a customer-centric approach that recognised that Tranz Rail's freight business was dominated by a small number of customers transporting a very small number of commodities (ISCR, 1999a, pp. 32–4). Tranz Rail benefited from this market segmentation, improved understanding of customers and focus on marketing to their largest customers. Volumes for the bulk-goods segment increased by 5.5% per year over 1994–97 in response to price falls of 7% per year. The export-goods segment was more elastic, with volumes growing at 12% per year in response to price falls of 4.4% per year. The distribution (logistics) segment had small price and volume growth in response to an improved quality of service (ISCR, 1999a, p. 42).

It was not until 1996 that Tranz Rail sought to directly measure operational indicators that had been identified as important to service quality. The limited data available showed somewhat variable results through to 1997 (ISCR, 1999a, pp. 39–40). Significant improvements were reflected in customer satisfaction surveys conducted in 2000 and 2003, with positive responses to the question 'Would you recommend Tranz Rail to another potential customer?' increasing from just over 30% to nearly 80% (Tranz Rail Holdings Limited, 2003).

Under private ownership Tranz Rail further improved productivity and returned the first operating profits for rail in many years. Costs were reduced, including by cutting uneconomic services. Freight volumes grew, peaking in 2000 (see Figure 7.3), while rail's share of the land freight market peaked at 29% in 1998 (Richard Paling Consulting, 2008, p. 4).

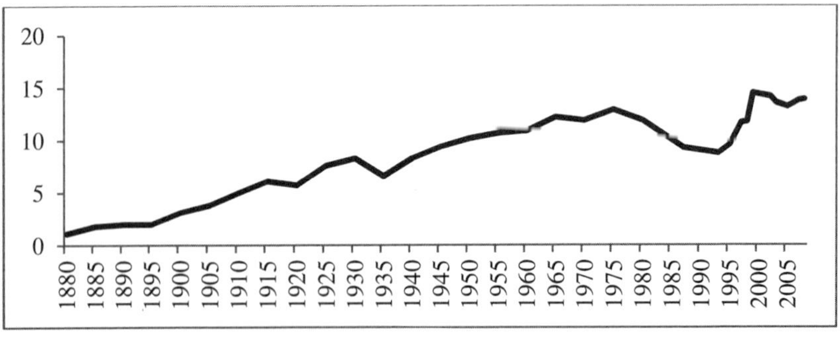

Figure 7.3 Rail Freight in New Zealand, 1880–2005 ('000 tonnes).
Source: Rockpoint (2009) p. 103.

However, Tranz Rail's debt levels were rising at the same time. Its profits were insufficient to cover the opportunity costs of capital (shown in Figure 7.4) and both the track and the rolling stock continued to suffer from insufficient investment in maintenance, renewal and upgrades (KiwiRail, 2012a; Heatley, 2009, p. 35). Nor did Tranz Rail perform well for its shareholders. From a high point of NZD9/share in 1997, the value of Tranz Rail shares fell steeply to NZ39 cents in 2003. Those who had bought shares in the public float in 1996 and retained them through to 2003 got back only 28% of their original investment[4] (Gaynor, 2008; Heatley, 2009, p. 31).

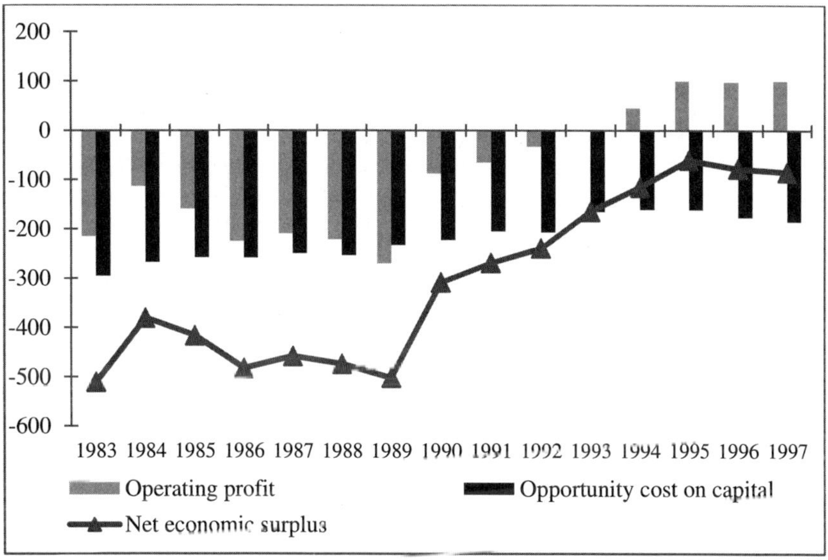

Figure 7.4 Tranz Rail's Profit could not Sustain its Operations ($NZ million at 1997 prices). ***Source:*** Heatley (2009) p. 28.

At the time of privatisation, the government retained ownership of the land under the rail tracks, leasing it to Tranz Rail through the Core Lease. Assuming that the initial objective of privatisation was greater economic efficiency, the Core Lease arrangement worked to undermine it. If a line was not economic, the rail operator was unable to make the economically rational decision to sell the land for a more productive use. This suggests that, although the government had at one level embraced the new era of privatisation, it was reluctant to abandon rail to market forces entirely.

[4] By contrast, the original investors did very well indeed, realising a total of NZD470 million on their initial equity of NZD105 million when they sold their shares in 1997 – a transaction that subsequently became the focus of an insider-trading inquiry.

What went wrong with privatisation? One problem was the assumption that – despite rail's history – simply changing the ownership model would 'fix' the underlying economics of rail in New Zealand (see Box 7.1). Secondly, the government's willingness to intervene when the

Box 7.1 Constrained by Geography and Population.

New Zealand – population 4.44 million – is an economy comprising two narrow, mountainous main islands, whose nearest neighbour is 1,500km away. These facts place certain inescapable limits on rail operations and have dictated some significant decisions. For example, the economy's challenging topography was instrumental in the early choice of narrow-gauge tracks, which were cheaper to build in mountainous terrain. Japan, Indonesia and Tasmania chose the same option for similar reasons. Unfortunately, this decision placed technological and commercial constraints on rail's development, which took decades to overcome (Leitch and Stott, 1988, p. 5).

The problems caused by New Zealand's low population density (16 people/km2) are insurmountable. This has made it difficult to achieve the 'economies of density' essential for successful rail services – in other words, there is insufficient population to justify running more trains on existing tracks (The Treasury, 2009, p. 25). Frequent, high-speed passenger trains may be viable in similarly-sized island nations such as the United Kingdom and Japan, but those economies' population density is far greater, at 338 and 251 people/km2 respectively. New Zealand's low urban population density and a trend to dispersed employment have also contributed to the demise of commuter rail services in all but two cities, Auckland and Wellington. Thus, in New Zealand today, freight, and not passengers, is the lifeblood of rail.

The viability of freight services, too, is constrained by physical factors. The fact that the railways still follow routes mapped out more than 100 years ago, often through difficult terrain, means freight may have to travel more slowly and over longer distances to reach the same destinations served by roads. Rail's competitiveness is also constrained by the low volume of bulk freight and the short distances it is carried, relative to international standards. For the 30 years to 2008, the average freight journey was just under 300km, well below the distance at which rail is found to be competitive internationally for all but point-to-point transport of bulk commodities (Heatley, 2009, p. 25). New Zealand's lack of borders, and the obvious inability to connect with other economies' rail networks is an important factor here.

In combination with the low population and other factors, it means New Zealand's rail freight density – calculated as the average number of tonnes of freight transported per kilometre of track – is very low by international standards (see Figure 7.5).

Despite all these constraints and their impact on rail's economic performance, the size of New Zealand's rail network in 2010 (4,000km) remained unchanged from 1991. However, since 2010 over 500km of minor lines have been 'mothballed', that is taken out of active service and retained for possible reopening in the future (KiwiRail, 2012b). This includes the 391km Napier-Gisborne line, which was generating only NZD1 million of revenue against NZD3.4 million of operating and maintenance costs, before a storm caused NZD4 million of track damage (KiwiRail, 2012c).

owners sought to rationalise services and close unprofitable lines demonstrated that it still wanted substantial control over rail. Not only did this create difficulties at the time, but it is likely to have long-term ramifications too: any future government wishing to pursue privatisation may find it cannot credibly commit to non-interference (Heatley, 2009, p. 46).

7.4 The Government Returns to Rail

The government's return to the rail business began with its purchase of the Auckland suburban rail network from Tranz Rail in 2002. The Auckland Regional Council's transport agency, the Auckland Regional Transport Authority, became responsible for services (which were later contracted out to Veolia Transport: see Box 7.5). In 2003 the government began discussing the possibility of buying a stake in Tranz Rail, but this stalled when Australian transport and logistics company Toll Group moved to take over Tranz Rail.

Toll Group saw Tranz Rail as complementing its New Zealand activities, and considered that it could operate the business profitably (KiwiRail, 2012; Toll Holdings Ltd, 2004; Toll Group, 2003). In 2003 it bought an 84% stake in Tranz Rail at NZD1.05/share (valuing Tranz Rail at NZD232 million) and renamed the business 'Toll NZ'. A year later the government struck a deal with Toll, buying the whole track network for NZD1. It was to be managed by ONTRACK, a business unit formed as part of the New Zealand Railways Corporation (NZRC). It could be argued that Toll had thus secured itself an attractive deal: it had bought into rail relatively cheaply and retained the only part of the business that was ever likely to be profitable, while the intrinsically loss-making part (the track network) was now the government's responsibility.

This observation may seem counter-intuitive: a track network with its high fixed and sunk costs seems a promising candidate for a natural monopoly, and the opportunity to earn monopoly rents. However, the allocation of rents is only pertinent if there are rents to be allocated. As argued in this chapter, New Zealand rail (as a whole) is uneconomic relative to its competition; therefore there is no natural monopoly.

Under its agreement with Toll NZ, the government committed to spending NZD200 million on network upgrades and renewal. For its part, Toll NZ would spend NZD100 million on new rolling stock, and pay the government an annual track charge for exclusive access to the rail network. These access rights were subject to a 'use-it-or-lose-it' provision: if Toll NZ's traffic fell below 70% of average freight levels for 2002–04 on any line segment, it would no longer have exclusive rights to that segment (The Treasury, 2004, p. 12). It must be considered very unlikely that this provision would have led to the appearance of a serious above-rail competitor to Toll, as the competitor's operations would have been restricted to those isolated line segments where there was declining demand for rail freight (Heatley, 2009, p. 47). In any case there was no competitive entry between 2004 and 2008, when the agreement was effectively cancelled.

The access charge became a serious sticking point over the next few years. When the government sought to raise the charge to help fund upgrades, Toll NZ argued that this would lead to substantial losses unless freight prices were increased – and this would inevitably mean losing customers to road transport. Nonetheless, Toll NZ said in October 2007 that it remained 'absolutely committed to rail in New Zealand and freight was increasing on a number of its services' (*Sydney Morning Herald*, 2007).

In the access charge negotiations between Toll and the government, both parties were in the position to 'hold up' the other and extract a 'profit' at the expense of a larger loss incurred by the other party.[5] Both the track (an exclusive sunk investment) and operations (with exclusive access conferred by contract) could be considered as 'bottleneck facilities', relative to each other.[6]

[5] The 'hold up problem' in economics is that a party that has a relationship-specific investment is vulnerable to a threat by other parties to terminate that relationship. The threat enables these parties to obtain better terms than initially agreed (Milgrom and Roberts, 1992).

[6] This does not, however, make them bottleneck facilities in the economy as a whole – for that to be the case there would need to be a lack of close substitutes for the services offered by those facilities.

The question was, 'Who had the greater bargaining power in the negotiations?'

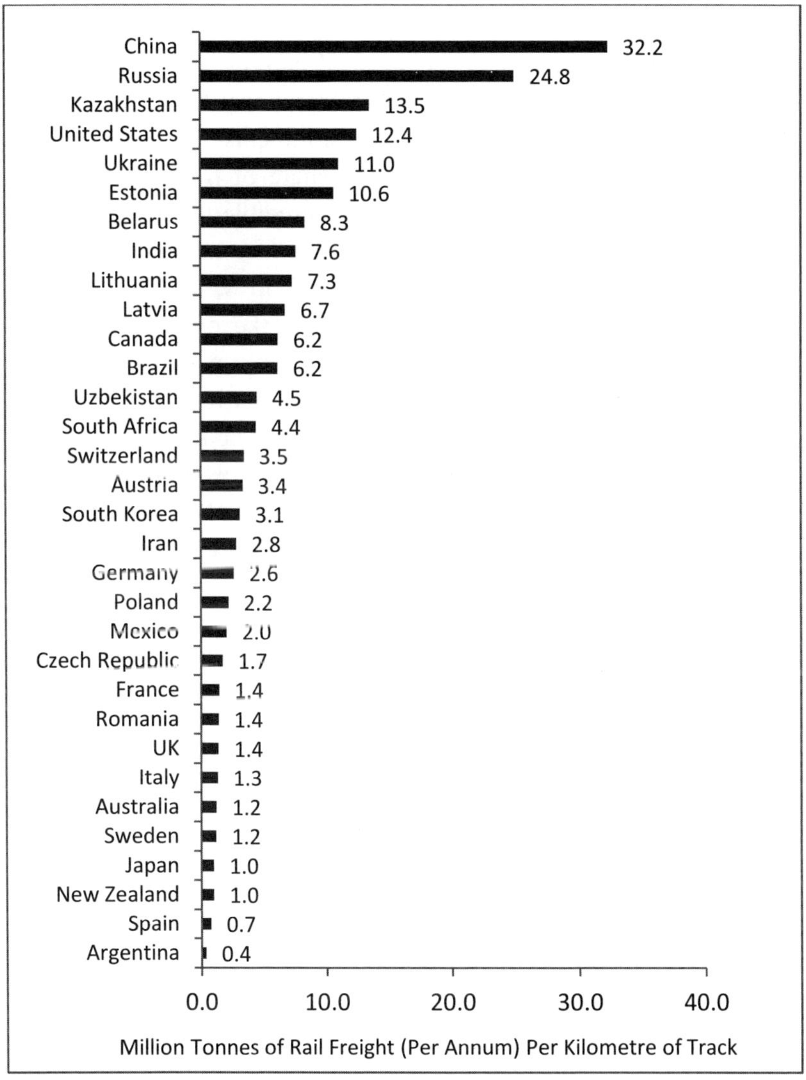

Figure 7.5 A Comparison of Rail Freight Density Internationally (million tonnes of rail freight (per annum) per kilometre of track).
Source: Heatley (2009) p. 21

Toll had a credible threat: to withdraw selected services from rail, and shift their operations to road and/or sea transport. This threat was credible because they had an existing road and sea transport business, and their shareholders would demand that Toll exit any business in which there was no reasonable prospect of earning an economic profit. Withdrawal of services would create a political cost for the government, which had made explicit policy commitments to invest in rail infrastructure and to move an increasing share of freight from road to rail. The government, however, lacked any credible threats against Toll. They were contractually committed to maintain or improve the rail infrastructure (The Treasury, 2004, p. 20). If Toll withdrew services, the contract allowed for a new rail operator to take over those services. While a lack of scale would mean that the new operator would likely face a higher cost structure than Toll, the contract meant that the terms for new entrants (including access charges) could be no more favourable than those faced by Toll (The Treasury, 2004, p. 14). The putative entrant, with higher costs, would have little chance of earning a profit on a service that Toll decided to exit because it was uneconomic. Hence, there was no credible threat of entry.

Thus, the 2004 agreement had left Toll with substantially greater bargaining power. The government's frustration at Toll exercising this power (combined with some unrealistic ideas about the potential of rail) led it to purchase the rail operator on terms very favourable to Toll. However, the costs of resolving this bargaining problem (approximately NZD2 billion to the end of 2012) have exceeded the costs of living with it (perhaps an access charge subsidy of NZD70 million per year[7]).

In this instance, the contractual allocation of rights determined the locus of the bargaining power. With hindsight, other strategies may have been more successful for the government than the 2004 agreement with Toll, for example:

1. Encouraging the rail operator to withdraw from uneconomic services (in order to ensure the operator's ongoing viability);

[7] http://www.treasury.govt.nz/publications/informationreleases/rail/purchase/pdfs/rp-tsy-em-4dec06.pdf, accessed on 25 January 2013.

2. Making an equity injection into the integrated rail operator (so that the government and private shareholders faced the same incentives);
3. Purchasing the distressed integrated rail operator at a bargain market price before (or in competition with) the takeover offer from Toll; and
4. Letting the rail operator fail, cancelling the exclusive access rights and introducing a new ownership and access model (for example, one with sections of track owned by major users or port operators and cross-licensing arrangements for access).

In May 2008 the government moved to purchase the rail (and inter-island ferry) business from a reluctant Toll NZ, citing the impasse over the access charge. Toll NZ retained its road transport and logistics arm, Toll TranzLink, which became New Zealand's largest road freight operator.

The change of ownership came into effect in July 2008. The government rebranded the business 'KiwiRail' and transferred it to the New Zealand Railways Corporation. ONTRACK was relabelled 'KiwiRail Network'. The now re-integrated business reported to the NZRC Board.

In principle, there were still no barriers to competition within rail. Under the Railways Act 2005, any operator who met safety-related licence conditions could start running a rail service – providing they could negotiate access to the rail network.

Despite the public battles over the track access charge, the Labour-led government's buy-back of rail was primarily driven by ideology. Firstly, it expressed their belief that a strong rail network was essential to New Zealand's future economic and environmental performance. With freight volumes forecast to rise by 75% over the next 25 years, the government considered rail had a significant economic role to play. It was essential for regional development, and for New Zealand's vital export industries that benefited from rail's ability to carry large volumes of bulk commodities (such as coal and dairy products) comparatively cheaply (Cullen, 2008a). The government also argued that the purchase was integral to the development of a more environmentally sustainable and integrated transport system. Even more fundamentally, however, the purchase confirmed the government's view that, if it was going to have to subsidise the rail network – which rail's performance under successive ownership structures had shown to be inevitable – it was preferable to subsidise a government-owned enterprise, rather than a foreign-owned private company. The Deputy Prime Minister of the time said that his government would not allow 'New Zealand taxpayers [to] indefinitely subsidise a private, foreign operation and then not make sure that the investment would deliver social and economic returns for New Zealand' (Cullen, 2008b).

There was considerable criticism of the price that taxpayers paid for the railways. At NZD690 million, even the government admitted it had paid 'a premium price' (Young, 2008). However, it said that the price reflected the need to buy Toll out of its long-term monopoly rights (Bridgman, 2008). It was also argued that the buy-out was preferable to the alternatives: "continuing to subsidise a foreign-owned company failing to invest sufficiently in basic infrastructure, increased expenditure required on roading, increased accidents on the road, and increased greenhouse gas emissions at a direct cost to the taxpayer" (Young, 2008).

The government made an immediate commitment to investment. In July 2008 it appointed a Rail Development Group (RDG) to make recommendations about rail's future. The RDG confirmed that deferred capital expenditure was a pressing issue, but said that remedying this would go only some way towards making rail commercially viable without government subsidy (RDG, 2008b, p. 6). It called for more than NZD1 billion to be spent over five years on replacing locomotives, rehabilitating key sections of the network, upgrading information technology and creating freight hubs. As a first step, in October 2008 the government announced an injection of NZD121 million for rail industry improvements in that fiscal year, in addition to previously forecast spending (Cullen, 2008c).

7.4.1 *The Turnaround Plan*

The following month, there was a change of government. The new National-led government had already pledged not to sell any public assets in its first term, so government ownership of rail until at least 2011 was guaranteed. The government stressed there was now a strong expectation that the rail network should deliver 'a commercial rate of return. Any taxpayer subsidies to the freight side of the business should be provided transparently and should not be at the expense of other transport modes' (Joyce, 2009a).

After its first year back in government ownership, rail's economic performance problems remained. KiwiRail made an accounting loss of NZD187 million in 2008/09, largely due to depreciation expenses on network assets (KiwiRail, 2009, p. 76). The total government funding of NZD425 million almost exceeded operating revenue of NZD518 million.

In May 2010 the National government announced the "KiwiRail Turnaround Plan". This 10-year, NZD4.6 billion plan was 'designed to see the rail freight business become sustainable within a decade by getting it to a point where it funds its costs solely from customer revenue... The government is committed to retaining and improving the rail freight network and is providing KiwiRail the capital investment to demonstrate it can become commercially viable and make a valuable contribution to the New Zealand economy" (Joyce, 2010). The government committed itself to three annual contributions of NZD250 million, saying that KiwiRail would need to fund the remaining NZD3.85 billion from operational cost savings and increased customer revenue.

Public documentation of the Turnaround Plan at the time of release was thin, and offered scant justification for the government's outlay (Heatley, 2010). Further details have emerged over time; these were summarised by the Productivity Commission in April 2012 as: "the Government is planning to provide: (a) funding (in the form of an equity injection) to cover the expected shortfall between EBITDA[8] and planned capital expenditure between 2010/11 and 2014/15; (b) reinvestment of operating profits between 2015/16 and 2019/20; (c) a restructure of KiwiRail's balance sheet so that future financial returns to the government are judged relative to an enterprise value of NZD1.1 billion,

[8] Earnings before interest, tax, depreciation and amortisation.

rather than the economic cost of the enterprise" (New Zealand Productivity Commission, 2012, p. 174).

This can be restated as the government will pay a subsidy until 2014/15, receive zero until 2020/21, and receives a financial return after then – but one insufficient to cover the full economic costs of the resources allocated to rail.

In June 2012 the Government announced details of the restructure of the group's balance sheet (English and Ryall, 2012). This included the government agreeing to write off NZD322.5m of debt – an action economically equivalent to a one-off subsidy of the same amount. This amount was additional to the subsidies announced as part of the Turnaround Plan.

By late 2012, two years into the plan, it was clear that KiwiRail's performance had not met the targets in the plan. Bennett (2012) commented that the "Government's NZD4.6 billion KiwiRail turnaround plan is coming off the rails with State Owned Enterprises Minister Tony Ryall yesterday admitting the rail company is unlikely to find the NZD3.85 billion the plan originally called for." KiwiRail's *Infrastructure and Engineering Business Plan 2013-2015* outlines reductions in planned spending – largely through delays in infrastructure investment and a consequent acceptance of a higher level of service disruption (KiwiRail, 2012b). The 'turnaround' – the date from which the business will become 'self-sustaining', has likely been pushed further into the future.

7.5 Regulation, Competition and Structural Reform

7.5.1 *Minimal regulation*

The 1980s New Zealand model of structural reform has been labelled 'light-handed regulation' (Evans *et al.*, 1996, p. 1885). It sought to minimise government and regulatory intervention and to place reliance on actual and potential competition for the regulation of prices and monopoly behaviour.

When the New Zealand Railways Corporation became a government-owned corporation in the 1980s and was subsequently privatised, a raft of regulations was discarded – including, most importantly, the regulatory restrictions on road transport first introduced in 1936 to allow rail to remain competitive. As already noted, deregulation had a major impact on the business, with rail losing one-third of its share of the freight market between 1980 and 1988. Today there is only minimal regulation of the sector and it focuses almost entirely on safety. The sector regulator is the Rail Regulation Section of the New Zealand Transport Agency, the government agency responsible for planning and funding land transport. Its rail-related responsibilities are confined to administering the Railways Act 2005, monitoring accidents, and licensing organisations that control and use rail networks. Licences are granted to rail providers and operators that meet specified safety standards.

Rail is also affected by the provisions of the Resource Management Act 1991, the principal legislation dealing with the use of the natural environment and its resources. Under the Act, rail operators wanting to build or expand infrastructure need to embark on planning and resource consent processes that can be both costly and time-consuming.

The largely 'hands-off' approach to rail regulation reflects the present (2012) government's thinking about infrastructure regulation in general. A 2009 Treasury paper described the objective of regulation as "to ensure sufficient certainty and consistency for business to operate competitively and with confidence, and with minimum transaction costs". It also expressed concern that the costs of compliance may be contributing to New Zealand's relatively low productivity performance: it ranked 22nd of 30 OECD economies (The Treasury, 2009, p. 95).

7.5.2 *No barriers to entry*

As described above, under the Railways Act 2005 any operator who meets safety-related licence conditions can start a rail service when they negotiate access to the rail network. The real competition lies with those other transport modes that manage to respond to changes and challenges more rapidly than rail – with its high fixed costs and 'sunk' assets – has been able to. Most rail costs (e.g. the cost of providing tracks or signalling equipment) are fixed: they do not change depending on the volume of freight or passengers. In addition, rail infrastructure is a very long-lived asset that gets more expensive to maintain and renew as it ages. Most of New Zealand's fixed rail assets are sunk: the value of tunnels, bridges, etc. cannot be recovered if they are no longer used for railways (Heatley, 2009, p. 20).

In practice, KiwiRail has no competitors in either the rail freight or long-distance passenger rail markets. Nor is there much likelihood of competitors emerging, given rail's perennial lack of profitability and KiwiRail's ability to access government financial support. The only scenario a potential new entrant might consider would be to service a profitable subset of routes or customers. KiwiRail could be expected to vigorously oppose such competitive entry, as the company relies on its profitable routes to cross-subsidise its less profitable ones, and its integration with KiwiRail Network gives it substantial power to exclude competing rail operators.

Recent overseas trends towards supply-chain integration have seen port operators taking control over their supply chains by purchasing the rail networks servicing their hinterlands (e.g. in Europe; Notteboom, 2008). Similarly, some large exporters (such as Australian mining companies) own the railways that connect their operations to ports. Such arrangements are unlikely to arise in New Zealand, as both major political parties appear committed to a national rail network with a single owner.

Urban commuter rail is in a slightly different situation. In 2004 services in Auckland were contracted out via competitive tender. The successful tenderer was the French-owned multinational Veolia Environment (see Box 7.2).

Commuter services in Wellington, owned and operated by KiwiRail under contract to the Wellington Regional Council at the time of writing, are expected to be similarly tendered out in 2016.[9] Assuming the successful tenderer is a new entrant to the market, the total number of

---

[9] http://www.transport.govt.nz/ourwork/rail/Documents/Metro%20rail%20Oct%2009.pdf, accessed on 25 January 2013.

significant rail operators will climb to four. The three existing operators are KiwiRail, Veolia Transport and Taieri Gorge Railway Ltd. Taieri Gorge Railway is the largest of the economy's 60 heritage rail operators (the others are mainly small, non-profit organisations).

7.5.3 *Structural integration favoured*

For much of its history New Zealand rail has been structurally integrated, with a single organisation responsible for both infrastructure and rail services. There was, however, a period of structural separation from 2004 to 2008 when ONTRACK was responsible for below-rail infrastructure and Tranz Rail provided above-rail services. 'Below-rail' in this context means the non-moving parts of the rail network, including the rails themselves.

Elsewhere in the world, structural separation has often been introduced to enhance competition. However, results have been mixed, with some economies (such as the United States) reporting a reduction in efficiency (Heatley, 2009, p. 46). In New Zealand, however, the case for structural separation was made for somewhat different reasons. It arose at a time when the private rail operator, Toll NZ, was seeking government subsidies in order to maintain the national network. Rather than continuing to make direct subsidies, the government elected instead to create ONTRACK as a separate entity with which Toll would negotiate a track access agreement. As Nick Wills-Johnson (2007, p. 2) has argued in relation to Australia, "by investing in the below-rail infrastructure only, government can [ensure] that its investment is not affected by future inefficiencies elsewhere in the railway, or even by the railway operation becoming insolvent". For the New Zealand government, then, structural separation was a less risky (and perhaps more politically acceptable) way of investing in rail.

In the event, information-sharing difficulties soon arose between ONTRACK and Toll. For example, the former needed accurate forecasts of future freight volumes in order to plan its capital works programme. Was supplying such information in Toll's interests when ONTRACK might have used it to justify a higher track access charge? Impasses such as this contributed to the return to vertical integration in 2008.

Box 7.2 Competition for Auckland Commuter Rail Services.

When the Auckland Regional Council (ARC) called for tenders for the operation of Auckland's commuter rail system in 2002, Tranz Rail chose not to tender. Instead, it sold the Auckland metropolitan rail network to the Crown for NZD81 million.

In November 2003 the successful tenderer was announced: Connex Group Australia (then known as Veolia Transport Auckland, part of the French multinational Veolia Environment). Connex was one of three tenderers; British firms Serco and Stagecoach were unsuccessful.[10] Connex took over operation of the trains from July 2004. In parallel with these changes the ARC moved to consolidate passenger transport planning, asset management and service delivery in one organisation. ARC formed the Auckland Regional Transport Authority (ARTA) in 2004 to own stations and passenger trains and take responsibility for service planning. Under the contract terms, Veolia receives payment for its costs plus a management fee. All fare revenue goes directly to ARTA.

Ownership of the track network and responsibility for signals and corridor infrastructure was transferred to publicly-owned enterprise NZRC, which adopted a new trading name ONTRACK.

As a result of the new public–private partnership structure, substantial investment in new infrastructure and fare subsidies, train patronage in Auckland doubled between 2005 and 2010 (Figure 7.6).[11] ARTA attributes the increase in patronage to the following changes:

- More trains, more often. With the double tracking of the Western Line almost complete, trains run every 15 minutes at peak times, and five to six trains run an hour at peak times on the Southern and Eastern lines. Services increased from 635 per week in 2005 to 1,475 in 2009 with 49 carriages added to the network.
- More punctual. In March 2005 only 76.6% of trains arrived on time. This figure steadied at over 85% for most of 2009.
- Better stations, better trains. 21 of the 41 stations on the network have been upgraded over five years. Six train carriages have been fitted this year with new seating, carpet and upgraded air conditioning (ARTA, 2009, p. 1).

The doubling in passenger numbers, however, came from a very low base. While rail in 2010 serviced 12.5% of public transport trips in Auckland, public transport was dominated by the use of private vehicles.

The fare subsidies required to reach this level of patronage are significant: rail requires a NZD7–8 operating subsidy per passenger trip (ARTA, 2006, p. 26). These subsidies do not include a contribution to capital costs.

Central government has committed to a NZD1.6 billion upgrade of Auckland's commuter rail system, including electrification of the network at a cost of NZD1

---

[10] http://tvnz.co.nz/content/238981, accessed on 25 January 2013.

[11] http://www.arta.co.nz/newsroom/media-releases.html?releaseid=dfdd9285-5056-a41f-9226-f3c70938762c22, accessed 25 February 2010.

Box 7.2 (Continued)

billion. ARTA expects these upgrades to enable it to provide fast, reliable journeys at 10-minute frequencies and attract 15.7 million passengers to rail by 2016. ARTA's modelling suggests that at this level of patronage the operating subsidy per passenger can be reduced to NZD4 per passenger trip (ARTA, 2006).

The structural split between ONTRACK and ARTA created integration issues (Mein, 2008) and continuing disputes between central and local government about who pays for rail. Transport Minister Stephen Joyce summed up the situation neatly: "everybody loves [rail], but nobody wants to pay."[12]

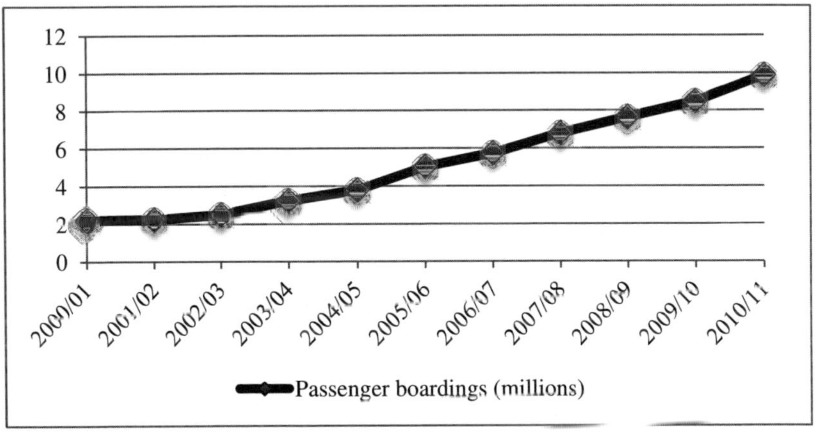

Figure 7.6 Growth in Auckland Passenger Rail, 2000–2011 (millions of passenger boardings).
Source: Ministry of Transport[13].

7.6 The Gap to Best Practice in Structural Reform

As at 2012, the current government favours minimal regulatory intervention, and has a review programme in place to identify and

[12] http://www.guide2.co.nz/politics/news/councils-need-to-pay-for-regional-rail-use-minister/11/15796, accessed 25 January 2013.

[13] http://www.transport.govt.nz/ourwork/TMIF/Pages/TV020.aspx accessed 8 December 2012.

remove "unnecessary and superfluous regulation".[14] Government ownership of transport infrastructure should be the exception rather than the norm, as evidenced by the following policy:

> All things being equal, the Government will favour the distributed decision-making power of a competitive market for the provision of infrastructure. This is because the commercial disciplines that come from investors risking their own money are difficult to replicate in the public sector. However, the Government does have a role providing goods and services where:
>
> - the goods and services have the characteristics of being 'public goods' in the technical sense;
> - the service is a monopoly and there are advantages in regulating through direct ownership rather than through the Commerce Act or other regulatory vehicle; or
> - distributional and equity objectives are better achieved through in-kind provision than through income support. (The Treasury, 2010, p. 25)

It would be hard to argue that railway freight and long-distance passenger services meet these criteria. Urban passenger rail may meet the criteria insofar as it can deliver public goods such as reductions in urban road congestion. The current (2012) government might prefer rail to be privately owned, but they are constrained by their own policy commitments and a general public distrust of privatisation. There is a substantial gap between a publicly owned and operated railway, and one that harnesses the 'distributed decision-making power of a competitive market'. The cost of this gap is difficult to establish. The direct costs of this policy to the taxpayer are measurable: the ongoing operational and capital subsidies to rail. Indirect costs include the opportunity costs of the land and other assets allocated to rail but potentially not being used for their most productive purpose in the economy. For example, the

[14] http://www.treasury.govt.nz/economy/regulation/statement/govt-stmt-reg.pdf, accessed on 25 January 2013.

government is earning a zero financial return on the approximately NZD6 billion of land under the rail network.

As rail is generally a price taker in a competitive freight market, it is unlikely that public ownership of rail has a significant impact on freight prices. However, ongoing public ownership and subsidy of rail is restraining private investment in other transport modes, particularly in coastal shipping (Rockpoint, 2009, p. 219). Distorted investment signals can be expected to lead to the creation or maintenance of an economically inefficient freight transport network with higher average prices over time.

As noted above, competition within the rail sector is unlikely to emerge. Close substitutes exist for almost all of the freight products offered by New Zealand railways (Mackie, Baas and Manz, 2006, p. 2). Rail faces substantial competition from both road and coastal shipping, and entry barriers in these sectors have been low in New Zealand since the 1980s (ISCR, 1999a, pp. 15, 28). Competition in rail's product markets (and threats of further entry there) should be sufficient to ameliorate monopoly power and drive efficiency gains.

While the existing regulatory arrangements are technically an open-access regime, entry is unlikely: the rail operator is in government ownership, rail freight is unprofitable, the operator is subsidised and the government is unable to credibly commit to future non-interference in the sector. These problems would need to be overcome before access regime changes had any material effect in the sector. Moreover, reforms designed to foster competition within the rail sector (e.g. structural separation and improved access regimes) would lack credibility given the government-owned and funded incumbent, and likely involve significant costs for little benefit.

7.7 Where to Now for Rail in New Zealand?

7.7.1 *Drivers for reform*

From the current (2012) government's perspective, the key drivers for reform appear to be:

- a wish not to be seen as supporting rail over other transport modes, and hence unwillingness to continue subsidising unprofitable services;
- the need for significant investment in rail infrastructure;
- concerns that the Turnaround Plan will not succeed in enabling KiwiRail to eventually meet its own renewal and capital development costs;
- a wish to be seen to be actively addressing road congestion in Auckland;
- a tight fiscal situation following the global financial crisis and recession in New Zealand; and
- competitive and political pressure from the road transport and coastal shipping sectors, requiring rail to be more narrowly focused on providing only services where it has a competitive advantage.

7.7.2 *Barriers to reform*

Major barriers to reform include:

- a commitment to retaining KiwiRail in public ownership;
- public perception that New Zealand went too far with structural reform in the 1980s and 1990s;
- ongoing operational and capital subsidies which reduce the incentives for efficiency improvements and structural change; and
- the risk of policy capture by the incumbent publicly-owned firm, which faces the weak market discipline inherent in a corporatised structure.

There is a strongly-held public perception that the rail network was run down by its private owners and that this situation has been ‘fixed’ by re-nationalisation, regardless of the evidence to the contrary. In fact, neither private nor public owners maintained rail infrastructure at anywhere near replacement levels from 1991 to 2008 (Heatley, 2009, pp. 34–5). Advocates of structural reform will need to overcome this public perception.

A possible impediment to change is emphasis on over-detailed centralised transport network planning, under various labels including 'logistics' and 'integrated planning'. While the goals of such activities are laudable, the vast majority of transport supply and demand factors are outside the control of the planners. The Treasury (2010, p. 88) recognises this when they state "the parts of the [rail freight] network that thrive, and those that decline, will be determined to a large extent by the decisions of our major exporters and by the configuration of our ports". There is a risk that integrated planning is used as a delaying tactic that supports the status quo, rather than as a true search for efficiency. Supply and demand uncertainties need to be acknowledged as such, and not unduly delay decision-making. Technical coordination – the efficient interchange of passengers and freight where transport modes interconnect – needs little central coordination; it will happen where demand is present and transport suppliers can profit from it.

7.7.3 *Small steps to support reform*

One useful reform would be to structurally separate the urban commuter services from the freight operator, with distinct branding and reporting. Advocates of the status quo frequently rely on arguments that ascribe commuter rail benefits to the freight network and vice versa. Functional and structural separation could allow for a more rational debate of these logically separate businesses.

The advocates of policy reform are at a substantial information disadvantage to KiwiRail. The level of financial detail (in particular breakdowns by business unit) and frequency of reporting declined under public ownership compared with the situation under private ownership (Heatley, 2010). A small but useful step in enabling the effective advocacy of structural reform would be to improve the financial reporting to the public, permitting effective evaluation of the rail sector by competitors and independent commentators.

A further measure would be to ensure that the assessment of road and rail infrastructure projects was coordinated in order to allocate public capital to where it can add most value (New Zealand Productivity Commission, 2012, p. 175).

7.7.4 *More questions than answers*

In 2010 rail faced an uncertain future and, for policy-makers, there were more questions than answers. How best to address rail's long legacy of under-investment and deferred maintenance (e.g. locomotives with an average age of 31 years, more than 550 bridges over 80 years old and dilapidated passenger services)? Much work was already in progress: major urban rail upgrades underway in Wellington and Auckland, new locomotives and carriages purchased and some heavily used parts of the freight network upgraded. The total cost of overcoming this legacy, however, was estimated to be as much as NZD2 billion over the five years to 2015 (The Treasury, 2009, p. 85). In addition, quite apart from 'catch up' funding, there was a need to invest in new technology and infrastructure that would allow KiwiRail to take advantage of emerging business opportunities. It could not be assumed that competing transport modes would stay stagnant – KiwiRail's new infrastructure would be competing for customers against more efficient coastal shipping and larger trucks with improved fuel efficiency running on better roads.

The 2009 government-appointed RDG concluded that while KiwiRail's commercial revenue might be sufficient to fund its operating costs, it would be well short of the level required to provide a return on capital, or to fund asset renewals and new investment. Nor would it be sufficient to "maintain ongoing operating capability at a level to achieve the government's desired policy outcomes" (RDG, 2008b, p. 6).

The clear need for ongoing government support was recognised when the government allocated NZD90 million in operating grants to KiwiRail for 2009/10. Was it prepared, however, to keep on subsidising rail to this extent, and for how long? How could the government both deliver subsidies *and* incentivise good commercial decision-making aimed at maximising financial returns? Finally, should government subsidies be used to keep on supporting parts of the network that have long been non-commercial?[15]

[15] RDG (2008c, p. 2) noted that some routes had a good commercial rate of return (15–20%) while others were operating on negative returns.

The government's expectation was "that all investments in the national rail network provide a commercial rate of return. Taxpayer subsidies should be provided only as a last resort and where there is clear evidence that it will improve service and provide a decent return on taxpayers' money" (Joyce, 2009b).

The government has continued to support commuter rail. KiwiRail provides some passenger services, in some cases in conjunction with private operators. In terms of KiwiRail's core freight business, a clear message emerged: the government expected the company to generate enough revenue to meet its own cash requirements – not necessarily to the point of providing the government (as owner) with a return on its investment, but sufficient to meet its own renewal and capital development costs.

The government did not wish to be seen as supporting rail over competing modes of transport, and this position moved it marginally closer to that goal. It is interesting to note that when the first National Infrastructure Plan was released in March 2010, rail was not among the government's eight 'key' or 'emerging' infrastructure priorities (The Treasury, 2010, p. 15).

Other policy questions surrounded the extent to which rail could deliver other economic and environmental benefits – the 'positive externalities' used by the previous government to justify its buyback of the railway. Research by the New Zealand Institute for the Study of Competition and Regulation (ISCR) in both 1999 and 2009 suggested that the magnitude of these externalities had been overstated. In some cases the benefits sought – such as reducing greenhouse gas emissions or congestion – could best be achieved by other means, such as a carbon tax, emissions trading scheme, commuter rail subsidies or road user charging. The research found that while rail did have some positive effects on economic development and the quality of the environment, they were not enough to outweigh rail's negative contribution to New Zealand's overall economic performance (ISCR, 1999b, p. 85; Heatley, 2009, p. 58).

The Treasury made similar observations in its paper 'Infrastructure: Facts and Issues' – a discussion document intended to guide the preparation of the first National Infrastructure Plan. It noted that economic benefits are likely to be realised only on heavily used parts of the network. Treasury offered the following analysis:

> The argument for ongoing public subsidisation of the network tends to rest on the premise that rail offers positive externalities (e.g. reduced congestion, emissions and accidents) and that road transport does not pay for its full social costs, reducing the ability of rail to compete. There is little current evidence to support this.
>
> Much of the New Zealand rail network is uneconomic, even when taking into account the environmental value of rail's greater fuel efficiency. While there may be a case for subsidising rail up to a certain point, based on its social and environmental contribution, it is an unresolved question about whether this would be sufficient to cover the full capital costs of the entire rail network. (The Treasury, 2009, p. 29)

Environmental benefits respond to the same economies of density that drive railway economics. The fixed (economic) costs of rail incur environmental costs in parallel. The main inputs into railway construction and maintenance are earthmoving (diesel), transport (diesel), steel and concrete. All have significant environmental costs, including being substantial sources of greenhouse gas emissions. On the operational side, heavily used lines are more likely to carry full trainloads, and these offer significantly better fuel efficiencies than partial trainloads. It follows that the most environmentally beneficial parts of the network are likely to be those in least need of government subsidy.

It has been suggested that the most economically rational course would be to largely abandon rail (Malpass, 2009). This view acknowledges that rail has placed an enormous burden on New Zealand taxpayers for decades, and the situation is unlikely to change. Without the loss-making railways, hundreds of millions of dollars could be diverted to more socially and economically beneficial uses.

A less extreme course would be to reduce the size of the network to only its most economic components (widely considered to comprise around 1500–2000km: see RDG, 2008b, p. 3, and Heatley, 2009, p. 69) and focus on rail's competitive advantages: the point-to-point transport of large volumes of bulk freight and carefully planned commuter rail. Under this scenario, line closures and land sales would fund the upgrade of the network to modern standards (Heatley, 2009, pp. 70–2). However, the government saw the retention of the national network as no more costly than having a disjointed smaller network, as that could necessitate some duplication of rolling stock across its disparate parts.

The course that the government was advised to take by the RDG in 2008 avoided any such potentially controversial steps as dismantling the national network. While the RDG recognised that, on a purely financial basis, "rail is not commercially sustainable without a significant reduction in the size of the existing network" (RDG, 2008c, p. 2), its ultimate recommendation was to retain the network at its present size through ongoing government support.

The government in 2010 faced some difficult decisions. What role did it want rail to perform, and how much was it willing to spend on it? Was it prepared to wear the political consequences of making tough decisions about rail, with any economic and social changes that may flow?

The 2010 KiwiRail Turnaround Plan was the government's response to these dilemmas. The package was crafted to deal with these issues from both a political and economic perspective. It incorporated time-limited subsidies and a 'turnaround' in rail's performance, leading to 'commercial viability' in the future, all under continuing government ownership.

In 2012, the Turnaround Plan is under-delivering on its promise. The plan is undergoing further modification, but may well prove inadequate to deliver on these goals. The economic issues underlying rail's dilemmas remain to be resolved. Fundamentally, to echo the words of the Railways Minister nearly 90 years ago, there is still a need to decide: what are 'the true interests' of New Zealand when it comes to rail?

7.8 Some Lessons from the New Zealand Experience

7.8.1 *Rail-specific lessons*

New Zealand's experience with rail may be different to that of other economies, but it is by no means unique. There are close parallels with the experiences in Australia – of the states of Victoria (2007) and Tasmania (2009), where those governments purchased previously privatised rail networks following near-abandonment by their owners. Successful structural reform requires a solid understanding of the economics of rail in general, and how they play out given the specific circumstances and history of an economy's transport system. While applying lessons from one economy to another should be done cautiously, the following observations from New Zealand are pertinent.

- Rail assets are very long-lived, but the demand for specific types of rail services has changed over significantly shorter timeframes. When combined with the high costs and sunk nature of rail infrastructure, this makes the problem of determining the optimum type and level of investment very difficult indeed.
- The long life of rail assets means that it is possible to boost short-term financial performance by deferring maintenance and upgrades, and incentives exist for both public and private owners to defer these costs. The inevitable long-term consequence is a dilapidated and uncompetitive rail system.
- The economic performance of rail in New Zealand has long been poor. Unable to cover its capital costs, it relies on taxpayer subsidies to cover its financial deficit. This performance can be attributed to the convergence of distinctive physical factors (low population density, topography and geographical isolation) with rail's underlying economic characteristics: high proportions of sunk fixed costs, expensive maintenance and renewals, and diminishing returns on infrastructure investment.
- Simply changing the ownership model – from public to private and back again – has not changed the fundamental economics of rail.

- A lack of competition within the rail sector does not give a rail operator a natural monopoly. KiwiRail competes with other transport modes – with trucks and coastal shipping for freight, and with aeroplanes, buses and private cars for passengers. It is thus unhelpful to consider rail in New Zealand in terms of a natural monopoly.
- Any given rail service may or may not have net environmental benefits – the existence and level of such benefits can only be determined once details of that specific service are known. The most environmentally beneficial services are likely to be those in least need of government subsidy.
- The New Zealand experience suggests that increasing or maintaining the size of the network to achieve so-called economies of network size does not enhance economic performance. Railways are driven by the economies of density, which can be achieved by using a rail network more and better. In New Zealand economies of density might be best achieved by focusing on a smaller, more heavily used subset of the existing network – a scenario which would also allow rail's potential economic and environment benefits to be realised.

7.8.2 *Structural reform lessons*

Some more general lessons about structural reform also emerge from this case study:

- Structural reform needs to be very clear about its goals and how the reform will achieve those goals. All underlying assumptions should be clearly identified.
- The goals of structural reform will shift over time. It is more appropriate to compare the outcomes of reforms against their original goals than against newly defined ones.
- Intervention to reverse previous structural reforms is likely to have long-term ramifications: any future government wishing to pursue reform may find it cannot credibly commit to non-interference.

- New Zealand experience points to an inherent conflict between financial and political goals for rail. Structural reform is unlikely to resolve such conflicts.
- Reforms designed to create competition within a sector may not be necessary (or even desirable) if the sector faces effective competition in its product markets.
- Some economic problems may be too large to be 'fixed' by structural reform. It may be necessary to recast the problem in a wider context.
- The mere existence of externalities is insufficient cause for specific government interventions. Externalities need to be quantified, and if material, a least-cost approach should be adopted for their mitigation. The least-cost approach identified may be cross-sectoral or even focused on other sectors entirely.

Chapter 8

Maritime Transport in Australia and the United States[1]

Fabien Bertho[2]

8.1 Introduction

This chapter analyses the maritime transport sector in Australia and the United States of America (US). In particular, it deals with commercial and competition regulations in international and domestic shipping. This analysis examines the reforms that occurred during the last decade (i.e. 2002-2012), the ones which are still being debated and others which are obviously necessary for reasons such as poor performance, congestion and bottlenecks. It explains the drivers of past and potential reforms, highlights the consequences of these reforms on economies and provides recommendations, as appropriate, to show room for progress.

---

[1] This chapter is based on a paper produced with funding from the Asia Pacific Economic Cooperation's Policy Support Unit and material from that paper is reproduced with its permission. Information is taken from 'The Impacts and Benefits of Structural Reforms in the Transport, Energy and Telecommunications Sectors in APEC Economies', APEC#211-SE-01.1. The views expressed in this paper are those of the authors and do not necessarily represent those of the APEC Secretariat or APEC Member Economies.

[2] The University of Adelaide and Groupe d'Economie Mondiale (Sciences Po, Paris) (fabien.bertho@sciencespo.org). I thank Howard Dick (Universities of Melbourne and Newcastle), Henry Ergas (University of Canberra), David Jacks (Simon Frazer University, Burnaby, British Columbia) and Michael Sutton and Susan Bell (Australian Department of Infrastructure, Transport, Regional Development and Local Development) for extremely helpful discussions and comments. Any errors are the author's.

In particular, four types of regulations that are specific to the sector are the focus of this chapter: cargo reservations, coastal shipping regimes, tax exemptions and subsidy schemes and exemption from competition rules in the liner shipping segment.

For a long time, the Australian and US maritime transport regulatory regimes have been considered as the less and the most restrictive of the developed world, respectively. On the one hand, the US pursues a policy of explicit support to the maritime industry, which means to both the fleet and the shipyards. The cornerstone of this policy is security of supply. The aim is to ensure that the fleet is sufficient to carry US water-borne foreign and domestic trade and is capable of serving as a naval military auxiliary in times of emergency. On the other hand, the Australian regulatory framework was one of the most open and liberal in the world. However, in 2012, to prevent the decline of the Australian-flag fleet and to make the country less dependent on foreign vessels, the Labor government reformed policy applying to the sector. An important part of this reform consisted of implementing protectionist-inspired measures.

For different reasons maritime transport is of crucial importance for Australia as well as the US. Concerning Australia, it is for geographical reasons. However, at first sight this does not show up from data on world-wide maritime transport. As of January 2010, the Australian-flag registered fleet represented just a tiny share of the world fleet—0.17% (UNCTAD, 2010). Moreover, in 2009 Australia's merchandise trade represented only 1.3% of world merchandise trade in value (UNCTAD, 2010). By volume, however, the picture was quite different. Despite Australia being a modest trader of general and containerised cargoes, it is a huge exporter of bulk cargoes. Indeed, in 2010 Australia's sea-borne export volume of coal and of iron ore represented one-third and 40% of the world's coal and iron ore sea-borne trade, respectively (UNCTAD, 2011).

Regarding the US, its focus on security follows from the significance of maritime transport in US trade. In 2009, 44% of the value of international trade was transported by sea and 11% of domestic trade was transported by water (US Department of Transportation, 2011; and BTS, 2012). Maritime transport also represents an important part of the US economy, accounting for USD34.2 billion of gross output and employing over a quarter of a million workers (in 2009, of whom about a quarter were in transportation, a third in port services and the balance (40%) in the shipbuilding and repair sector). In 2009, the US accounted for a large share of world sea-borne trade (15.5%), mostly petroleum products (47% of the total volume) and containers (in 2009 US container traffic represented 17% of world traffic).

8.2 The Australian and US Regulatory Frameworks

This section deals with the Australian and US maritime transport regulatory regimes, emphasising their similarities and differences. The US regulatory framework is restrictive with respect to Australia and other developed economies. This is mainly due to the fact that the US maintains significant restrictions limiting access to the markets of international transport of some type of cargo and domestic shipping. In contrast, the Australian regulatory regime was considered as one of the most liberal. Nevertheless, in July 2012, the Australian government implemented a reform aimed at revitalising the industry that was 'losing steam'. The reform consists of protecting the Australian-flag fleet in the coastal shipping market and supporting the Australian maritime industry through tax exemption schemes. It also establishes an international shipping register. Considering the first two measures, the Australian reform leads to convergence with the US regulatory regime.

In Australia as well as in the US, international shipping involves no barriers to entry in the market for domestic providers by way of licensing requirements or restriction on the number of providers. In contrast, there are significant barriers to entry for foreign providers. Regarding cross-border trade, the most significant restriction is cargo preference—also called cargo reservation. This type of measure is applied in the US. According to the General Agreement on Trade in Services (GATS), cargo preferences are a restriction to market access under mode 1. (GATS splits supply of services into four modes. Mode 1 is cross-border supply, and it applies when service suppliers resident in one economy provide services in another economy, without either the supplier or the 'buyer or consumer' moving to the physical location of the other [Francois and Hoekman, 2009]). According to this restriction, some types of cargo (e.g. government-impelled, strategic, military or that financed by certain government programmes)[3] can only be transported by vessels that fly the flag of the economy. At the same time, requirements to fly the US flag are quite restrictive: the vessel must be owned by a US entity (but may be owned up to 100% by non-citizen interests), crewed by US citizens or lawful permanent residents, all licensed officers must be US citizens and the vessel must be certified by the US Coast Guard. Foreign seafarers are allowed to work on US-flag vessels in domestic and international trade if they hold a green card but are limited to only 25% of the licensed crew members.

Cargo reservation in the past has widely applied in the maritime transport industry across nations. Nevertheless, although since the 1970s and 1980s most economies have repealed this type of restriction, the US is one of the OECD economies that still applies it. Moreover, as can be seen in Table 8.1, cargo preference laws in the US cover many types of cargoes. Additionally, considering cross-border trade restrictions, the US is party to a bilateral maritime agreement with Brazil. This agreement includes a cargo-sharing clause; that is, it establishes a system of 'cargo reservation' between partners based on shares of bilateral or international trade transported by sea. The agreement signed with Brazil states that "National-flag carriers of each party shall have equal and discriminatory access to the government-controlled cargo of the other party". Nevertheless, according to the Brazilian Maritime Transport Agency (Agência Nacional de Transportes Aquaviários), the reservation is not applied (Brazilian Maritime Transport Agency e-mail, 2009).

---

[3] Government-impelled cargo is cargo that is moving, either as a direct result of Federal Government involvement, or, indirectly through financial sponsorship of a Federal programme, or in connection with a guarantee provided by the Federal Government (MARAD, 2012).

Table 8.1 US Cargo Reservation Schemes.

Types of cargo reserved	Regulation associated	Share reserved to US-flag vessels
Military cargo [a]	Military Cargo Preference Act (1904)	100%
Government-impelled cargo [b]	Cargo Preference Act (1954)	At least 50% of the GT
Petroleum	Cargo Preference Act (1954)	
Agricultural cargoes under some foreign assistance programs [c]	Food Security Act (1985)	At least 75%
Exports for which a government agency makes export loan or credit [d]	Public resolution 17 (1934)	100%

Sources: MARAD website, 2012.
Notes: [a] Including military contract cargoes, commercial contractor cargoes, personal property cargoes, POV shipments. [b] Of which Congressional supplementary for Iraq reconstruction, Federal Transit Administration, AID loans and grants, etc. [c] Including the following programmes: P.L.480 (Title I to III), Food for Progress, Section 416(b) and Food for Education. [d] Ex-Im Bank.

Regarding mode 1, Australia maintains one minor measure that should not be considered as protectionist. Liner shipping operators providing transport services to or from Australia must be represented in ports by a resident. Even though this measure is considered by the GATS to be an impediment to trade, its main objective is not protectionist: it establishes practical jurisdiction over maritime incidents in Australian waters and ensures that ships do not leave port without paying their bills. In other words, this measure aims at responding to a market failure (information asymmetry) rather than protecting domestic and national producers.

In regard to commercial presence (mode 3), there are almost no restrictions to trade for foreign providers in Australia and the US. Only one measure affecting the establishment of foreign firms is applied in both economies. In Australia as well as in the US, international shipping activities cannot be conducted by a branch. This requirement is considered by GATS as a restriction on the form of commercial presence. However, again, this measure is not protectionist because it is applied for reasons of tax collection and the management of legal liability.

Turning to domestic shipping, before July 2012, the Australian regulatory regime was considered as one of the most liberal in the world. Many economies reserve coastal shipping for vessels flying their own flag. Although these requirements are burdensome, they are restrictions on foreign ownership and on the employment of foreign crews. Australia did not reserve domestic shipping for Australian-flag vessels. According to the previous regulatory framework (Part VI of the Navigation Act 1912), two systems co-existed in coastal shipping: a general scheme (the licence system) and a special scheme (the permit system) (Australian Parliament, House of Representatives, 2008). To be licensed, carriers had to comply with two main requirements. Firstly, the vessel's crew had to be paid at Australian wages, and secondly, the vessel must not have been subsidised in the previous 12 months. Permits to transport coastal trade were issued without these licence requirements but under certain conditions: where there were no suitable licensed ships available and where the issuing of the permit was considered desirable in the public interest.

In 2012, the reform of the coastal shipping sector consisted of giving preference to Australian flagged and crewed vessels (the Coastal Trading Act 2012). Foreign vessels are still allowed to compete under a new short-term licence system. Now, the Australian coastal shipping regulatory regime is comparable to the ones applied in most developed economies. Importantly, the new coastal shipping regime was coupled with two other measures: the implementation of tax exemptions (Tax Laws Amendment (Shipping Reform) Act 2012) and the establishment of an international register Shipping Registration Amendment (Australian International Shipping Register) Act 2012.

In comparison, the US has remained one of the most (if not the most) protectionist economy in the world regarding cabotage. Indeed, according to the 'Jones Act' (Merchant Marine Act of 1920) that rules coastal shipping in the US, vessels must be registered under the US flag and also be owned by a US corporation, of which the maximum amount of foreign equity is 25% and at least 75% of its employees must be US citizens. The requirements in order to provide cabotage service are more demanding in the US since it reserves cabotage for vessels built in the US. This building requirement has the effect of providing support for US shipyards. The US defines cabotage as "cargo services between two points in the US, including its territories and possession either directly or via a foreign port". According to the cabotage regulations, any domestic leg of an international journey is also considered cabotage. This is an important restriction and more inclusive than that used by some other economies, even if, in practice, many waivers are issued (as reported by experts in 2009). There are exemptions from the Jones Act. For instance, there is no building requirement for the transport of crude oil from Alaska. Also, with the exception of activities reserved for the US government, the US territories of American Samoa, Virgin Islands and Northern Mariana Islands are also exempt. These restrictions stem in part from the long decline in the size of the US maritime industry prior to World War I. In 1913 the US fleet was very small in comparison to the US's engagement in international trade. From the beginning of World War I foreign-flag ships were diverted away from US routes. In order to satisfy the demand for shipping for commercial and military purposes, the US government subsidised the shipbuilding industry. As a result, the shipbuilding industry obtained not only substantial financial resources but also experience of interaction with policy-making, adding to its capacity to influence the content of the Jones Act.

With regard to tax exemptions and subsidies, the US maintains an important scheme supporting the maritime industry as a whole. The US support programmes, described in Table 8.2, consist in supporting the US-flag fleet, the vessels' owners and operators or US shipyards. They can be applied to both international and domestic trade vessels and take various forms: subsidies, credit guarantees and tax deferrals. Before 2012, Australia maintained a minimal subsidy system in liner shipping, the Bass Strait Freight Equalisation Scheme that aimed at avoiding transport cost disadvantages for Tasmanians. According to this programme, the government subsidises shippers transporting certain types of cargo between Tasmania and mainland Australia. As part of the 2012 reform, four tax exemptions schemes have been established. Their goal is to help the Australian fleet to compete in the international and domestic shipping markets—tax exemptions are detailed in section 8.3, Table 8.10.

Table 8.2 Support Programmes to the US Maritime Transport Industry.

Programmes	Support	Mechanism
The Maritime Security Program (MSP)	US flag merchant marine - operators	Fixed payment to US-flag vessel operators
Voluntary Intermodal Sealift Agreement Program (VISA) [a]	US flag merchant marine - operators	Participants obtain priority consideration in the award of Department of Defence peacetime ocean freight contracts
Title XI - Federal Ship Financing Program	US merchant marine and shipyard	Credit guarantee to private entity seeking to finance the construction or modernization of vessels in US shipyards and for US shipyards seeking to invest in technology
Capital Construction Fund (CCF)	US flag merchant marine - owners and operators	Deferment of Federal income taxes on certain deposits of money or other property placed into a CCF
Small Shipyard Grant Program	Smaller shipyards	Grants for capital and related infrastructure improvements
Technical Assistance Program	Shipbuilding	Various programmes to aid the development of more advanced technologies

Source: Global Insight (2009); MARAD website, 2012.
Note: [a] VISA is not really a subsidy. Nevertheless, the effect of the programme is similar as it ensures a given level of resources for the carriers involved.

Finally, Australia and the US still maintain an exemption from domestic competition laws on international liner shipping agreements (Box 8.1). The rules governing exemptions are quite similar in both economies. In Australia, agreements containing any anti-competitive provisions must be registered under Part X of the Trade Practices Act (renamed the Competition and Consumer Act 2010) in order to qualify for the exemption. Carriers of registered agreements must publish specified details in a public register and they are also required to negotiate with, and provide information to, representative shipper bodies. In the US, agreements among liner operators and marine terminal operators to discuss, fix, or regulate transportation rates and other conditions of service or cooperate on operational matters must also be filed with the Federal Maritime Commission (FMC). The FMC reviews them to avoid anti-competitive behaviour. A crucial difference between the Australian and US regimes deals with individual actions of conference members. Contrary to the Australian exemption, the US regime mentions that confidential contracts between conference members and shippers must be allowed.

8.3 Forces for Policy Change

This section deals with regulations which have been subject to recent policy changes and reforms or which face policy challenges in Australia and/or the US, including the US cargo preferences system, coastal shipping rules, tax exemption and subsidy programmes and the exemption of shipping agreements from competition rules. For details about recent policy changes that occurred in both economies, see the Appendix.

Box 8.1 A Typology of Agreements in Liner Shipping.

Historically, economies exempt liner shipping carriers' agreements from the competition rules. The objectives of this measure were to:

- make the service more reliable;
- make the market more stable; and
- take advantage of economies of scale.

Various types of agreement have different aims and different competitive outcomes. We classify these agreements into three categories:

Conferences are route-specific agreements between carriers on conditions for the carriage of cargo. The main characteristics of the conferences are the regulation of capacity and the application of uniform or common freight rates. They can be seen as a kind of *entente* between carriers that restrict competition.

Operational agreements provide for cooperation by means of technical, operational or commercial coordination. They take various forms: vessel-sharing agreements, managing port installations and managing marketing activities. They do not affect competition directly and may improve the efficiency of market outcomes.

Discussion agreements are non-binding agreements between conferences or between conference and non-conference members servicing a particular route. They are forums to discuss and share commercial information relevant to a specific route -- e.g. forecast, introduction of a new capacity.

Source: Productivity Commission (2005).

8.3.1 *Cargo preferences in the US*

The US government grants preference to US-flag vessels for transporting various types of cargo. From 2006 to 2009 the volume of cargo transported under preference schemes represented a very small share of the total US foreign trade (1.1–1.2% of total US sea-borne trade depending on the year). Nevertheless, the revenue generated by cargo preferences transportation was sizable (Table 8.4). For each of the fiscal years between 2006 and 2009 it represented from USD1.3 billion to USD2.1 billion. Thus, it represents an important share of the total revenues of carriers operating US-flag vessels.

Military cargo preference is the most important scheme in volume and in value. In 2009, the scheme represented 80.2% of the volume of cargo reserved and 75.5% of the revenue generated. The share generated by military cargo over the last number of years has undoubtedly been inflated by the conflicts in Iraq (2003-2011) and Afghanistan (2001 to date). Nevertheless, the share of cargo that should be reserved according to the law and the share of cargo actually reserved are noticeably different.

This discrepancy is most likely due to the limited shipping capacity of the US-flag fleet. Because the general fleet is relatively small in size, the first issue is gross capacity. There is also the issue of the Department of Defense's demand for specialised carriers, such as Roll-on/Roll-off (Ro/Ro) ships, of which there are insufficient numbers in the US-flag fleet. Moreover, the share reserved to US-flag vessels.

Table 8.3 Importance of Various Cargo Preference Schemes from Fiscal Year 2006.

	FY2006			FY2007		
	Total tonnage (1,000)	Share really reserved [a]	US revenue (1,000)	Total tonnage (1,000)	Share really reserved [a]	US revenue (1,000)
Military cargoes	14,283	88.3	784,848 [d]	17,660	73.6	919,363
Agricultural cargoes [b]	3,654	72.8	414,403	2,553	83.1	319,760
Civilian agencies [c]	926	92.6	139,608	888	89.3	113,443
Total	18,864	85.5	1,338,859 [d]	21,103	75.4	1,352,566

	FY2008			FY2009		
	Total tonnage (1,000)	Share really reserved [a]	US revenue (1,000)	Total tonnage (1,000)	Share really reserved [a]	US revenue (1,000)
Military cargoes	15,644	76.3	1,208,009	14,690	81.0	1,642,195
Agricultural cargoes [b]	2,795	79.3	430,788	2,964	83.2	435,166
Civilian agencies [c]	848	93.8	100,317	521	92.0	95,907
Total	19,288	77.5	1,739,114	18,176	81.7	2,173,268

Source: MARAD website and email, 2012.

Note: [a] Share really reserved is expressed in percent of the total tonnage, weighted average. [b] Including the following programmes: P.L.480 (Title I to III), Food for Progress, Section 416(b) and Food for Education. [c] Including Ex-Im Bank, Resolution 17. [d] Does not include revenue for petroleum.

comes with the condition "to the extent that such vessels are available at fair and reasonable rates", which means that the various agencies are allowed to contract for foreign-flag vessels if there is a documented lack of availability of US-flag vessels.

From a trade policy point of view, cargo reservation works much like a quota, by protecting the vessels registered under the American flag. In the US, contrary to the situation in most other economies, there are no restrictions on foreign ownership in order to fly the flag. However, the cost of operating a foreign-flag vessel is lower than the cost of operating a US-flag vessel. Therefore, the operating cost differential comes, above all, from the American crew requirement, which makes for higher labour costs (Table 8.4). Thus, wage costs are from 5.1 to 5.7 times higher in US-flag than foreign-flag vessels—depending on the type of vessel considered. Protection of the domestic fleet leads to an increase in the price of shipping services, which results in an opportunity cost for the reserved cargoes' shippers—to transport the cargo on a US-flag ship rather than on a cheaper foreign ship. Most reserved cargoes are consumed by US government departments (e.g. Defense, Agriculture and Transport) so that it is the taxpayers who bear the cost.

Table 8.4 Daily Operating Costs for US- vs. Foreign-Flag Vessels, 2010 ($US).

	Containership		Ro/Ro		Bulk Carrier [a]	
	US	Foreign	US	Foreign	US	Foreign
Cost Categories						
Wages [b]	14,872	2,698	12,618	2,450	11,490	2,013
Stores & lubes [c]	1,053	2,200	1,251	513	1,362	638
Maintenance & repair	2,866	3,237	3,035	1,837	3,019	1,736
Insurance	959	868	1,047	535	1,527	745
Overhead [d]	1,444	581	1,249	580	257	676
Total operating costs	21,194	9,584	19,200	5,915	17,655	5,808

***Source*:** MARAD, 2011.

Notes: [a] Includes Handymax and Supramax sized vessels (25,000-65,000 dwt). [b] Generally include basic wages, subsistence, overtime, travel costs, training, pensions, and union fees. [c] Generally include paints, ropes, wires, tools, lubricating oils, greases, chemicals, washers, gaskets, cleaning equipment and materials, galley supplies, laundry needs, etc. [d] Generally include accounting, legal, communications, marketing, policy and planning, procurement needs, 'employment or chartering' decisions, flag registration fees, etc.

There is little information in terms of impact assessments relating to cargo preferences, as there has not been regular analysis allowing for the monitoring of this policy. Furthermore, there is only one analysis dealing with all schemes in combination, as most studies focus on one particular type of reservation scheme only.

Table 8.5 shows the results from various studies. The highest estimated cost is associated with military cargo—with estimates ranging from USD352 million to USD969 million according to the year and the study. The difference between assessments can be explained by the different methodologies used to compute the cost of the measure as well as the variation of the quantity of cargo transported under the various schemes. This is particularly true for military cargo, where the difference between cargo transported in peacetime and in wartime is important. Finally, the various impact assessments do not focus solely on the pecuniary costs of the measures; e.g. the 1990 assessment by the US Government Accountability Office (GAO) highlights the impact of cargo preferences on the quality of services provided. According to the report, because of the schemes a sizable share of cargoes are loaded late (GAO, 1990).

For all these reasons it is very difficult to draw general conclusions from this work beyond the assessment that cargo preferences are costly for the American economy. While the main objective of cargo preferences is to support the US-flag fleet involved in international trade, Figure 8.1 shows that this objective has not been reached. Indeed, the US-flag fleet decreased substantially over the two decades to 2008. Cargo preferences have not prevented the decline in the size of the US-flag fleet. It may also isolate carriers operating US-flag vessels from international competitive standards and reinforce the fleet's inefficiency.

Table 8.5 Results of Various Impact Assessments.

Authors	Period assessed	Schemes Assessed	Methodology	Main conclusions
White (1988)	1984	Agricultural commodities (P.L. 480), Strategic Petroleum Reserve, other shipments	-	Cost for the Federal government are respectively of USD130, 43 and 93 million
GAO (1990)	1986-1988	Food Aid (P.L. 480)	Based on ocean freight differentials	The cost differential is in average USD128.1 million per year - i.e. 9.5% of total programme expenditures
GAO (1994)	1989-1993	All schemes	Comparison with charges to carry cargo on foreign vessels	Federal agencies' transportation costs are increased by USD578 million per year
Department of Defense (1994) [a]	-	Military cargo scheme	-	Additional costs of USD476 million on a total bill of USD1.15 billion for the DoD
Barrett and Maxwell (2005)	1999-2000	Section 416(b) and Food for Progress	-	A premium of 78% is paid for ocean freight due to cargo preference
Bageant, Barrett and Lentz (2010)	2006	Food aid and agricultural cargo preference	Analysis of every USAID food aid shipment transactions.	Cargo reservation requirements cost US taxpayers roughly USD140 million -- 46% mark-up over competitive freight rates.

Sources: Various reports, for details see the references.
Note: [a] Not available, information reported from OECD (2001).

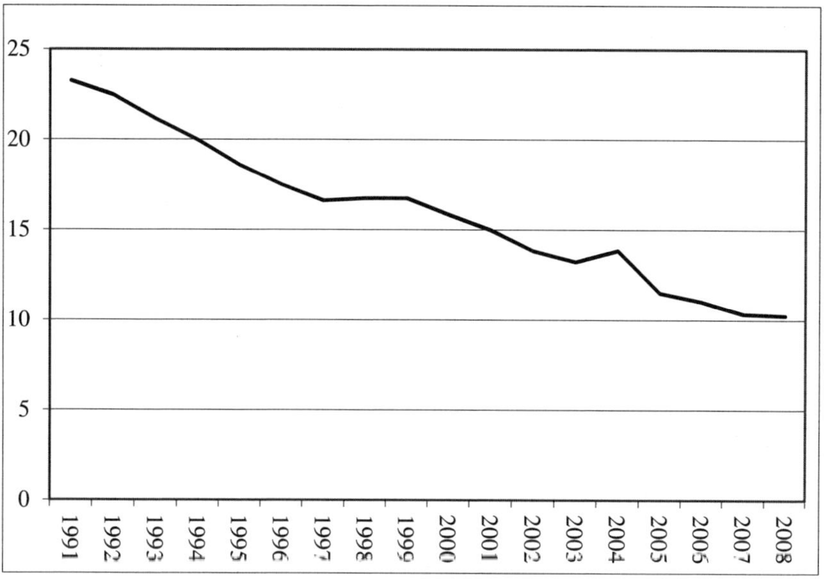

Figure 8.1 Size of the US-flag Merchant Fleet, Ocean-going Ships of ≥1,000 Gross Tons, 1991–2008 (million dwt).
Source: BTS, 2012.

8.3.2 *Subsidy schemes and coastal shipping regulatory regimes*

This section deals with tax exemptions, subsidy programmes and coastal shipping. In Australia (after the reform) and the US, both types of regulations are connected and work in conjunction.

US regulation

This section examines two programmes: the Maritime Security Program (MSP) and the Voluntary Intermodal Sealift Agreement (VISA). It also focuses on Title XI and the Capital Construction Fund (CCF) programmes (Table 8.2). The objective of these programmes is to support the fleet involved in international trade, whereas the aim of the MSP and VISA programmes is more specific. The MARAD website states that "These programs are designed to assure the availability of sufficient US commercial sealift capability and the US intermodal system to sustain US military operations overseas in an emergency." The MSP establishes a fleet of privately-owned, militarily useful vessels and the operators involved in the MSP have to make their ships and commercial transportation resources available on the request of the Secretary of Defense. With the VISA programme participants commit to capacity in exchange for priority consideration in the award of Department of Defense peacetime ocean freight contracts. The MSP was created in 1996 because cargo preferences were not able to support the fleet and to achieve the national security objective.

Table 8.6 Importance of Each Subsidy Scheme, Various Years.

Programmes	Budget	Associated fleet
The Maritime Security Programme (MSP)	USD174 million authorised annually for 2009-2011 and USD186 million for 2012-2015	60 vessels - of which 37 containerships. 2.5 million of dwt - of which 2 million of dwt for containerships
Voluntary Intermodal Sealift Agreement Programme (VISA) [a]	-	49 Companies, 133 Ocean Going Ships, 178 Tugs, barges and other vessels (More than 90% of the militarily useful vessels in the U.S.-flag fleet are committed to the VISA programme)
Title XI - Federal Ship Financing Programme [b]	Commitment of USD178 million in 2005, no new commitment in 2006-2008, USD351 million for 2009	In 2009, for 5 articulated tug or barges (185,000 bbl), 9 asphalt tank barges and 30 open hopper barges
Capital Construction Fund (CCF) [b]	n.a	-
Small Shipyard Grant Programme	USD10 million in 2008	-
Technical Assistance Programme	n.a	n.a.

Sources: MARAD website, 2012.

Notes: [a] The VISA programme is not strictly a subsidy. Nevertheless, the programme's effects are similar as it ensures a given level of resources for carriers involved. [b] These programmes are directly linked to the Jones Act.

The MSP and VISA programmes as a consequence work in conjunction, so that more than 90% of the militarily useful vessels in the US-flag fleet are committed to the VISA programme and over 77% of that capacity comes from MSP vessels.[4] Carriers can legally be engaged in either or both of the MSP and VISA programmes and at the same time transport reserved cargo, which means they can benefit from multiple support schemes. For instance, since military cargo is reserved for US-flag vessels and consequently is highly lucrative for carriers, the Department of Defense pays them to commit to capacity in the VISA programme. Clearly, because of this 'double dipping', this type of support is more costly for the taxpayer but without any corresponding enhancement of benefits. As shown in Figure 8.1, the creation of the MSP in 1996 may have prevented the decline of the fleet's size for a few years, however, after only three years the MSP was already insufficient and the decline began again. Furthermore, the complexity of the system leads to a lack of transparency, which further complicates the effective monitoring of these programmes. Finally, the MSP subsidises the operators of US-flag vessels even though maritime regulation does not require national ownership in order to fly the flag. Hence, an important share of the US-flag fleet is operated by foreign carriers. This leads to the situation where the US government, in supporting its fleet by allowing preferences, is directly subsidising foreign carriers. For instance, as of 1 December 2011 the container ship fleet in the MSP programme represented 2 million dwt (deadweight tonnage) and more than 80% of the capacity of the entire MSP fleet. Among this fleet, 98% of the deadweight tonnage was operated by four foreign-owned carriers.[5]

---

[4] Carriers with vessels enrolled in the MSP agree to make their ships available to the department if VISA is activated. In Stage III of VISA, those ships which receive the MSP subsidy must devote 100% of their capacity to Department of Defense cargo; those ships which opt into VISA but do not receive the MSP subsidy, however, devote only 50% of their capacity to Department of Defense cargo.

[5] They are APL Marine Services (subsidiaries of Neptune Orient Line, Singaporean ownership), Maersk Line Ltd and Farrell Lines (subsidiaries of AP Moller-Maersk Group, Danish ownership) and Hapag Lloyd (German ownership). The fifth carrier, Waterman Steamship Corporation, is US owned.

Table 8.7 Results of Various Jones Act Impact Assessments.

Authors	Period Assessed	Methodology	Cost estimation
White (1988) [a]	1984	Based on government transfers	Higher cost of USD2 billion to transport goods in the coastal trade
Congressional Budget Office (1994) [a]	1983	Based on government transfers	Cost of USD1.3 billion for the US economy
Hufbauer and Elliott (1993)	1990	Partial equilibrium model	Net cost of USD1.1 billion for the economy
USITC (1995)	1992	Computable General Equilibrium (CGE)—Operating and capital costs [b]	Net welfare gain of USD2.8 billion in case of repeal of the Jones Act
USITC (1999)	1996		Net welfare gain of USD1.3 billion in case of repeal of the Jones Act. Gain of USD380 million for the build liberalisation only
USITC (2002)	1999		Net welfare gain of USD656million in case of repeal of the Jones Act. Gain of USD261 million for the build liberalisation only
USITC (2004 and 2007)	No quantitative assessment		

Sources: Various reports, see references.
Notes: [a] The report is not available, information comes from Papavizas and Gardner (2009). [b] Partial equilibrium for assessing the removal of the domestic build requirement of the Jones Act.

Concerning cabotage, the Jones Act in effect works like a cargo preference system, reserving domestic maritime transport for US built and operated vessels. This adds to the costs of providing the services, due to the higher building costs and crew costs compared to ships from the rest of the world. There are, however, subsidies to offset this cost increase for the shipyards and for companies that want to buy a Jones Act vessel—Title XI and the CCF, respectively, see Table 8.2. Table 8.7 lists impact assessments that have computed the cost of the Jones Act system. The first conclusion is that the Jones Act is much more costly than other support programmes. This is, above all, due to the huge differential in construction costs. The difference is presented in Table 8.8. The price of a vessel built in an American shipyard was two, three or even four times higher than the representative new construction price reported by UNCTAD for an equivalent, or a larger, vessel of the same category in the same period. The additional operating and construction costs are supported by taxpayers via subsidies and by the consumers of the services, that is, first the shippers, but ultimately the final consumers of the goods.

Table 8.8 Major US Commercial Shipbuilding Programmes and Representative New Building Prices, Selected Years ($US million).

Original Name	Builder	Capacity	Delivery	Price	Representative new building price	Price differential (%)
Crude Carriers						
Polar Endeavour	NGSS Avondale	140,000 dwt	2001	166	41 [a]	405
Alaskan Explorer	GD/ NASSCO	193,000 dwt	2005	210	58 [b]	362
Alaskan Adventurer	GD/ NASSCO	193,000 dwt	2005	210	58 [b]	362
Alaskan Legend	GD/ NASSCO	193,000 dwt	2006	210	81 [c]	259
Container-ships						
Manulani	Aker Philadelphia	2,500 TEU	2005	145	42 [d]	345
Maunalei	Aker Philadelphia	2,500 TEU	2006	145	46 [e]	315

Sources: Shipbuilding history website, 2012; UNCTAD, 2009.

Notes: This table presents prices for buyers. Hence, data include subsidies directly paid to shipyards. [a] For tanker of 110,000 dwt, 2000. [b] For tanker of 110,000 dwt, 2005. [c] For tanker of 110,000 dwt, 2006. [d] For full container ship of 2,500 TEU, 2005. [e] For full container ship of 2,500 TEU, 2006.

The various methodologies explain the variability of the results presented in Table 8.7. Nevertheless, contrary to the assessments of cargo preferences, the studies of the Jones Act are more interesting for the purposes of this case. Of particular interest will be the most recent of the periodically released United States International Trade

Commission (USITC) assessments because, as they use a similar methodology, they will allow a comparison with the Jones Act's cost over time. According to various USITC studies since 1995, the cost of the Jones Act to the US economy has decreased. The USITC computed that if the Jones Act had been repealed in 1992 there would have been a welfare gain of USD2.8 billion; for 1996 the welfare gain of the repeal had decreased to USD1.3 billion; and to USD656 million for a repeal in 1999. Interestingly, the reduction in the cost of the Jones Act could potentially be explained by the decrease in the volume of domestic shipping as shown in Figure 8.2 (USITC, 2002).

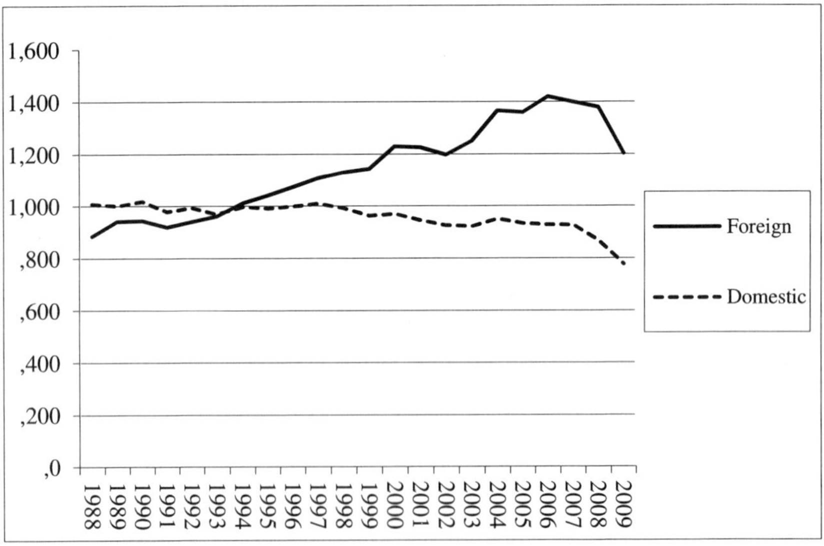

Figure 8.2 Volume of Foreign and Domestic Shipping, 1988–2009(Millions of Tonnes).
Source: BTS, 2012.

During the same period the daily operating cost differential for US- vs. foreign-flag vessels had increased—for example, between 2002 and 2005, from USD8,700 to USD11,300 for a tanker and from USD11,500 to USD12,070 for a container ship (Table 8.4 and USITC; 2007 and 2004). The building cost differential is presumed to have increased as well. Thus, the decrease in cost could be explained by a volume effect and not a price effect.

Furthermore, the Jones Act has resulted in a high cabotage service price. Moreover, between 2003 and 2008 the producer price of coastal shipping increased much more than the freight trucking rate. The producer price for rail transport increased at the same rate (US Department of Labor, Bureau of Labor Statistics, 2010). Hence, consumers substituted other modes of transport for coastal shipping (Figure 8.3). This in turn has reduced the volume of domestic shipping and thus raised the cost of the Jones Act. The reduction in volume can also be explained by reductions in domestic production and the shipment of crude oil. Additionally, substituting rail and road transport for domestic shipping leads to congestion on land.

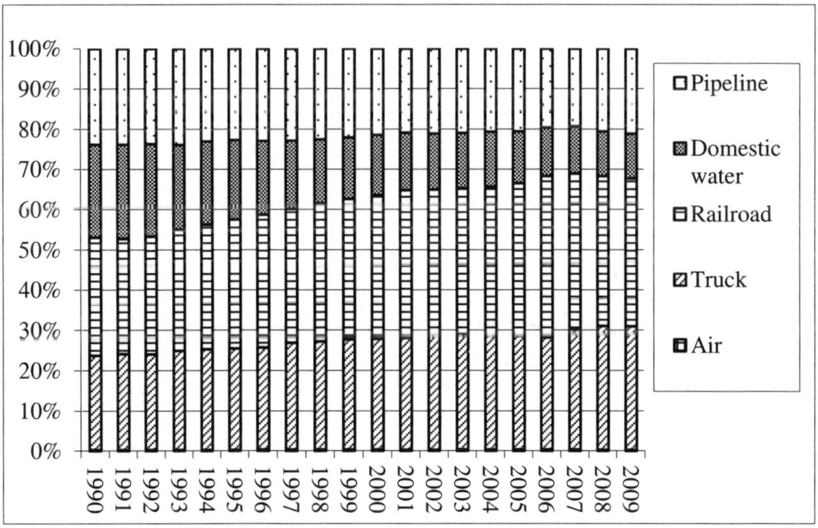

Figure 8.3 US Domestic Transport Share by Modes, 1990–2009(Ton/Miles of Freight). ***Source*:** BTS, 2012.

The combination of cargo preferences (on various types of international trade and on domestic shipping) and the various subsidy programmes could not prevent the decline of the US-flag fleet (Figure 8.1). Additionally, since the mid-1980s, the Jones Act and related subsidies have not prevented the decline of the shipbuilding sector.

There has been a strong decrease in the number of shipyards and in employment in the shipbuilding and repair sector (Figures 8.4 and 8.5).

In conclusion, cabotage regulation has had an important impact on the cost of domestic shipping but it has also had implications for international shipping. The definition of cabotage used by the US includes the domestic part of an international journey. In theory, foreign carriers providing international shipping services cannot call at multiple US ports without employing a 'Jones Act vessel'. Thus, the law prevents carriers involved in international shipping from rationalising the use of their vessels. It leads to higher costs for providers and higher prices for consumers. Even if waivers are issued, according to experts the system is burdensome and inefficient.

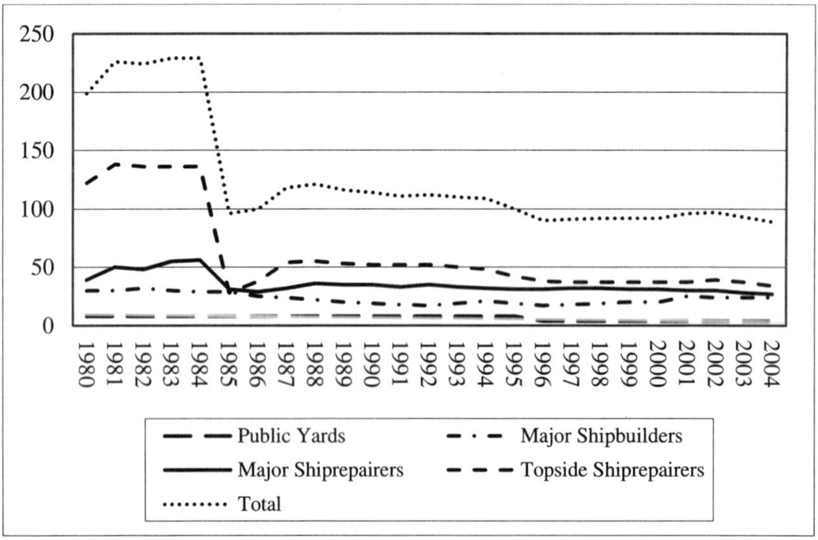

Figure 8.4 The Number of Shipyards in the US, 1998–2004.
Source: Shipbuilding History Website, 2012.

The Australian case

Before the July 2012 reform, the core legislation regulating coastal shipping in Australian waters was the Part VI of the Navigation Act 1912. The Act was supported by the Ministerial Guidelines for Granting Licences and Permits to Engage in Australia's Domestic Shipping (hereafter, the Ministerial Guidelines) which provided guidance for administering the coastal trade provisions of the Act.

Although the Australian coastal shipping legislation had not changed much over several decades, its interpretation and application by the government has changed a good deal. Until the early 1990s coastal shipping permits were issued to foreign-flag vessels in exceptional circumstances only and the share of coastal trade transported under the permit system was small (Figure 8.6).

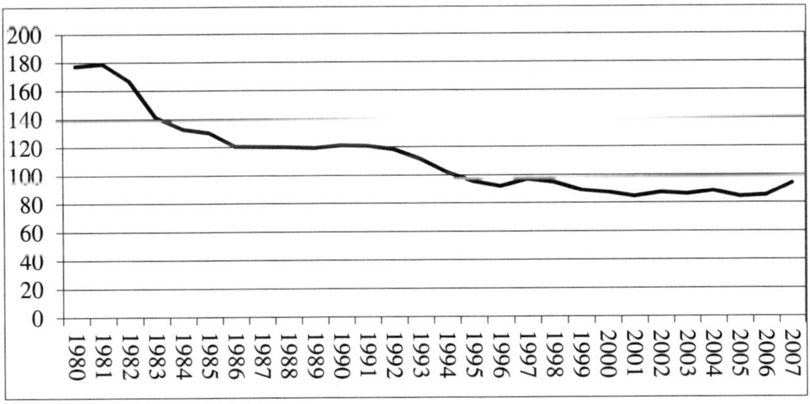

Figure 8.5 Employment in the Shipbuilding and Repairing Sector, 1998–2007 ('000).
Source: Shipbuilding History Website, 2012.

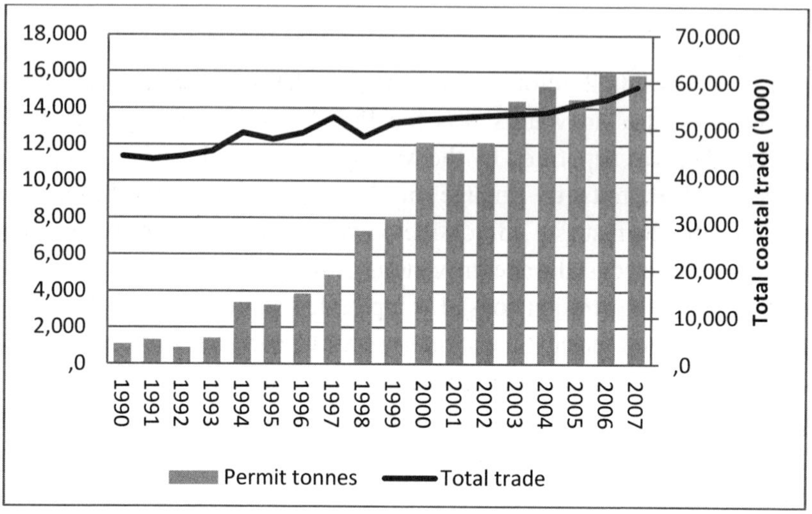

Figure 8.6 Total Coastal Trade and Permit Tonnage Issued by the Government, 1998–2007 ('000).
Source: Department of Infrastructure, Transport, Regional Development and Local Government, 2009.

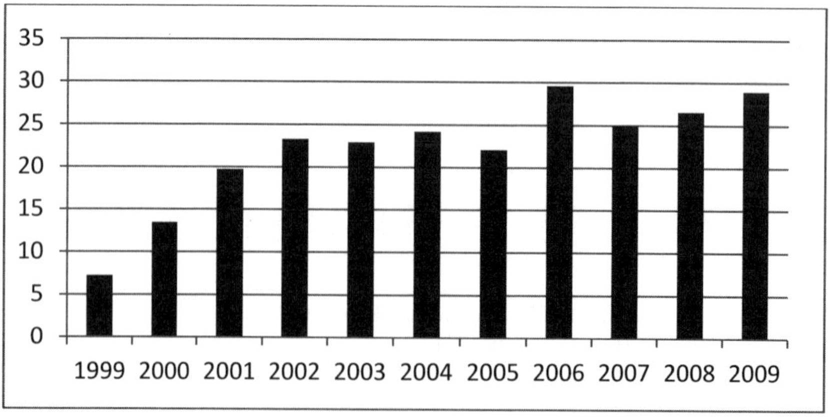

Figure 8.7 Share of Coastal Trade Transported Under Permits, 1999–2009 (%).
Source: BITRE, various years.

In the early 1990s, the combination of the licensing requirements and the small number of permits issued was a means for the government to protect the national fleet. Thus, in spite of high Australian labour costs, the Australian-flag vessels had continued to serve the market.

However, from the mid-1990s (to the end of the 2000s) the government decided to take a more liberal approach in order to reduce the cost of coastal shipping. Indeed, a parliamentary report on Australian coastal shipping stated that the gap between operating a foreign and an Australian crew ranged from AUD1 million to AUD3 million per year, depending on the size of the vessel (Australian Parliament, House of Representatives, 2008).

The relaxation of cabotage in the 1990s had two effects. At first, due to technological factors and the rationalisation of manning scales introduced by the Australian government, it sustained a downward trend that had been observable in real interstate non-bulk freight rates from the early 1980s. The impact of the change in coastal shipping policy was clear from the mid-1990s, however, as the decrease in freight rates for journeys to and from Perth accelerated despite rising fuel prices (Figure 8.8).[6]

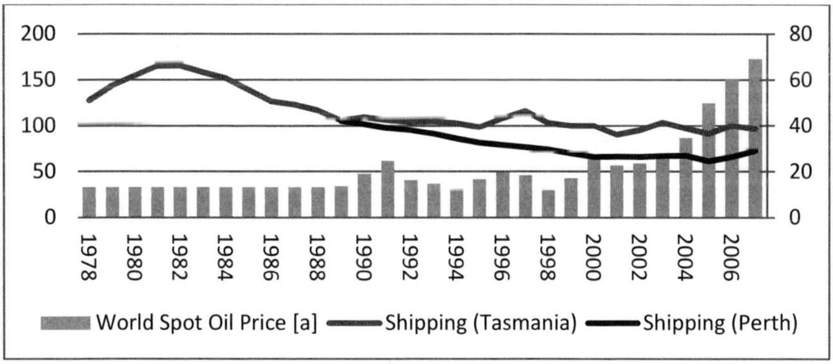

Figure 8.8 Real Interstate Non-Bulk Freight Rates (Index Numbers) and World Oil Price, ($AUS), 1978–2006.
Sources: BITRE, 2008; Energy Administration, 2010.

[6] There are two reasons for using Perth freight rates as the example. Firstly, the increase in the number of permits did not affect freight rates on the Tasmanian route because of the support of the Australian government through the Bass Straight Freight Equalisation Scheme. Secondly, coastal shipping to and from Perth represents more than 50% of the total interstate coastal shipping activity (in billion tonne kilometres) and the majority of this is transported in permit vessels. The port of Perth is Fremantle.

The second effect is more obvious. The Australian fleet decreased in deadweight tonnage by more than half between 1999 and 2009, with the much larger decrease in the coastal fleet (Table 8.9). This is a direct effect of the market share loss of Australian-flag vessels in favour of foreign permit vessels (Australian Parliament, House of Representatives, 2008). From 1994 the permit tonnage has increased much faster than the total coastal trade. Hence, the share of coastal trade transported under permits increased steeply from around 7% in 1999 to around 25% in 2007 (Figure 8.7). However, the decrease in the size of the Australian-flag coastal shipping fleet had been accompanied by an increase in the productivity of the fleet. Indeed, in 1999, the ratio of costal trade transported by the Australian-flag fleet (in tonnes) divided by the capacity of the Australian-flag fleet dedicated to coastal shipping (in dwt) was 27.7; in 2007 the ratio was 66.9 (computed from BTE [2000], BITRE [2009] and Department of Infrastructure, Transport, Regional Development and Local Government [2009]).

Table 8.9 Summary of the Australian Registered Trading Fleet, 1999 and 2009.

	Number of vessels		Deadweight tonnage ('000 tonnes)		
	1999	2009	1999	2009	Change (%)
Coastal trade	41	27	1,562.6	720.6	-53.9
Overseas trade	10	5	673.5	392.3	-41.7
Total	51	32	2,236.1	1,112.9	-50.2

Source: BTE, 2000; BITRE, 2011.
Note: Vessels have a capacity greater than 2,000 dwt.

In 2007 a Labor Government replaced the long-serving conservative coalition. The new government held the view that it was in the national interest to maintain a strong Australian fleet and industry, for strategic reasons that included security of trade and to provide a training ground for the maritime expertise necessary to an island economy.[7] The Labor Government reformed the sector in two stages.

[7] Of 32 Australian flagged vessels in 2009, three were tankers (one for crude oil and two for petroleum product) and three were LNG tankers (BITRE, 2011).

First, soft regulation was used to encourage Australian vessels to provide coastal shipping services but not to give preference to Australian-flag vessels in international trade. The new policy was implemented through two reforms of the Ministerial Guidelines in 2008 and 2009. According to a new preamble to the guidelines in 2008, the government's intention was "to enhance the competitiveness and sustainability of the Australian coastal shipping sector". In 2009 some terms of the guidelines were clarified in the interests of transparency and accountability. For example, one condition for the issuing of a permit was that there was "no suitable licensed ship available". The new guideline defined what were an 'available licensed ship' and a 'suitable licensed ship'. As shown in Figure 8.7, this did not lead to a decrease in the share of coastal shipping transported under permits. Nevertheless, the main policy change at this first stage of reform has been wrought through the coverage of licensed and permit vessels in the Fair Work Act (FWA), the legislation that governs employment terms and conditions in Australia. According to the new 2010 regulation, licensed vessels were subject to scrutiny (licensed vessels were required to offer Australian crew wages and conditions before the coverage by the FWA, but there was no formal inspection regime). According to the Seagoing Industry Award 2010, from 2011 permit vessels also had to comply with requirements in terms of minimum wages, hours of work and rest periods. These requirements had been applied during less than two years since a deeper and stronger reform occurred in mid-2012.

Indeed, after considering the sector's situation and consulting the stakeholders, the government decided to adopt a package of measures relating to the shipping sector as a whole. Regarding cabotage, the Coastal Trading Act 2012 replaced the Part VI of the Navigation Act 1912. The regulation establishes a new licence system and removes the permit system. The reformed system is based on three types of licences: general, temporary and emergency licences. General licences are reserved to vessels registered in the Australian General Register—the reform also establishes a double register system, for more details see Box 8.2, 'The Australian International Shipping Register'. To obtain a general licence, vessels are required to be crewed by Australian citizens or foreigners satisfying the immigration legislation. General licences provide an unrestricted access to the domestic shipping market for five years. In contrast, temporary licences are granted to vessels registered under the Australian International Shipping Register, they are also granted to foreign-registered vessels. Temporary licences are much more restrictive than the general ones. First, temporary licences provide access to the journeys authorised by the licence only—when they apply for a temporary licence carriers have to detail the number of journeys, the type and volume of cargo, the loading and discharge ports, etc. Second, temporary licence applications are submitted to the general licence holders. A temporary licence is issued only when no general licence holders are able to transport the cargo.[8] Third, temporary licences are issued for a period up to 12 months. Then, emergency licences are of minor interest since they are available in special circumstances only—e.g. when life or the environment is threatened. Finally, a five-year transition system has been implemented in order that producers and consumers adapt to the new regulation. Under the transitional system, licences and permits granted through the previous system are valid until end October 2012. In addition, transitional general licences have been granted to foreign-flag vessels holding a licence issued during the previous system. This gives foreign-flag vessel operators the time to change the registration of their vessels.

The new cabotage regime and international register are coupled with a third measure that establishes a system of tax exemptions (The Tax Law Amendment (Shipping Reform) Act 2012). Tax exemptions benefit from vessels registered under the General as well as International Registers. Their objective is to support owners and operators of Australian-flag vessels (Table 8.10) involved in the markets of international and domestic shipping. Tax exemptions are likely to help the Australian fleet to compete with foreign-flag vessels by filling the competitive gap and by promoting investment in the industry—that enables to renew the fleet and to make productivity improvements. Finally, two tax breaks are specifically designed to

[8] If the general licence holders are able to transport the cargo, the temporary licence application is withdrawn. If the general licence holders are able to transport a part of the cargo, the temporary licence application continues on the remaining part.

encourage the employment of Australian seafarers. Indeed, the main Income Tax Exemption (ITE) scheme depends on crew management and training requirements. Furthermore, another exemption is restricted to employers of Australian seafarers.

Box 8.2 The Australian International Shipping Register.

The second measure taken as part of the maritime transport reform consists of establishing two separate shipping registers: the Australian General and International Shipping Registers (Shipping Registration Amendment (Australian International Shipping Register) Act 2012). The General Register corresponds to the previous register and requirements to fly the Australian flag under this register are the same. Specifically, the vessel must be at least 50% owned by Australian nationals (or provide evidence that the vessel is being operated by an Australian entity under a demise charter[9]); the majority of officers and crew must be Australian citizens or residents; and the vessel must comply with high security, safety, environmental, and labour standards. The main difference with respect to the pre-reform register is that only vessels registered under the General Register can obtain a long-run licence to enter the cabotage market. Regarding the International Register, some requirements are relaxed with respect to the General Register. Thus, concerning crew requirements, at least two senior positions (engineering and deck officers) must be Australian citizens or residents. Furthermore, labour terms and conditions are also relaxed with respect to the General Register. However, they still comply with international regulation set by the International Labour Organization (ILO) Maritime Labour Convention 2006.

The objective of the International Register is to encourage the participation of Australian vessels in international trade. It aims at being a competitive option for Australian owners and operators involved in international shipping. The final objective is to promote the Australian maritime industry and develop its skills. The establishment of international registers is a strong global trend. The first international register was established in Norway in 1987. Then several economies such as Denmark (1988), Germany (1989), Japan (1996), Korea (1998) and France (2005) adopted this measure. In all economies, international registers consist of relaxing crewing rules and sometimes giving fiscal advantages. It is meant to compete with flags of convenience. In most economies the measure is likely to be a success since it leads to a substantial increase in the economies' fleets.

---

[9] A demise charter is an arrangement for the hiring of a vessel whereby no administration or technical maintenance is included as part of the agreement. Demise chartering is common for tankers and bulk-carriers.

Table 8.10 Support Programmes to the Australian Maritime Transport Industry.

	Eligibility criteria	Additional Requirements
Income Tax Exemption (ITE) [a]	Operators of Australian registered vessels—primary or international [b].	Management and training requirements [c]
Accelerated depreciation and rollover relief	Owners of Australian registered vessels—primary or international.	-
Refundable tax offset	Employers of Australian seafarers.	-
Exemption from royalty withholding tax	Foreign owners of vessels leased under a bareboat or demise charter to an Australian operator.	-

Source: Australian Government, Department of Infrastructure and Transport website, 2012.

Notes: [a] On qualifying shipping income. [b] Australian General register or Australian International Shipping Register. For details on these registers, see Box 8.2. [c] According to the Management requirements, the applicant must conduct crew management in Australia and at least one of the following activities must be conducted in Australia: strategic, commercial or technical management. According to the training requirements, the applicant must demonstrate that it had in place a training plan for the previous income year.

8.3.3 *Exemption from competition rules and price-fixing agreements*

Since the 1990s, the influence of price-fixing agreements (i.e. conferences and discussion agreement, see Box 8.1) has decreased sharply world-wide. While as of 2001, 150 conferences operated in the world; in 2010, less than 30 survived (OECD, 2002, and Containerisation International, 2010). As shown in Tables 8.11 and 8.12, Australia and the US are no exceptions. Indeed, conferences and discussion agreements appear to serve fewer and fewer routes to or from these two economies. In the US, the passage of the Ocean Shipping Reform Act (OSRA) in 1998 lead to the disappearance of significant conferences on its routes. This is mainly due to the provision that consists in making confidential individual contracts mandatory and that makes conferences obsolete. In contrast, discussion agreements are relatively active, both in terms of number and market shares. However, since they are non-binding agreements, they are likely to have a minor impact on competition.

Table 8.11 Active Liner Shipping Agreements Calling at Australian Ports—as of July 2010.

Type of agreement	Name	Journey	Countries
Conference	Australian & New Zealand/Eastern Shipping Conference (ANZESC)	To or from	Japan, Korea, China, Taiwan, Hong Kong, Philippines, Australia, Papua New Guinea and New Zealand
Conference	Australia Northbound Shipping Conference	From	Japan, Korea, China, Hong Kong, Taiwan and Philippines
Discussion agreement	Asia-Australia Discussion Agreement	To	Japan, Korea, Taiwan, Philippines, Hong Kong and China
Discussion agreement	Australia/Fiji Discussion Agreement	From	Fiji
Discussion agreement	Australia/New Zealand Discussion Agreement	From	New Zealand
Discussion agreement	Canada Australia New Zealand Discussion Agreement	To	Canada
Discussion agreement	United States/Australasia Discussion Agreement	To	United States
Trade Facilitation Agreement (TFA) [a]	Australia/North and East Asia Trade Facilitation Agreement (TFA)	From	Japan, Korea, PRC, Hong Kong, Taiwan and The Philippines
Trade Facilitation Agreement (TFA) [a]	Australia/South East Asia Trade Facilitation Agreement (TFG)	From	Singapore, Malaysia, Thailand, Indonesia, Brunei, Vietnam and Cambodia

Source: Containerisation International (2010).

Note: [a] Trade facilitation and stabilisation agreements are similar to discussion agreements.

Table 8.12 Active Liner Shipping Agreements Calling at US Ports—as of July 2010.

Type of agreement	Name	Journey	Countries
Discussion agreement	Central American Discussion Agreement	To or from	Central America: Costa Rica, Honduras, Guatemala, Nicaragua, Panama and El Salvador
Discussion agreement	Hispaniola Discussion Agreement	To or from	Puerto Rico, Dominican Republic, Haiti
Discussion agreement	West Coast of South America Discussion Agreement	To or from	Chile, Peru, Ecuador and Colombia
Discussion agreement	United States/Australasia Discussion Agreement	From	Australia and New Zealand
Discussion agreement	Middle East Indian Subcontinent Discussion Agreement	To or from	Bahrain, Bangladesh, India, Iran, Iraq, Jordan, Kuwait, Oman, Pakistan, Qatar, Saudi Arabia, Sri Lanka, UAE, and Yemen
Stabilisation agreement [a]	Transpacific Stabilization Agreement	To or from	Japan, Korea, Taiwan, Hong Kong, China, Singapore, Malaysia, Thailand, Indonesia, Philippines, Vietnam, Cambodia, Laos, Myanmar and Russia

Source: Containerisation International (2010).
Note: [a] Trade facilitation and stabilisation agreements are similar to discussion agreements.

Other external factors explain the decreasing importance of price-fixing agreements. First, since the end of the previous century, new carriers from emerging economies (notably from Asian economies) have entered the market. The increasing number of shipping lines in the market made the sustainability of agreements more complicated. Second, the repeal by European economies of the block exemption for liner shipping conferences (Regulation 4056/86) in 2006 also played a major role.

Considering the now minor importance of price-fixing agreements, it may be said that exemptions from competition rules are a non-issue in

Australia and the US. This situation is unlikely to change until demand for liner shipping catches up with the overcapacity that existed even before the 2008 global financial crisis.

Finally, as a response to the decreasing importance of price-fixing agreements, new types of agreements emerged such as operational agreements and global alliances. Nowadays, shipping lines prefer to enter into these types of agreements which are more operational and flexible. However, operational agreements and global alliances are less controversial than price-fixing agreements since their impact on competition is likely to be marginal.

8.4 Consequences of Changes and Scope for Further Reform

8.4.1 *The US case*

The last policy change in shipping was the OSRA in 1998. It dealt with the exemption from competition law of liner carriers' agreements. In spite of many proposals to reform the maritime regulatory framework, in particular the Jones Act and cargo preferences, nothing has been done since that time. This section considers why those changes have not occurred and discusses the most recent changes that have occurred in container and intermodal infrastructures.

US policy is motivated by concerns about the security of supply. It involves the use of cargo preferences and cabotage regulation. However these are costly for consumers and taxpayers with significant effects on the allocation of resources within the economy. Some of the consequences of the policy are apparently inconsistent with its purpose, since even the legislation which was designed to support US-flag vessels could not prevent the decline of the US fleet. In these respects, it might be expected that the policy package would come under pressure for change. There are, however, several sources of countervailing pressure. The first difficulty for policy-makers comes from the likely impact of reforms on employment. The maritime transport sector employs hundreds of thousands of people (Table 8.13, Figure 8.5). Repealing the cargo preferences measure would directly affect the shipboard jobs of 6,000 Americans (GOA, 1994). According to the

USITC report (2002), abolition of the Jones Act would affect about 7,700 maritime workers (full time equivalent; FTE) and about 3,100 FTE workers in the shipbuilding sector. These changes would be associated with responses through the political system.

Another difficulty in reforming the maritime transport policy comes from the fact that the 'losers' are diffuse and not easily organised whereas the 'winners' are few and very well organised. Government support to the maritime industry represents an important share of the revenue of some carriers. In relation to cargo preferences, 118 US-flag vessels participated in moving preferential cargo in 2006. At the same

Table 8.13 US Employment in Water Transport and Related Industries, 2004–09 ('000).

	2004	2005	2006	2007	2008	2009
Transportation	56.4	60.6	62.7	65.5	67.1	63.7
Port Services	91.5	93.9	99.3	100.1	98.6	92.6
Cargo Handling	40.8	42.8	45.6	46.2	45.9	41.5
Other	50.7	51.1	53.7	53.9	52.1	51.1
Shipbuilding and Repair	90.8	92.2	95.1	101	104.8	101.5
Total	238.7	246.7	257.1	266.6	270.5	257.8

Source: MARAD (2011).

time, more than 50% of the revenue of some operators was derived from this trade in preferential cargo (Global Insight, 2009). Whereas the aim of the system was to support the fleet, in fact it only subsidises a very few companies. In relation to the Jones Act, at the end of 2010 only two carriers operated Jones Act container vessels—Horizon Lines Inc. and Matson Navigation Inc.: 67% and 55% of the fleets of these carriers, respectively, were involved in the cabotage market. At the end of 2010 the domestic container transport was a duopoly, with Horizon Lines operating 55% of the fleet and Matson Navigation 45%. Experiences from various studies of regulation indicate that the more concentrated a market, the easier it is to organise and defend a favourable regulation. There are groups in the US which oppose the Jones Act. In 1995 an initiative called the Jones Act Reform Coalition, mostly comprised of shippers, was formed with the objective to repeal, or at least to reform, the regulations on cabotage. The coalition relied on the economic arguments surrounding the inefficiency of the present system. In the same year, by way of reply, some carriers, shipyards and other maritime interests involved in the domestic shipping market formed the Maritime Cabotage Taskforce. Despite the evidence provided, the efforts of the coalition were not seriously considered by Congress (Papavizas and Gardner, 2009).

8.4.2 *The Australian case*

The objective of the current Australian maritime transport reform is to 'revitalise' the industry. There is a substantial benefit to Australia as an island economy in maintaining a viable maritime industry of its own, with the supply of skills to all ancillary areas that this entails. From a security and political point of view, protecting and supporting a strategic industry is a legitimate objective. Economically, it raises two questions: (i) what is the cost of the protection or support and (ii) who bears this cost?

According to the Australian Department of Infrastructure and Transport: "The reform will deliver benefits not only for the Australian shipping industry but for the Australian economy as a whole" (Australian Department of Infrastructure and Transport website, 2012). The first part of the sentence is likely to be true, the Australian shipping industry will benefit from the reform—at least in the short run. However, some doubts could arise concerning the second part of the sentence. Indeed, theoretically, the protection of Australian-flag vessels in the coastal shipping market and (to a lesser extent) the support of the fleet through tax exemptions will lead to a welfare loss for the society as a whole.

Concerning coastal shipping, we can expect an increase in the price of the service. Nevertheless, it is difficult to provide a precise assessment of the cost of the new regulation. The impact and the cost of the measure will depend on the way that the new regulation is applied. Indeed, as explained in the previous section, in the 1990s and 2000s the Conservative and Labor governments applied the same regulation very differently. Thus, the impact of the coastal shipping reform will depend on the number of temporary licences issued. The less the administration issues temporary licences, the more operators of Australian-flag vessels (registered under the General Register) will be protected and the more the domestic shipping services will be expensive. In 2010, crude materials represented 54% of coastal freight, and mineral fuels, lubricants and related materials represented 22.5% (BITRE, 2011). Since these types of products cannot easily be switched to other modes of transport, their prices will increase. In addition, because these products transported by coastal shipping are inputs, the new regulation will affect the competitiveness of the Australian industry as a whole. It is likely to bear on future investment decisions (Deloitte, 2012), and we can expect that jobs saved or created in maritime transport will be lost in other industries.

The impact and the cost of the tax exemption schemes will depend on their ability to attract the registration of new vessels. This will depend on the capacity of tax exemptions to fill the competitive gap between Australian and foreign-flag vessels. Specifically to General Register vessels, the cost will also depend on the number of temporary coastal shipping licences issued—the more Australian-flag vessels registered under the General Register are protected, the more tax exemptions will be granted. Basically, this measure leads to a tax revenue loss for the government. This loss splits into two parts: a direct loss from vessels that were registered in Australia before the reform and a shortfall coming from new vessels that will be attracted by tax exemptions. Considering the size of the Australian fleet, the loss for the government will be minimal. From a trade policy point of view tax exemptions have two advantages. First, the cost of this type of measure is predictable. Second, tax exemptions (such as production subsidies) induce small distortions in markets; hence, they are considered as more efficient than other instruments of protection and support. Eventually, making two tax exemption schemes (i.e. the ITE and the 'refundable tax offset') contingent on training or hiring requirements is a good way not to miss the final policy target.

Contrary to the two other measures, the establishment of the international register is an almost free measure. It only entails a loss for seafarers crewing vessels registered under the new register. Indeed, labour standards of crews working in International Register vessels are set by the International Labour Organization (ILO) while they are set by Australian specific standards in General Register vessels. Considering that Australian standards are higher than the international ones, seafarers that will switch from General to International Register vessels could expect a loss in terms of wage and working conditions—e.g. holidays, rest periods, compensations in case of death or injury, etc.

International registers had contrasting outcomes in economies where they were introduced. According to Sletmo and Holste (1993), they are successful when the economy has a strong cluster of shipping activities. Again, it is too early to know if the initiative will be a success. In general, economies establishing an international register also introduce a tonnage tax to complete the framework.[10]

In the short run, protection and support measures will have a positive impact on the sector—in terms of registration, employment, etc. However, in the long run these impacts are likely to diminish until being negligible. From this point of view, the US example is interesting to consider. Since the competitive gap between Australian and foreign-flag vessels is increasing, the protection of the coastal shipping market and tax exemptions prevent the decline of the fleet for a few years but they could not address the issue in the long run. This trend forces the US to invest even more to maintain protection and fill the increasing competitive gap.

Finally, it is important to underline that the Australian government anticipated a monitoring system to assess the impact of the reform. It enables the provision of transparent information on the costs and benefits of the reform and improves the decision-making process.

8.5 Conclusion

While governments pursue non-economic objectives, there are often a variety of policy tools available for those purposes. Some are more costly than others, and may also be less effective. Regular processes for

---

[10] A tonnage tax is an alternative to corporation tax to which certain shipping companies may elect to have their profits charged, subject to certain conditions.

making policy more transparent and then assessing policy in quantitative terms relative to its objectives can contribute to effective structural reform. The case of shipping policy in the US highlights the value of establishing these processes and also linking them to policy-making processes. Australia introduced such monitoring processes as part of its reform, and it will be interesting to pay attention to the information transmitted and how it is used.

US policy is designed to support the US-flag fleet and American shipyards. The policy which applies to both international and domestic shipping entails costs for the American economy, according to a series of assessments. One objective of the policy is to have a strong fleet that will help to maintain maritime skills within the workforce. Another is for security reasons. These objectives are laudable. Nevertheless, the policy package has incurred significant costs. Furthermore, measures to curb the costs did not reach their goals. In order to cut major sources of inefficiency, and to be in line with the OECD's maritime regulations, the US would have to repeal cargo preferences and abandon its building requirement in cabotage. The cargo preference system represents only a tiny share of the economy's waterborne international trade and this would be a symbolic reform. The building requirement of the Jones Act would lead to much higher gains. Yet despite the economic analysis, the government maintains all these policies in place at a cost to consumers and taxpayers and to the benefit of a limited number of carriers (and even foreign carriers). The difficulties of reform can be explained in part by the operations of well-organised interest groups and the effectiveness of their efforts compared to those who are in favour of reform.

Australia was characterised by fairly open maritime transport markets under liberal commercial regulations. Coastal shipping was the best example of the openness of Australia in comparison with many overseas regimes. Justified by the strategic need of an island nation to sustain a maritime capability, Australia decided to adopt a mix of protectionist measures (preference given to Australian-flag vessels employing Australian seafarers in coastal shipping), supporting measures (tax exemptions), and more liberal measures (the use of the international register). First, the protection of the cabotage market will be costly and even risky for the Australian economy as a whole. Second, tax exemptions are likely to have a limited cost but also a limited impact on the sector—in spite of their interesting conditionality requirements. Third, the establishment of the international register is also likely to have a limited impact since it has not been coupled with the introduction of a tonnage tax, which has besides been discussed in Australia since the early 2000s. Meanwhile, the reform is not likely to attain its own objectives—i.e. check the decline of the Australian fleet and maritime industry and maintain maritime skills in Australia.

The final observation is that the exemption of liner shipping agreements from the competition rules is no longer an issue because the liner shipping market is now highly competitive and price-fixing agreements no longer have binding force. Nevertheless, the registration system could be simplified to maintain transparency but reduce the cost and burden of administration.

Appendix

Table 8. A1 Recent Policy Changes in Maritime Transport in Australia and the US.

Country	Sector	Area of policy change	Associated regulation	Year	Description of change
Australia	Coastal shipping	Regulation	Coastal Trading Act 2012	2012	Establishment of a new license system and removal of the permit system. A preference is given to Australian-flag vessels
Australia	International and domestic shipping	Tax and fiscal policy	Shipping Reform Act 2012	2012	Implementation of four tax incentives to support owners and operators of Australian-flag vessels and employers of Australian seafarers
Australia	International and domestic shipping	Registration	Shipping Registration Amendment Act 2012	2012	Establishment of an international register
Australia	Coastal shipping	Regulation	Review of the Ministerial Guidelines	2009	Clarification of key terms in a concern of transparency and accountability
					Coverage of licensed and permit vessels by legislation that governs workplace relations
				2008	Introduction of a preamble setting new objectives of the government
Australia	Liner shipping	Competition rules	Review of Part X of the Trade Practice Act [a]	2005	Introduction of new provisions on contract's confidentiality

Table 8. A1 (*Continued*).

Country	Sector	Area of policy change	Associated regulation	Year	Description of change
United States	Liner shipping	Regulation and competition	Ocean Shipping Reform Act	1998	Abolition of the obligation for carriers to publish publicly freight rates and service contracts. Shippers and carriers are allowed to engage in confidential agreements

Notes: [a] Renamed the Competition and Consumer Act 2010.

Chapter 9

Road Transport in Thailand[1]

Narong Pomlaktong, Rattana Jongwilaiwan, Prakai Theerawattanakul and Rapee Pholpanich[2]

9.1 Introduction

Many of the important issues in road transport policy development in Thailand are related to the population in Bangkok. Its size has made it difficult to create a well-designed urban public transportation system that meets the needs of the entire population. Related issues are the heavy focus on mega-projects in urban areas and their associated infrastructure, without considering the development of secondary roads, the regulation of passenger vans, and price distortions such as lack of congestion and pollution charges.

We begin this chapter with a review of the situation in Bangkok followed by a discussion of the road transport industry. We then examine particular issues in the passenger markets.

---

[1] This chapter is based on a paper produced with funding from the Asia Pacific Economic Cooperation's Policy Support Unit and material from that paper is reproduced with its permission. Information is taken from The Impacts and Benefits of Structural Reforms in the Transport, Energy and Telecommunications Sectors in APEC Economies APEC#211-SE-01.1. The views expressed in this paper are those of the authors and do not necessarily represent those of the APEC Secretariat or APEC Member Economies.

[2] Thailand Development Research Institute: Narong Pomlaktong (pom@tdri.or.th), Rattana Jongwilaiwan (rattana@tdri.or.th) and Prakai Theerawattanakul (prakai@tdri.or.th).

9.2 Bangkok and Its Impact

The Bangkok metropolitan population is almost eight times as large as Chiang Mai, the second largest city in Thailand. Bangkok is not only the capital city but it has also become the centre of political, financial and business activities. It is estimated that the population of Bangkok and its nearby provinces will reach 13.6 million (over 19% of Thailand's population) by 2017. There are two major consequences:

- Bangkok has become crowded due to the rising number of rural-urban migrants, leading to problems with housing shortages, a lack of basic infrastructure and impact on the public health service; and
- The land price in Bangkok has been soaring due to urban development and speculation.

As a result of the rising land price, rural migrants and the poor live in densely settled and run-down areas, which have turned into slum communities, and many people live in outer areas where the land price is lower than in the urban area. This, in turn, creates pressure for public transport services. The residents have to commute from the suburbs into the metropolitan area of Bangkok, thus contributing to traffic congestion in Bangkok.

Accordingly, the government has implemented a passenger transport policy with the goal of universal service to keep the public transport between the city and outer Bangkok at a low cost. This has led to poor quality public transport. The middle class then prefer to use old cars or motorcycles. Cars and motorcycles are more prevalent than other vehicles in Bangkok: they account for approximately 75% of the total vehicles used (Table 9.1).

9.3 Road Networks

The increase in the use of passenger vehicles has led to more traffic congestion and to air and noise pollution problems. The development of roads has also brought extensive negative social impacts. Examples are the deterioration of urban areas, the rise in slum areas, an increase in ineffective land use and environmental impacts (such as encroachment

Table 9.1 The Number of Vehicles in Use in Bangkok, 1994–2010.

Type of vehicle	1994	2003	2010	Average annual growth (%)	2010	
					Share of fleet in Bangkok (BMA)	Bangkok fleet as % of Thailand's
Car	716,951	1,162704	1,203,764	3.77	36.14%	53.59%
Micro-bus and passenger van	241,120	149,613	104,703	-5.78	3.14%	50.35%
Van and pick up	245,942	583,045	522,511	5.53	15.69%	20.44%
Urban taxi	22,256	63,228	49,224	5.83	1.48%	98.90%
Motor tricycle taxi (TukTuk)	3,645	7,394	4,876	2.10	0.15%	41.94%
Motor-cycle	851,853	857,460	1,299,637	3.06	39.02%	14.46%
Truck	73,145	75,800	61,732	-1.20	1.85%	14.39%
Bus	17,457	26,225	18,831	0.54	0.57%	27.26%
Other	13,220	11,248	65,298	12.09	1.96%	27.30%
Total	2,185,229	2,936,717	3,330,616	3.06	100.00%	22.51%

Sources: World Bank (2007), Department of Land Transport, Land Transport Promotion Center (2010).

on forest areas, carbon dioxide emissions, massive energy consumption and water pollution). Furthermore, the increase in the number of roads and in the volume of traffic has affected the rates of vehicle-related deaths and accidents in Thailand.[3]

[3] The accident rate declined from 1997 onwards as a result of road improvements (e.g. separated and wider road lanes). The 1998–2007 death toll was, however, still about

Due to the increased population and housing density in Bangkok (including in the Bangkok port area), the government launched an extended industrial estate policy, which has resulted in more extensive urbanisation and more sprawl. During three National Economic and Social Development Board (NESDB) plans (1982–96), the government implemented a decentralisation policy and invested heavily in projects such as the Eastern Seaboard Project which consists of the LaemChabang Deep Sea Port and Map Ta Phut Industrial Estateas well as the Northern Region Industrial Estate. Although the plans focused on investment in road transport infrastructure in Bangkok's outskirts, the development also extended to central and eastern regions, but Bangkok and its vicinity[4] was still the centre of development.

With sound economic growth, a rising population and changing lifestyles resulting in increasing demand for goods and services, the urban areas attract the modern retailers including the 'mega markets' (47 of Thailand's 166 mega markets – 28.3% – are located in Bangkok.). The entry of these modern businesses has had mixed effects on traffic issues. On the one hand, there is greater traffic congestion due to their location within inner Bangkok and this is also the case in the other large cities of Thailand. On the other hand, they have brought innovative urban freight logistics management. Regarding the urban logistics management, the modern retail businesses use information and communications technologies to improve the flow of their supply chains and optimise such supply chains by reducing the number of warehouses, centralising inventory and consolidating deliveries through a distribution centre or so-called 'hub and spoke' transport. The freight consolidation approach will lessen the number of vehicles and their trips by using bigger and

127,296 people (average of 12,729 per year). In 2007 the economic and social cost of road accidents to the nation was THB232,855 million (USD7,216 million). This was equivalent to 2.81% of the economy's GDP (Department of Highways (DOH), 2007). Some 1.5 million road crashes occur annually, resulting in about 9,000 disabilities, 210,000 serious injuries and 750,000 slight injuries. The fatality rate on Thailand's roads is about six times that of Japan's and Great Britain's (OECD database).

[4] This area includes Bangkok and and the five adjacent provinces of NakhonPathom, PathumThani, Nonthaburi, SamutPrakan and SamutSakhon.

fewer trucks, reducing the traffic at loading areas, reducing the supply chain cost, optimising inventory management as well as contributing to the improvement in air and noise quality and pollution in the city centre.

In the two decades to 2010 the Thai government has been investing heavily in a road network system. Road transport has become the most significant transport mode for the economy, despite its inefficiency in terms of energy consumption. The government's policy is to encourage the development of road transport since it may lead to the development of land use, and its surrounding estates,[5] which will finally bring about the economic growth needed for many regions. Not surprisingly, Thailand's transport sector of passengers and freight is dominated by roads. Thailand's Department of Land Transport (DLT), a government agency under the Ministry of Transport, is the main regulator for bus and truck transport. Established on 11 September 1941, the DLT is responsible for the regulation of land transport.

9.4 Passenger Transport

Passenger transport in Thailand consists primarily of personal vehicles, including cars, personal pick-ups and motorcycles. For passenger public transport there are four categories of fixed route (Table 9.2) and there are two government agencies that operate bus transport: the Transport Company Ltd and the Bangkok Mass Transit Authority (BMTA), both of which are government enterprises that have the government as the primary shareholder (51%), and private shareholders have 49% (details of characteristics of operators and route categories shown in Table 9.3). The Transport Company is permitted to operate the routes of Categories 2 and 3.

- The BMTA is permitted to operate the routes of Categories 1 and 4 in Bangkok; and

[5] Examples are new communities, new housing, new markets and new office buildings which would be located along the roads.

- Private companies are entitled to operate the routes of Categories 1 and 4 in the provinces, Categories 1 and 4 in Bangkok and Category 3.

The DLT is the government agency authorising public bus regulations:

(1) To supervise and control fixed-route buses to run on a fixed route and on the condition of picking up the passengers at specific locations according to a timetable, to collect bus fares at government-regulated rates and to stop at regulated bus terminals;
(2) To stipulate, improve and revoke the bus route and to renew or withdraw bus operation licences;
(3) To stipulate and improve the condition of vehicle operations, and the number and category of vehicles;
(4) To give the information of fixing the fare rate to the Central Land Transport Control Board (CLTCB) for approval;
(5) To stipulate bus standards, to supervise the service quality of the transport operators to service the passengers, to control bus safety (speed, duration for parking and the age of buses), and to control and to examine the operation of the transport operators, crew and vehicles; and
(6) To encourage and develop a system of mass transit by bus.

Regulating the passenger transport market is done by licensing conditions and pricing.[6]

---

[6] Fixed-route bus regulation in Thailand is implemented under Land Transport Act 1979 (BE2522) by having the Land Transport Policy Committee (LTPC), Central Land Transport Control Board (CLTCB) and Provincial Land Transport Control Board (PLTCB) that have the authority to approve fixed-route buses. The CLTCB has the authority as follows: (1) To stipulate the category of fixed-route bus; (2) Fix the routes, the number of bus operators and the number of vehicles for fixed routes in Bangkok, between provinces and between economies; (3) Fix the rates of transport charges and other service charges; (4) Designate the sites, arrange for or set up and regulate the bus terminal; (5) Specify the types or conditions of vehicles not acceptable for registration; (6) Prescribe the classes or categories of vehicles which must stop or park for picking up

Table 9.2 The Operations of Passenger Bus Transport Services by Government and Private Sectors.

Bus route category	Government and private operations	Maximum private equity permitted
Category 1 in Bangkok Has contiguous routes in the perimeter area by running on the main road in the community area which is crowded by people, business centre, school and university, government agency, etc.	From totally 360 route licences; The BMTA has 89% (of route licences (321) and allows the private sector to be sub-contractor. The Premier Metro Bus Company operates 10% of route licences (35). The Thonburi Bus Service Company has 1% of route licences (4).	The BMTA has the government share (51%) and the private share is 49%. The other two firms are 100% private equity.
Category 2 Route links Bangkok and the provinces.	The Transport Company has all licences and allows the private sector to be sub-contractors.	The Transport Company has the government share (51%). The private share is 49%.
Category 2 Route links Bangkok and the provinces.	The Transport Company has all licences and allows the private sector to be sub-contractors.	The Transport Company has the government share (51%). The private share is 49%.
Category 3 Interprovincial route which links one province with another province and may pass through other provinces.	Many private firms operate in the market under the licensing system.	100% private equity is permitted.

---

and setting down the passengers or for loading and unloading goods at the bus terminal; (7) To stipulate places for parking to pick up the passengers; (8) Lay down measures for the prescribing, permitting, and control of transport business; (9) Carry on other acts as provided in this Act and according to the regulations of the LTPC. The PLTCB has the authority on: (1) Fixing bus routes, number of transport operators, the number of vehicles in the provincial area; (2) Fix the rates of transport charges in the provincial area (the same criteria as prescribed by the CLTCB); (3) Carry on other acts as provided in the land transport regulation according to the LTPC and the CLTCB.

Table 9.2 (Continued)

Category 4 in Bangkok Route mainly on subordinate road and the feeder road to the main road to link with Category 1 in Bangkok	The BMTA operates 76% (113 routes) and allows private sub-contractors. Private firms operate 24% (36 routes).	100% private equity is permitted.
Category 4 in provincial areas Services the community (village, district and city) in the provinces.	Many private firms operate in the market under the licensing system	100% private equity is permitted.

Source: Thailand Development Research Institute (2010b).

Bus Route Category 1 in the provincial area is open for private company operation. Generally, the licence for a fixed route is THB7,000 (USD217) and is valid for seven years; for a non-fixed route it is valid for five years.[7] There is a policy of only 'one licence per one route'. Thus, each route is monopolised in the sense that once the operator is licensed to operate a route for seven years, the licence will be renewed so long as the firm complies with the DLT's conditions. However, there is considerable competition for new route licences through a tendering procedure; a firm is able to apply for a licence to provide service for a fixed term. The firm that receives a licence usually will not operate the whole fleet but will sub-contract some of its operations to other operators without competitive tendering. Routes compete with each other (and some licences have a duplicated route section), which reduces the incentive for dynamic efficiency, introducing new technology or improving services to increase profit.

The situation is different for the Bus Route Category 1 in Bangkok where only three companies have licences for the 360 routes. The BMTA is entitled to operate 321 routes, the Premier Metro Bus Company has 35 concessional routes and the Thonburi Bus Service Company is the airport express bus service provider with four downtown routes.

[7] Non-fixed route bus is a 'for hire' vehicle such as a taxi. The DLT only regulates the licence of drivers and vehicle standard. There is no regulation on entry to the taxi market.

The Transport Company, a government-owned enterprise, is entitled to provide services for all Category 2 routes, and private companies are allowed to be sub-contract operators of the Transport Company. BMTA can also sub-contract its routes to private operators. The companies collect a royalty fee which can be used to subsidise their loss-making routes. The royalty fee collected by the Transport Company is sufficient to subsidise its loss-making routes which enables the government to maintain universal services. The royalty fee collected by the BMTA is inadequate for its loss-making operations: the sub-contractor pays the BMTA THB200–300/vehicle/day (USD6.2–9.2) and THB100–150/vehicle/day (USD3.06–4.60) for air-conditioned buses and non-air-conditioned buses, respectively. Therefore, the government has to subsidise the BMTA by loan guarantees (Table 9.3).

Under this licensing and sub-contracting system, there are approximately 1,256 companies (all but the BMTA and the Transport Company are private companies). The majority of the bus companies are small and family-owned firms: only 0.1% of the private companies have more than 50 buses, around 8% have between two and 48 buses, and around 92%

Table 9.3 Characteristics of the Passenger Transport Industry.

Bus route category	Characteristics of competition
Category 1 in Bangkok	Concessions are granted to three operators. The government-owned BMTA is entitled to grant sub-contracts to private companies and collect the royalty fee. The passenger van is the new mode which serves the niche market.
Category 1 in provincial areas	One licence per one route policy is implemented. The firms which receive the licence are able to grant sub-contracts to the small scale operators. The market is highly competitive between overlapping route operators.
Category 2	Only the government-owned Transport Company is entitled to provide services for all routes and grant sub-contracts to private companies and collect the royalty fee. The passenger van is the new mode which serves the niche market.

Table 9.3 (Continued)

Category 3	One licence per one route policy is implemented, and this is a monopoly. The firms which receive the licence are able to sub-contract to small-scale operators. The market is highly competitive between overlapping route operators. The passenger van is a new competitor in this category.
Category 4 in Bangkok	One licence per one route policy is implemented, and this is a monopoly. The firms which receive the licence are able to sub-contract to small-scale operators. The market is highly competitive between overlapping route operators.
Category 4 in provincial areas	One licence per one route policy is implemented. The firms which receive the licence are able to sub-contract to small-scale operators. The market is highly competitive between overlapping route operators. The passenger van is the new mode which serves the niche market.

own only one bus (National Statistical Office and Thailand Development Research Institute (TDRI) survey). The BMTA and the Transport Company have the biggest market shares (21.02% and 13.77%, respectively) followed by four private firms (Cherd Chai Motor 5.06%, Nakornchai Air 2.11%, ThepSombat 1.74% and Bangkok Transport Company 1.29%). The market share of these six operators accounts for 45% of the sector. Other companies shared the rest of the market as shown for 2007 data in Table 9.4.

The public bus fare is regulated by the Land Transport Committee, the Land Transport Policy Committee, the Central Land Transport Control Board and the Provincial Land Transport Control Board (Table 9.5). Prices are based on a cost-plus formula, including a target rate of return and an allowance for an expected load factor. The fare rate (THB /km) is adjusted according to a change in the diesel price with 25 steps ranging between THB10.07 and THB40.57: for example, if the diesel price increases from THB28/litre to THB30/litre, the 17th fare rate (THB0.56/km) is used to multiply the actual operating vehicle kilometres to provide a new fare for travelling on that section. However, any increase in bus fares is a sensitive political issue in which the final decision is made by the Cabinet (Meakin, 2005).

Table 9.4 Characteristics of the Largest Passenger Transport Firms in Terms of Revenue, 2007.

Firm*	Year established	Government equity (%)	Domestic private equity (%)	Market share of total revenue (%)
Bangkok Mass Transit Authority[1]	1976	51	49	21.02
Transport Company	1930	51	49	13.77
Cherd Chai Motors Sales Company	1980	–	100	5.06
Nakornchai Air Company	1986	–	100	2.11
ThepSombat Company	1978	–	100	1.74
Bangkok Transport Company	1984	–	100	1.29
Others (1,250 registered firms)				55

Source: Based on Department of Business Development (2010) and survey data by Thailand Development Research Institute (accessed on 2 March 2010).
* All firms had not share of foreign equity.
Note: [1] The BMTA was established by Royal Decree BE2519 in August 1976

Table 9.5 Public Bus Pricing.

Bus route category	Pricing
Category 1 in Bangkok Category 4 in Bangkok	The Central Land Transport Control Board regulates the price based on the calculation of the cost/person/trip plus a 15% margin (excluding labour and fuel costs) and fluctuates according to the oil price.
Category 1 in provincial areas Category 4 in provincial areas	The Provincial Land Transport Control Board regulates the price based on the guidelines set by the Central Land Transport Control Board. The price differentiation depends on the cost of operation in each province. The calculation of margin is based on Minimum Retail Rate (MRR) plus 5% (i.e. MRR = 13 + 5, margin = 18%). Price adjustment is used to cope with the oil price fluctuation and is tabulated in 25 steps. Yet the real price adjustment is subject to negotiation between the DLT and bus operators rather than being adjusted automatically.

Table 9.5 (Continued)

Category 2 Category 3	The Central Land Transport Control Board regulates the price adjustment according to the fuel price. The price differentiation depends on the cost of operation in each province. The calculation of margin is based on MRR plus 5% (i.e. MRR = 13 + 5, margin = 18%). Price adjustment is used to cope with the oil price fluctuation and is tabulated in 25 steps. Yet the real price adjustment is subject to negotiation between the DLT and bus operators rather than being adjusted automatically.

Source: Thailand Development Research Institute (2010b).

The bus fare calculation is based on the assumptions of a maximum of seven years of vehicle use and a 70–90% load factor depending on the bus standard.[8] In fact, this cost-plus pricing does not take into account the addition to capacity and changes in load factor due to the issuing of new licences and the entry of passenger vans into the market, as described below. Therefore, regulated bus operations generally have a lower load factor and thus a lower margin of profit than the DLT's assumptions. The bus operators, therefore, have less incentive to invest in their services and the fare regulation process contributes to falling quality. Not only does quality suffer, but maintenance and replacement is also adversely affected. Furthermore, prices cannot respond to demand shifts in the market: as the population increases, so the gap between the quantity supplied and that demanded at the regulated price widens. This provides an incentive for the growth of an unregulated or 'illegal' sector (see below).

Public bus provision is unable to meet the demand for bus services in suburban residential areas. The BMTA could not provide adequate convenient and comfortable services for those commuters who travelled from suburbs to work in the city. Leopairojna and Hanaoka (2006) explain that passenger van services were started by investors who saw benefits in responding to the needs of commuters in suburban Bangkok. The number of vans grew steadily from the mid-1980s to 1996.

[8] The standard depends on many criteria such as the age of the bus and the efficiency of its mechanical systems.

However, these vans operated outside the regulatory system and were technically illegal. In 1984 the DLT promulgated that operating vans as bus-like services was illegal, and the Ministry of Transport introduced a policy to eliminate the van services in 1986.

The van operators can charge fares that cover their costs. These fares are usually higher than those of the regulated companies (see below). They also offer a different service quality (Table 9.6). Illegal vans provide alternative services on the profit-making routes. They offer shorter, faster routes with guaranteed seats and a door-to-door service. They are supposed to operate between passenger van terminals (in housing estates, markets or community centres) and they are not supposed to pick up passengers at bus stops (although in practice they do so). Although passenger van operations cause lower revenues for the normal bus services and the van drivers were often criticised as reckless and undisciplined, they can bridge the gap between the lack of public air-conditioned buses and the increasing demand from Bangkok-vicinity commuters. Leopairojna and Hanaoka (2006) found that passengers who travelled by van valued the shorter travel times and comfort from a guaranteed seat. The downsides according to those who travelled by bus were the narrower space and the higher fares.

Table 9.6 Advantages of Vans Over Buses by Category.

Bus route category	Advantages of vans over buses
Category 1 in Bangkok Has contiguous routes in the perimeter area by running on the main road in the community area which is crowded by people, business centre, school and university, government agency, etc.	Passenger vans have to pick up passengers only at origins and drop off them at bus stops along routes or at destinations. In fact, they undercut the bus operators since they operate on more profitable routes (cutting routes*), pick up and drop off passengers at the bus stops, residential areas, markets, and elsewhere in the community (more like a door-to-door service).

Table 9.6 (Continued)

Category 2 Route links Bangkok and the provinces. Category 3 Interprovincial route which links one province with another province and may pass through other provinces.	Buses of the Transport Company and its sub-contractors are required to pick up passengers at official bus terminals (only one or few terminals in a province). However, passenger van terminals are usually located in residential areas (in housing estates, markets or community centres) which are not proclaimed officially. They also provide a door-to-door service by charging extra, which is prohibited.

Note: * Cutting routes were the routes that vans could drive through which were the same as the buses used.

Leopairojna and Hanaoka (2006) report that average trip lengths for the vans were less than for buses. They say that the gap between van fares and bus fares increased with trip length. Bus fares tend to be flatter over long distances, so competition from vans on shorter routes undermined the ability of buses to cross-subsidise longer routes (to cater for low-income households living further from the city centre) from shorter ones. The study reports that the incumbent operators such as BMTA and its sub-contractors complained to the DLT. They identify research that showed a link between these complaints and the new policy on vans introduced in 1999. At that time, only BMTA was granted licences to operate passenger van services, but it was able to sub-contract this work to van drivers. The licences were allocated on the existing routes of the vans between important locations in the city and suburbs with distances of 8–56km. The services had to comply with DLT standards, have insurance for passengers and pay fees to BMTA. Maximum fares were also regulated. The quota of legal vans was set according to the number of van drivers who applied for a BMTA sub-contract and then was adjusted according to passenger demand. The van service was established originally by investors who constructed the van terminals and set up the services. Establishing the terminals required the "support from influential figures (who were) paid … in return" (Leopairojna and Hanaoka, 2006, p. 6). According to some passenger van operators, the drivers made an unofficial payment to the police who enforce the transport laws. The van drivers also had to be 'members' of the terminals for which they paid a membership fee. They report that in 1998 these fees were THB100,000 for entry and THB4,000/month. After the vans were legalised the fees rose to THB250,000 and THB5,000/month. This may reflect the expectation that the legalisation process might actually make it more difficult to enter the market.

Although the van fare in the Bangkok Metropolitan Region is more expensive than for the air-conditioned buses (Table 9.7), the number of legal vans has increased from a few hundred in 1995 to 5,555 in 2004 and 6,582 in 2008 (Table 9.8). However illegal vans continued to be operated. Illegal vans do not have to comply with the DLT's conditions and can operate on disallowed (profit-making) routes in peak hour, for example. Furthermore, they can charge more for offering extra services such as door-to-door and dropping passengers off in small Soi (lanes). Economies in vehicle size in passenger transport are also argued to be insignificant (Gwilliam, 2008). Leopairojna and Hanaoka (2006) report that a Senatorial Subcommittee found there were 8,000–9,000 vans in Bangkok in 2001.

Table 9.7 Characteristics of Urban Public Transport Modes in the Bangkok Metropolitan Region (Bus Route Category 1), September 2008.

Transport mode	Fare (THB/ride)
1. Non-air-conditioned bus	7
2. Air-conditioned bus	Regular bus: 11–19 Euro I and Euro II: 12–24
3. Micro bus	20–40
4.Mini bus (non-air-conditioned)	6.50
5. Van (legal)	10–45

Source: Department of Land Transport, Land Transport Promotion Center (2010).

Table 9.8 Number of Passenger Vans in the Bangkok Metropolitan Region (Bus Route Category 1).

	Before legalisation	After legalisation		
Year	*1995*	*1999–2002*	*2004*	*2008*[3]
Quota limit	n.a.	4,789–8,505 (115 routes)	3,964–5,574 (144 routes)	6,950 (127 routes)
Legal vans	Approx. 300	5,566	5,555	6,582
Illegal vans		unknown	3,690	unknown

Source: Leopairojna and Hanaoka (2006); APEIS (2004); BMTA (2010).

In 2009 the DLT legalised another 6,400 passenger vans to provide services in 60 routes from Bangkok to other provinces (Bus route Category 2). According to the DLT regulation, van route Categories 2 and 3 offer the same price as normal air-conditioned buses for the same section. However, passengers are willing to pay extra because the vans' size means they can provide a door-to-door service. These vans have pick-up and drop-off points in the city centre while the large buses (Bus Route Categories 2 and 3) must stop at the regulated bus terminals.

9.5 Conclusion

In Thailand's urban bus markets, attempts to provide a universal service in a regulated environment have created incentives for entry in substitute but unregulated markets. Since the existing regulation did not meet the market demand, there was a gap between the demand and the supply of legal bus services. This gap has been filled by the entry of illegal vans. Passengers have benefited from the wider options available.

The legalisation of passenger vans is a good lesson in basing regulatory reform on market-driven demand. The DLT, therefore, has a policy to legalise the operation of the vans. However, a large number of vans apparently continue to operate illegally which affects the number of passengers buying tickets on a legal route, particularly air-conditioned bus routes.

Thus the entry of passenger vans has challenged the capacity of the incumbents in the regulated markets to meet their service obligations. The significance of the impact of the growth of the unregulated sector is exaggerated in the absence of both pricing for traffic congestion and measures to capture other externalities associated with urban passenger transport systems.

Chapter 10

China's Services Policy Reform Before and After the Global Financial Crisis

Fan Ying

10.1 Introduction[1]

The services sector has become the most dynamic sector in China. According to the National Bureau of Statistics, its share of GDP grew from 23.9% in 1978 to 43.0% in 2010, while its share of employment grew from 12.2% to 34.1% between 1978 and 2009. Nevertheless, its relative significance still lags behind that in other economies — in 2007 the sector contributed 72% of GDP in industrialised economics and 54% of GDP in developing countries, with an average share of 69% in world GDP. Even in low income countries, the sector frequently contributes more than 50% of GDP. In this respect, China is still lagging behind other countries.

The services sector has also been the fastest growing segment of China's trade. Services exports grew at an average annual rate of 18% between 1990 and 2000 and 17% between 2000 and 2009. Services imports grew at 24% between 1990 and 2000 and 18% between 2000 and 2009. The growth of China's services trade exceeded world average growth between 1990 and 2009. As a result, China's position in world services trade increased from 12th to 5th in exports and from 10th to 4th in

[1] The author is grateful to John Whalley, Christopher Findlay, Philippa Dee and Xiaopeng Yin for their constructive comments. This paper is part of the research work under the International Development Research Centre/Centre for International Governance Innovation Project 'Young China Scholars Research and Policy Engagement Network'.

imports between 2001 and 2009. China has become one of the top five trading nations in services.

However, China's services trade is still much smaller than its goods trade, and it has long been in deficit. The share of services in total trade in China was below 10% between 1990 and 2009, whereas the world average was around 20%. China's services trade deficit was USD11.56 billion in 2008, and grew to USD29.6 billion in 2009, at the height of the global financial crisis. The low share of services in China's total trade reflects the bias in favour of merchandise manufacturing and heavy industries in China's development and trade, and is consistent with the low share of services in its GDP.

Temporary measures alone are not sufficient to correct imbalances in China's pattern of economic growth and development, which are macroeconomic and structural in nature. The global financial crisis has reinforced China's intention to undertake the longer-term structural reforms needed to diversify the economic and trade structure. The Chinese government regards the accelerated development of the services sector as an important way to promote the rationalisation of economic structure, to transform economic development and foreign trade and to create job opportunities. Services play a key role in competitiveness and trade facilitation. The potential gains from more open services trade are greater than those from liberalising goods. If sufficiently competitive, the services sector also has the potential in the long run to generate new jobs for surplus labour currently located in China's rural areas.

The next section surveys the impact of the global financial crisis on China's services trade. The following sections examine the current openness of China's services sector to global markets, both as a result of accession to the World Trade Organization (WTO) and from additional autonomous liberalisation. The subsequent section outlines the opportunities for, and challenges to, further services trade liberalisation as part of the long-term restructuring necessary for the Chinese economy. It also offers possible directions for further services trade policy reform.

10.2 Impacts of the Global Financial Crisis on China's Trade in Services

The global financial crisis from 2008 impacted international trade in two ways. On the financial side, the crisis directly impaired the environment for trade financing with tougher conditions, reduced credit lines and delayed trade settlement, thus adversely affecting international trade. On the real side, the financial crisis caused substantial depreciation in the value of financial assets, and the rapid reduction of wealth triggered a steep decline in investment and consumption, resulting in reduced demand for imports. The services sector was directly affected by the financial crisis because financing itself falls in the category of services, and trade in services by nature is highly conditional on the operation of the real economy. The downturn in demand for investment and consumption not only affected merchandise imports and exports, but also directly affected the demand for services.

During the financial crisis, China's trade in services fell noticeably. Figure 10.1 shows the impact of the crisis on the growth rates of China's services exports and imports. The growth of services exports turned negative in 2009, while the growth of services imports fell significantly, but still remained (barely) positive. The services trade deficit in 2009 increased by 150%.

Exports of traditional services were particularly adversely affected by the financial crisis, while services with high added value were less affected. A total of seven sectors showed negative export growth rates in 2009 — transportation, travel, communications, construction, royalties and licence fees, film and audiovisual services, and 'other' business services. Five sectors maintained positive export growth — insurance, financial services, computer and information services, consulting services, and advertising and public opinion polling. In the first half of 2010, almost all services sectors except communications services returned to rapid export growth.

On the import side, five sectors showed negative growth rates in 2009 — transportation, construction, insurance, consulting services and 'other' business services. Seven sectors maintained positive growth in 2009 — travel, construction, financial services, computer and information services, royalties and licence fees, advertising and public opinion polling, and film and audiovisual services. In the first half of 2010, almost all the services sectors except 'other' business services returned to rapid import growth.

In 2010, China's services trade recovered. According to balance of payments statistics by the State Administration of Foreign Exchange (SAFE), services exports increased by 32% and imports by 22% over the year before, while the services trade deficit declined by 43%. Thus the recovery of China's services trade has followed a V-curve, as seen in Figure 10.1, and the magnitude of the impact on services was felt to be not very large. There are several possible explanations.

- China's large stimulus package included vigorous and timely fiscal and monetary stimuli, which helped China's growth to recover following a large increase in unemployment from the initial shock to world trade. China's successful domestic stimulus not only helped to stimulate the domestic economy but also boosted Chinese demand for services imports. China was the only leading trading economy to maintain positive growth of services imports in 2009.
- Services trade is more robust than goods trade because there is less cyclical demand and less dependence on external finance.
- China's services sector is not totally integrated with the global market at present — services account for only about 10% of total trade, and most Chinese services firms are not involved in services trade.

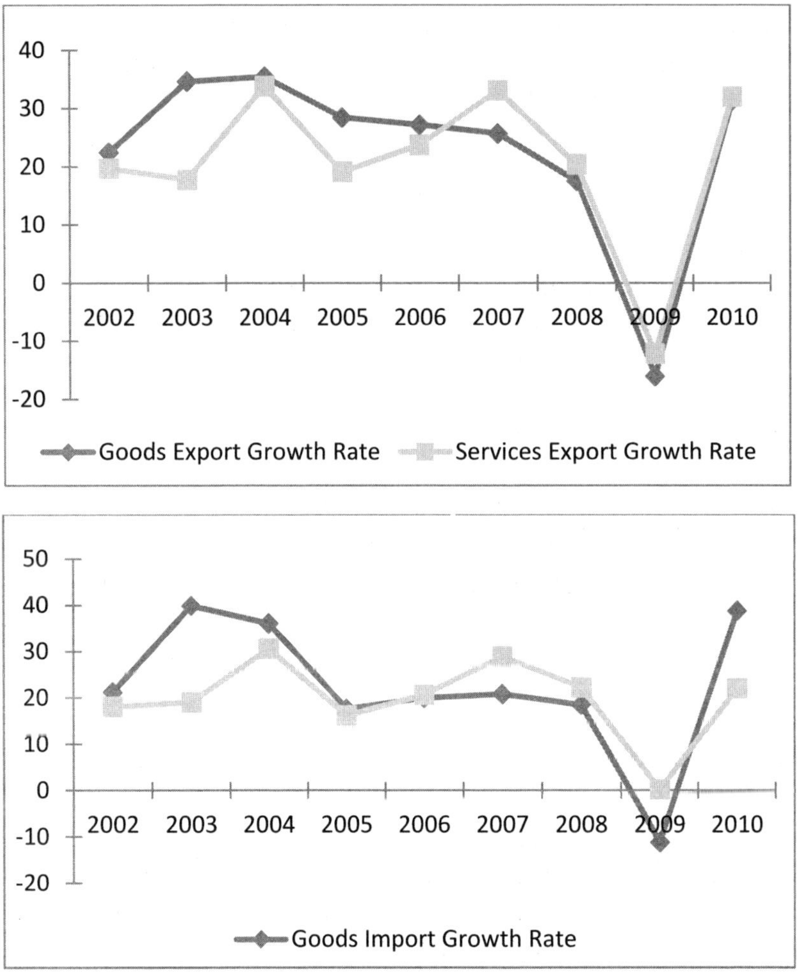

Figure 10.1 China's Goods and Services Trade Growth Rate, 2002–2010 (%). ***Source:*** MOC (2010) 'China Trade in Services Report 2010', Beijing: China Commerce and Trade Press; SAFE (2010) '2009 Statistical Bulletin of China's Outward Foreign Direct Investment', Beijing: National Bureau of Statistics, State Administration of Foreign Exchange, Ministry of Commerce.

10.3 The Structure of China's Services Trade

The global financial crisis did not affect China's services trade composition greatly in the short run (Table 10.1). On the export side, the share of China's traditional services sectors such as transport and tourism declined slightly, while other emerging services sectors such as insurance, computer and information services, and consulting grew in proportion. On the import side, traditional services maintained their dominance.

Not all services sectors run a trade deficit. Four sectors did so in 2008 — transportation, insurance, financial services, and royalties and licence fees. In 2009, the number had grown to six — transportation, travel, insurance, financial services, royalties and licence fees, and film and audiovisual services. Construction and some emerging sectors such as computer and information services, consultancy services and 'other' business services ran trade surpluses in both years.

Table 10.1 Sectoral Composition of China's Services Trade, 2007–2010(%).

Year	Transport and Tourism		All other sectors	
	Exports	Imports	Exports	Imports
2007	56.3	56.5	43.7	43.5
2008	54.1	54.8	45.9	45.2
2009	49.2	57.1	50.8	42.9
2010	47.0	61.5	53.0	38.5

Source: MOC (2010) 'China Trade in Services Report 2010', Beijing: China Commerce and Trade Press.

The services trade data presented so far are taken from balance of payments statistics. This does not capture services traded via commercial presence (mode 3). Such trade is significant owing to the opening up of trade and investment in services (see Figure 10.2).

In 2008, 14,582 foreign-invested enterprises were newly established in China's services sector, accounting for 53.0% of the total number of newly established foreign-invested enterprises in China that year. The actual utilisation of foreign investment in services amounted to USD54.94 billion, or 50.7% of the total. While the number of newly established foreign-invested enterprises in services was down 9.8% on the year before, their utilisation of foreign investment was up by 3.5%.

At the height of the global financial crisis in 2009, the number of newly established foreign-invested enterprises in the services sector was down to 11,461, or 48.9% of the total. The actual utilisation of foreign investment in services amounted to USD37.87 billion, accounting for 42.1% of the total foreign direct investment (FDI) in 2009.

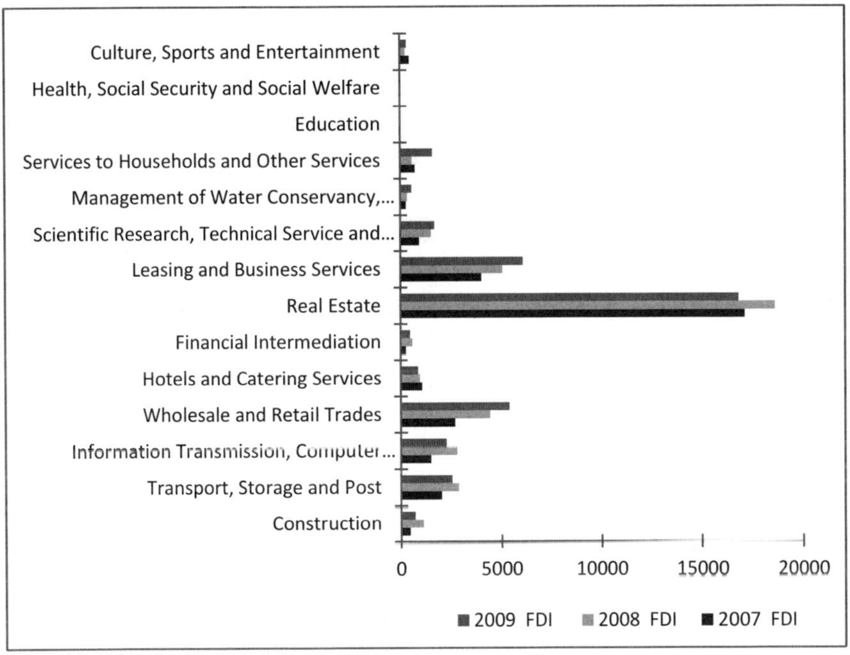

Figure 10.2 Sectoral Composition of China's Inward FDI in Services, 2007–2009 ($US million).
Source: SAFE (2010) '2009 Statistical Bulletin of China's Outward Foreign Direct Investment', Beijing: National Bureau of Statistics, State Administration of Foreign Exchange, Ministry of Commerce.

China's outward FDI in services is also significant. In 2008, this amounted to USD46.1 billion, up 136% over 2007 and accounting for 82.5% of China's total outward FDI. The sectoral composition is shown in Figure 10.3. In 2009, China's outward FDI in services sector fell to USD39.77 billion, or 70.4% of the total outward FDI.

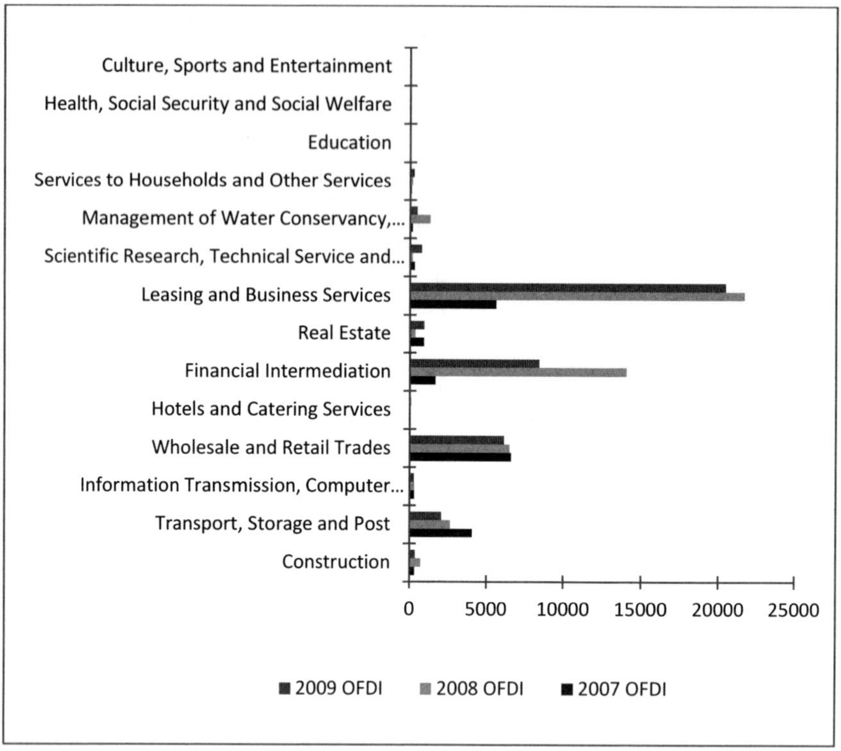

Figure 10.3 Sectoral Composition of China's Outward FDI in Services, 2007–2009($US million).
Source: SAFE (2010) '2009 Statistical Bulletin of China's Outward Foreign Direct Investment', Beijing: National Bureau of Statistics, State Administration of Foreign Exchange, Ministry of Commerce.

Hong Kong, the United States, European Union, Japan and ASEAN are the top five services trading partners of China. The trade value (sum of services imports and exports) of these five partners with China accounted for 68.2% of China's total services trade in 2008. The value of cross-border trade with these partners has fluctuated but the basic trade structure was not changed post-crisis.

Hong Kong is both the leading market for exports and source of imports for China in services trade. The sum of China's services imports and exports with Hong Kong amounted to USD68.18 billion in 2008, accounting for 22.4% of total services trade. The United States was the second largest trading partner with 15.2% of total services trade, the

European Union was third with 14.7%, Japan was fourth with 8.2% and ASEAN was fifth with 7.7%.

Despite having a large overall trade deficit in services in 2008, China ran a trade surplus of USD15.62 billion with Hong Kong. Australia was the largest trading partner with whom China ran a trade deficit in services, at USD5.52 billion. Other bilateral services trade deficits were USD3.86 billion with Japan, USD2.68 billion with South Korea and USD0.73 billion with the United States.

In 2009, China's services imports and exports were still concentrated with the same five partners. Exports to these major trading partners fell, but imports remained on the same scale as in the previous year. Hong Kong retained the largest bilateral trade surplus in 2009, at USD10.88 billion. The United States became the leading source of bilateral deficit, at USD7.46 billion.

Hong Kong and the European Union were China's main destinations for outward FDI in services. In 2009, China's outward FDI to Hong Kong's service sector was USD28.92 billion, accounting for 72.7% of China's total outward FDI in services. China's outward FDI to the European Union services sector was USD26.7 billion, accounting for 6.7% of China's services total.

10.4 China's Services Trade Policy

10.4.1 *GATS commitments*

China made relatively broad services trade commitments upon its accession to the WTO as a developing country. The coverage of its commitments under the General Agreement on Trade in Services (GATS) is close to that in the developed countries, with commitments covering 93 of the 160 GATS services categories. China has made commitments in all sectors except research and development, postal services, health and social services, and recreational services.

The breakdown of the commitments by mode of service delivery varies from sector to sector. Sectors committed are more often 'unbound' (i.e. with no commitments) under mode 1 (cross-border supply) than under other modes, while commitments under mode 2 (consumption abroad) tend to be unrestricted. A relatively high number of limitations tend to be attached to commitments under mode 3 (commercial presence) and mode 4 (movement of natural persons). Examples of limitations under mode 3 included foreign equity limits, restrictions on the type of legal entity and limitations on the number of suppliers. Mode 4 commitments are usually set out in the horizontal section of the Schedule.

10.4.2 *Subsequent liberalisation*

Since WTO accession, the Chinese government has established new rules and regulations to promote further opening up of its service sectors. These laws and regulations not only embody China's WTO commitments but also incorporate measures of autonomous liberalisation, demonstrating China's positive stand towards opening up its trade in services. The rules and regulations include: Regulation on Administration of Commercial Franchise; Detailed Rules for the Implementation of the Regulations on the Administration of Foreign-funded Banks of the People's Republic of China; Measures for the Information Disclosure of Commercial Banks; Measures for the Administration of Trust Companies; Measures for the Administration of Finance Leasing Companies; Measures for the Overseas Investment with Insurance Funds; Administrative Measures for Insurance Licences; and Measures for the Administration of Foreign Stock Exchanges' Representative Offices in China.

China has also made its trade regime more transparent, by introducing the Regulation on Open Government Information, which entered into force on 1 May 2008. In addition, the China Foreign Economic and Trade Gazette is a designated publication of the Chinese government to make trade-related laws and regulations public. It had published more than 3,300 laws, regulations and specific measures by the end of 2007.

Prior to China's WTO accession, foreign companies in many services sectors did not have an unqualified right to apply for a licence to establish or otherwise provide services in China. They could only apply for a licence if they first received an invitation from the relevant Chinese regulatory authorities, and even then the decision-making process lacked transparency and was subject to inordinate delay and discretion. In its accession agreement, China committed to licensing procedures that were streamlined, transparent and more predictable. China's Services Schedule called for the implementation of relatively minor additional commitments by 11 December 2007, in areas such as taxation services, management consulting services, travel and tourism services, and rail transport services. These commitments are the last ones scheduled to be phased in pursuant to China's scheduled commitments.

Since China's entry to WTO, China has gradually lifted the restrictions on foreign investment in services relating to equity, geographic location, and scope of business. Services sectors have become more open, attracting more foreign investment and a further expansion of commercial presence in China.

China has established new domestic laws and regulations to facilitate the further opening up of its service sectors. These include the Property Law, Enterprise Income Tax Law, Anti-Monopoly Law and Law on Enterprise Bankruptcy. These laws contribute to a more rule-based, predictable business environment, which is particularly important for foreign investors. China has thus been moving recently towards establishing a more level playing field for domestic and foreign investors.

10.4.3 *The restrictiveness of China's services trade*

China's services commitments at accession were recognised for their breadth and significance, and China has continued to open its services markets since. However, eight years after China's WTO entry, there are still some areas for improvement, including access by foreign companies; more transparency in China's domestic regulations; smoother administrative procedures, especially in licensing procedures; capital requirements for financial institutions; clearer guidelines on access to the telecommunications industry for joint ventures; and rules governing domestic distribution of foreign products.

In China, some services sectors are still subject to a certain degree of state control and lack competition. Several services sectors continue to be characterised by state involvement and the level of state interference in the economy is still noticeable, distorting market functioning. There are restrictions on foreign investment and private-sector activities in several of the individual sectors including banking, insurance, securities, asset management, and telecommunications services.

China's regulations have generated significant concerns with regard to the implementation of important commitments in some sectors. Capital requirements that are excessive and often apparently discriminatory by international norms continue to restrict market entry for foreign suppliers in sectors such as banking, securities, asset management, telecommunications and construction services. In addition, in banking, insurance and legal services, branching restrictions and related practices limit market access for foreign suppliers. In other sectors, particularly construction services, problematic measures appear to be taking away previously acquired market access rights.

National treatment concerns remain, particularly in the banking and insurance sectors. Particularly in insurance services, the licensing process is characterised by lengthy delays. China still does not allow foreign credit card companies and other suppliers to provide electronic payments processing and related services for domestic currency transactions in China.

Restrictions on trade in services impose costs, limit domestic and international competition, decrease efficiency and permit incumbent services suppliers to charge prices above those in a competitive market. Restrictions on services trade usually take the form of government regulation. Administrative regulation includes reporting, information and application procedures and burdens on start-ups. Both economy-wide and sector-specific administrative requirements can restrict domestic market mechanisms and curb international transactions. Economic regulation includes all other domestic regulatory provisions affecting product market competition such as state control and legal barriers to competition.

Borchert, Gootiiz and Mattoo (2012) calculated the overall restrictiveness of services trade policies of 56 countries in 2005. China belongs to the group of countries whose restrictiveness is above trend, and it has more restrictive services policies than most developed countries and some underdeveloped countries such as Cambodia, Nigeria and Mongolia. China's restrictiveness is lower than that of other Asian economies such as India, Indonesia, Thailand and the Philippines.

Further reductions in China's services barriers are essential to China's integration into the global economy and continued economic development. China's implementation of its WTO commitments in services already benefits China, but there is still a range of impediments to the growth of China's services sector, as well as services trade and foreign investment. China should remove these constraints in the future to realise the full potential economic benefits of trade and investment in services. China is also in a position to be more transparent about its regulating and trading regime. Greater transparency is in China's own interest, since this would preclude any unnecessary misunderstanding of its trade practices and measures, and foster better decision-making in China.

10.5 China's Post-crisis Services Trade Policy — Opportunities and Challenges

Most of the policies aimed at countering the effects of the global financial crisis were not specific to services. However, some were designed to stimulate and rebalance the economy, to increase consumer spending, to restructure and subsidise certain industries, and to boost incomes for farmers and rural poor. Examples were as follows.

- China's two-year RMB4 trillion (USD586 billion) stimulus package (equivalent to 13.3% of China's 2008 GDP) provided stimulus to services sectors including public transport infrastructure, rural infrastructure, environmental projects, technological innovation, health and education.
- In order to rely less on the manufacturing sector, the Chinese government has relaxed FDI restrictions on some services sectors, notably in telecommunication and tourism, and the central government has been delegating to local governments licensing

authority for the establishment and modification of operations of 'encouraged' foreign-invested enterprises (FIEs) and certain selected sectors, as well as certain types of FIEs, such as foreign invested joint-stock companies.

- China's central bank loosened monetary policy and provided directives to commercial banks for providing financing and funding to help firms invest overseas, including outward FDI in services sectors.
- China has continued to review, revise or amend its trade and related laws including the Anti-Monopoly Law (effective 1 August 2008), China's first comprehensive competition law and the Patent Law (effective 1 October 2009), which strengthened patent protection by increasing penalties against infringement. China has also reformed its tax system to render it more neutral. In particular, this involved the unification of enterprise income tax rates for all companies (domestic and foreign), and the transformation of value added tax (VAT) from a production-based tax to a consumption-based one.

10.5.1 *Opportunities*

The global financial crisis has generated challenges but also provided opportunities for China.

One opportunity is to be a major beneficiary of world trade in services. With the continued rise of world services trade, new trading opportunities, as well as new services, are being created by the rapid improvement in communications and large reductions in costs. Distance-related barriers that had previously disadvantaged suppliers and users in remote locations are becoming less relevant. Attitudes of governments and expectations of citizens are also changing. In many parts of the world, more services are being opened up to private commercial participation. The combination of technological and regulatory innovations has enhanced the 'tradability' of services and thus created new opportunities for all economies, including China.

China's transformation from a 'manufacturing industry-oriented economy' to a 'service-oriented economy' needs the further expansion of trade in services. The global financial crisis was a blow to foreign trade, and has prompted China to rethink its development strategies. China is facing the choice between growth driven by goods exports and growth driven by domestic demand. The need to find new and sustainable sources of growth in China is becoming crucial. For the welfare of the majority of people, China needs to resist protectionism and become more, not less, integrated into the global economy to continue to reap the benefits of global knowledge, technologies and innovation. Trade in services plays a special role in knowledge transfer and exchange. It can enable China to benefit from international research, contracts, use of new equipment that incorporates newer technology, and exchange of knowledge and experience. Knowledge transfers have been helped through trade in services in telecommunications, retailing, banking, and information technology training.

There is a large domestic services market in China generated by China's urbanisation and industrialisation. Urbanisation has become an important driving force to China's economic growth and social development. In the next ten years, China will meet the great historical turning point where urban population exceeds that in the rural areas. Emerging manufacturing and service industries will spread inland from the coastal areas, and thousands of cities will prosper. This will generate huge market demands for both goods and services and drive the long-term rapid development of China's economy. With the acceleration of China's industrialisation and urbanisation process, the market demand for services imports will grow rapidly.

China can sustain services-led growth because there is a great deal of room for catch-up and convergence. The globalisation of services provides opportunities for China to find niches beyond manufacturing where China can specialise, scale up, and grow. Comparative advantage can just as easily be in services as in manufacturing or agriculture. China's value added in services accounts for 40% of GDP, yet services only account for 11% of China's external trade. Taking advantage of this potential will require two sets of actions: one is a more neutral policy and incentives environment; another is supportive investments in the services sector.

In April 2010, the Ministry of Commerce released its 'China's Foreign Trade Development Strategy in the Post-Crisis Era' report, which stated clearly the goal of making the country a strong trading power by 2030. Specific targets for the year 2020 were a total trade value of USD5.3 trillion, breaking down to USD4.3 trillion in goods and USD1 trillion in services. China is expected to play a leading role in setting up international trade rules.

Liberalisation of trade in services will help to generate economic growth by creating bigger markets, which stimulate technology and encourage lower costs. Services liberalisation is strategically important for technology transfer and development. Producer services such as telecommunications, banking, insurance, construction and transport help to shape overall economic performance. FDI in services sectors typically brings with it new skills and technologies that spill over into the wider economy in various ways. Trade liberalisation can help increase the supply of services by offering an environment conducive to attracting foreign investment and by lowering cost through competition in China. The gains from more investment and greater domestic competition also go with building greater export competitiveness in both goods and services.

10.5.2 *Challenges*

There remain very substantial barriers to trade and investment in services and regulations impeding both domestic and foreign services suppliers in China. Not all of these are discriminatory but may stem from barriers to entry that apply to domestic and foreign suppliers equally. Integration for services has remained slow outside a few specific sectors such as telecommunications, road and air transport, and financial services. There are still significant restrictions, such as foreign participation limits, on foreign investment and private sector activities in some services sectors. In banking, stringent qualification requirements remain, and there are restrictions on the business scope of foreign banks. Nevertheless, the stock market in China has continued to develop during the period under review, and the process of converting shares of state-owned enterprises to be traded in the market has progressed.

Opening services markets can lead to long-term gains, but it is neither adjustment nor risk free in the short term. Moving towards a more competitive environment may take time and may impose significant burdens as the adjustment takes place. Services sectors that previously enjoyed heavy protection will lobby strongly against further trade liberalisation. Badly designed reforms may unnecessarily complicate the adjustment process, or even more seriously lead to monopoly rents being transferred to private, perhaps foreign, owners.

How to avoid unnecessary frictions and ensure the efficiency and viability of more open, market-oriented service regimes is a big problem facing the Chinese government. Instability might ensue if liberalisation of the services sector is not accompanied by adequate prudential supervision and regulation. The absence of well-designed universal service requirements on new services actors, especially private actors in the market, could also result in reduced access to services for vulnerable groups or geographically remote regions. How to design an institutional framework that will favour structural reform, while enhancing social dialogue and public understanding and acceptance of reform measures, is a big challenge.

How to harmonise the services trade-related policies of different regulators and coordinate services trade reforms across different policy areas is an additional problem facing China. The Ministry of Commerce regulates both domestic and foreign trade and works to attract foreign investment and is also the supervisory body of all distribution services in China. The Ministry set up a Department of Trade in Services in 2006, which is responsible for trade promotion in services. However, in China, there are many administrations responsible for the regulation of different services sub-sectors. For communications services, the national telecommunications regulatory authority is the Ministry of Industry and Information Technology. It has a nation-wide regulatory system comprising provincial branches called Provincial Telecommunications Administrations, which have regulatory functions in their respective provinces. The other two regulatory agencies in telecommunications are the State Administration of Radio, Film and TV and the National

Development and Reform Commission. The former is responsible for awarding licences for broadcasting and managing censorship of content. The latter is responsible for regulating basic telecommunication prices and interconnection charges.

For financial services, the situation is similarly complex. The China Banking Regulatory Commission is the main regulator of the banking sector along with People's Bank of China (the central bank) and the State Administration of Foreign Exchange. China's insurance regulator, the China Insurance Regulatory Commission, is responsible for the approval of operating licences. The China Securities Regulatory Commission is responsible for the regulation of the securities sector. How to harmonise the policies made by these regulators involved in services is a very difficult problem.

There is also a problem of harmonising the conflicting interests of the central and local governments in services trade policy-making. China is a country of multiple jurisdictions and each jurisdiction is more interested in its local development than the overall development of the country. This situation has led to the problem of contradictory decision-making and local protectionism. Each region has its own unique trade and investment barriers, and interpretation of regulations differs. It is not easy to balance the relationship between local community outcomes and the national long-term strategy. Future services policy reforms should encourage local authorities to focus on promoting the services sectors, consistent with the principles of sustainable development.

It is difficult for Chinese regulators to make an efficient framework of regulation that achieves legitimate domestic regulatory objectives while keeping regulatory burdens on enterprises to the necessary minimum, fostering competition and helping ensure genuine market openness in services. Chinese regulators' knowledge of regulation is sector specific. Often the focus of regulators is not on international trade or investment or on supporting the development of competition. The policy adjustment challenge faced by China differs both in nature and extent from that faced by the advanced industrialised economies. So too, therefore, does the required policy mix and the ability to implement policies.

10.5.3 *Possible future directions for services trade policy reform*

Effective policy system linkages in services need to be established. The cross-sector liaison mechanisms for policy coordination need to be strengthened. A liaison mechanism between the government and enterprises also needs to be established. Industrial associations for trade in services need to be encouraged throughout the country. A coordinating mechanism and a working system for promotion of trade in services can be formed by way of close cooperation between different sectors and tight liaison between the government and enterprises.

Trade promotion policy needs to focus on expanding exports of services by key sectors. This can be done by offering sector-specific Exports Guidance Catalogues. Trade promotion organisations in services can be developed to serve the enterprises' trade and investment strategies. Independent services export brands can be encouraged. Thereby a number of enterprises with core competencies in trade in services can be created.

Producer services, including transportation, telecommunications, logistics, distribution and financial services, are prerequisites to ensure and sustain economic growth. Trade in services has the advantage of being high in added value, and low in energy consumption and pollution. By developing trade in producer services, the quality of the growth of trade in goods can be upgraded. The aim is to achieve coordinated development between trade in goods and trade in services through the mutual complementary effects between the two.

Trade or investment barriers in services can be further reduced. These barriers include both discriminatory barriers against foreign services providers and domestic regulation that applies to all firms whatever their nationality. Restrictions on inward FDI, entry (ownership) limitations and operating requirements would have effects on foreign services providers. There is a positive relationship between FDI in services and the performance of domestic firms in services. Reducing barriers to trade and investment in services helps improve the productivity and competitiveness of services firms. China should take steps to further open services markets. It should open services markets by improving general services regulation and ensuring that regulations do not impede market access. It should also remove the discriminatory policies to increase both export and import opportunities for services providers.

China should accelerate the reform of its tax system to shore up the transition of its economic growth pattern from goods orientation to services orientation. The Chinese government will replace the sales tax with a VAT for services in five years, to unify the tax treatment of goods and services. According to the Ministry of Finance, beginning from 2011, the Chinese government started with a pilot programme to impose VAT on some producer services, while reducing the sales tax on them at the same time. The gradual unification of taxes on goods and services will boost the development of the services sector. Before 2011, VAT was levied only on manufacturing in China, while services were subject to a business tax that raised a much smaller amount. Given the heavy dependency of local governments on VAT revenue, they have had a strong incentive to promote manufacturing, rather than services. The current frame of China's finance and tax system, which was set up in 1994, can no longer adjust to rapid economic growth and solve emerging problems. Uniform VAT implementation on goods and services will offer incentives for local governments to promote the services sector. China will make better use of the role of taxes in accelerating the transition of the development pattern.

In addition, a preferential tax policy should also be implemented to help some small and medium-sized services enterprises, and the policy will aid services sub-sectors involved in protecting the environment and creating new jobs. Some services sub-sectors can not only provide fiscal revenue for local governments but also help create job opportunities for citizens and migrant workers and improve people's standard of living. Tax breaks should be offered to the enterprises in these sectors. More favourable tax policies should be implemented to support the efforts of qualified services enterprises to list on the stock markets. China will also give provincial-level governments the power to adjust local tax categories, rates, and cuts in the next five years to ensure their fiscal revenues in accord with administrative responsibilities.

There is a need for competition policy reforms to provide equal opportunities for all services providers. There is still a dominant presence of state-owned enterprises in the services sector, which constrains competitiveness and productivity. The high market concentration limits the entry of both new domestic and new foreign players, thus reducing the benefits of enhanced competition and liberalisation. Against this background, wide-ranging reforms are needed to turn services into an efficient and competitive sector. That would strengthen domestic sources of growth and support government efforts to rebalance the economy. Competition policy should be reformed by reducing market concentration in the sector. The resulting liberalisation and improved competitiveness would lower production costs and prices, and increase the quality of the services provided to both consumers and producers. Recent efforts by the Chinese government to better enforce the Antitrust Law are steps in the right direction to avoid abuses of dominant position in post-deregulation services markets. More openness toward foreign participation in sectors, including banking, telecommunications and professional services, will foster liberalisation efforts. In this regard, a reliable intellectual property rights regime, which is crucial for the development of services, where copyrights and trademarks are important, would help attract more overseas direct investment into the sector, and encourage domestic firms to innovate.

There needs to be financial policy reform for private and small and medium enterprises in the services sector. The inefficient allocation of financial resources enhances the dominance of state-owned enterprises in the provision of services. While significant progress in financial sector liberalisation has been achieved, the current system remains biased toward large state-owned enterprises, which absorb about two-thirds of total lending. In contrast, private enterprises, which tend to be more efficient and innovative, receive only one fourth of the available credit. Notwithstanding their significantly smaller allocation, private firms generate about 50% of GDP and are the primary source of employment generation in China. It is important to deepen financial sector reform for the improvement of capital allocation to move toward an innovation-based economy and grant wider access to finance. Given the superior performance of private companies in China, more efficient capital allocation would translate into higher GDP growth. Furthermore, more sophisticated capital markets will bring benefits to self-employed entrepreneurs, and small and medium-sized enterprises, which are critical players in a vibrant services sector-based economy.

China should negotiate further market access for China's services exports. Both the WTO and regional or bilateral trade agreements provide mechanisms for liberalising access to services markets. Trade agreements can potentially help the Chinese government implement policy reforms that enhance the contestability of services markets that are opposed by domestic interests groups. By committing to certain multilateral or bilateral trading rules, the Chinese government can make domestic policy reforms more credible. The trade agreements act as domestic policy reform anchors. China will make progressive liberalisation under the bilateral and regional framework of trade agreements through binding GATS-plus commitments and make progressive liberalisation under the WTO framework through binding GATS commitments. China should also stimulate services exports by improving market access through multilateral and regional negotiation channels.

The negative effects of trade liberalisation in services can be diminished by complementary policy reforms. Specific benefits are likely to result from the liberalisation of trade in services. However, services liberalisation also carries risks. Making appropriate regulation and other complementary policy reforms can help to ensure that liberalisation delivers the expected benefits. The trade-related policy reform challenges facing China are preference erosion and revenue loss. Policies are also necessary to provide adequate income support and make compensation to those suffering losses. Undertaking reforms across different policy areas in a complementary way can reduce the adjustment cost of policy reform. In a global environment, comprehensive policy reform is more effective than piecemeal strategies.

10.6 Conclusion

The share of services in GDP and employment is relatively low in China. The relative underdevelopment of the services sector is a direct consequence of the economic development model adopted by China, which favours manufacturing with the focus on manufactured exports.

As a result, policy incentives have directed investment into the production and export of goods, discouraging investment in services.

China's economy has come to a turning point because of the global financial crisis, but also because of the domestic tensions engendered by the export-led model. To have sustainable growth China has to rebalance its economy towards the domestic market and services sector.

A well-developed services sector plays a major role in improving production efficiency and promoting technical progress and innovation. More favourable policies aimed at boosting the services sector's development should be implemented, which would also boost China's trade in services.

While manufacturing greatly benefited from liberalisation brought about by the successful opening-up policy, openness has been limited in the services sector. The restricted exposure of the services sector to overseas direct investment, and its implicit technological transfer, has limited the expansion of the sector and the quality of the services provided. It has constrained the potential of trading services, too, which explains the persistent deficit observed in the services account of the balance of payments.

Despite the ambitious services liberalisation commitments that China agreed to when it joined the WTO, implementation and enforcement remain imperfect in some fields. There is still a dominant presence of state-owned enterprises in the services sector, which constrains competitiveness and productivity. The high market concentration limits the entry of new domestic and foreign players, thus reducing the benefits of enhanced competition and liberalisation.

The possible direction for China's policy reform in services should focus on strengthening the contribution of services trade to China's economic growth and removing the trade or investment barriers in services. Liberal trade and investment policies contribute to growth, innovation and competitiveness and avoid policy reversal. Because of downstream linkages, particular benefits are likely to arise from the liberalisation of trade in services.

China's services sectors can be liberalised further by building sound institutions, fostering an appropriate services policy framework and removing any anti-export bias, improving firms' access to international services markets and reducing other domestic barriers to services trade and investment.

Trade liberalisation policy should be backed by supportive action in other policy areas to complement the reform process. A comprehensive policy response is crucial for China.

Trade liberalisation in services also carries risks. Making appropriate regulation and other complementary policy reforms will help to ensure that liberalisation delivers the expected benefits.

Chapter 11

Services Sector Reforms in India: Update and Challenges

Rupa Chanda and Pralok Gupta

11.1 Introduction

The rapid growth of India's services sector in the post-2000 period has contributed to the country's emergence as one of the fastest-growing economies in the world since 2000. Real gross domestic product (GDP) growth averaged just over 8% a year between 2005–06 and 2011–12. The services sector grew at more than 9% over the same period. Communication services registered the highest growth rate of around 26%. Other rapidly growing service subsectors included trade, hotels and restaurants, construction, financing, insurance, and business services. Given its growth performance, the contribution of the services sector (including construction) to overall GDP has increased sharply, from 41% in 1990–91 to 63% in 2010–11 (Government of India, 2012).

The services sector has also facilitated India's integration with the world economy through trade and investment. Services exports have grown significantly, from less than $7 billion in 1995 to over $137 billion by 2011. India's share in global services exports has risen from 0.5% in 1995 to over 3% in 2011. The sector's share in the country's exports has risen from around 18% in 1995 to over 39% in 2011 (United Nations Conference on Trade and Development (UNCTAD), 2012). It was expected to surpass merchandise exports in 2012 as per a 2007 survey by the Federation of Indian Chambers of Commerce and

Industry.[1] However, the current export data for India suggest that it may take a few more years for services exports to surpass merchandise exports.

The current dynamism of India's services sector is largely a reflection of domestic liberalisation and growing linkages with external markets. A World Bank (2004) study showed a positive correlation between the extent of liberalisation in different Indian service subsectors and their corresponding rates of growth. Services that have been liberalised most in terms of trade and foreign direct investment (FDI) policies have typically experienced higher growth rates and creation of employment opportunities.

As evident from Figure 11.1, the highest growth segments have been business and communication services, which are 'significantly liberalised sectors', followed by banking and insurance services, which are 'moderately liberalised sectors'. Segments such as postal, railways, and storage services are 'non-liberalised' or restricted sectors and have registered the lowest growth rates. Sectors such as road and air transport have undergone 'moderate' liberalisation and experienced moderate growth rates. Some segments such as distribution services have registered reasonably high growth rates, despite their limited liberalisation, mainly because of the overall buoyancy of the Indian economy. Thus the service sector's growth dynamics reflect both domestic economic conditions and the outcome of liberalisation and reforms in this sector and in the wider economy.

Productivity estimates also corroborate the role of liberalisation and increased competition in improving the sector's efficiency. For instance, McKinsey estimates found that services such as telecommunications and software services have had higher productivity levels than other service sectors in India (World Bank, 2004). While it is difficult to identify the exact channels through which these efficiency gains have materialised, factors such as technological externalities, knowledge spillovers, improved management practices, and technology diffusion, which are

---

[1] Metrics 2.0 Business and Market Intelligence, 'India services exports to hit $310 billion and surpass merchandise exports by 2012', 5 April 2007, http://www.metrics2.com/blog/2007/04/05/india_services_exports_to_hit_310_billion_and_surp.html, accessed 10 August 2009.

facilitated by integration with world trade and capital markets, have certainly played a role. In addition, liberalisation in certain services such as telecommunications has also impacted positively on export opportunities in other areas, such as in IT-enabled services.

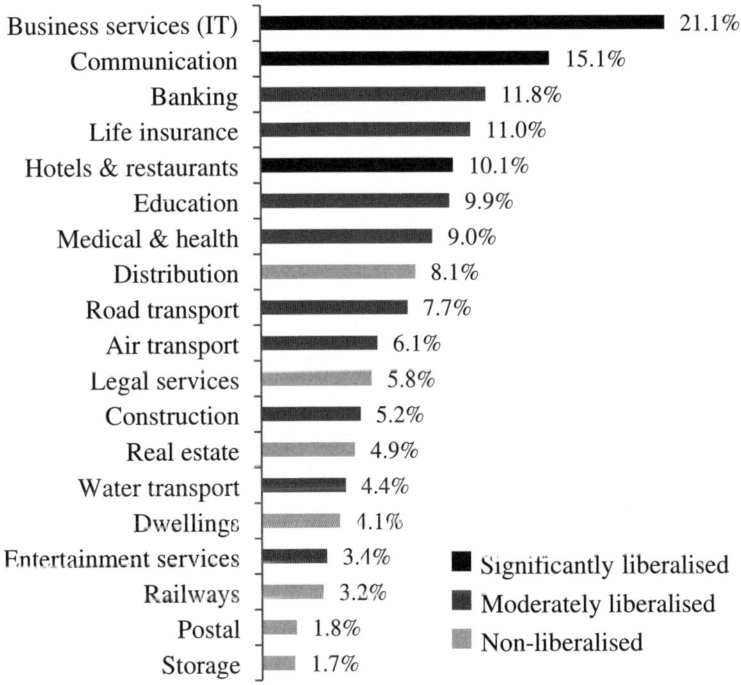

Figure 11.1 Liberalisation and Growth Linkages in India's Services Sectors.
Source: World Bank (2004).

Nevertheless, there has been debate and controversy in India over the desired pace, extent and implications of liberalisation and reforms, and the concerns have varied across different kinds of services. While there has been rapid and extensive liberalisation of some services for both domestic and foreign participants, the reform process has been slow and even halting in some cases. Key pieces of legislation have taken a number of years to be passed, because of domestic stakeholders' sensitivities, a lack of political will and consensus, and a variety of social and economic concerns.

The remainder of the chapter outlines the nature of the liberalisation and regulatory reforms that have been undertaken for selected services — telecommunications, retail distribution, accountancy, and legal services — and the debates, challenges and political economy constraints surrounding the process. The chapter concludes by highlighting the lessons to be learned from India's experiences of service sector liberalisation.

11.2 Telecommunications Services[2]

The telecommunications services sector is perhaps the showpiece of India's liberalisation and reform programme. Following the introduction of a major economy-wide reform programme in 1991, the roadmap for the telecommunications sector has been to expand and upgrade the country's network, privatise telecommunications services, introduce a more liberal foreign investment framework, and introduce new regulations and regulatory structures in this sector. The most significant aspect of these reforms has been the consistent liberalisation of FDI restrictions in both the basic and value-added segments and the gradual removal of restrictions on private players. The Department of Telecommunications (DOT) has been restructured and its monopoly status as a telecommunications service provider has been gradually reduced and eventually eliminated.

11.2.1 *Reform and liberalisation measures*

Telecommunications reforms began with the introduction of the National Telecommunications Policy (NTP) of 1994, which called for the systematic de-monopolisation of the telecommunications sector by

[2] The discussion on telecommunications services is primarily based on Kathuria (2008), Narsalay (2006) and Kathuria *et al.* (2003). It is supplemented by Virmani (2004), Hossain and Kathuria (2003) and various online documents. It is adapted from Chanda and Gupta (2011).

opening up basic services to private telecommunications companies and the setting up of an independent statutory regulatory body, the Telecommunications Regulatory Authority of India (TRAI) in 1997. The first major step in the sector's liberalisation was the entry of private players into the basic telecommunications services segment in 1997, in order to supplement the DOT's services and help achieve universal access targets. Entry was permitted on a duopoly basis, with both the DOT and private players participating. Licences were rationed and foreign equity participation in both basic and cellular mobile services was permitted only up to 49%. The TRAI's role was to oversee compliance and implementation, ensure fair competition, safeguard consumer interests, and to give directions to players in this sector. The DOT retained its role as policy-maker, licence issuer, and player, and retained its monopoly over long distance telephony for another five years.

The initial years of telecommunications reforms were not very successful as targets were not met and there was insufficient opening up of markets. This failure was mainly because of the lack of commitment on the part of the incumbent policy-maker, the DOT, which was reluctant to cede its monopoly status and revenues to private players. Although the market was divided into separate calling circles, private players could only provide intra-circle long distance services while the government provider was also permitted to provide inter-circle long distance calling services. Thus, although competition was permitted between the public provider and a limited number of private players, there remained an uneven playing field.

The regulatory framework was also to blame. There was a conflict of interest between the government (represented by the DOT) and the regulator (TRAI) arising from the latter's lack of autonomy to issue licences, place terms and conditions on providers, fix tariffs or override DOT decisions. Such conflicts adversely affected TRAI's credibility in the initial years of liberalisation. Problems were also caused by the failure of many private players because of financially unviable bids. Political instability at the centre further affected the progress of telecommunications reforms.

The second phase of telecommunications reforms began with the introduction of the NTP of 1999 under a new government. This policy stated its commitment to an independent regulator and more clearly defined the role of the TRAI. In accordance with the NTP 1999, national long distance telephony was opened up to private operators in January 2000. In 2001, unlimited entry was permitted in each policy circle for the provision of basic and mobile services. The licence regime was migrated from a fixed fee scheme to one of revenue sharing. In April 2002, the international long distance service was opened up to competition by privatising the public provider and removing restrictions on the number of operators in this segment. Other liberalisation measures undertaken post-1999 included the opening up of internet telephony, the disinvestment and corporatisation of public sector telecommunications providers in some metropolitan areas, the introduction of new technologies and forms of service delivery, and approval to internet service providers to set up international internet gateways.

In February 2005, the government increased the foreign holding limit to 74% for fixed line basic services, cellular services, unified access services, national and international long distance telephony, public mobile trunked services, global mobile personal communication services, and various value-added services such as voicemail and email services, up from an earlier ceiling of 49%. Subsequently, FDI was permitted up to 100% in value-added services such as email, voicemail, electronic data interchange, on-line information and data processing, and internet service provision without gateways (Narsalay, 2006). Thus, competition was encouraged, with the entry of both local and foreign providers, the granting of greater flexibility to existing players with the waiver of various obligations and permission to provide additional services, and substantial reductions in entry and licensing fee shares from providers.

While competition and efficiency were overriding objectives, considerations of affordable access and equity were also kept in mind. The TRAI also instituted guidelines for effective compliance with universal service obligations, including commitments to provide access to basic telecommunications services at affordable and reasonable rates. A Universal Service Support Policy and a Universal Service Obligation Fund were introduced in 2004. Under the latter policy, funds generated via a universal service levy of a certain percentage of licence fees charged from different service providers were to be used to subsidise universal service obligations.

Table 11.1 summarises the latest status of FDI regulations as well as entry terms and conditions in selected segments of the telecommunications sector in India.

Table 11.1 Current FDI and Other Regulations in India's Telecommunications Sector.

Sector/Activity	FDI Cap/Equity	Entry Route	Other Conditions
(a) Basic, cellular, unified access services, national or international long distance, V-sat, public mobile radio trunked services, global mobile personal communications services and other value-added services	74% (including foreign institutional investors, non-resident Indians, foreign currency convertible bonds, American depository receipts, global depository receipts and convertible preference shares held by foreign entity)	Automatic up to 49% Government route beyond 49% and up to 74%	Subject to licensing and security requirements notified by the Department of Telecommunications (www.dot.gov.in) Other Service Providers (OSPs) providing services such as call centres, business process outsourcing, tele-marketing, tele-education, etc, and are registered with DoT as OSP: 100% FDI is permitted.
(a) ISP with gateways (b) ISPs not providing gateways (both for satellite and marine cables) (c) Radio paging (d) End-to-end bandwidth	74%	Automatic up to 49% Government route beyond 49% and up to 74%	Subject to licensing and security requirements notified by the Department of Telecommunications (www.dot.gov.in)

Table 11.1 (Continued)

(a) Infrastructure provider providing dark fibre, right of way, duct space, tower (IP Category I) (b)Electronic Mail (c) Voicemail	100%	Automatic up to 49% Government route beyond 49%	Subject to the conditions that such companies will divest 26% of their equity in favour of Indian public in 5 years, if these companies are listed in other parts of the world. Also subject to licensing and security requirements, where required (www.dot.gov.in)

Source: DIPP (2012a).

The extent of liberalisation over time in the regulatory barriers affecting foreign suppliers has been calculated using a trade restrictiveness index that captures regulatory barriers of two types — 'at the border' barriers affecting foreign entry decisions, such as FDI limits and restrictions on legal forms of entry, and 'behind the border' barriers affecting ongoing operations of foreign firms, such as licensing requirements and the tax structure (Gupta, 2011). The index ranges between zero (least restrictive) and one (most restrictive).

The index values shown in Figure 11.2 indicate that there has been a significant decline in regulatory barriers over time. 'At the border' barriers have come down because of higher FDI limits, simplified FDI approval processes and the shift towards a more competitive market structure (Department of Industrial Policy and Promotion (DIPP), 2010). 'Behind the border' barriers have come down with the easing of licensing procedures, the removal of some restrictions on value-added services and the introduction of easier tax laws. The low values of the indices in 2010 indicate that the sector is now highly liberalised.

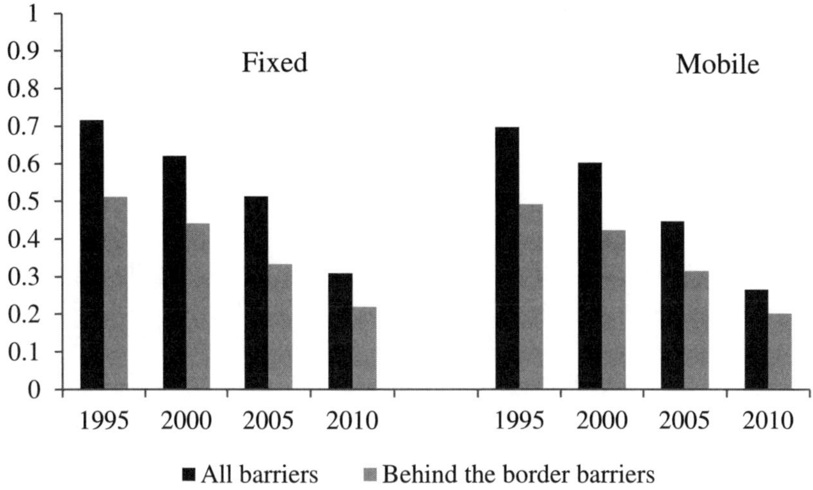

Figure 11.2 Trade Restrictiveness Index for Telecommunications Services in India, 1995–2010.
Source: Gupta (2011).

11.2.2 *Outcomes*

The outcome of reforms in telecommunication services has been striking. It is reflected in network expansion, productivity improvements, increased number of lines in operation, reductions in prices and waiting lists, increased demand for basic and value-added services, and increased teledensity in rural and urban areas. The sector has grown from a level of 22.8 million telephone subscribers in 1999 to 54.6 million in 2003, and to 935.2 million at the end of October 2012 (TRAI, 2012).

Reform measures and technological advances have also resulted in changes in the sector's profile. Value-added and mobile telephony have become the fastest-growing segments and growth drivers. The number of wireless connections rose from 3.6 million in March 2001 to 904.2 million by October 2012. Teledensity increased from 2.32% in 1999 to 76.75% at the end of October 2012 (TRAI, 2012). The internet services segment has also grown significantly, with 175 internet service providers operating as of January 2013,[3] and with a growing subscriber base. Several integrated public and private players have also emerged with significant presence across the value chain, across the national and international long distance as well as internet segments.

11.2.3 *Challenges*

The liberalisation and regulatory reform experience in the telecommunications sector has thus been successful, despite many challenges. It has required evolving regulations and frameworks, a redefinition of responsibilities for the regulator, and evolving approaches to market entry and equity. Notwithstanding the resulting growth and benefits, certain critical issues remain to be addressed.

One challenge is infrastructure, particularly the availability of spectrum, which is currently in short supply. Further reductions in bandwidth costs are essential, as first-mile costs for Indian business process outsourcing (BPO) providers remain higher than those abroad. Lower bandwidth costs would help to increase the competitiveness of Indian BPO providers.

There is also concern regarding transparency in spectrum allocation. The 2G spectrum[4] allocation process, which is under the scrutiny of Indian investigation agencies, revealed the possible misuse of decision-making power by the concerned authorities. The licences were awarded on a first-come, first-served basis, rather than through the process of auction, as stipulated under the NTP 1999. Moreover, the ministry reduced the cut-off time without consulting and informing other related

---

[3] See List of Internet Service Providers, available at Telecommunications Regulatory Authority of India (TRAI) website http://www.trai.gov.in/Content/ProviderListDisp.aspx?SERVICE_ID=3, accessed 22 January 2013.

[4] 2G is an acronym used for second-generation wireless telephone technology. After the launch of 2G technology, the previous mobile telephone systems were retrospectively classified as 1G. Radio signals on 1G networks are analog whereas these are digital for 2G networks. 2G networks offer many benefits over 1G networks, such as, digitally encrypted phone conversations; significantly more efficiency on the spectrum allowing for far greater mobile phone penetration levels; and data services for mobile (SMS text messages, etc.).

ministries and without mandatory approval from the cabinet committee for such important decisions. According to estimates of the Comptroller and Auditor General of India, the changing policy stance and non-transparency in 2G spectrum allocation has resulted in a loss of approximately INR[5]1.7 trillion to the exchequer.[6] In February 2012, the Supreme Court of India revoked the 2G licences and asked the government to undertake a fresh auction.

Another area of concern is the urban-rural divide, which has increased significantly post-liberalisation. This is mainly because of the largely urban coverage of the fast-growing mobile telephony segment, which has overtaken the fixed-line segment. At the end of October 2012, urban teledensity was 153.06% while rural teledensity was only 39.78% (TRAI, 2012).

Universal service obligations and regulatory mechanisms that promote equity with efficiency are also an important concern as India's telecommunication sector is liberalised further. The new competition regime under the Competition Commission of India, and the existing regulatory body in the telecommunication sector, TRAI, will both need to ensure that profitability and efficiency are not at the expense of social obligations. Social obligations are particularly important in light of India's goal of using telecommunications to create a knowledge-driven society, for which access to telecommunications services at affordable prices and wider geographic reach are essential. It is also important that these organisations avoid regulatory conflicts, especially given the growing convergence of communication services.

---

[5] INR is the internationally used acronym for the Indian currency 'rupees'.

[6] ArticlesBase.com, '2G spectrum scam – Allocation of spectrum or loot of spectrum?', 15 November 2010, http://www.articlesbase.com/banking-articles/2g-spectrum-scam-allocation-of-spectrum-or-loot-of-spectrum-3670753.html, accessed 11 March 2011.

11.3 Retail Distribution Services[7]

Liberalisation of India's retail services sector has been the subject of considerable political and social debate. It is one of the best examples of the political economy constraints to services sector liberalisation and lack of a principled stand by political parties.

India's retail industry is the fifth largest in the world and the largest private industry in the country. It is also the second largest single employer after agriculture. Although it is difficult to estimate the size of the sector given a large unorganised segment, according to various reports, the retail industry has grown from $394 billion in 2005 to around $550 billion in 2010 and is projected to grow to over $800 billion by 2015, with average annual growth of around 7.6% over the 2010–15 period. Strong economic growth, population expansion, increased disposable income and growth in organised retail infrastructure are seen as the major drivers of growth in India's retail industry.[8]

The retail distribution sector is characterised by the presence of a large number of intermediaries and a fragmented supply chain. Most retail outlets are in the form of mom-and-pop stores offering limited choice to consumers. Of late, new retail formats have emerged in the form of department stores, supermarkets, hypermarkets, and non-store formats such as direct selling, e-marketing (i.e. retailing on the internet) and television shopping. The concept of brands has developed and more and more manufacturers are branding their products. Many foreign brands have entered the Indian market. Indian business houses are increasingly investing in this sector and many others are planning to make huge investments. Interestingly, the retail boom is not just concentrated in the cities. Retailers are also venturing into smaller cities and sourcing their products from local small-scale industries. Some companies are entering into rural markets to source directly from

[7] This section draws on Mukherjee (2006).

[8] See http://www.ibef.org/artdispview.aspx?in=63&art_id=30569&cat_id=376&page=2, http://business.mapsofindia.com/india-retail-industry/, Business Monitor International India Retail Report.

farmers, to ensure product quality, and to set up the supply chain from the rural to the urban market.

11.3.1 *Reform and liberalisation measures*

The nature and extent of liberalisation of distribution services has varied across the different segments. While FDI in non-retail segments such as wholesale trading, export trading, cash and carry, and franchising is permitted up to 100% (earlier 51%) through the automatic route, the retail segment is only partially open. In 2006, the government allowed 51% FDI in single brand retailing subject to Foreign Investment Promotion Board approval and subject to certain conditions, namely:

- only single brand products were to be sold;
- products would be sold under the same brand internationally;
- single brand product retailing would only cover products that are branded during manufacturing; and
- any addition to product categories sold under a single brand would require fresh approval from the government.

To facilitate the growth of retail infrastructure, the government allowed FDI in real estate in 2005. Notwithstanding the opening up of single brand retailing to 51% FDI, cumulative FDI inflows in this segment during April 2000 to October 2012 were meagre, amounting to only $42.70 million (DIPP, 2012b).

The debate on multi-brand retailing has been particularly strident. Proposals to open this segment to FDI have been dropped in the past on account of strong opposition from small retailers (with the backing of several political parties) over the likely impact of large foreign retailers such as Walmart and Carrefour and large organised domestic players such as Reliance on unorganised retail businesses. Critics argue that the entry of big foreign retailers would lead to the displacement of small traders and cause unemployment among low-skilled workers, who would not have the requisite skills or training to find jobs in the modern retail formats. Proponents of liberalisation, however, argue that foreign entry would force consolidation within the sector and lead to the co-existence of large domestic players and foreign players. Further, they contend that foreign competition would in any case be limited by domestic constraints such as infrastructure and lack of quality manpower.

The political economy of liberalising retail services is evident from the fact that soon after the government announced a proposal to open up selected products such as electronics, furniture, stationery and sports goods to multi-brand retailing, it was forced to rethink its position and instead proposed a study to assess the desirability of, and approach to, further liberalisation of this sector. Contrary to expectations, the 2007–08 budget did not propose liberalisation of the multi-brand retail segment or further liberalisation of the single brand retail segment.

It is worth noting, however, that several restrictions have not been effective. Foreign entry has occurred in other forms, such as through local sourcing, franchising, setting up of manufacturing units, wholesale cash and carry trade, and joint ventures with local companies. Since FDI is not allowed, most international brands have established retail presence in India through the franchising route. A large number of foreign brands have also entered into shop-in-shop arrangements with leading department stores in India. Some brands have distribution offices in India that supply products to local Indian retailers. Thus the FDI cap in single brand retailing and the ban on multi-brand retailing have been bypassed to some extent.

In 2010, the government re-opened the debate on multi-brand retail. The Economic Survey for 2010–11 proposed that FDI should be phased in for multi-brand retailing, starting with the metropolitan areas, and called for modernisation of existing retail shops (Government of India, 2011). The DIPP put up a discussion paper proposing FDI in multi-brand retail and in July 2011 a Committee of Secretaries cleared the proposal to allow up to 51% FDI in multi-brand retail. This proposal was subsequently approved by the Union Cabinet in November 2011, with riders.

However, because of severe opposition from several political parties, including parties critical for the coalition government at the centre, this policy could not be introduced. The central government was put in an embarrassing position wherein its own coalition partners did not support its initiative to liberalise multi-brand retailing. It had to go back on its announcement to open up this segment. While the government was criticised by its coalition partners for introducing this proposal without taking them into its confidence, it was criticised by the private sector and the media for its inability to push through reforms and for continued policy paralysis.

Subsequently, in November 2011, the government notified an increase in the FDI limit in single brand product retailing from 51% to 100%. The Union Cabinet had earlier approved this increase, subject to government approval (though State Governments have the prerogative to disallow 100% FDI in single brand retailing in their respective states). To some extent, this step reflected the government's attempt to stem criticisms over its mishandling of the liberalisation of multi-brand retailing and to overcome the perception of a government that is unable to push through FDI reforms.

However, conditions have been imposed on FDI in single brand retailing to benefit local industries. For FDI beyond 51%, a mandatory requirement has been introduced that at least 30% of the value of the products sold must be sourced from domestic small and cottage industries, which have a maximum investment in plant and machinery of $1 million. This sourcing condition is aimed at providing a stimulus to domestic manufacturing value addition and to help in technical upgradation of India's local small-scale industries.

This notification opens up the possibility for global retail chains such as Gucci and Armani to fully own their Indian operations and to make the Indian market more attractive for global fashion brands by allowing them to buy out their domestic partners. It is also hoped that this policy will enhance the competitiveness of Indian firms by increasing their access to global technologies, management practices, and designs. The riders are that products by the global retail chains must be single brand only and must be sold under the same brand name internationally, that only products which are branded during manufacturing would be covered and that the foreign investor must be the owner of the brand.[9]

---

[9] See http://www.thehindu.com/news/national/article2790373.ece

In spite of opposition from several political parties including its allies, the government has indicated that it remains committed to opening up multi-brand retailing and has been working towards evolving a consensus with its political allies to permit 51% FDI in this segment. The DIPP has also undertaken consultations with state governments, representatives of consumer associations, micro and small industry associations, farmers' associations and representatives of food processing industry and industry associations to evolve a consensus on this issue. Partially successful in its efforts, with only a few states agreeing to FDI in multi-brand retail, the Government of India has announced 51% FDI in multi-brand retail in September 2012, subject to the following conditions:[10]

- retail sales outlets may be set up only in those states which have agreed, or agree in future, to allow FDI in multi-brand retailing;
- the establishment of the retail sales outlets will be in compliance with applicable state laws or regulations, such as the Shops and Establishments Act, etc.;
- retail sales outlets may be set up only in cities with a population of more than one million as per the 2011 Census and may also cover an area of 10km around the municipal or urban agglomeration limits of such cities;
- retail locations will be restricted to conforming areas as per the Master or Zonal Plans of the concerned cities and provision will be made for requisite facilities such as transport connectivity and parking;
- in states or union territories not having cities with population of more than one million as per the 2011 Census, retail sales outlets may be set up in the cities of their choice, preferably the largest city and may also cover an area of 10km around the municipal or urban agglomeration limits of such cities:
- at least 50% of total FDI brought in shall be invested in 'back-end infrastructure' within three years of the induction of FDI, where

[10] See http://www.firstpost.com/economy/full-text-cabinet-clears-fdi-in-multi-brand-retail-456276.html

'back-end infrastructure' will include capital expenditure on all activities, excluding that on front-end units; for instance, back-end infrastructure will include investment made towards processing, manufacturing, distribution, design improvement, quality control, packaging, logistics, storage, warehousing, agriculture market produce infrastructure, etc. Expenditure on land cost and rentals, if any, will not be counted for purposes of back-end infrastructure.

It is expected that allowing FDI in multi-brand retailing would address problems relating to food price inflation, low prices realised by farmers and investment gaps in post-harvest infrastructure for agricultural produce (Government of India, 2012). Several global retailers such as Tesco, Walmart and Carrefour are waiting to enter the Indian multi-brand retail segment.[11]

Table 11.2 summarises the current status of FDI policies in various segments of the trade and distribution services sector.

Table 11.2 Current FDI and Other Regulations in India's Trade and Distribution Services Sector.

Sector/Activity	FDI Cap/ Equity	Entry Route	Other Conditions
Cash and carry wholesale trading/wholesale trading (including sourcing from micro and small enterprises)	100%	Automatic	Subject to the guidelines and procedures prescribed by the Department of Industrial Policy and Promotion from time to time.

[11] See http://timesofindia.indiatimes.com/business/india-business/FDI-in-multi-brand-retail-still-on-govts-mind-FM/articleshow/11224948.cms and http://economictimes.indiatimes.com/news/news-by-industry/services/retailing/process-on-for-consensus-on-fdi-in-multi-brand-retail-says-pranab-mukherjee/articleshow/11980425.cms for a discussion of recent developments in multi-brand retail in India.

Table 11.2 (Continued)

E-commerce	**100%**	**Automatic**	**Such companies would engage only in business to business (B2B) e-commerce and not in retail trading, inter alia implying that existing restrictions on FDI in domestic trading would be applicable to e-commerce as well.**
Test marketing	100%	Government	Applicable for such items for which a company has approval for manufacture, provided such test marketing facility will be for a period of two years, and investment in setting up manufacturing facility commences simultaneously with test marketing.
Single brand product trading	100%	Government	Subject to the following conditions: (a) Products to be sold should be of a 'single brand' only. (b) Products should be sold under the same brand in one or more countries other than India. (c) 'Single brand' retailing would cover only products which are branded during manufacturing. (d) The foreign investor should be the owner of the brand. (e) In respect of proposals involving FDI beyond 51%, 30% sourcing would mandatorily have to be done from SMEs or village and cottage industries artisans and craftsmen.
Multi-brand retailing	51%	Government	(a) Retail sales outlets may be set up in those States which have agreed, or agree in future, to allow FDI in multi-brand retail. (b) Retail sales outlets may be set up only in cities with a population of more than one million as per the 2011 Census and may also cover an area of 10km around the municipal or urban agglomeration limits of such cities. (c) At least 50% of total FDI brought in shall be invested in 'backend infrastructure' within three years of the induction of FDI.

Source: DIPP (2012a), http://www.firstpost.com/economy/full-text-cabinet-clears-fdi-in-multi-brand-retail-456276.html and http://articles.economictimes.indiatimes.com/2012-09-14/news/33844067_1_village-and-cottage-industries-single-brand-small-industry.

11.3.2 *Outcomes*

It is thus evident that the liberalisation of retail services has been held back by strong political and domestic stakeholder interests, notwithstanding potential benefits in the form of increased sourcing and export opportunities, improved supply chain management, investments in related infrastructure and standardisation and efficiency spillovers. It is difficult to say how valid the concerns are over employment displacement and adverse fallout for the mom-and-pop stores in the context of further liberalisation of retail services. Some recent studies on the impact of modernisation and foreign entry in India's retail sector thus far suggest that the outcome may not be particularly adverse and that the unorganised segment is already adjusting to the changes brought about by modernisation. Some unorganised retailers have upgraded their store infrastructure and implemented technologies such as bar-coding to enhance efficiency. With modernisation, labour productivity in distribution has increased (Mukherjee and Patel, 2005, pp. 131-135). There have also been benefits through price reductions, greater consumer choice, and increased earnings for farmers and manufacturers. The emergence of modern formats has also improved the quality of employment and salaries and created new job opportunities in sectors such as food processing industries and logistic support services.

Although there have been some job losses due to the reduction in the number of intermediaries or middlemen, overall employment in this sector has increased significantly in the past few years and is likely to increase in the future. Some Indian retailers have also established retail outlets and distribution networks in other countries. A 2008 study conducted by the Indian Council for Research on International Economic Relations (ICRIER) on the impact of organised retailing on the unorganised sector finds that both segments will coexist and continue to grow and that if the retail sector remains dominated by the unorganised segment, then productivity improvements in agriculture and industry would be constrained (Joseph *et al.*, 2008).

11.3.3 *Challenges*

While overall economic growth and further liberalisation are likely to spur the growth of India's retail services, it is important to recognise several domestic regulatory and infrastructural constraints to this sector's growth and also the extent to which opportunities arising from liberalisation can be exploited. One such weakness is the lack of economies of scale in sourcing because of the presence of several intermediaries in the supply chain. It is thus difficult for unorganised retailers to develop a modern supply chain. Another weakness is the lack of supporting infrastructure and facilities in other segments of the distribution services sector. For instance, studies have shown that 40% of fresh fruits and vegetables get wasted in the supply chain because of inefficient distribution networks and poor storage facilities, which adversely affects the retail segment (Mukherjee and Patel, 2005, p. 154).

The retail sector is also plagued by a lack of supporting infrastructure. Expansion of organised retailing and franchising is dependent on the availability of approach roads, parking facilities, public transport facilities, electricity and communication systems, and real estate. In India, the lack of quality urban public transport discourages the development of shopping malls or hypermarkets in the outskirts of cities. Electricity charges are high and the supply is unpredictable. Shortage of electricity and frequent power cuts hamper efficient operation of the existing outlets and impose restrictions on shop opening hours. In order to overcome the accessibility problems, many organised retailers are forced to open their outlets close to residential areas. However, they face a variety of barriers that make real estate acquisition very costly. Factors such as restrictive zoning legislation, which limits the availability of land for retail or commercial purposes, non-availability of government land together with fragmented private holdings, lack of transparency and clear ownership or titles, and lack of proper planning in setting up retail establishments, make it difficult for retailers to acquire large plots of land and to set up large establishments.

The retail services segment is also constrained by significant restrictions on trade in some commodities, with different Indian states having their own policy with respect to production, distribution and taxation. The sector is subject to multi-level administrative control. There are restrictions on interstate movement of goods. Multi-point taxation makes it difficult to set up a centralised sourcing infrastructure, causing most retailers in India to source their products locally and affecting their economies of scale in sourcing. Inter-state differences in taxes encourage infiltration of products from states with lower taxes to states with higher taxes, resulting in black marketing.

The distribution sector is also subject to a plethora of laws at the central, state and local or municipal levels. Unlike developed countries, India does not have any specific legislation controlling distribution trade. There is also no nodal ministry to control and guide the operation of this sector. The laws governing the sector are very archaic. Another major barrier is lack of access to institutional funding. Since a large part of this sector is unorganised, very few banks are willing to invest in this sector. Retail services are also constrained by a lack of trained and quality manpower and low productivity levels. Many organised retailers find it difficult to recruit trained manpower and are forced to set up in-house training facilities. Furthermore, the rigid labour laws in India make it difficult for retailers or franchisees to employ staff.

Overall, India's retail services segment is likely to expand in the future, with the sector becoming more organised and consolidated over time. The AT Kearney's Global Retail Development Index (AT Kearney, 2012) ranked India at fifth position among 30 emerging markets for global retailers.[12] However, though foreign retailers have shown a keen interest in investing in the Indian market, actual investment will depend on the government's FDI policy in retailing. Further liberalisation of conditions on single brand retailing and opening up of multi-brand retail will be important for determining future trade and investment prospects in this sector. At present, however, the roadmap is not clear and political

---

[12] The AT Kearney Global Retail Development Index (GRDI) ranks the top 30 emerging countries for retail development and identifies windows of opportunity for global retailers to invest in developing markets. Published since 2002, the GRDI helps retailers prioritise their global development strategies by ranking the retail expansion attractiveness of emerging countries based on a set of 25 variables including economic and political risk, retail market attractiveness, retail saturation levels, and modern retailing sales area and sales growth.

economy constraints continue to slow down the reforms in this sector in the absence of a strong government at the centre.

11.4 Accountancy Services[13]

The liberalisation of professional services has similarly been subject to considerable debate and political economy considerations. The experience with both legal and accountancy services reveals that the main concern is over the implications of foreign commercial presence for domestic firms, given the existing market structure and nature of domestic regulation in these areas. The debates in these two services also reveal the important role played by professional councils in determining the pace and extent of liberalisation.

India's accounting sector is the second largest in the world, after that of the United States. Unlike the global accountancy sector which is dominated by a few large firms, the Indian accountancy sector is very fragmented, characterised by many small and medium-sized firms, typically with two to three chartered accounts and a few article clerks. The medium-sized firms employ around five to six chartered accountants. According to the Institute of Chartered Accountants of India (ICAI), there are more than 53,000 such audit firms in India, some of which are associates of the global big players. Less than 200 firms (or 0.5% of total accountancy firms) have more than 10 partners. According to a World Bank (2004) study, there are 100,000 chartered accountants in India, with an average of two chartered accountants per firm, compared to an average of between 350 and 1,500 chartered accountants in the 'big four' accounting firms.[14]

---

[13] This discussion is based on Pal (2006), findings from interviews conducted by the authors during December 2011-March 2012, and a roundtable discussion held on 8 February 2012 (organised jointly by IIM Bangalore, the British High Commission, Institute of Chartered Accountants of India and the Federation of Indian Chambers of Commerce and Industry) in New Delhi as part of a Foreign Commonwealth Office funded research project titled, 'Strengthening Regulatory Framework and Enhancing Capacity in India's Accountancy Services Sector: A Roadmap for Reforms'.

[14] The 'big four' are PricewaterhouseCoopers, Deloitte Touche Tohmatsu, Ernst and Young and KPMG.

Notwithstanding the fragmented nature of this sector, India's accounting profession is recognised as highly developed, with the potential to become internationally competitive. Increasingly, the larger Indian accounting firms are venturing overseas, becoming members of international networks, and becoming integrated into the international market. Some are also increasingly performing associated activities, such as management consultancy, corporate finance, and advisory services, in addition to conducting their core business of accounting, auditing, and tax services.

11.4.1 *Regulatory framework*

The accounts and audit segment of the sector is regulated by the ICAI under the 1949 Chartered Accountants Act and currently the Chartered Accountants (Amendment) Act 2006. The ICAI sets accounting and auditing standards, grants qualifications, and maintains discipline among its members. The cost accounting segment is regulated by the Institute of Cost and Works Accountants of India under the Cost and Works Accounts Act of 1959, while the company secretaries segment is regulated by the Institute of Company Secretaries of India. This discussion focuses on the chartered accountants' segment of the sector and the role of the ICAI.

As is the case with other professional services, the sector is subject to a variety of regulations aimed at maintaining standards and quality, minimising conflict of interest, and protecting consumers. Some of the key areas covered by regulation are training and certification, the size and scope of accounting firms, advertising and fees. There are stringent qualification requirements for Indian chartered accountants (which are seen to be on a par with or in some respects higher than those in other countries) and restrictions on practice by chartered accountants with foreign qualifications. Existing regulations prohibit an Indian accountant from paying a commission or brokerage or a share of profits from his or her business to or with any person other than an institute member, from soliciting clients or professional work by circular or advertisement (except as per the 2008 guidelines issued by the Council) and from responding to advertisements inviting applications for appointment of auditors. There are bans on the use of logos by individual chartered accountancy firms. The number of partners is restricted to 20, except for Limited Liability Partnerships (LLPs). There are also restrictions on the number of audits, with the number of clients limited to 45 tax audits (earlier 30) per partner. Indian regulations also proscribe inter-disciplinary professional models — accounting firms are not allowed to hire management professionals or engineers or lawyers to perform activities such as management consulting, technical analysis, or legal services, respectively.

In addition to these domestic regulations which affect the operations of domestic chartered accountancy firms and limit access to the Indian market by foreign chartered accountancy professionals, other major regulations control foreign commercial presence or FDI in this sector.[15] FDI is not permitted in accounting services. Multinational accounting firms (for example, the 'big four') cannot establish themselves in India for the purpose of conducting statutory audits of companies or for attest functions. (However, these firms are present in India to carry out management consulting services, as this segment is fully open to FDI).

The FDI restriction on audit services has led to the emergence of chartered accountancy firms that are affiliates of the multinational firms but registered as private limited companies in India (often with names that are a variant of the multinational firm name or new names) so as to carry out audit and attest functions, which constitute one of the most lucrative segments of this sector (ICAI, 2010). These private limited Indian chartered accountancy firms are basically part of an international network of the various multinational accounting firms and benefit from the latter through their access to a common pool of funds available to the international network, references to clients, and sharing of management practices and standards.

[15] Even under the WTO, India did not make any commitments in accounting services. In its revised offer for accountancy services, although India offered full commitments in accounting and bookkeeping services under mode 1 (cross-border trade) and mode 2 (consumption abroad), it kept mode 3 (commercial presence) unbound. Mode 4 (presence of natural persons) was left subject to horizontal commitments.

11.4.2 *Reform and liberalisation measures*

In recent years, there have been several regulatory reforms in this sector. The Companies Act was amended to permit LLPs and multidisciplinary firms between chartered accountants, cost accountants and company secretaries. It is hoped that in the near future, required amendments will be made in other professions to permit multidisciplinary partnerships with professionals outside the accounting sector (engineers and lawyers for instance).

The chartered accountancy profession in India is also increasingly benchmarking its qualifications and training requirements to global ones so as to facilitate the mobility of its professionals to other countries. It has entered into qualification recognition arrangements with accounting bodies in the United Kingdom, Australia, Canada and Ireland and signed Memoranda of Understanding with various countries to facilitate reciprocal access of chartered accountancy professionals to each other's markets. Accounting and auditing standards in the country are also increasingly being developed on the basis of international standards (such as the convergence with the International Financial Reporting Standards) so as to improve financial reporting and corporate governance in the country, though there is also an attempt to adapt these global standards to suit the Indian context and requirements.

The main debate over liberalisation of accountancy services has centred on whether to allow the multinational accounting firms to enter the audit services segment through commercial presence. In recent years, there has been considerable pressure from the United States and the United Kingdom to relax the current restrictions on FDI. This has sparked controversy within the Indian accountancy fraternity. Views are highly divided.

Proponents, who mainly consist of multinational accounting firms and their Indian affiliates, see only benefits arising from the full opening up of this sector. They argue that opening up of the sector could benefit India's large pool of qualified professionals and the industry as a whole. The potential benefits include reduced fragmentation of the industry, better employment opportunities, and higher standards. New opportunities could also emerge for Indian accountancy professionals in the form of back office services and the outsourcing of certain parts of the global operations of the international firms.

On the other hand, opponents, who mainly consist of Indian chartered accountants, small and medium-size Indian firms and regulatory bodies, are concerned that liberalisation could threaten the survival of Indian accountancy firms unless complementary measures, including amending some of the domestic regulations affecting Indian accountancy firms are also implemented. They argue that foreign firms operating in India prefer the 'big four' firms for their auditing work and that in joint venture firms, there are pressures from the foreign partner to use one of the 'big four' firms as a statutory auditor, hence pushing Indian chartered accountants into doing low value-added work. They also argue that such market segmentation is likely to drive the better qualified accountancy professionals towards the big firms and leave the lower quality professionals to serve the general populace, and that service costs are likely to rise following the entry of foreign firms. Thus the debate over liberalisation of accountancy services and in particular audit and attest services in India has to be viewed against the sector's fragmented market structure and the predominance of small firms. It is mainly a debate over large versus small-scale competition, similar to the case of retail services.

11.4.3 *Issues and challenges*

Several interesting issues have emerged in the course of this debate, though many of these are not clear cut and often tend to be coloured by vested interests of different stakeholders.

Supporting domestic reforms and a level playing field

The first issue is the importance of supporting liberalisation with complementary domestic reforms and creating a level playing field. Indian firms have resisted the opening up of the sector unless various domestic regulations on scale, scope and functioning are relaxed so that they can be on a level playing field with foreign firms. For instance, they argue that such restrictions result in small firms that are narrow in geographic scope and lack an all-India presence, which in turn makes it difficult for them to compete with foreign firms or to take advantage of global opportunities. They have thus called for amendments to the regulations governing multi-disciplinary firms and limited liability partnerships, the number of partners, the number of audits permitted per firm, and the use of firm logos and advertising of chartered accountants' products and services, so that domestic firms can compete with foreign firms.

However, discussions with various stakeholders suggest that the extent to which this position is valid is an open question. For example, although there is a restriction on the size of firms, with a maximum of 20 partners allowed for non-LLP firms, for the most part, Indian chartered accountancy firms are very small, with two to three partners on average. There are hardly any firms facing a binding constraint because of the ceiling on size. This would suggest that the regulation on size is perhaps not as critical a regulatory impediment as is made out by the chartered accountants and small firms. Discussions indicate that staying small and a preference for proprietary firms is in large part a reflection of mindset (for example, the firm is named after the chartered accountant who owns the firm) and the flexibility this permits individual chartered accountants in terms of the nature of practice and working conditions. Even though in recent years the ICAI has encouraged firms to network and consolidate into larger firms, very few have done so, suggesting that factors other than regulation may be at play. Of course, to the extent that multidisciplinary and LLP firms have now been permitted, Indian firms could become more competitive in due course, but much depends on the extent to which these new forms of operation are actually utilised.

Similarly, to what extent the level playing field argument is valid is not clear. Again, discussions with various stakeholders indicate that there is very little competition, even in the absence of liberalisation, between the small and medium Indian chartered accountancy firms and the larger affiliate firms of the multinationals. The fee structure is significantly different, so is the client base as well as the kinds of services provided. Hence, whether the entry of foreign firms through FDI presence in audit and attest services would really take away business or raise costs of services is not clear, as there is already a strong divide between foreign and domestic firms in terms of client profile, targets, products and services, prices, and modes of operation. Discussions with some larger firms also suggest that the real threat to the small Indian firms and proprietary concerns may come from their old-fashioned ways of practice, lack of professionalism and lack of growth opportunities because of the limited range of services offered, all of which are causing graduating chartered accountants to move into industry as opposed to private practice. Hence, in the long run, there is the likelihood of existing small proprietary concerns dying out, a gradual consolidation of the number of firms and a decline in the number of practitioners, not from foreign competition but from the gradual evolution of the sector.

Reciprocity

A second issue that characterises the debate over liberalisation of accountancy services in India is that of reciprocity. The ICAI and individual chartered accountants have argued that foreign firms should not be allowed to enter unless Indian firms are given reciprocal market access in other countries, thus linking FDI liberalisation to the recognition of Indian accountancy professionals and their right to practise in other markets. The ICAI has also sought the removal of other barriers such as residency conditions, commercial presence requirements, and visa regulations that restrict the movement of Indian accountancy professionals. They have argued that such complementary efforts are also required if the sector is opened up so that Indian professionals are on an equal footing in accessing overseas opportunities. As highlighted earlier, progress has been made in this regard with the signing of several mutual recognition agreements with other countries, though the utilisation of these agreements remains limited to date, mainly because of other conditions on residency and visas which undermine the mutual recognition agreements. This issue is a valid one and it is generally accepted even by the proponents of liberalisation that reciprocal access should be sought by Indian chartered accountants if market access is granted in India.

Disciplinary mechanisms and governance

A third issue highlighted by the debate in India's accountancy services is that of disciplinary mechanisms and governance of chartered accountancy firms, foreign and domestic, and to what extent the existing regulatory bodies are in a position to discipline the large foreign firms. Given recent cases of auditing fraud in both India and abroad (the Satyam and Enron cases),[16] the ICAI and individual Indian chartered accountants are concerned about possible malpractices by foreign firms and the regulator's inability to hold these firms responsible in such cases, with the liability falling entirely on the Indian affiliate or partner. They also point out that discipline on foreign firms is also eroded because existing FDI restrictions are being bypassed through 'surrogate presence', as noted earlier, whereby the foreign accountancy firms provide management consulting, advisory and other value-added services while the statutory audit services are carried out through their local associates under a different name (often pre-merger names). The regulator and the government have not been able to discipline these affiliate practices. The ICAI had even put forward a proposal in 2003 to prohibit the 'big four' from offering management consulting services under their current names, to prevent such affiliate practice in the audit segment.

While the concern about the ICAI's and the government's inability to govern the operations of multinational accounting firms has validity, proponents of liberalisation argue that this is the case only because foreign firms are not allowed to practise under their own name and because the sector is not open. If it is the Indian affiliate firm that has to undertake the audit, then it is natural that it would be the liable party and not the foreign firm, which has not been allowed into this segment in the first place. They also argue that the affiliate firms are Indian firms and

---

[16] The Satyam Computer Services scandal was a corporate scandal that occurred in India in 2009 where its Chairman confessed that the company's accounts had been falsified. The Enron scandal, that eventually led to the bankruptcy of the Enron Corporation (American energy company), was revealed in October 2001. It is considered as one of the biggest audit failures in American history. It also resulted in the dissolution of Arthur Andersen, one of the five largest audit and accountancy partnerships in the world at that time.

not surrogates as they only share management practices and a common global kitty of resources, but they are separate Indian private limited companies. Moreover, they are not bypassing or violating local regulations but rather following a common practice, as most chartered accountancy firms worldwide are members of international networks in order to derive a variety of benefits.

It is hard to come to a final position on this issue until one fully understands how the affiliations actually operate and the extent to which the foreign firm is culpable for any malpractice done by the Indian partner. As pointed out by several Indian respondents, although the foreign firm may not be liable in the strict legal sense, ethically there may still be a case to hold it accountable. However, the concern is whether the Indian regulatory framework would have the required disciplinary mechanisms and enforcement capability to do so. Hence, the questions of disciplinary action, codes of conduct and governance are complex.

Other issues

Other issues have been highlighted in the ongoing debate about opening up accountancy services. These include:

- standards, particularly whether global standards such as the International Financial Regulatory Standards should be adopted, whether these should be aligned to suit local requirements, and how the adoption of standards should be phased in;
- availability of financing in order to scale up Indian firms;
- modernisation of infrastructure and processes to improve efficiency;
- diversification and provision of value-added services in order to strengthen the sector and improve competitiveness;
- the role of the regulator and its ambit and whether this gives rise to conflicts of interest impeding the growth of the sector;
- the powers of the regulator versus the government ministry in shaping legislation and regulatory reforms; and
- training and qualification requirements and alignment to changing requirements.

Most of these issues are about domestic regulations and frameworks that will need to be addressed and operating practices that will require a change in outlook, whether or not liberalisation is undertaken.

Overall, the Indian accountancy sector provides an interesting example of a profession where there are diametrically opposite views about liberalisation and reform, reflecting a very strong protectionist mindset on one hand and a very strong pro-liberalisation mindset on the other. However, it is clear that many archaic regulations need to be removed or amended if the sector is to be strengthened and ready to face more competition from foreign firms in future. Incremental steps through the permission of multidisciplinary LLPs, relaxation of advertising regulations and signing of mutual recognition agreements are moves in this direction, but without a change in mindset and without a more balanced assessment of the issues by all concerned parties, the sector is likely to be marked by continued debate in the near future.

11.5 Legal Services[17]

It is difficult to estimate the true size, composition, and growth trends in India's legal services market. However, it is widely believed that this sector, especially the corporate legal services segment, has grown rapidly over the past decade or so, in large part because of the liberalisation of the economy and relaxation of FDI norms in 1991. From a mere seven to eight leading law firms in 1991–92, the number has grown to over a hundred. Legal activities have emerged in areas such as project finance, intellectual property rights, competition law, corporate taxation, infrastructure contracts, investment, dispute resolution, IT, e-commerce, anti-trust, and telecommunications. Hence, employment in this sector has grown significantly with the growing demand for legal professionals from Indian companies and multinationals operating in India.

[17] Much of the discussion in this section is based on Rangan and Dasgupta (2006), unless otherwise indicated.

11.5.1 *Regulatory framework*

The legal services sector, like the accountancy services sector, is closed to foreign commercial presence. Foreign law firms are not allowed to establish in India and provide legal services under their name. There are also restrictions on foreign legal professionals, because only natural persons who are Indian citizens can provide legal services in an individual capacity, unless the Indian national is permitted similar opportunity in the foreign national's country. Moreover, foreign legal professionals must have a Bachelors degree in law that is recognised by the apex regulatory body, the Bar Council of India. Foreign legal professionals cannot be appointed as partners and cannot sign any legal document or represent in court. They can only be employed as employees or consultants.

11.5.2 *Reform and liberalisation measures*

As with accountancy services, there has been a lot of domestic opposition to liberalising FDI in legal services, though the stand taken has been slightly different. The regulatory body in legal services, the Bar Council of India, has maintained that it is neither interested in accessing international markets nor in allowing entry to foreign law firms. The grounds for its opposition are similar to those in accountancy services. They stem from the uneven playing field for Indian law firms because of domestic regulations that prevent Indian firms from having more than 20 partners, prevent multidisciplinary practice and limited liability partnerships (though there is a recent proposal on LLPs), and restrict Indian lawyers from advertising. Joint ventures involving revenue sharing between local and foreign law firms are also not permitted. Such regulations clearly make it difficult for Indian law firms to grow in size and scope and to benefit from partnerships with foreign law firms.

Apart from raising the issue of domestic regulatory constraints, the Bar Council has also called for the recognition of Indian qualifications and reciprocal treatment of Indian legal professionals. Overall, the legal fraternity in India is concerned that the entry of foreign law firms will make it difficult for small Indian law firms to survive, and that it would segment the market and cause the cost of legal services to rise following liberalisation, thus hurting the Indian public. The Bar Council has maintained its opposition to FDI liberalisation in the face of growing pressure from the United States and the United Kingdom in particular to open up the Indian legal market, given the growing Indian economy, the increasing presence of multinationals and the need for expertise in global and Indian corporate law, and the pool of qualified and low cost Indian legal professionals.

The Council has also voiced concerns that despite the restriction on foreign commercial presence, foreign law firms are already present in the market through other means such as liaison offices, advisory work, regional offices, and informal tie-ups with Indian law firms. While some of the foreign firms maintain that they provide only information gathering and disseminating work in India to provide information to their other offices, some do advise on issues such as mergers and acquisitions, commercial agreements, and joint ventures. Several firms work in the Indian market in an advisory capacity. Several have Memoranda of Understanding with Indian law firms. Even state governments in India have turned to foreign law firms for advice. Thus, there is surrogate presence of foreign law firms, as in the case of accountancy services, and the FDI restriction has not been fully effective. A group called the 'Lawyers Collective' has even taken the matter to court over the presence of Ashurst of the United Kingdom and White and Case of the United States, which had opened liaison offices in India and were reportedly engaging in active legal practice, in breach of statutory requirements.

The extent of the debate against the liberalisation of legal services is evident from the strong statements that have been made by the Bar Council. According to one senior advocate and ex-chairman of the Bar Council of India- "The conspiracy is to concentrate and monopolise the entire legal profession in India or as a consequence of globalisation, in the hands of a few mega establishments controlling the legal profession" (Mittal, 2005, p. 16). It is perceived that the suggested increase in employment opportunities from opening up would only accrue to a few resourceful families and not to the younger members of the Bar. The small and medium-sized law firms are particularly concerned that they might be forced to close down and their lawyers would be left jobless if foreign firms were allowed to set up in India. There is also concern that the gradual entry of foreign firms could have adverse implications for the judiciary system and the structure of the legal services sector in India.

In line with the position taken by the Bar Council, the large Indian law firms have campaigned and lobbied strongly against the opening up of this sector and have kept it outside the scope of India's commitments under the General Agreement on Trade in Services (GATS). They fear losing their share of the Indian market. Some law firms have collectively formed a Society of Indian Law Firms as a platform for opposing the entry of foreign law firms in the country and to pressure the Bar Council to resist any government steps to liberalise the sector. It is understood, however, that a Cabinet Committee has been constituted to draft a proposal that would allow 26% FDI in legal services. The aim of this proposal is to encourage Indian law firms to enter into joint ventures with foreign firms and to eventually change their position about opening up this sector.

Although those opposing the liberalisation of legal services have been more vocal, there are also proponents who have argued for greater competition and internationalisation of this sector. According to this group, while it is true that Indian law firms are at present not ready to face competition from their foreign counterparts, such opening up is inevitable. Global commerce, investment, protection of intellectual property rights, technological advances, and the growing integration of economies will necessarily require the internationalisation of legal services. Hence, they argue that the required amendments in domestic legislation must be carried out immediately so as to prepare the sector for international competition. This group has also argued that foreign legal professionals have already been providing advisory services in India, to corporates, state governments, and public sector enterprises for more than a decade and that the Indian legal profession should take advantage of the entry of organised law firms to obtain a portion of their business in areas where Indian professionals have greater expertise about the local market. They also argue that entry of foreign law firms can only lead to more demand for both junior and senior Indian lawyers to work as associates and partners in the Indian offices set up by these firms and even overseas, to the benefit of the Indian legal fraternity.

The proponents of liberalisation have also questioned the resistance to opening up of this sector. For instance, they have noted that since foreign law firms are likely to compete in the corporate law domain, it is unlikely that the general populace would be affected by higher costs of litigation and other advisory services. Moreover, even if corporate legal services become more expensive, corporate houses or governments in India would not be willing to pay exorbitant fees and thus some reasonable ceiling would be maintained. In this group's view, it is the large Indian law firms that have created myths about the fallout from liberalisation as they have a vested interest in keeping their market share. The supporters of liberalisation further argue that there would be potential benefits in terms of standards, better expertise and knowledge transfer in certain domains, and increased outsourcing opportunities if the sector was opened up.

It is to be noted that in a recent judgement in July 2012, the Supreme Court of India directed the Reserve Bank of India not to allow foreign law firms to open liaison offices in the country. It also clarified that under section 29 of the Advocates Act, 1961, the term 'practice' covers consultation, legal drafting and all other non-litigious matters, besides litigious matters. As the issue of entry of foreign law firms in India has to be examined strictly in accordance with the provisions of the Act of 1961 and the Act does not permit so, foreign law firms are not allowed to practice in India.[18]

Overall, the legal services sector has been witness to much debate, with perhaps the critics of liberalisation dominating the debate. However, the debate has shifted from one of strident opposition to one where different opinions are now being voiced and consideration is being given to how best the sector could be opened up, keeping in mind the market structure, public interest concerns, and stakeholder sensitivities.

---

[18] See http://articles.economictimes.indiatimes.com/2012-07-05/news/32551798_1_foreign-law-firms-advocates-act-open-liaison

11.6 Summarising the Key Lessons

The preceding discussion has highlighted the liberalisation experience in a representative set of services — infrastructural, commercial, and professional. Several common issues are highlighted across the sectors.

First, the reform experience has not been smooth in any of the services discussed. It has taken time to introduce new legislation and at times, proposals and bills have been delayed or remain stalled for long periods and have not been passed into legislation. Lack of political will and the absence of a strong central government have to a large extent been responsible for these delays.

Second, in several services, the process has been evolutionary, marked by learning-by-doing. In the face of unforeseen outcomes, regulatory frameworks have evolved, the roles of regulators have been defined and redefined, legislation has been amended and policies have been changed in the course of opening up. In many ways, the phasing in of liberalisation through the step-by-step relaxation of FDI ceilings has also reflected the gradualist and sometimes hesitant approach to liberalisation, first getting evidence on the benefits and challenges following partial liberalisation before liberalising further.

A third feature of the liberalisation experience has been conflicts of interest among different stakeholders, be it the government versus the private players, the government versus independent regulators, the public sector entities versus the private players, the large versus the small private domestic players, the large domestic versus the large foreign players, and the regulatory bodies or professional councils versus the government or versus foreign players. Each sector has been characterised by its own sets of interest and spheres of conflict, which have often caused the delays in pushing ahead with reforms.

A fourth issue highlighted by the various cases is that the market structure and domestic policies and frameworks have shaped the pace and extent of liberalisation across different services. The presence of fragmented market structures with a large number of small unorganised players and related concerns about displacement and market concentration following liberalisation have hindered liberalisation in sectors such as accountancy, legal, and retail services. In others such as telecommunications, the dominance of public sector entities and the government's reluctance to give up control have been the main stumbling block.

A fifth important issue highlighted by these sectors is the difficulty in balancing equity and efficiency concerns, in balancing public and private interests, and in ensuring the right balance between institutional autonomy and regulation so that players are not burdened with onerous regulations but at the same time do not function in ways that go against the larger public interest.

A final important point highlighted by the experiences is that instituting appropriate regulatory bodies, clearly defining their roles, and improving governance, are just as important as pursuing liberalisation. Very complex regulations and regulatory structures or excessively stringent conditions imposed on players that cannot be monitored, ultimately tend to be ineffective and do not serve their purpose. Thus, liberalisation has to be supported by regulatory and legislative reforms, as well as strengthening of regulatory and enforcement capacity. In the absence of the latter, liberalisation can lead to undesirable outcomes and some of the concerns may be validated.

Liberalisation of services has been undertaken as part of India's general economic reform programme and has been shaped by domestic compulsions. Where opening has not been possible, the sector has not figured in the multilateral negotiations or has figured only in a limited manner. Multilateral commitments and offers have typically lagged behind the autonomous liberalisation process and there are few occasions of pre-commitment. Also, multilateral commitments and offers have largely been less than the status quo, indicating an overall conservatism in the negotiating strategy and a strategy of keeping room for future leveraging of the negotiations in certain services (Chanda and Sasidaran, 2007). While regional or bilateral commitments have on occasion been more liberal than those made multilaterally, autonomous and non-binding reforms have led the way in almost all services.

Chapter 12

Services Trade Reform in the European Union — The EU Services Directive[1]

Anne McNaughton and Paul Furlong

12.1 Introduction

In 2006 the European Council and European Parliament signed off on 'Directive 2006/123/EC of the European Parliament and of the Council of 12 December 2006 on Services in the Internal Market' — the EU Services Directive. The passage of the directive was highly controversial and the resulting instrument much more moderate in certain respects, than the Commission's original proposal. Member States were required to give effect to the obligations set out in the directive before 28 December 2009.

This chapter sets the directive in its legal and political context. It outlines its scope, and more importantly, the work that has been done by the EU Commission and the Member States since the directive's enactment to give effect to its aims and obligations. The chapter seeks to present a model of services reform 'European-style'. In our concluding comments, we consider the lessons such reform may have for other countries.

As noted above, the version of the directive that was finally enacted was, in certain respects, a more moderate instrument than the original draft. The main controversy centred on the apparent reliance on the principle of mutual recognition, set out in the original wording of Article

[1] This chapter is also part of the research output from Australian Research Council Linkage grant LP 0990000 'Australia and the European Union: A Study of a Changing Trade and Business Relationship'.

16. That article stipulated that service providers would be subject to the regulation of their home state and not the host state.

It is conceivable (although we suggest, highly unlikely) that if the directive had been enacted with the original wording of Article 16 (providing that services would be subject to 'home country regulation' rather than host country regulation), considerable work and expense at the EU and Member State levels may have been saved. However, if the history of market integration within the EU is any guide, in fact such an outcome would have been highly unlikely. Had Article 16 been left in its original form, the onus would still have been on the Member States to do whatever was necessary in order for service providers from other Member States to be able to provide their services, whether by moving temporarily into the host state to provide the service; establishing themselves in the host state to provide the service, or by providing the service across borders, without themselves moving. At the risk of stating the obvious, the mere fact that Member States were bound to allow those services that were already being provided in the service provider's own 'home' state, without requiring the service providers to comply with any further requirements imposed by the host state, by no means meant that from one day to the next, service providers could freely and without obstacles provide their services in the host state. History shows that the Member States of the EU have not always responded uniformly and with alacrity to the removal of such obstacles to trade. We suggest that the directive will in fact achieve the kind of liberalisation of services and integration of the services market to which the proponents of the instrument in its original form aspired. However, it will achieve this because of the provisions in Chapter II of the directive concerning administrative simplification, the provisions in Chapter VI on administrative cooperation, and in Chapter VII on the convergence programme.

12.2 The EU as a Legal System and Legislative Background of the EU Services Directive

As indicated above, the true innovation introduced by the directive is the set of measures directed to simplifying administrative procedures, enhancing cooperation between Member States' administrative agencies and in so doing, reducing or indeed removing the administrative barriers to the free movement of services and service providers within the internal market. In order to fully appreciate these measures and the way in which implementation of the obligations under the directive is monitored and managed, it is necessary first, to talk briefly about the European Union as a legal system.

The European Union is a *sui generis* legal system; it is more than the usual regional trading bloc based on a multilateral trade agreement. The EU itself came into existence in November 1993 when the Treaty on European Union came into force. The EU was based on three so-called pillars:

- the European Communities Pillar;
- the Common Foreign and Security Policy Pillar; and
- the Police and Judicial Cooperation in Criminal Matters Pillar (originally named the Justice and Home Affairs Pillar).

The European Communities Pillar contained three treaties, the most significant of which for market integration and development is the European Community (EC) Treaty. It is the provisions of that treaty, as amended, that are referred to in this chapter.

Following a failed attempt to introduce a Treaty Establishing a European Constitution,[2] the Member States signed the Lisbon Treaty on 13 December 2007, and it came into force on 1 December 2009.[3] Significant changes were made to the provisions of the Treaty on European Union and the EC Treaty, with the name of the latter being changed to The Treaty on the Functioning of the European Union (TFEU). With the entry into force of the Lisbon Treaty, the European Community was replaced and succeeded by the European Union which, for the first time in its short history, was expressly granted legal personality.

---

[2] Treaty Establishing a Constitution for Europe [2004] OJ C 310/01.This treaty was signed by all Member States (25) at the time. However, in 2005 citizens in France and the Netherlands rejected the treaty in national referenda and it was not adopted.
[3] Treaty of Lisbon [2007] OJ C 306/01.

At the heart of the EC Treaty were the 'Four Freedoms' on which the internal market is built. These were:

- Free Movement of Goods;
- Free Movement of Persons;
- Free Movement of Services; and
- Free Movement of Capital.

Article 14 of the EC Treaty provided for the establishment of the internal market:[4]

1. The Community shall adopt measures with the aim of progressively establishing the internal market over a period expiring on 31 December 1992, in accordance with the provisions of this Article and of Articles 15, 26, 47(2), 49, 80, 93 and 95 and without prejudice to the other provisions of this Treaty.
2. The internal market shall comprise an area without internal frontiers in which the free movement of goods, persons, services and capital is ensured in accordance with the provisions of this Treaty.
3. The Council, acting by a qualified majority on a proposal from the Commission, shall determine the guidelines and conditions necessary to ensure balanced progress in all the sectors concerned.

12.2.1 *Institutional structures*

The treaties establishing the European Communities did not simply set out the policy areas on which the Member States agreed to cooperate. More significantly, the treaties established a set of institutions that were independent of the Member States and had different responsibilities for achieving the objectives set out in the treaties. What follows is a basic overview of the key functions of the main EU institutions relevant to the discussion of the Services Directive.

---

[4] This article is now modified and renumbered as Article 26, TFEU. This provision was introduced into the treaty regime by the Single European Act 1986.

The Council of Ministers was, in effect, the legislative body of the European Communities. The Commission was responsible for initiating legislation and monitoring Member States' compliance with their treaty obligations. The European Court of Justice, among other things, was responsible for ruling on matters of interpretation concerning the treaties and instruments created under them, as well as for hearing matters brought before it by the Commission, concerning the failure of Member States to comply with their treaty obligations. What is now the Parliament was originally simply called the Assembly and was a passive review body ostensibly created to represent the interests of EC citizens but with no significant voice or power. It was quite a different institution to the European Parliament of today.

The two institutions of particular relevance for the following discussion are the Commission and the European Court of Justice (ECJ). As noted above, the Commission's responsibility was — and is — to ensure, among other things, that the Member States comply with their obligations under the treaties and other secondary EU law such as directives. Apart from directives, which are only binding on the Member States in terms of the *outcomes* to be achieved, the other instruments of EU law binding on Member States are regulations and decisions. As we will see below, the Commission has the power to adopt decisions and these are binding in their entirety on the parties to whom they are addressed. Where the Commission considers that a Member State has failed to fulfil its obligations under the treaties (including obligations set out in secondary instruments such as directives and decisions), it is to give the state in question an opportunity, in effect, to explain its failure, after which the Commission is to deliver a reasoned opinion to the Member State. If the Member State fails to comply with the reasoned opinion within a stipulated time frame, the Commission may then take the matter to the ECJ. This is what is meant by an 'infringement procedure' and is relevant to the continuing monitoring of Member States' compliance with their obligations under the Services Directive.

Early in the history of the European Communities, the ECJ created two doctrines of EC law: that of *direct effect* and that of *supremacy.* Direct effect was established by the European Court of Justice in a decision in 1962.[5] The ECJ held that the Member States of the EEC had limited their sovereign rights within limited fields, transferring that sovereignty to the institutions of the EEC which they themselves had brought into existence through the EEC Treaty. As a consequence, the subjects of this new legal system created by the treaties comprised not only the Member States but also their nationals:

> Independently of the legislation of Member States, Community law therefore not only imposes obligations on individuals but is also intended to confer upon them rights which become part of their legal heritage. These rights arise not only where they are expressly granted by the Treaty, but also by reason of obligations which the Treaty imposes in a clearly defined way upon individuals as well as upon the Member State and upon the institutions of the Community…[6]

Not only are treaty provisions capable of being directly effective, provisions in directives, if they satisfy the elements of the doctrine of direct effect, are also capable of being relied upon by *nationals* of Member States once the period for the transposition of the directive into national law has passed. The broader significance of this is explained shortly.

The doctrine of supremacy was established by the ECJ in 1964 in a decision building on its earlier finding that the Member States had created 'a new legal order' of international law:

> By contrast with ordinary international treaties, the EEC Treaty has created its own legal system which, on entry into force of the Treaty, became an integral part of the legal systems of the Member States and which their courts are bound to apply… The

---

[5] Case 26/62 *NV Algemene Transporten Expeditie Onderneming van Gend en Loos v Nederlandse Administratie der Belastingen* [1963] ECR 1.

[6] Case 26/62 *NV Algemene Transporten Expeditie Onderneming van Gend en Loos v Nederlandse Administratie der Belastingen* [1963] ECR 1 at p. 12.

> transfer by the states from their domestic legal system to the Community legal system of the rights and obligations arising under the Treaty carries with it a permanent limitation of their sovereign rights, against which a subsequent unilateral act incompatible with the concept of the Community cannot prevail.[7]

The doctrine of supremacy is by no means uncontentious, particularly when the Constitutional Courts of the Member States are involved. Notwithstanding this, the supremacy is, on the whole, an accepted and settled doctrine of EU law.

Since its inception the ECJ has had jurisdiction to give so-called preliminary rulings on matters concerning the interpretation of the treaties and the validity and interpretation of acts of the institutions, bodies, offices or agencies of the European Union. Member State nationals have always been able to raise such questions of interpretation before their own national courts and tribunals. Those institutions, in turn, have had either a discretion or an obligation to refer such questions to the ECJ for a preliminary ruling in circumstances where the position under EU law is unclear or unsettled. It is unnecessary for present purposes to go into the detail of how the preliminary ruling mechanism works. Suffice to say that the effect of this mechanism, combined with the doctrines of 'direct effect' and 'supremacy', is to empower Member State *nationals* to monitor the compliance of Member States (including their own) with their obligations under the treaties and measures of EU law such as directives. This is one of the (many) ways in which the EU legal structure differs from a conventional trade agreement. Dee and McNaughton (2011) provide evidence that this empowerment of nationals has been an important driver of domestic reforms in Member States.

12.2.2 *The Services Directive in its legal context*

The treaty provisions dealing with the Four Freedoms were in the original European Economic Treaty of 1958. They have, to a greater and

[7] Case 6/64 *Flaminio Costa v ENEL* [1964] ECR 585, at pp. 593–4.

lesser extent, been the subject of judicial consideration by the ECJ since the establishment of the European Communities.

The right of establishment and the freedom to provide services have had direct effect since 1974.[8] Through the application of the doctrine of direct effect, the laws of the Member States were 'negatively harmonised' (meaning that barriers to establishment and services provision were removed) but 'positive harmonisation', through EC legislation, was slower to develop. Indeed, during the first 27 years of the EC's existence, integration was driven more by the case law of the ECJ than by legislative activity of the Commission and Council. That being so, why was it necessary to develop something like the Services Directive? It would seem that relying on this process of 'negative harmonisation' was not the most effective approach:

> There was a strong suspicion that the European Court of Justice, in its case-law, only dealt with the proverbial tip of the iceberg and that most impediments to trade in services remained hidden under the surface because the Commission failed to identify them in its infringement investigations, because the individual persons or firms suffering from those restrictions failed to take legal action, and because national courts, when confronted with such cases, failed to enforce the Treaty and/or to refer preliminary questions to the European Court of Justice. This suspicion — that many humanly and economically obnoxious impediments to the cross-border provision of services continue to exist in the post-1992 European Community — would seem to be confirmed by the marked increase of services cases before the ECJ in recent years... Whatever the reasons, the growing amount of ECJ cases — assuming that they still only constitute the tip of the iceberg, though perhaps a slightly bigger tip than before — seems to indicate that there are serious problems with the

[8] In the case of the right of establishment, this was as a result of the decision in Case 2/74 *Reyners v Belgium* [1974] ECR 631. In the case of the freedom to provide services, this was as a result of the decision in Case 33/74 *Van Binsbergen v Bestuur van de Bedrijfsvereniging voor de Metaalnijverheid* [1974] ECR 1299.

> effective application of the internal market rules on services. (de Witte, 2007, p. 6)

Professor de Witte makes the further important point about the ECJ's case law and the principle of 'mutual recognition' as adopted by the court:

> [t]he principle ... simply meant that the host state must take into account the laws and regulations to which the service provider is subject in its home state, so as not to create unjustified double burdens. This is not the same thing as imposing, as a matter of principle, the application of the laws of the country of origin. (de Witte, 2007, p. 8)

These concerns are echoed in recital 6 of the preamble of the Services Directive; they were reasons enough to legislate for a more effective and efficient integration of the services market.

In an attempt to realise the objectives of the Community regime, a programme of legislative reform was launched through the Single European Act of 1986 which entered into force in 1987.[9] The Services Directive is not, however, a direct consequence of that programme, although it is certainly in conformity with it. Rather, it is a result of the European Commission's (2000) Strategy Paper, 'Internal Market Strategy for Services'. This paper was prepared in response to the 'Lisbon Agenda', the agenda set by the European Council at its meeting in Lisbon in March 2000. The Presidency Conclusions from that meeting set a new strategic goal for the EU of becoming the most competitive and dynamic knowledge-based economy in the world. The Commission's Strategy Paper was intended to respond to that challenge. In particular, it aimed to prepare the internal services market for the new opportunities for cross-border supply provided by information and communications technology, thereby enhancing competitiveness, growth and employment creation.

---

[9] Official Journal L169 of 29 June, 1987. The provisions of Article 14 referred to above were introduced into the treaties with this programme.

The strategy paper set out many obstacles faced by operators in providing services across borders, ranging from administrative difficulties and legal barriers to lack of information and excessive bureaucracy. Rules on authorisation or planning could present an obstacle to establishing a business, while rules on employment conditions or access to capital could present obstacles to ongoing business operations. The Commission considered that it was imperative to remove unjustifiable barriers so as to enhance the quality and competitiveness of its services industries.

Accordingly, in 2004 the Commission sent to the Council and the European Parliament its Proposal for a Services Directive (European Commission, 2004). Under the original proposal, barriers to establishment and to the free provision of services were to be eliminated in three ways (Flower, 2008).

- First, there was to be a programme of deregulation over a period of years, beginning with administrative simplification, the abolition of discriminatory national regulations, the evaluation of existing requirements by Member States themselves, and the creation of points of single contact at which businesses could complete most formalities required to provide a service in another Member State.
- Second, the *country of origin* principle was to apply to temporary service providers as distinct from those seeking to establish themselves in a Member State other than their own.
- Third, measures were to be introduced to protect the recipients of these services, so as to underpin the country of origin principle. Such measures would include harmonised requirements for provision of information about service providers, rules for professional services, encouraging voluntary measures to facilitate quality standards, and establishing administrative co-operation between Member States.

The legal bases of the directive are Articles 47(2) and 55 EC.[10] Both these treaty provisions stipulated the use of what was then called the co-

---

[10] Now Articles 53 and 62 TFEU.

decision procedure, set out in Article 251 EC,[11] for the promulgation of legislation. The essential points about this procedure are that it became the 'default' legislative procedure in Community law and under this procedure, if the European Parliament did not consent to the measure in question, it did not become Community law.[12] It is now called the ordinary legislative procedure.

In her paper on the negotiation of the Services Directive, Flower (2008) noted the politically highly charged nature of the project. A range of interest groups lobbied effectively to bring about significant changes to the Commission's original proposed directive, notably in respect of labour law and the application of the *country of origin* principle. As a consequence, the application of the country of origin principle was replaced with a mechanism requiring Member States to respect the right of service providers to supply services and guaranteeing "free access to and free exercise of a service activity" within a Member State. This hybrid principle of regulation is set out in Article 16 of the directive, 'Freedom to Provide Services'. In a very real sense, this new approach, developed by the European Parliament in response to the Commission's initial proposal, ensured the directive's survival:

> … the controversy over the country of origin principle in the Commission's original proposal threatened to derail the entire Directive and the Parliament's ingenious new hybrid mechanism essentially broke the log-jam in the co-decision process. (Flower, 2008, p. 232)

---

[11] Now Article 294 TFEU.

[12] It is necessary to understand that the European Parliament is not a parliament in the traditional Westminster sense. As noted earlier, it began life as a very passive forum — the nascent representation of the citizens of Europe and champion of their interests. Over time, through successive treaty amendments, the European Parliament went from an institution that was not recognised as anything more than a consultative body to one which has the power to veto the vast majority of legislation, the default voting procedure for Community legislation now being the ordinary legislative procedure set out in Article 294 TFEU.

12.2.3 *The Services Directive in its political context*

Why did the European Commission promote this contentious piece of legislation at such a sensitive time, in 2004–5, as the European Constitutional Treaty was being considered in referenda and by parliaments across Europe? The political context to the Lisbon Agenda, and to the Commission's strategy paper, helps explain both the timing and the content, and how the final version came about. Perhaps just as importantly, it may contribute to an understanding of how the directive may work in practice.

A simple answer is that the European Commission miscalculated badly in not anticipating the impact of the coincidence with the ill-fated European Constitutional Treaty. Students of the Commission will not find this surprising. This is not the full explanation, however. The Services Directive had to be promoted, and had to be promoted at the chosen time, because it is an integral part of the reform process that had been re-launched with the Lisbon Agenda of 2000. The single market programme resulting from the 1986 reforms is widely regarded as having achieved the free movement of goods through the reform of tariff and non-tariff barriers to trade, and has been associated with (though probably is not responsible for) the process of de-regulation of financial flows within Europe. Indirectly, the programme also helped to stimulate the successful introduction of the single currency, the Euro, in 2001.

However, it did not prevent Europe slipping further behind other large trading blocs in rates of economic growth. The Lisbon Agenda can be seen as an attempt by some European leaders to respond to globalisation by radically transforming the European economy, focussing on openness, flexibility, exchange of skills and above all on the characterisation of Europe as a leading 'knowledge economy'. It does this by promoting, among other things, a relatively new form of policy-making known as the 'open method of co-ordination'; the purpose of this is to apply new public sector management principles to the multi-level, multi-actor European Union policy process, bypassing the European Parliament and the European Council of Ministers, or at least restricting their capacity to block policy change.

If we then ask how the Services Directive fits into this context, it seems to apply in two ways. First, the directive seeks to extend the single market to the main sector of the economy left largely untouched by integration, that of services. In 1986 this was already the largest sector of some large national economies in the EU, especially the UK, and by 2000 the sector was the most important numerically in the EU economy, accounting for over 50% of the active workforce and of GDP across the EU. Notwithstanding this predominance, growth in the sector was slow, especially compared to the emerging large economies in Asia. This was attributed, in the Commission's thinking, to the many complex obstacles in Member States that prevented service professionals, whether as employees of large companies or as individuals, from offering their skills outside their own country. The failure to achieve free movement of services was therefore regarded as one of the main inhibitors of economic growth in the EU area.

Second, to a certain extent the directive represents a return to previous methods and ideas. The successful use of directives for major policy change reached its peak between 1986 and 1992; thereafter the Commission found it increasingly difficult to promote integration through direct legislation, for various reasons we do not address here. The diminishing effectiveness of directives encouraged the adoption of the open method of co-ordination referred to above. The Services Directive is in that sense an anachronism — a complex and significant policy change on a sensitive subject engineered through the Commission's traditional heavyweight procedure. It is also a throwback to the economic thinking of the single market programme, with its emphasis on the removal of supply-side obstructions so as to promote competitive markets.

In some respects, the original draft directive can be seen as an attempt by the Commission to clarify and build on existing case law in the area, especially the strong assertion of the country of origin principle. The omission of this from the final text marks a retreat from the position achieved before the directive was published, though in other respects the text does bring some order to a vexed and confused subject. However, the political debate in 2004 was not what it was in 1990. In the debate about the Lisbon Agenda, some of the tensions and contradictions emerging from the single market programme achieved a political salience that the directive did not help resolve. In particular, the Lisbon Agenda and the promotion of economic growth and competitiveness, especially through labour market reform, were subject to much more criticism and debate, centring on the division between the global integration approach (allegedly Anglo-American and neo-liberal) and the more protectionist Social Europe model.

The foregoing discussion to a certain extent places the Services Directive in its legal and political context. To fully understand this instrument and the extent to which it will facilitate market integration in the services sector, however, it is necessary to look at the directive itself in more detail.

12.3 The Content of the Services Directive

12.3.1 *Structure*

The Services Directive begins with a large number of recitals, 118 in total. As noted above, the negotiations of this directive were highly contentious. During the course of negotiations, it became clear that there was no real opportunity to negotiate substantial changes to the European Parliament's proposed mechanism to facilitate the free movement of services — the mechanism that replaced the country of origin principle. According to Flowers (2008), placing desired text in the recitals became the next-best option, while conceding such text became a bargaining chip. Recitals do not form part of the substantive legislative instrument and are of little use in judicial interpretation where the provisions of that instrument are clear. However, apart from their importance in securing agreement, they can be used as an aid to interpretation where provisions are ambiguous.

The substantive part of the directive is set out in eight chapters containing 46 articles in all. General principles of European Community law are referred to explicitly in the directive. The principle of non-discrimination can be found in Articles 15, 16 and 20, for example. The principles of necessity and proportionality are also found in Articles 15 and 16. The principle of necessity is the requirement for a national measure that derogates from that state's obligation under EU law to be justified for reasons of public policy, public security, public health or the protection of the environment. The principle of proportionality is the requirement that the derogation must be suitable for attaining the objective pursued, and must not go beyond what is necessary to attain that objective.

Chapter I sets out the scope of the directive, its relationship with other provisions of European Community law and certain definitions. Chapter II contains the provisions simplifying the administrative requirements for accessing a service activity and for exercising such an activity. Chapter III deals with authorisation arrangements for the establishment of service providers. This chapter includes a provision prohibiting Member States from making access to or the exercise of a service activity subject to compliance with certain requirements (Article 14). Where Member States are permitted to impose certain potentially restrictive requirements on accessing or exercising a service activity, these states are required to evaluate such measures according to conditions set out in Article 15(3) to ensure that they are non-discriminatory, necessary and proportionate to the objective being pursued.

Chapter IV of the directive deals with the free movement of services. This chapter contains Article 16, the provision that sets out the mechanism developed by the European Parliament to replace the Commission's proposed country of origin principle. In its original form, Article 16(1) provided

> Member States shall ensure that providers are subject only to the national provisions of their Member State of origin which fall within the coordinated field. (European Commission, 2004, p. 55)

In its final form, this provision reads

> Member States shall respect the right of providers to provide services in a Member State other than that in which they are established.[13]

Chapter IV also deals with derogations from the freedom to provide services, case-by-case derogations and the rights of recipients of services. Chapter V contains provisions addressing the quality of services, and Chapter VI sets out provisions for administrative cooperation. Chapter VII sets out the convergence programme, which is aimed at developing, at the Community level, codes of conduct to facilitate the "provision of services or the establishment of a provider in another Member States, in conformity with Community law" (Article 37(1)). The last chapter, Chapter VIII contains the provisions dealing with the transposition of the directive into domestic law in the Member States, the date of entry into force of the directive and its addressees.

12.3.2 *Scope*

Despite the universal title, the Service Directive is far from universal or exhaustive. According to Article 1, the directive establishes general provisions facilitating the exercise of the freedom of establishment for service providers and the free movement of services. However, the same article states that the directive:

- does not deal with the liberalisation of services 'of general economic interest', reserved to public or private entities;
- nor the privatisation of public entities providing services;
- nor the abolition of monopoly service providers;
- nor with state aid;
- does not affect national or Community measures taken to protect or promote cultural or linguistic diversity or media pluralism;
- does not affect Member States' rules of criminal law;
- nor labour law.

---

[13] Directive 2006/123/EC of the European Parliament and of the Council of 12 December 2006 on services in the internal market, OJ 2006 L 376/36, Art. 16(1).

On the other hand, the directive does not affect the exercise of those fundamental rights as recognised in the Member States and by Community law, nor does it affect the right to negotiate, conclude and enforce collective agreements or to take industrial action in accordance with national law and practices which respect Community law.

The expression 'services of general economic interest' is not defined in the directive, nor in the EC Treaty, although as noted below, these services are explicitly excluded from the core disciplines on services. These services are a subset of a broader group of services referred to as 'services of general interest'. In its Green Paper on this broader category of services, the Commission (2003) noted that:

> … in Community practice there is broad agreement that the term [services of general economic interest] refers to services of an economic nature which the Member States or the Community subject to specific public service obligations by virtue of a general interest criterion. The concept of services of general economic interest thus covers in particular certain services provided by the big network industries such as transport, postal services, energy and communications. However, the term also extends to any other economic activity subject to public service obligations. (European Commission, 2003, p. 6)

The directive also excludes a range of other services from its application. According to Article 2(2), these include:

- non-economic services of general interest;
- financial services, such as banking, credit, insurance and re-insurance, occupational or personal pensions, securities, investment funds, payment and investment advice;
- electronic communications services and networks;
- services of temporary work agencies;
- healthcare services whether or not they are provided via healthcare facilities, and regardless of the ways in which they are organised and financed at national level or whether they are public or private;

- audiovisual services, including cinematographic services, whatever their mode of production, distribution and transmission, and radio broadcasting;
- gambling activities which involve wagering a stake with pecuniary value in games of chance, including lotteries, gambling in casinos and betting transactions;
- social services relating to social housing, childcare and support of families and persons permanently or temporarily in need which are provided by the state, by providers mandated by the state or by charities recognised as such by the state; and
- private security services.

Although healthcare services, audiovisual services and gambling activities are excluded, the European Court of Justice has ruled that these areas are already covered by Article 49 EC.[14] It is thought, therefore, that the treaty provisions will continue to apply to these areas (Barnard, 2010).

Article 3 deals with the relationship between the directive and other provisions of Community law. Where a provision of another Community act deals with services activity but conflicts with the provisions of the Services Directive, the provision of the other Community act shall prevail. The article goes on to list a number of Community acts that would prevail over the provisions of this directive to the extent of any conflict.[15] However, the list is not exhaustive.

Despite the considerable number of services excluded from the application of the directive, it still applies to services that account for more than 45% of EU GDP, according to the European Commission (2012a). The Commission assesses that considerable gains have already been made as a result of structural reform in the internal market for services following the implementation of the directive, but that still

---

[14] Now Art. 56 TFEU,

[15] Directive 96/71/EC the 'Posted Workers' Directive; 'Regulation (EEC) No 1408/71, which deals with the application of social security schemes to employed and self-employed persons and family members; Directive 2005/36/EC, on the recognition of professional qualifications'.

further gains can be made. It has set out in this initial report to the European Parliament and Council the ways in which this can be achieved. These suggestions are discussed in more detail later in this chapter.

12.3.3 *Disciplines on services*

The term 'services' is defined in Article 4 to mean "any self-employed economic activity, normally provided for remuneration, as referred to in Article 50 of the Treaty."[16] According to Barnard (2010), this definition is in accordance with the definition of services in the General Agreement on Trade in Services.

Chapter III of the Services Directive addresses the elimination of obstacles to the freedom of *establishment* of service providers. As noted above, Articles 9–13 in Chapter III set out certain principles that must be respected by authorisation schemes that Member States implement. Articles 14–15 prohibit certain particularly restrictive legal requirements that may still be in force in certain Member States, and oblige Member States to assess the compatibility of certain other legal requirements with the conditions laid down in the directive, particularly proportionality.

Chapter IV deals with the elimination of obstacles to the free movement of *services,* and in its original incarnation, contained the application of the country of origin principle in Article 16. This caused great concern about the risk of 'social dumping', and the fear that if the free movement of services were subject only to the application of the country of origin principle, re-regulation would be impossible. The principle was ultimately replaced by a hybrid mechanism proposed by the European Parliament. In the third paragraph of Article 16(1), Member States are prohibited from making access to or the exercise of a service activity in their territory subject to any requirements that do not respect the three principles of non-discrimination, necessity and proportionality.

As noted above, the directive's definition of necessity includes public policy in its list of express derogations, as well as public security, public

[16] Now Art. 57 TFEU.

health and the protection of the environment. The directive makes no reference to the judicially developed public interest requirements: presumably, the drafters of the directive decided not to apply these requirements to those activities covered by the directive. However, Barnard (2007) argues that, as indicated in the Preamble, 'public policy' may well be interpreted more broadly than the ECJ has done so far.

Barnard describes the difference between the country of origin principle and the current approach under Article 16 thus:

> Under the country-of-origin-principle, the principal regulator would have been the home state… [r]einforced by the presumption that the host state could not impose any additional requirements unless there were very good reasons… On one view, the present Article 16 comes close to the country-of-origin principle… Another reading is that the current approach appears to reverse the country-of-origin principle: it accepts that the host state can impose its own restrictions on the service provider where there are good reasons for so doing, account being taken of the protection already provided in the home state. This latter reading broadly reflects the case law of the Court, under Article 49.[17] In practice, the difference… may well be one of emphasis rather than substance: the country-of-origin principle raises a strong presumption of illegality of the host state measure; the current approach may raise a weaker presumption of illegality. (Barnard, 2010, p. 409).

In addition to the services excluded entirely from the operation of the directive by Article 2, Article 17 sets out some additional services to which the core services disciplines in Article 16 shall not apply. Of particular note are the exclusions of 'services of general economic interest', defined above, and measures (such as visas, residence permits or reporting requirements) that may be applied to certain third country nationals who move cross-border to provide a service. Article 18

[17] Now Art. 56 TFEU.

provides for further derogations from the operation of Article 16 *in exceptional circumstances only* for the purpose of taking measures relating to the safety of services. Any such derogations must fulfil conditions set out in the article itself.

Where Member States do impose national requirements on cross-border service provision consistent with Articles 16 or 17, the Member State where the service is provided is responsible for supervising the activity of the provider in its territory. The conditions for this are laid out in Articles 3, 30(1) and 31(1).

12.3.4 *Provision for mutual evaluation*

We suggest that the true innovation of the directive was always in Chapter VII on the convergence programme and in Chapter II on administrative simplification (discussed later), rather than in Chapter IV.

Chapter VII sets out a mutual evaluation process to be conducted by Member States as the means by which those 'humanly and economically obnoxious impediments to the cross-border provision of services' referred to earlier in this chapter can, ideally, be identified and removed.[18] It would be unrealistic to expect that all such impediments could be identified and removed: the services market is a dynamic one and it must be expected that administrative, legal and cultural barriers will arise from time to time as new services are offered or innovations are made to the way in which they are or can be delivered. Innovation in a dynamic market will always create unforeseen and unexpected consequences, including barriers to trade. The significance of the mutual evaluation system, however, is not that it could achieve the removal of these restrictions on cross-border trade in services because clearly it could not. The strength of this system is the way in which it requires Member States to reflect on the measures they do have in place, to report on those measures and to explain how they are consistent with the Member State's obligations under the directive. In so doing, Member

[18] Chapter VII also contains provision on further harmonisation, but this is limited to the activity of judicial recovery of debts; and private security services and transport of cash and valuables.

States must, in effect, defend the measures they have in place. This process raises awareness on the part of the institutions and agencies of the Member States and, we suggest, should engender a change in their institutional cultures over time.

The outcomes of the initial mutual evaluation process are now available and are discussed in more detail below. Thereafter, Member States are required to transmit to the Commission any changes in their requirements including new requirements, together with the reasons for them. The Commission, in turn, will communicate these transmitted requirements to other Member States. The Commission shall then, on an annual basis, provide analyses and orientations on the application of these provisions in the context of the directive.

Unlike the initial mutual evaluation process, the directive does not stipulate that these subsequent requirements would also be subject to mutual evaluation by the Member States. It would seem that the transmission by the Commission to the other Member States of these subsequent requirements is for information only. It would appear that, after the initial mutual evaluation process, the onus is in fact on the Commission and not the other Member States to evaluate these requirements and the Member States' justification of them. Nothing in the directive prevents Member States from adopting these subsequent requirements. It would therefore seem that, should the Commission (or indeed another Member State) form the view that such a requirement was not in fact consistent with a Member State's obligations under the directive, the Commission would initiate infringement proceedings under Art. 258 TFEU.

Conducting this clean sweep of measures that constitute an obstacle to cross-border trade in services should significantly reduce the number of measures in respect of which the Commission then needs to confer with individual Member States and initiate infringement proceedings. Article 41 requires the Commission to provide the European Parliament and Council with "a comprehensive report on the application of this Directive". The report is, in particular, to address the application of Article 16 but it is also to "consider the need for additional measures for matters excluded from the scope of application" of the directive. Where appropriate, the report is also to be accompanied by proposals for amendments to the Services Directive "with a view to completing the Internal Market for services". The first of these reports was to be presented to the European Parliament and Council by 28 December 2011. It was delivered on 8 June 2012. The Commission is required to provide such a report every three years thereafter, so the next report would be due at the end of 2015.

12.4 The First Round of Mutual Evaluation

The main results of the mutual evaluation process (in European Commission 2011a) were presented to the European Parliament, the Council, the European Economic and Social Committee and the Committee of the Regions on 27 January 2011. This Communication was accompanied by a more detailed document (European Commission, 2011b) describing the work that was undertaken during the mutual evaluation process. Given the magnitude and complexity of the task, the mutual evaluation process, described as an evidence-based exercise of peer review, was indispensable for ensuring a high level of engagement by all Member States with the implementation of obligations under the Services Directive.

12.4.1 *Process*

In October 2009, the Commission, the High Level Group of the Competitiveness Council and the Member States all agreed on the methodology to be used for this major exercise involving 30 countries[19]and covering close to 35,000 requirements. As reported in European Commission (2011a), Member States began meeting in clusters of five countries, between January and March 2010, to discuss the situation in those individual countries and to prepare for further discussions. Between March and October 2010, work continued with plenary meetings at which specific requirements and the main services sectors covered by the directive were examined. The Member States

[19] Iceland, Lichtenstein and Norway, all members of the European Economic Area, also participated.

identified a range of services they considered to have priority for consideration. These services were: construction and property related services; tourism and related services; food and beverage services; services of regulated professions; wholesale and retail services; business services and private education services. Between June and mid-September 2010, a public consultation was also held at which interested parties were invited to share their views. In its Communication, the Commission observed that

> [b]y putting in place a structured dialogue between Member States it has created transparency as to the results of the implementation of the Services Directive and it has helped identify and promote good regulatory practices. Discussions have also helped to foster a habit of dialogue. Contact and exchange of information between Member States (from bilateral and 'clusters' contacts to larger groups) have multiplied all along the process and have been key to its results. (European Commission, 2011a, p. 6)

Even allowing for, with the greatest of respect, a certain level of self-congratulation, these conclusions are undoubtedly valid. In addition to these gains, the mutual evaluation process enabled a detailed picture of the state of an important part of the Single Market for services to be drawn up. For the first time in the history of the European Union, Member States and the Commission conducted a thorough assessment of national rules affecting service activities. This assessment concerned not only rules at national, regional and local levels but also rules set by professional associations with regulatory powers. According to the Commission, the mutual evaluation process

> has had an unprecedented "Single Market effect" within Member States as all levels of national administrations were called upon to critically assess their own rules and those existing in other Member States from a Single Market perspective. (European Commission, 2011a, p. 6)

A further benefit of the mutual evaluation process was that those involved were able to identify the remaining obstacles for the Single Market and to lay the basis for future policy actions in the service sector. Such obstacles were not only within the legal and administrative structures of the Member States, they also resulted from the inconsistent or uncoordinated application of a number of rules of EU law that have been adopted over the years. Among the recommendations for future action, the Commission has identified the need for other single market instruments such as the Directive on the Recognition of Professional Qualifications and the E-Commerce Directive to be applied "in a streamlined way" (European Commission, 2011a, p. 12).

12.4.2 *Outcomes*

In total, Member States reported over 34,000 requirements that they felt it necessary to maintain. Most of these requirements were authorisation schemes and requirements imposed on cross-border services. It is not possible here to give a complete overview of the results of the mutual evaluation process. Such an analysis is a topic in its own right. The regulatory landscape revealed by the mutual evaluation process is a highly nuanced and rather dynamic one. In the words of the Commission:

> The different sections [of the report] focus on the requirements that have been maintained after the implementation period. They also indicate requirements that have been abolished as a result of implementation, but it should be borne in mind that Member States did not have to report all the requirements that they abolished... A number of Member States are still in the process of amending existing legislation… In those cases, certain parts of the information provided may no longer be up to date. (European Commission, 2011b, p. 9)

Section 4 of the report deals with establishment-related requirements identified by Member States. In Section 5, requirements relating to cross-border services are covered. Section 6 then deals with the situation in specific services sectors, and Section 7 sets out the results of stakeholder consultation (European Commission, 2011b).

Following the Commission's presentation of the results of the mutual evaluation process to the European Parliament and Council, a further process of 'performance checks' was launched. These 'performance checks' were designed to assess the way in which different pieces of EU legislation interact and were applied 'on the ground' in Member States. They were carried out in three significant economic sectors that had previously been identified by Member States as having priority for attention: construction, business services and tourism. This exercise enabled the Commission and Member States to identify further barriers faced daily by businesses operating in the internal markets — barriers that could not be eliminated solely by the Services Directive. The mutual evaluation process and the 'performance checks' process also identified instances of incomplete implementation of the Services Directive within the Member States.

12.5 Performance Checks

12.5.1 *Process*

Although the three areas selected for case studies represented relatively small percentages of GDP (construction 6.3%, business services 11.7% and tourism 4.4%), they were selected because of their potential for cross-border service trade within the EU. The performance checks were built around three sector-specific case studies: construction, architecture and related services; business services (tax advisers); and tourism services (tourist guides, travel agents and tour operators). The process provided the opportunity for a holistic assessment of the impact of various pieces of EU legislation on business activities.

Member States were provided with questionnaires and asked to provide a detailed explanation of the way in which national rules implementing the relevant directives would be applied on the ground to potential service providers wishing to establish themselves or provide cross-border services in their territory.

The construction sector case study involved the combined application of the Professional Qualifications Directive; the E-Commerce Directive; the Services Directive and the primary rules of the Treaty on the Functioning of the European Union (TFEU); the Directive on Misleading and Comparative Advertising; the Directive on Energy Performance of Buildings; the Directive on Waste; and the Regulation on Certain Fluorinated Greenhouse Gases. The business services case study involved the combined application of the Professional Qualifications Directive, the E-Commerce Directive, the Services Directive and the primary rules of the TFEU. The tourism case study also involved the combined application of the Professional Qualifications Directive, the E-Commerce Directive, the Services Directive and primary rules of the TFEU, together with the Package Travel Directive and the Unfair Contract Terms Directive.

This process was also useful in raising internal market awareness within competent authorities at all levels. National authorities responsible for supervising different policies were called upon to cooperate in assessing the cumulative impact that the concrete implementation of their respective rules could have on the internal market for services from the perspective of services providers.

12.5.2 *Outcomes*

The Commission Staff Working Document (European Commission, 2012b) sets out in detail the results of these performance check case studies. It is useful to set out a summary of those findings.

12.5.3 *Barriers common to the three sectors*

The performance checks highlighted a number of instances of deficient implementation of the internal market rules, including those contained in directives. A considerable part of the ECJ's jurisprudence is built on preliminary ruling matters in which the national of a Member State (individual or entity) has challenged a measure of domestic law in their own court system on the basis that the measure is incompatible with the

Member State's obligations under a directive. In order for such an action to succeed, however, the national needs to establish that the provision in the directive has direct effect and so provides them with rights under EU law that the national court must uphold and protect. If it is not possible to establish an appropriate, directly effect provision in the directive, or there is not enough time, energy or money on the part of nationals to challenge the apparently defective national measure, then it remains in place, applicable and, as the performance checks process seems to have demonstrated, a barrier to cross-border trade.

Other challenges identified concern situations in which Member States have exercised their rights under the TFEU or secondary EU legislation to derogate from measures designed to facilitate the functioning of the internal market. The performance checks revealed significant divergences in the regulation of professions across the Member States, for example. Such divergent regulatory practices, even if permitted under EU law, add to the complexity of providing professional services in the internal market.

Obstacles were also noted in relation to the existing body of consumer protection law and practices in the EU (the so-called '*acquis*').[20] Much of the existing *acquis* is based on minimum harmonisation: Member States are permitted as a matter of EU law, to introduce higher levels of consumer protection where they see this is appropriate. The difficulty with this is that services providers seeking to operate across borders must adapt their services to differing levels of consumer protection regulation. This was made particularly evident in the tourism case study.

All three case studies also revealed difficulties concerning insurance obligations.

> A significant number of Member States do not take account of insurance obligations complied with in the Member State of establishment, which results in the duplication of insurance coverage costs borne by businesses in tourism (in particular for

[20] The term '*acquis*' is used to refer to the entire body of EU law, developed since the creation of the European Communities and includes both hard and soft law.

> travel agencies and tour operators), business services and construction sectors. (European Commission, 2012b, p. 7)

Service providers are also confronted with the practical difficulty of finding appropriate insurance cover for providing cross-border services.

12.5.4 *Sector-specific barriers*

In the construction case study, businesses and professionals were found to have problems because of a "lack of mutual recognition clauses in sector-specific EU legislation that provides for authorisation or registration schemes or the certification of experts" (European Commission, 2012b, p. 8). The business services case study revealed that, despite the implementation of the Services Directive, many Member States have kept in place certain limitations on corporate structure and capital ownership requirements in respect of certain professional services. It was also revealed that not all total bans on a form of commercial communication for regulated professions have been removed. The tourism case study revealed certain practical difficulties in the application of the distinction between the establishment and the cross-border service provision requirements. Tourist guides are often subject to the rules concerning establishment when all they want to do is provide their services across the border. The divergence of consumer protection rules governing package travel sales was also identified as a problem specific to the tourism sector. While this problem in generic form was also identified as one facing all three sectors, it is to be expected that those sectors of the services economy having considerable contact with consumers will carry a heavier burden in this regard than will other sectors of that economy.

12.5.5 *Conclusions*

The conclusions drawn from this process, along with the results of the mutual evaluation process, inform the proposed actions contained in the Commission's 'Services Package' for 2012–15 (discussed further below). It is not enough to ensure that existing EU legislation is given its full effect through appropriate implementation. It is also essential that such implementation translates into benefits on the ground for businesses and professionals. Indicators that this is happening include updated Points of Single Contact and evidence of better use of the IMI (Internal Market Information system). Other challenges concern smoothing out the differences resulting from legitimate regulatory divergence across Member States in certain areas (for example, in regulated professions, in the recognition of professional qualifications, and in consumer protection). Addressing questions concerning the availability of appropriate insurance products is also to be addressed in the responses to the outcomes of the performance checks process.

12.6 Administrative Simplification

According to Chapter II, Article 5 of the Services Directive, Member States are required to examine their procedures and formalities concerning accessing and exercising services and to simplify them. The Commission is empowered to introduce at the EU level harmonised forms equivalent to certificates, attestations and any other documents required of a service provider. Arguably, however, the most significant article in Chapter II is Article 6. This requires Member States to establish Points of Single Contact through which providers can complete all procedures and formalities needed for access to the service provider's activities. In particular, providers should be able to use the Points of Single Contact to complete "all declarations, notifications or applications necessary for authorisation from the competent authorities, including applications for inclusion in a register, a roll or a database, or for registration with a professional body or association; and any applications for authorisation needed to exercise the service activities".[21] The Points of Single Contact have been an important development in removing a significant number of administrative barriers. They are connected to the Internal Market Information system (IMI) that was launched in 2008 to enhance administrative cooperation (European Commission, 2011c).

---

[21] Article 6 (1).

In Chapter VI, Administrative Cooperation, Article 28 stipulates that Member States shall designate one or more liaison points, the contact details of which shall be communicated to the other Member States and the Commission. National IMI coordinators may be nominated as these liaison points (European Commission, 2009). When IMI was first launched, it supported the revised Directive on the Recognition of Professional Qualifications. Since December 2009, Member States have also been required to use IMI to fulfil their information exchange obligations set out in the Services Directive (European Commission, 2011c). IMI is a secure, reusable, multilingual, online electronic application developed by the Commission in partnership with the Member States. The idea underpinning IMI is to "replace the very high number of bilateral relationships linking EU Member States with a single interface, the IMI network" (European Commission, 2011c, p. 3).

At the end of 2011, 6,802 authorities were registered in IMI, 1,065 more than the previous year (European Commission, 2012c). There are still authorities in the Member States not registered with IMI. It is to be expected that this will change over time, as awareness of the IMI is raised. It should also be unavoidable as work continues on developing and improving the Points of Single Contact across the EU.

12.7 Services Package 2012–15

In its 'Services Package', launched on 8 June 2012, the Commission proposed a set of actions intended to stimulate further growth in the services sector. These proposals are based on the outcomes of the mutual evaluation and 'performance checks' processes. The Commission will focus on those service sectors regarded as having significant economic weight and 'above average' growth potential (European Commission, 2012a):

- business services, representing 11.7% of GDP;
- construction, representing 6.3% of GDP;
- tourism, representing 4.4% of GDP; and
- retail, representing 4.2% of GDP.

The Commission intends to follow a 'zero tolerance' policy for non-compliance with the unequivocal obligations imposed on Member States by the Services Directive. This approach will apply in the first instance to the examples of non-compliance already identified through the mutual evaluation and 'performance checks' processes. No doubt, as other examples come to light, they too would be subject to this 'zero tolerance' policy. This means that the Commission will use the infringement procedures under the TFEU, referred to earlier in the chapter, where Member States fail to comply with their obligations under EU law.

There are a number of instances where Member States have discretion in implementing the obligations under the directive. This means that, although Member States may not be failing to comply with their obligations, the extent to which permissible measures vary across Member States can create its own barrier to cross-border trade. To deal with this, the Commission proposes working with the Member States to launch "a peer review process and exchange of best practices focusing on requirements limiting company structures and capital ownership and on the freedom to provide services clause" (European Commission, 2012a, p. 6).

Member States will be required to eliminate all restrictions and authorisations which are not justified on the basis of the directive. In particular, they will be required to review the necessity and proportionality of requirements imposed on service providers and to assess the economic benefits of eliminating any remaining, legitimate restrictions. The Commission will make country-specific recommendations on priority actions in the context of the European Semester for 2013. In light of these outcomes, the Commission may propose further legislation on specific issues. Member States are also required to improve their efforts to enhance the use of the IMI and will be assisted by the Commission in these efforts (European Commission, 2012a).

Other actions in the Commission's Services Package include improving the regulatory framework for professional services in Member States; encouraging the promulgation of a modernised Professional Qualifications Directive; 'vigorously' enforcing the Professional Qualifications and E-Commerce Directive; and "ensuring an increased use of mutual recognition clauses in future proposals of sector-specific legislation setting up authorisation schemes for experts providing specialised services" (European Commission, 2012a, p. 9). Specific attention has also been given to further developing the Points of Single Contact (PSCs) in the Member States:

> Member States must make their PSCs fully compliant with the requirements of the Services Directive as a matter of urgency. By the end of 2014 Member States, assisted by the Commission are encouraged to develop the second generation PSCs which should (1) cover all procedures during the business life cycle, (2) be multilingual, and (3) be more user-friendly. The Commission will agree with Member States criteria for the second generation PSCs in the form of a 'PSC Charter'. The Commission will launch a communication campaign on PSCs in 2013, coordinate with Member States to improve the internet presence of PSCs and engage with business organisations to make businesses more aware of PSCs and further promote their use. (European Commission, 2012a, p. 12)

The full Communication from the Commission makes very interesting reading and the agenda is unquestionably ambitious. The extent to which further integration of the services market in the EU succeeds will be due in no small part, we suggest, to the dedication and engagement of the Commission, the European Parliament and Council and the Member States themselves. As awareness of these developments grows at the 'grass roots' level, there should also be an added impetus coming from service providers, those accessing services and consumers more generally.

Though it was ambiguous on some important points, to supporters of the Social Europe model the failed European Constitutional Treaty of 2004 appeared to give too much of a commitment to a neo-liberal understanding of economic integration — in other words, to emphasis on the openness of the single market. In political terms, therefore, the publication of the draft text of the Services Directive during the referendum campaigns on the European Constitutional Treaty produced a direct resonance with the debate over the directive, and achieved for it a much greater prominence than it might otherwise have had. The directive as amended and approved, to put it somewhat simply, bears much more of a Social Europe stamp than the original, excluding public sector policy areas such as health and, as we have seen, allowing the country of destination to apply potentially restrictive requirements relating to health and safety, pension provision and labour law.

12.8 Lessons for Other Countries

In its Communication on the mutual evaluation process, the Commission acknowledged that the success of the process was thanks to the active engagement of the Member States who took ownership of the process and actively participated in it. According to the Commission, this high level of engagement was also supported by strong political backing, including from the European Parliament and the Council (European Commission, 2011a). It is important not to underestimate the significance of these two elements: the level of ownership of the process on the part of the Member States and the strong political support given the enterprise at all levels of the EU legal structure. It is questionable whether the mutual evaluation process would have achieved the results it did if either, let alone both of these elements had been missing.

Much of the success of market integration in services in the EU will depend on the extent to which the Member States and the Commission and other EU institutions work together to achieve this. It must be remembered, however, that the Commission has available to it the 'stick' of the infringement procedure with which to back up any exhortations to Member States to comply with their obligations under EU law. The 'zero tolerance' policy set out in the Services Package is a clear statement that the Commission intends to use this procedure sooner rather than later where clear breaches of EU law are identified. We suggest, however, that the value of the procedure is not so much in the punitive aspect of being taken before the ECJ, although this is not to be underestimated. Rather, the value of relying on this procedure as a 'regulatory tool' is that it ensures that conversations about services and improving market integration continue between Member States and Member States and the Commission. This is part of the behavioural and cultural change that will have lasting benefits flowing to other areas of EU law, regulation and policy.

12.9 Conclusion

In its final form, the Services Directive is notably different to the original proposal. It achieves certain useful administrative simplification and co-operation aimed at reducing obstacles to the free movement of services and the freedom of establishment. Craig and de Burca (2008) are of the view that the regulatory provisions in Articles 16–18 are weaker and more complicated as a result of the change. In view of the reactions to the country of origin principle however, the survival of the directive depended on a pragmatic adjustment that could promote the further integration of the internal market for services in the EU.

It is worth noting that though the debate and outcome may seem to have resulted in a policy defeat for the European Commission, the long-term consequences are more mixed. The services reform covers a major proportion (up to 40%, according to the Commission) of EU economic activity and had the potential either to wither in the face of unmanageable numbers of cases going to the European Court of Justice, or to the Commission itself for adjudication, or alternatively to achieve the most significant extension to the Single Market since 1992. In practice, though it is too early to say whether the boost to economic integration can be achieved, the introduction of mutual evaluation and performance checks appears to have gone a long way towards avoiding the log-jams and Member State inertia that impeded the implementation of many previous ambitious initiatives in the single market programme. In developing this policy tool, the Commission has found a new instrument of implementation in mutual evaluation based on bilateral and multilateral interaction between Member States that may be applicable in other sectors. The report of the Internal Market Committee of the European Parliament on the Services Directive, approved in October 2011, criticised the delays of some Member States in implementing the directive but welcomed the development of mutual evaluation and called for it to be used more widely as a flexible instrument on a case-by case basis, suggesting that "the tool should be proposed in a targeted manner for inclusion in selected directives of a 'horizontal' nature which imply numerous transposition measures and provide for a wide margin of discretion for the Member States" (European Parliament, 2011, p. 8.)

The Commission will continue to be involved in promoting convergence of standards and practice, in monitoring procedures relating to administrative co-operation and in developing Community-wide codes of conduct to facilitate the growth of cross-border service provision. Under the Lisbon Agenda, the Commission already has the structures, procedures and powers to engage in this kind of policy-making. Paradoxical as it may seem, a directive which started life as a classical piece of single market legislation may yet prove to be an extension of the open method of coordination. The Services Directive is only one of a number of EU acts addressing the integration of the internal market for services. Its contribution to economic integration may yet prove to be significant not only for the practical benefits of increased intra-EU trade in services in terms of economic growth and innovation, but also as a prototype of new forms of 'flexible instruments' available to the European Commission in this policy sector.

References

Abdurafikov, R. (2009) 'Russian electricity market: Current state and perspectives', VTT Working Papers 121, http://www.vtt.fi/inf/pdf/workingpapers/2009/W121.pdf, Accessed on 10 February 2010.

Abe, T. (2007a) 'Challenges to regulating the utilities', Speech to Port Moresby Chamber of Commerce Inc., 5 October, ICCC, Port Moresby.

Abe, T. (2007b) 'Time to get the facts straight on mobile competition', Press statement, 30 July 2007, ICCC, Port Moresby.

Alliende, M.P. (2001) 'La Construcción de los Ferrocarriles en Chile 1850-1913', *Revista Austral de Ciencias Sociales*, 5(enero), pp. 143-161.

Asia Pacific Economic Cooperation (APEC) various years. Individual Action Plans. Available at http://www.apec-iap.org/, Accessed between June 2009 and September 2012.

Asia Pacific Energy Research Centre (2003) Natural Gas Market Reform in the Asia Pacific Region, http://www.ieej.or.jp/aperc/pdf/project2002/gas-market.pdf Accessed on 1 February 2013.

Asian Development Bank (ADB) (2009) Strategy and Action Plan for the East-West Economic Corridor.

Asian Development Bank Institute (ADBI) (2009) 'Transport Infrastructure and Trade Facilitation in the Greater Mekong Sub-region', Working Paper Series No. 130.

Asian Transportation Research Society (ATRANS) (2008) 'Transportation Research Challenges in Thailand Sub-Project on Thailand Road Safety', Special Research Project 2007 Project No: A-07/ 003-1.

Asia-Pacific Economic Cooperation (APEC) (2005) *Thailand's Transport Progress towards the Bogor Goals*, September 2005.

Asia-Pacific Environmental Innovation Strategy Project (APEIS) (2006) Research on Innovative and Strategic Policy Options (RISPO), Good Practices Inventory, Van Transit System in Bangkok Metropolitan Region.

Asmild, M., Holvad, T., Hougaard, J.L. and Kronborg, D. (2005) 'Railway reforms: Do they influence operating efficiency?, Discussion Papers 08-05, Department of Economics, University of Copenhagen.

AT Kearney (2012) 'Global Retail Expansion: Keeps on Moving', available at http://www.atkearney.com/consumer-products-retail/global-retail-development-index, Accessed on 22 January 2013.

Atack, J., Bateman, F., Haines, M. and Margo, R.A. (2009) 'Did Railroads Induce or Follow Economic Growth? Urbanization and Population Growth in the American Midwest, 1850-60', NBER Working Paper No. 14640.

Atkinson, N. (2007) *Trainland: How railways made New Zealand*, Random House: Auckland.

ATON (2010) 'Electricity distribution: RAB must go on', ATON LLC, 4 February 2010.

ATON (2012) Electricity supply: Sector undermined by regulatory changes. Equity Research – Utilities. ATON LLC. 22 March 2012.

ATS (2010) 'Wholesale Price Report 2008', Administrator of Trading System, http://www.atsenergo.ru/idc/groups/rt_cost_review/documents/ats_download/ats078093.pdf, Accessed on 20 February 2010.

Auckland Regional Transport Authority (2006) *A Step-change for Auckland. Rail Development Plan 2006*, http://www.aucklandtransport.govt.nz/improving-transport/plans-proposals/IntegratedTravel/Documents/Original/AT_ARTA_Policy_Rail DevelopmentPlanSeptember2006.pdf, Accessed on 8 December 2012.

Auckland Regional Transport Authority (2009). *Annual Report 2009*, http://www.aucklandtransport.govt.nz/about-us/publications/Reports/Documents/AT-ARTA-Report-AnnualReport2009.pdf, Accessed on 8 December 2012.

Australian Parliament, House of Representatives (2008) 'Rebuilding Australia's Coastal Shipping Industry'.

Bageant, E.R., Barrett, C.B. and Lentz, E.C. (2010) 'Food Aid and Agricultural Cargo Preference', Cornell University Policy Brief, November 2010.

Bangkok Post (2009) http://www.bangkokpost.com/business/economics/30175/ptt-sees-gas-subsidy-cost-rising-25, dated 29 December 2009, Accessed on February 2010.

Banomyong, R. (n.d., c. 2006) 'Logistics impact on trade and economic development in Lao PDR: the Thai factor', Report written for the World Bank, Thammasat University.

Barnard, C. (2010) *The Substantive Law of the EU: The Four Freedoms,* 3rd edn, Oxford: Oxford University Press.

Barrett, C.B. and Maxwell, D.G. (2005) *Food Aid After Fifty Years: Recasting Its Role*, London, Routledge.

Batten, A, Gouy, J. and Duncan, R. (2009) 'Papua New Guinea Survey: from boom to gloom?' *Pacific Economic Bulletin,* 24(1): 1–26.

Baumgartner, O. (2009) 'Further rise in tariffs inevitable – Support for investment activity still lacking', *Nezavisimaya Gazeta,* 11 August 2009. http://wwww.ng.ru/energy/2009-08-11/12_tarify.html, Accessed on 13 February 2010 (in Russian).

Belyaev, L. (2005) 'The need for a regulation of the generation capacity development in a competitive electricity market', Power Tech, 2005 IEEE Russia, 27–30 June.

Belyaev, L.S., Marchenko, O.V. and Podkovalnikov, S.V. (2002) 'Expected consequences of transition to market in Russian electric power industry', Power System Technology, 2002, Proceedings, PowerCon 2002, International Conference on Power System Technology Proceedings Vol. 1 Digital Object Identifier: 10.1109/ICPST.2002.1053497, pp.24–28.

Belyaev, L.S., Voropai, N.I. Chudinova, L.Y. Podkovalnikov, S.V. and Savelyev, V.A. (2005) 'Prospects of electricity infrastructure in East Asia', Power Engineering Society General Meeting. IEEE Digital Object Identifier: 10.1109/PES.2005.1489190, Vol. 2, pp.1536–39.

Bennett, A. (2012) 'Govt admits cash not there for KiwiRail turnaround', 15 August, *New Zealand Herald,* http://www.nzherald.co.nz/business/news/article.cfm?c_id=3&objectid=10827019, Accessed on 8 December 2012.

Borchert, I., Gootiiz, B., and Mattoo, A. (2012) 'Policy barriers to international trade in services : evidence from a new database', Policy Research working paper; no. WPS 6109. Washington D.C. - The Worldbank. http://documents.worldbank.org/curated/en/ 2012/06/16441100/policy-barriers-international-trade-services-evidence-new-database, Accessed on November 11 2012.

Bosworth, M. and Duncan, R.C. (2002) 'Facilitating the accession of ESCAP developing countries to WTO through regional cooperation', in *Current status of the WTO accession process and the experience of ESCAP acceding countries*, ESCAP Studies in Trade and Investment 49, United Nations, New York.

Bridgman, D. (2008) 'Treasury papers show government was sucker punched over rail deal', *National Business Review*, 16 September, http://www.nbr.co.nz/article/treasury-papers-show-government-was-sucker-punched-over-rail-deal-35245, Accessed on 13 February 2010.

Brooks, M. (2009) 'Liberalization in Maritime Transport', International Transport Forum Paper 2009-2, OECD/ITF, Paris.

Bureau of Infrastructure, Transport and Regional Economics (BITRE) 2011, 'Australian Sea Freight 2009-10', http://www.bitre.gov.au/statistics/maritime/australian_sea_freight.aspx, Accessed on September 2012.

Bureau of Infrastructure, Transport and Regional Economics (BITRE) 2008, 'Australian Sea Freight 2006-07', http://www.bitre.gov.au/statistics/maritime/australian_sea_freight.aspx, Accessed on September 2012.

Bureau of Infrastructure, Transport and Regional Economics (BITRE) various years, 'Australian Sea Freight', http://www.bitre.gov.au/statistics/maritime/australian_sea_freight.aspx, Accessed on September 2012.

Bureau of Infrastructure, Transport and Regional Economics (BITRE) various years, 'Waterline', http://www.bitre.gov.au/statistics/maritime/index.aspx, Accessed on September 2012.

Bureau of Infrastructure, Transport and Regional Economics (BITRE) (2008) Freight Rates in Australia 1964–65 to 2007–08, Information Sheet 28, October 2008, http://www.bitre.gov.au/publications/2008/files/is_028.pdf, Accessed on September 2012.

Bureau of Transport and Regional Economics (BTRE) (2006) 'Freight Measurement and Modelling in Australia', Report 112, March 2006.

Bureau of Transport Economics (BTE) (2000) 'Coastal Freight in Australia 1998-99', available at http://www.bitre.gov.au/publications/2000/files/ip_046.pdf, Accessed on September 2012.

Bureau of Transportation Statistics (BTS) (2012) 'National Transport Statistics', http://www.bts.gov/publications/national_transportation_statistics/, Accessed on September 2012.

Chanda, R. and Gupta, P. (2011) 'Service Sector Liberalisation in India: Key Lessons and Challenges', Occasional Paper No. 88, Johannesburg: South African Institute of International Affairs.

Chanda, R. and Sasidaran, G. (2007) 'GATS and Developments in India's Services Sector', in S. Karmakar, R. Kumar and B. Debroy (eds), *India's Liberalization Experience: Hostage to the WTO?*, New Delhi: Sage Publications: 169–212.

CITRA (2008) *Análisis de la Seguridad en el Transporte Ferroviario*, for Ministerio de Transportes y Telecomunicaciones de Chile.

Containerisation International (2010) Online database at http://www.ci-online.co.uk/, Accessed on July 2010.

Cooke, D, Antonyuk, A. Murray, I. (2012) *Toward a More Efficient and Innovative Electricity Sector in Russia. Consultation* Paper, International Energy Agency Insights Series 2012 International Energy Agency/OECD, Paris.

Craig, P. and de Burca, G. (2008) *EU Law: Text, Cases and Materials,* 4th edn., Oxford: Oxford University Press.

Cullen, M. (2008a) Address to the All Aboard Rail Conference, 26 October, http//www.beehive.govt.nz/speech/address+all+aboard+rail+conference, Accessed on 13 February 2010.

Cullen, M. (2008b) 'New Zealand's rail back in New Zealand hands', 1 July, http://www.beehive.govt.nz/speech/rail+returns+to+new+zealand+hands, Accessed on 13 February 2010.

Cullen, M. (2008c) '$121 million investment boost for rail', 1 October, http://www.beehive.govt.nz/speech/121+million+investment+boost+rail, Accessed on 13 February 2010.

de Witte, B. (2007) 'Setting the Scene: How did Services get to Bolkestein and Why?', EUI Working Papers, 20/2007, Florence: European University Institute.

Dee, P. (2012) 'Measuring and Modelling Regulatory Restrictions in Services', Chapter in 1 in *Priorities and Pathways in Services Reform – Volume 1: Modelling and Quantitative Studies*, World Scientific, Singapore.

Dee, P. and McNaughton, A. (2011) 'Promoting Domestic Reforms through Regionalism', ADBI Working Paper No. 312, Tokyo: Asian Development Bank Institute.

Deloitte (2011) 'Economic Impacts of the Proposed Shipping Reform Package', Deloitte Access Economics, February 2012.

Department of Business Development (2010) Business Online data, http:// www.thairegistration.com, Accessed on 10 January, 2010.

Department of Communication and Information (2008) 'National Information and Communication Technology (ICT) Policy', April 2008, Government of Papua New Guinea, Port Moresby.

Department of Communication and Information (2009) 'National ICT policy: phase 2 reforms (final report)', March 2009, Government of Papua New Guinea, Port Moresby.

Department of Land Transport, Land Transport Promotion Center (2010) http://www.ltpcenter.com, Accessed on January 12, 2010.

Digicel PNG (2008) 'A monopoly on international communications will mean poorer service and less competition', Media release, 26 March 2008, http://www.digicelpng.com/about/article_printversion.php?aid =10101&pn=in_the_media, Accessed on 24 June 2010.

DIPP (2012a) 'Consolidated FDI Policy', New Delhi: Ministry of Commerce and Industry, Government of India.

DIPP (2012b) 'Factsheet on Foreign Direct Investment (FDI): From April 2000 to October 2012', New Delhi: Ministry of Commerce and Industry, Government of India, available at http://dipp.nic.in/English/Publications/FDI_Statistics/2012/india_FDI_October2012.pdf.

DIPP (Department of Industrial Policy and Promotion) (2010) 'Consolidated FDI Policy', New Delhi: Ministry of Commerce and Industry, Government of India.

DPEIDC (Department of Public Enterprises, Information and Development Co-operation) (2006) 'National Information and Communication Technology (ICT) Policy', September 2006, Government of Papua New Guinea, Port Moresby.

DPEIDC (Department of Public Enterprises, Information and Development Co-operation) (2007) 'National Information and Communication Technology (ICT) Policy', May 2007, Government of Papua New Guinea, Port Moresby.

Dravitzki, V. and Lester, T. (2006) *Economics drove our first sustainable urban transport system and the unsustainable one that followed*, http://www.thesustainabilitysociety.org.nz/conference/2007/papers/DRAVITZKI-Economics DrivesUs.pdf, Accessed on 8 December 2012.

Drugov, S. (2008) *Guarding security of the Far East energy system*, 'Energorynok' (Energy Market), No. 7, http://www.e-m.ru/er/2008-07/23510/?phrase_id=23106 (in Russian), Accessed on 20 February 2010.

EFE (2009) 'El Futuro Del Sistema Ferroviario', position paper by the Board of Directors of EFE.

EFE (2011) *Memoria Anual 2011,* Santiago, Chile.

Energy Administration (2010) Website http://www.eia.gov/petroleum/data.cfm#prices, Accessed June 2010.

Energy Strategy 2030, http://minenergo.gov.ru/activity/energostrategy/ (in Russian), Accessed on 25 February 2010.

Energy website n.d. http://www.energy.go.th/en/knowledgeDetail.asp?id=118, Accessed on February 2010.

English, B. and Ryall, T. (2012) 'Next steps in KiwiRail's Turnaround Plan', from http://www.national.org.nz/Article.aspx?articleId=38833, Accessed on 8 December 2012.

EPPO(n.d.) http://www.eppo.go.th/thaienergynews/Energy_News/Articles/ArticleShow Detail.aspx?ObjectID= 349., Accessed on February 2010.

European Commission (2000) 'Communication from the Commission to the Council and the European Parliament: An Internal Market Strategy for Services', COM (2000) 888, Brussels: European Commission.

European Commission (2003) 'Green Paper on Services of General Interest', COM(2003) 270 final, Brussels: European Commission.

European Commission (2004) 'Proposal for a Directive of the European Parliament and of the Council on Services in the Internal Market', COM (2004) 002 final, Brussels: European Commission.

European Commission (2009) 'Commission Decision 2009/739/EC of 2.10.2009 setting out the Practical Arrangements for the Exchange of Information by Electronic Means between Member States under Chapter VI of Directive 2006/123/EC of the European Parliament and of the Council on Services in the Internal Market', [2009] OJ L263/32, 7.10.2009 Brussels: European Commission.

European Commission (2011a) 'Communication from the Commission to the European Parliament, the Council, the European Economic and Social Committee and the Committee of the Regions Towards a better functioning Single Market for services – building on the results of the mutual evaluation process of the Services Directive', COM (2011) 20 final, Brussels: European Commission.

European Commission (2011b) 'On the Process of Mutual Evaluation of the Services Directive. Accompanying document to the Communication from the Commission to the European Parliament, The Council, the European Economic and Social Committee and the Committee of the Regions.

European Parliament, the Council, the European Economic and Social Committee and the Committee of the Regions: Towards a better functioning Single Market for services – building on the results of the mutual evaluation process of the Services Directive', Commission Staff Working Paper SEC (2011) 102 final, Brussels: European Commission.

European Commission (2011c) 'Communication from the Commission to the European Parliament, the Council, the European Economic and Social Committee and the Committee of the Regions: Better Governance of the Single Market through Greater Administrative Cooperation: A Strategy for Expanding and Developing the Internal Market Information System (IMI)', COM (2011) 75 final, Brussels: European Commission.

European Commission (2012a) 'Communication from the Commission to the European Parliament, the Council, the European Economic and Social Committee and the Committee of the Regions on the Implementation of the Services Directive. A partnership for new growth in services 2012–2015', COM (2012) 261 final, Brussels: European Commission.

European Commission (2012b) 'Commission Staff Working Document on the Result of the Performance Checks of the Internal Market for Services (Construction, Business Services and Tourism). Accompanying the document Communication from the Commission to the European Parliament, the Council, the European Economic and Social Committee and the Committee of the Regions on the Implementation of the Services Directive. A partnership for new growth in services 2012–2015', SWD (2012) 147 final, Brussels: European Commission.

European Commission (2012c) 'The Internal Market Information System (IMI) Operation and Development in 2011', Staff Working Document (2012) 26 final, Brussels: European Commission.

European Conference of Ministers of Transport (2005) *Railway Reform and Charges for the Use of Infrastructure,* OECD.

European Parliament (2011) 'Report 4 October 2011 on the Mutual Evaluation process of the services directive (2011/2085/INI)', Committee on the Internal Market and Consumer Protection, Rapporteur Malgordata Handzlik.

Evans, L., Grimes, A. and Wilkinson, B. with Teece, D. (1996) 'Economic Reform in New Zealand 1984–95: The Pursuit of Efficiency', *Journal of Economic Literature*, 34 (December): 1856–902.

FAS (2009a) 'Analysis of the electricity (capacity) retail distribution market in 2008', 28 December 2009, Federal Antimonopoly Service, Russian Federation. http://www.fas.gov.ru/analisys/tek/a_28410.shtml, Accessed on 16 February 2010.

FAS (2009b) 'Attention small businesses: Technological connections to electric networks', Electrical Energy Supervision Department. http://www.fas.gov.ru/monopoly/power/a_25269.shtml?print, Accessed on 9 July 2009.

Federal Maritime Commission (FMC) Website. http://www.fmc.gov/, Accessed September 2012.

Flower, J. (2008) 'Negotiating European Legislation: The Services Directive' in C. Barnard (ed.) *Cambridge Yearbook of European Studies, 2006–2007*, Cambridge: Cambridge University Press: pp.217-38.

François, J. and Hoekman, B. (2010) 'Services Trade and Policy', *Journal of Economic Literature*, American Economic Association, 48(3): 642-92, September.

Francois, J.F. and Hoekman, B. (2009) 'Services Trade and Policy', Johannes Kepler University Economic Working Paper, March 2009.

FSS (2010a) 'Electrical energy balance of Russia, 2008', Federal Statistical Services of Russian Federation. http://www.gks.ru/free_doc/new_site/business/prom/el_balans.htm, Accessed on 20 February 2010 (in Russian).

FSS (2010b) 'Industry of Russia 2008', Federal Statistical Services of Russian Federation', http://www.gks.ru/bgd/regl/b08_48/Main.htm (in Russian), Accessed on .

Gaynor, B. (2008) 'Government Toll buy a sad indictment', *New Zealand Herald*, 10 May, http://www.nzherald.co.nz/business/news/article.cfm?c_id=3&objectid=10509183, Accessed on 22 February 2010.

General Accounting Office (GAO) (1990) 'Cargo Preference Requirements - Their Impact on USA Food Aid Programs and the USA Merchant Marine, Report to the Chairman, Committee on Agriculture, House of Representatives, June 1990', GAO-NSIAD 90-194, GAO, Washington DC.

General Accounting Office (GAO) (1994) 'Cargo Preference Laws – Estimated Costs and Effects, GAO Report to Congressional Requesters, November 1994', GAO/RCED-95-34, GAO Washington DC.

Global Insight (2009) 'An Evaluation of Maritime Policy in Meeting the Commercial and Security Needs of the United States', 7 January 2009, http://www.ihsglobalinsight.com/gcpath/MARADPolicyStudy.pdf, Accessed on February 2010

Gore, O., Viljainen, S., Makkonen, M., Kuleshov, D. (2012) 'Russian electricity market reform: Deregulation or re-regulation?', *Energy Policy* 41, pp. 676–85.

Government of India (2011) 'Economic Survey 2010–11', New Delhi: Ministry of Finance, Government of India.

Government of India (2012) 'Economic Survey 2011–12', New Delhi: Ministry of Finance, Government of India.

Greacen, C. (2005) 'Privatization of profits, socialization of costs and risks: privatization in Thailand's power sector', PowerPoint presentation, Windsor Hotel, Bangkok, 16-17 July 2005.

Greacen, C.S. and Greacen, C. (2004) 'Thailand's Electricity Reforms: Privatization of Benefits and Socialization of Costs and Risks', *Pacific Affairs*, Vol. 77(3): 517–541.

Gupta P. (2011) 'Regulatory Barriers Affecting Factor Mobility in International Trade in Services: Measurement and Implications', PhD thesis, Mimeo, Bangalore: Indian Institute of Management, March.

Gwilliam, K.(2008) 'Bus transport: Is there a regulatory cycle?', *Transportation Research Part A: Policy and Practice*, 42(9), 1183–94.

Heatley, D. (2009) *The history and future of rail in New Zealand*, NZ Institute for the Study of Competition and Regulation Inc., http://www.iscr.org.nz/f511,14914/The_history_and_future_of_rail_in_New_Zealand_RR_.pdf, Accessed 8 December 2012.

Heatley, D. (2010) 'Level crossing: collision ahead?', *Competition and Regulation Times*, 32, July, http://www.iscr.org.nz/f584,16670/ISCR_July_2010_2_.pdf, Accessed on 9 December 2012.

Hossain, M. and Kathuria, R. (2003) 'Telecommunications Reform and the Emerging New Economy — The Case of India', presented at the DSA conference, 10-12 September, University of Strathclyde, Glasgow.

Hufbauer, G.C. and Elliott, K.A. (1993) *The Costs of US Trade Barriers*, Washington, Institute for International Economics.

Hunt, L.C. and Mantajit, J. (2005) 'The Thai Gas Industry: A Comparative Study of the Efficiency and Technological Progress'. http://www.seec.surrey.ac.uk/people/lhunt/Research/H&MMimeoForWebAugust2005.pdf, Accessed on 1 February 2013.

ICAI (Institute of Chartered Accountants of India) (2010) 'Report on Operation of Multinational Network Accounting Firms in India', New Delhi: Institute of Chartered Accountants of India.

ICCC (Independent Consumer and Competition Commission) (2006) 'Introduction of Competition in Mobile Phone Networks', Media release, Office of the Commissioner, ICCC, Port Moresby.

ICCC (Independent Consumer and Competition Commission) (2007) 'Time to get the facts straight on mobile competition', Media release, Office of the Commissioner, ICCC, Port Moresby.

IEA (2005) Russian Electricity Reform: Emerging Challenges and Opportunities, International Energy Agency/OECD, Paris.

IEA (2009) 'Key world energy statistics', International Energy Agency, Paris, 2009. http://www.iea.org/Textbase/nppdf/free/2009/key_stats_2009.pdf, Accessed on.

Inter RAO-UES (2008) Investors' presentation, April 2008.

Inter RAO-UES (2009) 'Russian Energy Trip. Presentation May 13, 2009', http://www.Inter RAO.ru/_upload/editor_files/file0529.pdf, Accessed on 8 February 2010.

ISCR (1999a) *The Privatisation of New Zealand Rail: Part 1: Assessment of History, Markets and Data*, New Zealand Institute for the Study of Competition and Regulation, http://www.iscr.org.nz/f249,4986/4986_tranzrail_part_1_100899.pdf, Accessed on 13 February 2010.

ISCR (1999b) *The Privatisation of New Zealand Rail Part 2: Quantitative Cost Benefit Analysis*, New Zealand Institute for the Study of Competition and Regulation Inc., http://www.iscr.org.nz/f251,5018/tranzrail_part_2_100799.pdf, Accessed on 8 December 2010.

Islands Business (2007) 'Digicel issue raised with government', *Islands Business Online*, http://www.islandsbusiness.com/news/index_dynamic/containerNameToReplace=Middle Middle/focusModuleID=130/focusContentID=9935/tableName=mediaRelease/overide SkinName=newsArticle-full.tpl, Accessed on 24 June 2010.

Japan External Trade Organization (JETRO) (2008)'Current Status and Issues of Logistics Network in ASEAN-Outline of ASEAN Logistics Network Map Project', Workshop on Statistics of Asian Traffic and Transportation, March 2008.

Japan International Cooperation Agency (JICA) (2007)'The research on the Cross-border Transportation Infrastructure: Phase 2, Final Report', December 2007.

Joku, H. (2008) 'Telecommunications: Digicel tightlipped on gateway issue', *Islands Business Online*, http://www.islandsbusiness.com/islands_business/index_dynamic/ containerNameToReplace=MiddleMiddle/focusModuleID=17940/overideSkinName=iss ueArticle-full.tpl, Accessed on 24 June 2010.

Joseph, M., Soundararajan, N., Gupta, M. and Sahu, S. (2008) 'Impact of Organized Retailing on the Unorganized Sector', New Delhi: Indian Council for Research on International Economic Relations.

Joskow, P. (2006) 'Competitive electricity markets ad investment in new generating capacity', AEI-Brookings Joint Center for Regulatory Studies, Working Paper 06-14, May 2006.

Joskow, P. (2008a) 'Capacity payments in imperfect electricity markets: Need and design', *Utilities Policy* 16, pp. 159–170.

Joskow, P. (2008b) 'Lessons learned from electricity market liberalisation', *The Energy Journal*, Special Issue 'The Future of Electricity: Papers in Honor of David Newbery' http://econ-www.mit.edu/files/2093, Accessed on.

Joskow, P.L. (2008) 'Lessons learned from electricity market liberalization', *The Energy Journal,* Special issue. The Future of Electricity: Papers in Honor of David Newberry.

Joyce, S. (2009a) 'Taxpayers pay big for Labour's rail dream', 4 June, http://www.beehive.govt.nz/release/taxpayers+pay+big+labour%e2%80%99s+rail+dream, Accessed on 13 February 2010.

Joyce, S. (2009b) Speech to the Australasian Rail Association, 30 April, http://www.beehive.govt.nz/speech/speech+australasian+rail+association, Accessed on 12 February 2010.

Joyce, S. (2010) 'Government investment for rail turnaround', 18 May, http://beehive.govt.nz/release/government-investment-rail-turnaround, Accessed on 8 December 2012.

Kathuria, R. (2008) 'Prospects for the Telecommunication Sector under the Indo-EU Trade and Investment Agreement', New Delhi: Indian Council for Research on International Economic Relations.

Kathuria, R., Singh, H.V. and Soni, A. (2003) 'Telecommunications Policy Reform in India', in A. Mattoo and R. Stern (eds), *India and the WTO*, Washington DC: World Bank and Oxford University Press: 81–116.

Kim, D.-W., Knittel, C. and Cho, H.-S. (2006) 'Regulatory Restructuring and Plant Efficiency in the Korea Electricity Market', *Research Paper 519*, Korea Institute for Economics & Trade.

Kim, J. and Kim, K. (2008) 'The electricity industry reform in Korea: Lessons for further liberalization', Mimeograph.

KiwiRail (2009) Annual Report, http://www.kiwirail.co.nz/uploads/Publications and Reports/KiwiRail Annual Report 09 (web).pdf, Accessed on 12 February 2010.

KiwiRail (2012a) 'Brief Rail History', http://www.kiwirail.co.nz/about-us/history-of-kiwirail.html, Accessed on 8 December 2012.

KiwiRail (2012b) *Infrastructure and Engineering Business Plan 2013-2015*, 24 August, http://www.kiwirail.co.nz/uploads/Publications/Infrastructure%20and%20Engineering%20Business%20Plan%202013-2015.pdf, Accessed on 8 December 2012.

KiwiRail (2012c) *Napier Gisborne Line: Assessment of the Commercial Viability of the Line*, 18 May, http://www.kiwirail.co.nz/uploads/media/Napier%20Gisborne%20Line%20-%202012-05-18%20(Redacted).pdf, Accessed on 9 December 2012.

Kuleshov, D., Viljainen, S., Annala, S., Gore, O. (2012) 'Russian electricity market reform: Challenges to retail competition', *Utilities Policy* doi: 10.1016/j.jup.2012.05.001.

Kurronen, S. (2006) 'Russian electricity sector – reform and prospects', Bank of Finland, BOFIT Institute for Economies in Transition BOFIT Online 6/2006, http://www.bof.fi/NR/rdonlyres/C60670F4-B7BB-4267-95BC-3788A1A76C9/0/bon0606.pdf, Accessed on 15 January 2010.

Laoonual, Y., Sumrerng, J., Somchai, C. and Chollacoop, C. (2007) 'An Analysis of Composition Variation of Natural Gas for Vehicle (NGV) in Thailand', paper presented at The Third National Energy Network Academic Seminar, 23–25 May, 2007, Bangkok, Thailand.

Larraín, F. and Vergara, R. (eds) (2000) *La Transformación Económica de Chile*, Centro de Estudios Públicos, Santiago, Chile.

Lee, S.-S., Kim, Y.-C., Han, J.-K., Park, J.-K., Lee, S.-H., Osawa, M., Moon, S.-I. and Yoon, Y.-T. (2007) *Northeast Asia Power Interconnection Routs and Representative.*

Studies in South Korea Power Tech, 2007 IEEE Lausanne Digital Object Identifier: 10.1109/PCT.2007.4538606, pp. 1893–98.

Lee, Y.-S. and Kim, J. (2008) 'Restructuring toward a competitive electricity market', KEEI discussion paper 08-05.

Leitch, D. and Stott, B. (1988) *New Zealand Railways: The First 125 Years*, Heinemann Reed: Auckland.

Leopairojna, S.K. and Hanaoka, S.(2006) 'Market analysis of passenger vans in Bangkok'in R. Macario, J.M.Viegas and D.Hensher (eds) *Competition andOwnership in Land Passenger Transport: Proceedings of 9th International Conference on Competition and Ownership of Land Passenger Transport*, Elsevier.

LIBRA (2007) 'Estudio de Diagnóstico del Modo de Transporte Ferroviario', for Ministerio de Transportes y Telecomunicaciones de Chile.

LIBRA (2008) 'Análisis de la Seguridad en el Transporte Ferroviario', for Ministerio de Transportes y Telecomunicaciones de Chile.

Mackie, H., Baas, P. and Manz, H. (2006) *The contestability of New Zealand's road freight task by rail*, Transport Engineering Research New Zealand Limited, http://www.ternz.co.nz/Publications/The%20Contestability%20of%20New%20Zealand%27s%20Road%20Freight%20Task%20by%20Rail.pdf, Accessed on 3 May 2010.

Malpass, L. (2009) *KiwiRail: Doomed to Fail?*, Centre for Independent Studies http://www.cis.org.au/issue_analysis/IA115/IA115.pdf, Accessed on 2 March 2010.

MARAD – see US Department of Transportation, Maritime Administration.

McKinnon, A. (1998) 'The abolition of quantitative controls on road freight transport: the end of an era?' *Transport Logistics*, 1(3): 211–23.

Meakin, R. (2005) A Study of Urban Public Transport Conditions in Bangkok. A Case Study Forming an Input to the Global Toolkit on Bus Transport Reform.

MED (2007) 'Concept of long-term growth to 2020 for Russian Federation', Ministry of Economic Development of the Russian Federation, 31 October 2007. http://wcm.economy.gov.ru/minec/activity/sections/strategicPlanning/concept/doc1193835322297, Accessed on 25 February 2010.

MED (2010a) 'Report on the outcomes of implementation of the new rules for technological connection to electric networks for small businesses', Ministry of Economic Development of the Russian Federation, http://wcm.economy.gov.ru/minec/activity/sections/naturMonopoly/doc20100209_0.

MED (2010b) 'Summary indicators of social-economic development of Russian Federation in 2009', Ministry of Economic Development and Trade, 3 February 2010, http://www.economy.gov.ru/minec/activity/sections/macro/monitoring/doc20100203_01, Accessed on 31 March 2010.

Mein, B. (2008) 'Transport Governance in Auckland. Situation Analysis', *Auckland Governance, Volume 4: Research Papers*, Royal Commission on Auckland Governance, http://www.royalcommission.govt.nz/rccms.nsf/0/D18FC80DE3314853CC257586000CEE50/$FILE/Vol4Part6.pdf?open, Accessed on 3 May 2010.

Meyrick and Associates (2007) 'International and Domestic Shipping and Ports Study, May 2007'.

Milgrom, P. and Roberts, J. (1992) *Economics, Organisation and Management*, Prentice Hall: Upper Saddle River, New Jersey.

Milov, V. (2005) 'Regulatory framework in the Russian power sector: trends and challenges', Institute of Energy Policy/Center for Strategic Research, Presentation, Moscow, 14 July 2005.

Milyutin, D. (2011) 'Regulation on long-term capacity market', Presentation at the 10th ERRA Energy Investment and Regulation Conference, St Petersburg, Russia. 17 May 2011, http://www.energy-regulators.eu/portal/page/portal/EER_HOME/EER_INTERNATIONAL/CEER-FTS/3rd%20FTS-CEER%20meeting, Accessed on 20 February 2010.

Minenergo (2010a) http://minenergo.gov.ru/activity/powerindustry/powerdirection/energorynok/ (in Russian), Accessed on 20 February 2010.

Minenergo (2010b) 'Report on the results and projected future activities of the Ministry of Energy, Russian Federation, for 2010-2012', http://minenergo.gov.ru/activity/plan/2010-2012_3/1.php, Accessed on 31 March 2010.

Ministry of Energy (2012) 'Analysis of the performance of electric power industry in 2011, 2012 forecast', http://minenergo.gov.ru/upload/iblock/d6f/d6fb1b2ad5fa7be6db40215f7bc3e5b6.pdf, Accessed on 1 February 2013.

Ministry of Transport website http://www.mot.go.th, Accessed on 15 January, 2010.

Mittal, K.C. (2005) 'WTO and its Impact on Legal Profession', *Popular Jurist*, May-June: 16–18.

MOC (2009) 'China Trade in Services Report 2009', Beijing: China Commerce and Trade Press.

MOC (2010) 'China Trade in Services Report 2010', Beijing: China Commerce and Trade Press.

MOC (Ministry of Commerce of the People's Republic of China) (2008) 'China Trade in Services Report 2008', Beijing: China Commerce and Trade Press.

Mukherjee, A. (2006) 'India's Trade in Distribution Services', in R. Chanda (ed.), *Trade in Services and India: Prospects and Strategies*, Centre for Trade and Development, New Delhi: Wiley-India: 145–76.

Mukherjee, A. and Patel, N. (2005) *FDI in Retail Sector: India*, New Delhi: Academic Foundation.

Narsalay, R. (2006) 'Liberalisation of India's Telecommunications Sector under the WTO and Preferential Trade Agreements', in R. Chanda (ed.), *Trade in Services and India: Prospects and Strategies*, Centre for Trade and Development, New Delhi: Wiley-India: 119–44.

Nathan Associates Inc. (1995) 'Economic Analysis of Federal Support for the Private Merchant Marine', prepared for DTEI on behalf of the Australian Maritime Group (AMG), January 1995.

NESDB (1991)The Seventh Plan Urban and Regional Transport (SPURT) Final Report, Office of the National Economic and Social Development Board.

New Zealand Productivity Commission (2012) *International Freight Transport Services Inquiry*, April, http://www.productivity.govt.nz/sites/default/files/FINAL%20 International%20Freight%20Transport%20Services%20PDF%20with%20covers_1_0.pdf, Accessed on 9 December 2012.

Nigmatullin, B. (2011) 'Electric power industry in Russia: Current state and challenges', Presentation at Workshop on 'Current problems of energy supply in the real sector of economy and power industry development', Institute of Problems of Natural Monopolies, Moscow, Russia, 20 September 2011.

Nikomborirak, D. and Cheevasittiyanon, S. (2009) 'Telecom Regulatory and Policy Environment in Thailand: Results and Analysis of the 2008 TRE Survey (2008), http://lirneasia.net/wp-content/uploads/2009/07/TRE_Thailand_Final_2008Nov11.pdf., Accessed on 1 February 2013.

Nikomborirak, D. and Sirikarn, L. (2009) 'Business Concentration in Thailand', paper presented at the TDRI Annual Seminar', November 25–26, 2009, Bangkok, Thailand.

Notteboom, T. (2008) *The relationship between seaports and the intermodal hinterland in light of global supply chains – European challenges*, OECD/ITF Joint Transportation Research Centre, Discussion Paper No. 2008-10, March 2008, http://www.internationaltransportforum.org/jtrc/DiscussionPapers/DP200810.pdf, Accessed on 8 December 2012.

OECD (2001) 'Report on Regulatory Issues in International Maritime Transport', August 2001, OECD, Paris.

OECD (2002) 'Liner Shipping Competition Policy Report', Division of Transport, April 2002, OECD, Paris.

Ofa, S.V. (2008) 'The telecommunications sector in the Pacific: a regulatory policy survey', *Pacific Economic Bulletin,* 23(3): 69–100.

Ofa, S.V. (2009) 'The WTO's telecommunications commitments and the credibility of telecommunications regulatory reforms in small island developing states', *Pacific Economic Bulletin,* 24(3): 39-57.

Ofa, S.V. (2011). 'Telecommunication regulatory reforms and the credibility problem: case studies from Papua New Guinea and Tonga', Ch. 4 in R. Duncan (ed.), *The political economy of economic reform in the Pacific,* Pacific Studies Series, Asian Development Bank, Manila.

Oksanen, M., Karjalainen, R., Viljainen, S. and Kuleshov, D. (2009) 'Electricity markets in Russia, the US, and Europe', EEM 2009, 6th International Conference on the European Energy Market, Leuven, Belgium 27–29 May 2009, Digital Object Identifier: 10.1109/EEM.2009.5207214 pp. 1–7.

Pal, P. (2006) 'Liberalizing Accountancy Services in India', in R. Chanda (ed.), *Trade in Services and India: Prospects and Strategies*, Centre for Trade and Development, New Delhi: Wiley-India: 177–206.

Palamarchuk, S.I. and Voropai, N.I. (2006) 'Russian's power industry restructuring: current state and problems', Engineering Society General Meeting, 2006, IEEE 6.

Palamarchuk, S.I. and Voropai, N.I. (2009) 'Status and development of the Russian electricity market', Power and Energy Society General Meeting, 2009, PES '09, IEEE, pp. 1–5.

Palamarchuk, S.I., Lamoureux, M.A. and Voropai, N.I. (2008) 'Status of Russian power sector liberalization', Electric Utility Deregulation and Restructuring and Power Technologies, 2008, The Third International Conference on Electric Utility Deregulation and Restructuring and Power Technologies, Nanjing, China, pp. 82–8.

Papavizas, C.G. and Gardner, B.E. (2009) 'Is the Jones Act Redundant?', *USF Maritime Law Journal*, 21(1), May, pp. 95-137.

Pollitt, M. (2007) 'Liberalisation and Regulation in Electricity Systems: How can we get the balance right?', CWPE 0753 and EPRG 0724 Working Paper. October 2007, http://www.eprg.group.cam.ac.uk/wp-content/uploads/2008/11/eprg0724.pdf, Accessed on 31 March 2010.

Post Courier September 2008.

Productivity Commission (2005) 'Review of Part X of the Trade Practices Act 1974: International Liner Cargo Shipping'.

Productivity Commission (2009) 'Annual Review of Regulatory Burdens on Business: Social and Economic Infrastructure Services'.

PTT Annual Report (2009) 'History of Gas Transmission', www.pttplc.com/Files/Document/Pdf/Gas/Gas_en2.pdf, Accessed in February 2010.

PTT website (2007) http://www.pttplc.com/Files/Document/51_en/compl_e.pdf, Accessed in February 2010.

Rangan, V. and Dasgupta, A. (2006) 'Liberalizing Legal Services in India', in R. Chanda (ed.), *Trade in Services and India: Prospects and Strategies*, Centre for Trade and Development, New Delhi: Wiley-India: 207–48.

RAO-UES (2003) 'Concept strategy for RAO UES of Russia for 2003-2008 '5+5'', United Energy Systems of Russia, http://www.rao-ues.u/ru/reforming/kon/show.cgi?kon_main.htm, Accessed on 1 February 2010.

RDG (Rail Development Group) (2008a) *Report 5: Outline Purchase Contract and Financial Model*, ONTRACK, http://www.ontrack.govt.nz/news/2009/Documents/RDG%20paper% 205%20(OIA%20version).pdf, Accessed on 16 February 2010.

RDG (Rail Development Group) (2008b) *Report 2: Subsidy*, ONTRACK, http://www.ontrack.govt.nz/news/2009/Pages/RailDevelopmentPapersreleased.aspx, Accessed on 16 February 2010.

RDG (Rail Development Group) (2008c) *Report 4: Capital investment*, ONTRACK, http://www.ontrack.govt.nz/news/2009/Pages/RailDevelopmentPapersreleased.aspx, Accessed on 16 February 2010.

Renaissance Capital (2005) *Utilities: Form and Substance*, 30 August 2005.

Richard Paling Consulting (2008) *National Freight Demands Study*, New Zealand Ministry of Transport, http://www.transport.govt.nz/research/nationalfreightdemands study/, Accessed on 22 February 2010.

Rietveld, P. and Stough, R.(2004)Barriers to Sustainable Transport: Institutions, Regulation and Sustainability.

Rockpoint Corporate Finance Ltd (2009) *Coastal shipping and modal freight choice*, retrieved from http://www.nzta.govt.nz/resources/domestic-sea-freight-development-fund/coastal-shipping-and-modal-freight-choice/docs/rockpoint-coastal-shipping-report-1.pdf, Accessed on 13 April 2010.

SAFE (State Administration of Foreign Exchange) (2010) '2009 Statistical Bulletin of China's Outward Foreign Direct Investment', Beijing: National Bureau of Statistics, State Administration of Foreign Exchange, Ministry of Commerce.

Samil Consultant (2003) 'Gencos' management performance after divestiture', unpublished report in Korean.

Shipbuilding history website (2012) http://www.shipbuildinghistory.com/, Accessed in September 2012.

Sinclair, J. (1984) *Uniting a Nation: The Postal and Telecommunication Services of Papua New Guinea,* Oxford University Press, Melbourne.

Sinclair, J. (1993) *Uniting a Nation Through the 1980s*, Crawford House, Bathurst.

Sletmo, G.K. and Holste S. (1993) 'Shipping and the competitive advantage of nations: the role of international ship registers', *Maritime Policy and Management*, 20(3), July, pp. 243-255.

SO (2010a) 'Forecast of reaching system limits and conditions to ensure operations within the limits', System Operator. 31 January 2010 (in Russian). http://www.so-ups.ru/fileadmin/files/company/reports/disclosure/ 2010/tech-disc-jan2010.pdf, Accessed on 8 February 2010.

SO (2010b) 'United Energy Systems (UES) of Russia 2009 operations report', System Operator, 31 January, 2010 (in Russian), http://www.so-ups.ru/fileadmin/files/company/reports/disclosure/2010/ues_rep_2009.pdf, Accessed on 16 February 2010.

Solanko, L. (2011) 'How to liberalize a thousand TWh market? – Restructuring the Russian power sector', BOFIT Online 1/2011, http://www.suomenpankki.fi/bofit_en/tutkimus/tutkimusjulkaisut/online/Documents/bon0111.pdf_, Accessed on 1 July 2012.

Sovacool, B.K. (2009) 'Energy Policy and Cooperation in Southeast Asia: The History, Challenges and Implications of the Trans-ASEAN Gas Pipeline (TAGP) Network', *Energy Policy*, 37: 2356–67.

Standard & Poor's (2008) 'Restructured Russian distribution companies are facing an increase in debt and new regulatory regime' (in Russian), 8 September 2008. http://www.standardandpoors.ru/article.php?pubid= 4524&sec=pr, Accessed on 12 February 2010.

Stanley, L. (2008a) 'The development of information and communication technology law and policy in Papua New Guinea', *Pacific Economic Bulletin,* 23(1): 16–28.

Stanley, L. (2008b) 'Regulating the telecommunications sector in Papua New Guinea', *Pacific Economic Bulletin,* 23(3): 135–40.

Supreme Court of Papua New Guinea (2008) 'PacLII Databases – Telikom PNG Ltd v Independent Consumer and Competition Commission PGSC5; SC906 (28 March 2008), http://www.paclii.org/pg/cases/PGSC/2008/5.html, Accessed on 18 December 2008.

Sydney Morning Herald (2007) 'Toll could exit NZ rail market', October 8, http://www.smh.com.au/news/Business/Toll-could-exit-NZ-rail-market/2007/10/08/1191695805849.html, Accessed on 22 February 2010.

Tatenergo (2009) 'Wholesale electricity market rules in the transition period: main features', Powerpoint presentation, www.tatenergo.ru/download/presentation_02.ppt, Accessed on 19 February 2010.

Thailand Development Research Institute (TDRI) (2005) 'Transport Liberalization and Competition Concerns in ASEAN', *TDRI Quarterly Review*, December.

Thailand Development Research Institute (TDRI) (2010a) Sharing the Benefits from Transportation Linkages and Logistics Improvements in the GMS: A Study of the East-West and North-South Corridor, Bangkok, Thailand.

Thailand Development Research Institute (TDRI) (2010b) *The Study of Bus Cost Structure*, Bangkok, Thailand.

The Korean Society for Electricity Industry Study (2005) 'Enhancing competition among Gencos', unpublished report to government in Korean.

The Korean Society for Electricity Industry Study (2007) 'Improving efficiency of electricity market', unpublished report to KPX in Korean.

The National, 12 September 2007.

The Treasury (2004) 'National Rail Access Agreement', http://www.treasury.govt.nz/publications/informationreleases/rail/transaction/pdfs/rt-mof-toll.pdf, Accessed on 3 May 2010.

The Treasury (2009) *Infrastructure: Facts and Issues*, http://www.infrastructure.govt.nz/plan/ifi, Accessed on 4 February 2010.

The Treasury (2010) *National Infrastructure Plan*, http://www.infrastructure.govt.nz/plan/mar2010, Accessed on 8 December 2012.

Thompson, I. (1999) 'Concessions and road and rail transport optimization', *ECLAC Review*, 67, 177–89.

Thompson, I. and Angerstein, D. (1997), *Historia del Ferrocarril en Chile*, Ediciones de la Biblioteca Nacional de Chile, Santiago, Chile.

Thompson, L.; Budin, K.J. and Estache, A. (2001) 'Private Investment in Railways: Experience from South and North America, Africa and New Zealand', PTRC Conference, Cambridge.

Toll Group (2003) 'Intention to Make Full Takeover Offer for Tranz Rail', 29 May, http://www.toll.com.au/media/56833.pdf, Accessed on 24 February 2010.

Toll Holdings Limited (2004) *Annual Report*, http://www.toll.com.au/media/2004/166498.pdf, Accessed on 24 February 2010.

TRAI (Telecommunications Regulatory Authority of India) (2012) 'Press Release No. 231/2012', available at http://www.trai.gov.in/WriteReadData/WhatsNew/Documents/PR-TSD-Oct2012.pdf, Accessed 22 January 2013.

Tranz Rail Holdings Limited (2003) *Annual Report*, Auckland.

Udaltsov (2005) 'Critical challenges and strategy for facing the power sector reform transition', Presentation at World Bank workshop 'Russian Electricity Reform', Moscow, 14 July 2005.

UNCTAD (United Nations Conference on Trade and Development) (2012) 'International Trade in Services', UNCTADStat, available at http://unctadstat.unctad.org, Accessed 31 December 2012.

UNCTAD various years, 'Review of Maritime Transport', UNCTAD, Geneva.

UniCredit (2008) 'Global Equity Research: Sector Flash – Electric power', Russia/CIS, Accessed on 24 January 2008.

US Central Intelligence Agency (2009) https://www.cia.gov/library/publications/the-world-factbook/rankorder/ 2180rank.html, Accessed on February 2010.

US Department of Labor, Bureau of Labor Statistics, Producer Price Index Industry Data; www.bls.gov/data/sa.htm, Accessed on September 2012.

US Department of Transportation, Maritime Administration (MARAD) (2012), http://www.marad.dot.gov, Accessed on September 2012.

US Department of Transportation, Maritime Administration (MARAD) (2011) 'Comparison of US and Foreign-Flag Operating Costs', September 2011, MARAD, Washington DC.

US Department of Transportation, Maritime Administration (MARAD) (2011) 'US Water Transportation Statistical Snapshot', February 2011, MARAD, Washington DC.

US International Trade Commission (USITC) various years, 'The Economic Effects of Significant Import Restraints', USITC, Washington DC.

Virmani, A. (2004) 'Telecommunication Reforms in India', New Delhi: Indian Council for Research on International Economic Relations.

Voropai, N.I. and Kucherov, Y.N. (2000) 'Russia and the EU electricity directive', *Power Engineering Review, IEEE*, vol. 20, no. 4 Digital Object Identifier: 10.1109/ 39.833011, pp. 19–21.

White, L.J. (1988) 'International Trade in Ocean Shipping Services: The United States and the World', Ballinger, Cambridge, MA.

Wills-Johnson, N. (2007) 'Competition Policy and Railway Investment in Australia', SSRN eLibrary, http://papers.ssrn.com/sol3/papers.cfm?abstract_id=965608, Accessed on 15 February 2010.

Woods, N. (1935) 'The Birth of Our Railways', *The New Zealand Railways Magazine*, 10(3), June 1935, http://www.nzetc.org/tm/scholarly/tei-Gov10_03Rail-t1-body-d13.html, Accessed on 23 February 2010.

World Bank (2004) Sustaining India's Services Revolution: Access to Foreign Markets, Domestic Reform and International Negotiations, South Asian Region, New Delhi: World Bank.

World Bank (2007) 'Diagnóstico estratégico de EFE y opciones de política Asistencia Técnica', for Ministerio de Hacienda de Chile.

World Bank (2007) *Strategic Urban Transport Policy Directions for Bangkok*, http://siteresources.worldbank.org/INTTHAILAND/Resources/333200-1177475763598/2007june_bkk-urban-transport-directions.pdf, Accessed on January 15, 2010.

World Bank (2008) *Thailand Infrastructure Annual Report*,http://www.awex.be/fr-BE/Infos%20march%C3%A9s%20et%20secteurs/Infossecteurs/Pages/THAILANDE_DOC_THAILANDEINFRASTRUCTUREANNUALREPORT2008.aspx, Accessed on January 12, 2010.

World Bank (2012) Services Trade Restrictions database at http://iresearch.worldbank.org/servicestrade/default.htm, Accessed in September 2012.

World Bank and NESDB (2009) *Thailand: Making Transport more Energy Efficient*, World Bank and NESDB, Bangkok, March.

WTO (2008) 'Trade Policy Review—United States', WTO, Geneva.

Yoon, J., Park, D. and Kim, H. (2006) 'Feasible power exchange model between the ROK, the DPRK and Russia', Power Engineering Society General Meeting, IEEE Digital Object Identifier: 10.1109/PES.2006.1709195.

Young, A. (2008) 'Govt: We paid top dollar for rail', *New Zealand Herald*, 2 July, http://www.nzherald.co.nz/nz/news/article.cfm?c_id=1&objectid=10519449&pnum=0, Accessed on 1 February 2010.

Yyudashkina, G. and Pobochy, S. (2007) 'Regulation of the electricity sector in Russia: regional aspects', *Quantile*, 2007, issue 2, pp. 107–30, http://quantile.ru/02/02-YP.pdf (in Russian), Accessed on 20 February 2010.